NEWS

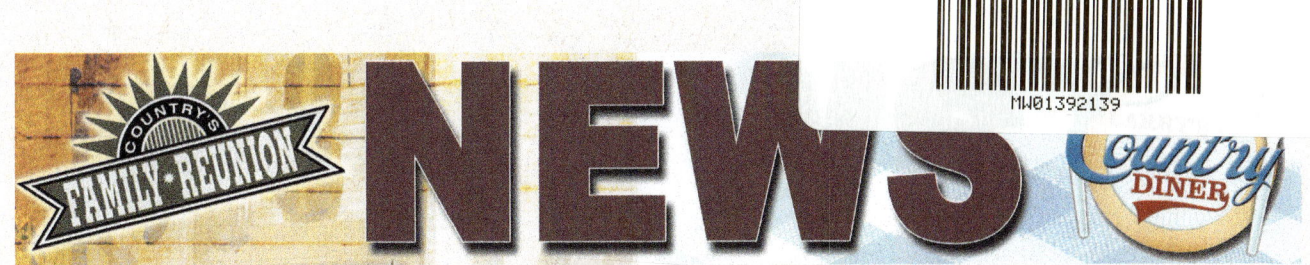

Our Monthly Newspapers from Year 4

January - December 2015

© 2016 Gabriel Communications, Inc.
All rights reserved
Including the right of reproduction in whole or in part in any form

ISBN: 978-0-98939891-6

Published by Gabriel Communications, Inc.
916 Harpeth Valley Place
Nashville, TN 37221

To order more copies:
www.cfrvideos.com
www.larrycountrydiner.com
800-820-5405

CONTENTS

January
Remembering Ray Price — 5
Hank Williams Past and Present — 10
Cowboy Church — 14
Mt. Faith — 19

February
Country Music loses Little Jimmy — 24
Ernest Tubb Past and Present — 28
Musical Sweethearts — 35
Stage Clothes — 38

March
Jim Ed Brown in Remission — 39
Tex Ritter — 41
Brenda Lee in Victoria Secret — 46
2015 Cruise Photos — 47
Honky Tonk Reunion — 52

April
Don Hurron of Hee Haw passes — 56
Southern Raised — 57
Opry loses James "Spider" Wilson — 59
Wade Hayes, honky tonk singer — 60
Duke of Paducah Past and Present — 61
Randy Travis improving — 64

May
Keith Bilbrey Radio Hall of Fame — 76
T. Graham Brown and Chordbuddy — 79
Don Williams 2015 Tour — 80
George Hay Past and Present — 81
The Next Generations — 87
Midnight Jamboree closes — 93

June
Rory Feek 50 & making a movie — 96
John Conlee law enforcement song — 99
Faron Young Past and Present — 101
George Jones Museum opens — 103
Roy Clark Hobbies and Interests — 108

July
Jim Ed Brown loses battle — 114
Glen Campbell condition — 119
Lee Greenwood new book of America — 120
Moe and Gene New TV Special — 123
Johnny Russell Past and Present — 130

August
Larry Black Hospitalized — 132
Dale Watson honky tonk artist — 137
Bob Luman Past and Present — 143
Aaron Tippin Road Story — 149

September
Lynn Anderson dies unexpectedly — 152
Charlie Louvin — 157
Celebrating Marty Robbins 90th Birthday — 166
Tammy Wynette Past and Present — 172

October
Larry's Country Diner breaks ground — 173
William Lee Golden weds — 176
Smathers Family Scrapbook — 179
50 Years of Exile — 180
Little Jimmy Dickens Past and Present — 190

November
Diner moving back to Thursdays — 192
Larry's Country Diner at the Starlite — 200
Mo Pitney engaged — 208
Hawkshaw Hawkins Past and Present — 210

December
Jean Shepard celebrations 60 at the Opry — 211
Charlie Dick dies at 81 — 216
Hoosier Hotshots — 220
Skeeter Davis Past and Present — 230

JANUARY

Remembering the life & legacy of Ray Price

During the taping, Larry Gatlin grabbed Janie and started dancing, much to the delight of everyone there.

Ray Price, one of the greatest voices of country music, revolutionized the genre with Number One hits like "Crazy Arms" and "City Lights," was honored with a Country's Family Reunion Tribute. The DVD series was recorded in September 2014 with a room full of some of the greatest entertainers singing his praises and his songs. Price's widow Janie was there to watch it all as they celebrated his life and legacy.

Noble Ray Price was born January 12, 1926 on a farm near the small, now gone, community of Peach, near Perryville in Wood County, Texas. Price was three years old when his parents divorced and his mother moved to Dallas, Texas. For the rest of his childhood he split time between Dallas and on the family farm, where his father had remained. Price's mother and step-father were successful fashion designers and wanted him to take up that line of work, but he wasn't interested. Price began singing and playing guitar as a teenager but he chose a career in veterinary medicine.

After serving as a Marine in World War II, and finishing college, Price rethought his decision to continue schooling to be a veterinarian. He was considered too small to work with large cattle and horses, the backbone of a Texas veterinarian's practice. While helping around his father's ranch he also began singing at various functions around the Abilene, Texas area. This eventually led him to begin singing on the radio.

He joined the Big D Jamboree on Dallas radio station KRLD-AM in 1949, and when the show was picked up for broadcast on the CBS radio network Price had his first taste of national exposure. It was around this time Ray Price became friends with Lefty Frizzell.

Price relocated to Nashville in the early 1950s, rooming for a brief time with Hank Williams. When Williams died, Price managed his band, the Drifting Cowboys, and had minor success.

In 1953, Price formed his own band, The Cherokee Cowboys. Among its members during the late 1950s and early 1960s were; Roger Miller, Willie Nelson, Darrell McCall, Van Howard, Johnny Paycheck, Johnny Bush, Buddy Emmons, Pete Wade, Jan Kurtis, Shorty Lavender and Buddy Spicher.

Price became one of the staunch supporters of 1950s honky tonk music, with hit songs such as "Talk To Your Heart" (1952) and "Release Me". He later developed the famous "Ray Price Shuffle," a 4/4 arrangement of honky tonk music with a walking bassline, which can be heard on "Crazy Arms" (1956) and many of his other recordings from the late 1950s.

During the 1960s, Ray experimented with the Nashville sound, singing slow ballads and utilizing lush arrangements of strings and backing singers. Examples include his 1967 rendition of "Danny Boy", and "For the Good Times" in 1970 which was Price's first country music chart No. 1 hit since "The Same Old Me" in 1959. Price had three more No. 1 country music successes during the 1970s: "I Won't Mention It Again", "She's Got To Be A Saint", and "You're the Best Thing That Ever Happened To Me." His final top ten hit was "Diamonds In The Stars" in early 1982. Price continued to have songs on the country music chart through 1989.

On November 6, 2012, Ray Price confirmed that he was fighting pancreatic cancer. Price told the San Antonio Express-News that he had been receiving chemotherapy for the past six months. An alternative to the chemo would have been surgery that involved

January 2015

removing the pancreas along with portions of the stomach and liver, which would have meant a long recovery and stay in a nursing home. Said Price, "That's not very much an option for me. God knows I want to live as long as I can but I don't want to live like that." The 87-year-old Country Music Hall of Famer also told the newspaper, "The doctor said that every man will get cancer if he lives to be old enough. I don't know why I got it – I ain't old!" Price retained a positive outlook.

Although in February 2013 the cancer appeared to be in remission, Price was hospitalized in May 2013 with severe dehydration. On December 2, 2013, Price entered a Tyler, Texas, hospital in the final stages of pancreatic cancer, according to his son, then left on December 12 for home hospice care. Price died at his home in Mt. Pleasant, Texas, on December 16, 2013

After leaving Nashville Price lived his time off the road on his east Texas ranch near Mount Pleasant, continuing to dabble in cattle and horses. Ray Price married twice. He and his first wife divorced in the late 1960s. Price married second wife Janie in the early 1980s and they remained together until his death. He has a son from his first marriage, Cliff Price.

Dawn Sears, vocalist with Time Jumpers dies of cancer

Dawn Sears, a vocalist for the Grammy-nominated Western swing group the Time Jumpers, passed away December 11 after a battle with lung cancer. She was 53 years old.

Sears was born in East Grand Forks, Minn. and made her way to Nashville, where she recorded for Warner Bros. and Decca Records in the '90s, charting with a single titled 'Runaway Train.' She was also an in-demand backing vocalist for artists including Tracy Byrd, Ronnie Milsap, Jim Lauderdale, Patty Loveless and Merle Haggard.

As a longtime friend of Vince Gill's, she worked in his touring band for years. The two also worked together in the Time Jumpers, garnering four Grammy nominations over the course of two albums.

Sears was diagnosed with Stage 3B lung cancer in March of 2013. She continued to perform at the Time Jumpers' weekly gigs in Nashville during her treatment, as long as she was feeling up to it.

She tried to maintain a positive outlook to the end and received cards and letters from four continents as she fought the disease.

"This is going to sound crazy, but I think this disease is going to be a blessing in many ways, and you never know how much of an impact you're going to make," she told Nashville's WSMV in July. "All I ever heard in the music business when I had record deals was what was wrong, not anything good."

Sears attended a fundraising concert held in her name on Nov. 30 in Gallatin, Tenn., featuring Reba McEntire, the Time Jumpers and Riders in the Sky. The event brought in more than $100,000 for the Vanderbilt-Ingram Cancer Center.

She is survived by her husband, Time Jumpers fiddler Kenny Sears, and daughter Tess.

Down Home
with Carol Bass

You have heard the saying, "You can tell the year a woman graduated from high school by the way she wears her hair and makeup!" Just like hair and make-up, a home can show its age too. Here are some dead give-a-ways known as age spots, see if you recognize any. But more importantly, here are some simple practical fixes.

THE FLORAL ARRANGEMENT

Floral arrangements don't last forever. Really, they don't! These dust collectors quickly turn into age spots. The key is the type and style. Faux greenery falls into this category too. If you are using faux plants and florals, did you know you should change your arrangements at least every two years to stay current? It saves on dusting too. How many of you have floral arrangements that date back to 1994? Do you still have a dried flower arrangement? Could I see a show of hands please? Ouch! What about the ficus tree in the corner?

PRACTICAL SIMPLE FIX

The day of the big bushy ivy or philodendron has given way to a single stem in a tall glass vase. The big round floral in the center of the dining room table has changed to a series of objects repeated. A centerpiece composed of three to five identical pieces, or a grouping of unusual objects, perhaps apothecary jars filled with fun seasonal items will work beautifully. Work in odd numbers.

SECRET TIP

To clean silk plants and flowers spray them with cheap hairspray, I mean real cheap like Aqua Net or White Rain. The high alcohol content captures the dust and it just falls away.

Hope you found this information helpful. Tune in next month for the next instalment in the series; "Is your Room Showing Its Age Spots!"

Carol Bass, The Practical Decorator, Decorating for real people in real homes with real budgets and teaching other to do the same. 1-888-800-7507. www.ThePracticalDecorator.com

Have A Talent For Decorating?

Interior Redesign, Styling and Staging
Professional Certification Workshop
Nashville, TN

Practical decorating for real people in real homes with real budgets

carol bass THE PRACTICAL decorator
1-888-800-7507
carol@thepracticaldecorator.com
ThePracticalDecorator.com

The CFR News
is published monthly by
Gabriel Communications, Inc.
P.O. Box 210796, Nashville, TN 37221
615-673-2846
Larry Black, Publisher
Renae Johnson, General Manager
Paula Underwood Winters, Editor
Subscriptions: $29.95 yearly

TOUR DATES & TICKETS

Dates	Venue	Location
May 5, 6, 7, 8, 9	Starlite Theatre	Branson, MO
Sept. 22, 23, 24, 25, 26, 27	Starlite Theatre	Branson, MO

For more information: www.starlitetheatre.com or (417) 337-9333

January 2015

Behind the Scenes — Spotlight

Catherine Malkiewicz

Catherine provides the craft service for Larry's Country Diner and Country's Family Reunion tapings.. Her company, Table Charms, provides food of all varieties to all the workers on the set and the behind the set guests.

Before she started her company, she worked at the famous 101st Airborne restaurant in Nashville as a waitress and designing the brunch buffet. She soon had requests to cater weddings.

Growing up in New York she came from a long line of cooks, but she actually hated cooking. She says, "They're all in heaven now, but it's their joke that I'm a caterer."

Catherine has catered for the Music City Awards, Dove Awards, Backstreet Boys tour rehearsals in Nashville and other large events.

She has worked with Larry Black for several years. "Larry and Luann have taken me on many wonderful journeys. Mr. Larry Black is the only host/producer who starts the day with "The Promise" and a prayer. He does not waiver in this. I am very grateful that God sent him and his lovely family my way."

A typical day at the Diner tapings start at 7 a.m. The crew arrives knowing the eggs and coffee will be ready. She then moves on to prepare snack items for everyone to enjoy throughout the day.

"I love the joy the Diner shows bring to Hometowns across America! It's not your typical day at the office!"

January 2015

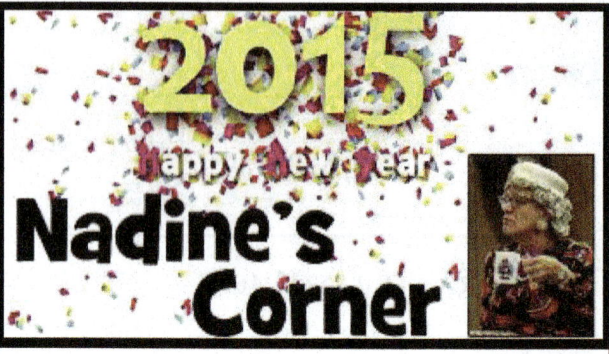

Nadine's Corner

Senior's New Year's Resolutions

For seniors, like me and Homer setting New Year's resolutions feels like old hat by now. After all, we've had enough opportunities to get it right. Personally, I think it is fun to set new goals and plans for the new year. In fact, I spent this past weekend free writing, making plans, and writing lists for what I would like to accomplish in 2015. Seniors and New Year's resolutions should go hand in hand after all your not dead yet. Everyone of us , no matter how old we are can renew old acquaintances, plan for better health and spend more time with the man upstairs.

Here's my New Year's prayer:

God, grant me the senility to forget the people I never liked anyway. The good fortune to run into the ones that I do. And the eyesight to tell the difference.

Top 10 New Year's Resolutions!

New Year's Eve has always been a time for looking forward to the coming year. Did your New Year resolutions make our top ten list?

#1 Spend More Time with Family & Friends

Recent polls show more than 50% of Americans vow to appreciate loved ones and spend more time with family and friends this year.

#2 Get Out of Debt

Millions of Americans have resolved to spend less this year getting a handle on their finances. Try to make a budget and stick to it!

#3 Lose Weight

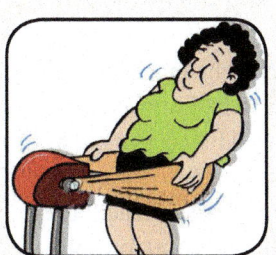

Over 66 percent of adult Americans are considered overweight or obese by recent studies, so it is not surprising to find that weight loss is one of the most popular New Year's resolutions. Setting reasonable goals and staying focused are the two most important factors in sticking with a weight loss program.

#4 Quit Smoking

If you have resolved to make this the year that you stamp out your smoking habit, over-the-counter availability of nicotine replacement therapy now provides easier access to proven quit-smoking aids. Even if you've tried to quit before and failed, don't let it get you down. On average, smokers try about four times before they quit for good. Start enjoying the rest of your smoke-free life

#5 Enjoy Life More

Given the hectic, stressful lifestyles of millions of Americans, it is no wonder that "enjoying life more" has become a popular resolution in recent years. It's an important step to a happier and healthier you!

#3 Quit Drinking

Many heavy drinkers fail to quit cold turkey but do much better when they taper gradually, or even learn to moderate their drinking. If you have decided that you want to stop drinking, there is a world of help and support available.

#7 Get Fit

Regular exercise has been associated with more health benefits than anything else known to man. Studies show that it reduces the risk of some cancers, increases longevity, helps achieve and maintain weight loss, enhances mood, lowers blood pressure, and even improves arthritis. In short, exercise keeps you healthy and makes you look and feel better.

#8 Learn Something New

Whether you take a course or read a book, you'll find education to be one of the easiest, most motivating New Year's resolutions to keep. There are lots of senior groups that offer classes in everything from finances to quilting! Find one that interests you!

#9 Help Others

A popular, non-selfish New Year's resolution, volunteerism can take many forms. Whether you choose to spend time helping out at your local library or mentoring a child, there are many nonprofit volunteer organizations that could really use your help

#10 Get Organized

On just about every New Year resolution top ten list, organization can be a very reasonable goal. Whether you want your home organized enough that you can invite someone over on a whim or just want to be able to find things easier, organization is key.

January 2015

COUNTRY LEGENDS PAST AND PRESENT   BY TOM WOOD

HANK WILLIAMS

Jett Williams and dad, Hank

Has any artist had such a profound effect on country music in as short a time as Hank Williams?

It certainly wouldn't be hard to argue a strong case for the uber-impact of Jimmie Rodgers, who came a generation earlier and is widely considered the Father of Country Music by music historians.

But those who would contend that Hank Williams' plaintive, yodeling style was equally if not more important to the development and proliferation of country music, well, those assertions are not without merit.

Both had short, but prolific careers and died way too early.

Both entertainers were among the Original Three inductees into the Country Music Hall of Fame in 1961, along with songwriter / music publisher Fred Rose.

And both continue to have considerable influence on the genre today, even among a new generation of glitzy, glamorous, polished country music stars.

Jimmy Rodgers churned out 109 recordings between 1927 and his death in 1933 at age 35 from complications of tuberculosis. Perhaps his biggest hit was "Blue Yodel No. 1 (T for Texas)" in 1927.

Between 1947 and his 1953 death at age 29 from drugs and alcohol, Hank Williams put 35 on the charts' Top 10 and he had 11 singles reach No. 1, including three after his death.

Hank's first song to make climb into the top 10 was "Move It On Over" in 1947 and his first No. 1 was "Lovesick Blues" a year later. "Hey Good Looking" in 1951 was Hank's fourth No. 1 and stands out among fan favorites along with and "I'm So Lonesome I Could Cry" (1949) and "Jambalaya (On The Bayou)" (1952).

These were all soulful songs and lyrics that bared the rawest emotions and touched common folk. Ironically, or perhaps prophetically, the last Hank recorded in late 1952 before his January, 1953 death was "I'll Never Get Out of This World Alive". It became a No. 1 hit following news of Hank's death, as did "Your Cheating Heart" and "Kaw-Liga".

Some critics have suggested that Williams would not have had the same impact had he not died when he did, that his fast-rising star was on a downward spiral when his untimely death occurred.

We'll never know, of course, and such speculation is easily discounted.

But what cannot be dismissed is the fact that Hank's body of work continues to be honored and rediscovered in this new century. He has ranked at or near the top of favorites' lists by media such as CMT and Rolling Stone magazine in the past decade; the Pulitzer Prize Board cited Williams' contributions as a songwriter in 2010; in 2011, his "Lovesick Blues" was inducted into the Grammy Hall of Fame; and more recently "lost" Hank Williams' material has made its way back into the spotlight.

And of course his legacy is carried on by his family, including son Hank Jr., daughter Jett, grandson Hank III and granddaughters Hilary and Holly Williams.

Hank with wife Audrey, daughter Lycrecia, and son Hank Jr.

January 2015

Country Questions
By Dick Boise, CI

Send questions to:
Dick Boise, , c/o CFR News,
P.O. Box 201796, Nashville,
TN 37221.

Q. Dear Dick, I purchased a CD at an estate sale by Stu Stevens and would like to know is he alive, where is her performing. He's a great singer.

Johnny Howton, Birmingham, AL

A. Thank you for your question about this artist. Questions like these cause me to learn more about folks like Stu Stevens. The reason we haven't heard about him is he was born in Nottinghamshire, England 1937. He won a talent contest in 1965 and made his first recording with EMI records. He has appeared in Nashville during the 1973 disc jockey convention. His touring has been in England and it is reported that after the death of his 19 year old son, Stu began to withdraw from the music scene. He did record a new album for Ash records titled "The Voice" in 2003.

Q. I enjoy reading CFR News and have a question for you. What ever happened to Carol Lee Cooper and her mother Wilma Lee?

June Alberts

A. First it is sad to report that the great Wilma Lee Cooper passed away September 13, 2011. She had been a Grand Ole Opry member since 1957 and was loved by many. As for her daughter, Carol Lee Cooper, she retired March 2013 due to some health and voice related issues. She was the leader of the Opry's backup vocalists, The Carol Lee Singers for many years.

Q. I saw a Merle Haggard concert last October in Minot, ND and we thought that he didn't put on a good concert. We were wondering how old he was? Thanks. Opal Bachmeier, Minot, ND

A. Thanks for your letter, Opal, and as to Mr. Haggard's age, he was born April 6, 1937. That would make him about 77 years young. About the concert performance, it is really hard to say. He might have been having an off day from the road travel. I know in my lifetime, I've gone to work on an off day and I'm sure I was not up to par in my work those days.

Q. I seem to remember a song about Little Green Apples several years ago and would like to know who sang it and who wrote it? Am I allowed two questions!

Candee H., Morris, NY

A. We will allow you two questions because my Mother always told me that Candee is sweet. The song you asked about was written by Bobby Russell. It was recorded by several artists and it was the 1969 Grammy winning Country Western Best Song for that year. Roger Miller's recording went to number 6 on the country charts and made the 39 spot in the top 40 Billboard pop charts.

It was also recorded by Bobby Goldsboro, who is also known for his recording of the song Honey, a song also written by Bobby Russell.

Some of the questions asked have already been answered in past columns or articles in the CFR News.

You can find the answers to these in the CFR News Books, available for $29.95 through CFR Videos.

January 2015

Road Stories

By Claudia Johnson

Hank Williams' Final Tour

Every musical genre has its tales of immeasurable losses during tragic tours – bluesmen Robert Johnson and Stevie Ray Vaughan, rockers Buddy Holly and Ronnie Van Zant, pop stars Jim Croce and Ricky Nelson, R&B singers Otis Redding and Aaliyah and big band leader Glenn Miller are among the sad examples. Country music, too, has lost its share of legends while touring, including Patsy Cline, Cowboy Copas and Hawkshaw Hawkins in 1963 and Jim Reeves in 1964.

Before any of these, however, as the new year of 1953 began, music lost one of its most talented songwriters and performers somewhere between Knoxville and Oak Hill, W.Va. when 29-year-old Hank Williams slipped into eternity in the back of a pale blue 1952 Cadillac.

For Williams, 1952 had been a trip of its own. Within the year he'd divorced the mother of his son, Hank Williams Jr., and had remarried in October. A pregnant lover was expecting his daughter, now known as Jett Williams, who was born within a week of his death. He moved at least four times among three states, continued to suffer from alcohol abuse, deteriorating health and chronic pain and had been banned from the Grand Ole Opry. Yet, eternal classic "Jambalaya" was among the many hits that made him the biggest selling country music artist for 1952.

Williams' holiday schedule had him set to perform in Canton, Ohio, on Jan. 1, 1953, after a New Year's Eve concert in Charleston, W.V. Arrangements were made for Charles Carr, a 17-year-old Auburn University student and son of one of Williams' most trusted friends, to drive the singer from Williams' home in Montgomery, Ala., to Knoxville, where he would catch a flight to the West Virginia venue. Though the plane left the airport as planned, it soon returned Williams and his teenage driver to Knoxville due to treacherous fog, and the performance was cancelled.

Carr and Williams checked into Knoxville's Andrew Johnson Hotel, where Williams was supposed to eat and rest. Pain-ridden and troubled throughout the trip (as well as all his adult life), Williams had been ingesting substantial amounts of alcohol along with the prescription drug chloral hydrate and had received several shots of morphine to ease back pain in the days and hours before Carr helped Williams into the back of the Cadillac when they left Knoxville around 11 p.m. to drive through the darkness to Ohio.

During interviews in the years since that final road trip, Carr has recounted his memory of being stopped for speeding near Blaine, W.Va., and sometime later, his discovery of Williams' cold, stiff body between the rural West Virginia towns of Mount Hope and Oak Hill. Though most historians agree that Williams died after crossing the Tennessee state line at Bristol, that mystery of where the tour ended for Williams may never be solved.

An Associated Press story printed Jan. 1, 1953, in The Los Angeles Times identified the deceased Williams as a "onetime shoeshine boy" who was "a singer and composer called the King of the Hillbillies by his followers." The article reported that he was employed by KWKH radio in Shreveport, La., and was under contract to MGM Recording Co. and MGM Pictures.

"Williams sang doleful mountain ballads in a nasal voice accompanying himself on a guitar, which he began playing at age 6," the AP story stated. "The lanky singer shot to fame with his recording 'Lovesick Blues.' The record sold more than one million copies."

January 2015

At the time of the AP story's distribution, no cause of death had been released. By Jan. 2, 1953, Dr. Diego Nunnari had signed Williams' death certificate, determining that death was from "acute rt. ventricular dilation." William's occupation was given as "radio singer.

On Sunday, Jan. 4, 1953, family members viewed Williams' body before it was transported four blocks to Montgomery's Municipal Auditorium, where as many as 25,000 mourners were estimated to have passed by the open silver casket. More than two tons of flowers were sent.

According to an Alabama state historic marker, some 2,750 mourners crowded inside for the actual service, while another 20,000 stood outside in the cold. Williams' band, the Drifting Cowboys, reunited to sing, and other performances included Ernest Tubb singing "Beyond the Sunset" followed by Roy Acuff with "I Saw the Light" and Red Foley with "Peace in the Valley." He was buried at Oakwood Annex in Montgomery, and his Cadillac's last trip was to the Hank Williams Museum in Montgomery.

Sadly, the most memorable road stories are those from which there is no return.

Artist Jack Terry now makes Tennessee home

Artist Jack Terry recently moved to Tennessee from Texas and visited Larry on the set of Larry's Country Diner to present him with one of his paintings. He said his moving here was a spiritual thing.

Jack was born in West Texas as a fourth generation Texan. He began his art career as a young child drawing inspiration from his rancher grandfather and west Texas painting grandmother. With support and encouragement from his parents, Terry pursued his love of painting and by the age of 16 won more than 130 awards.

As a graduate of the University of Texas, he studied anatomy and design while displaying his paintings in various galleries throughout the State. His big break came at 26 when he was named Bicentennial Artist of Texas; he had a one-man show in the Texas Capitol Rotunda and was commissioned to paint the late President Lyndon B. Johnson.

In addition to his long list of accomplishments he has written and illustrated: "The Great Trail Ride" A Cowboy's Faith, "Reflections of a Horseman", "Prayers Along the Trail", "Wide Open Spaces",

"Good Ol' Cowboy Stories and "Good Ol' Cowgirl Stories. His illustrations for celebrated authors include "Child of the Promise", by Stormie Omartian and "Friend to Friend by Dee Appel.

January 2015

Jack's paintings hang in prominent collections throughout the world including: The King Ranch, actor Burt Reynolds, cultural icon Dick Clark, President George W. Bush, country singer Travis Tritt, PGA Champion Hal Sutton, Governor Ann Richards, the Lyndon B. Johnson Library and Exxon-Mobil.

Jack has his studio at his home. He doesn't currently have a gallery, but his paintings and prints can be purchased through his website www.jackterryart.com.

Jack and his wife Anita have four beautiful children and twelve wonderful grandchildren.

Ever consider going to Cowboy Church?

Cowboy churches are mostly found in rural areas, but they have now expanded into more urban areas. Nashville, TN even has a Cowboy church that meets on Brick Church Pike.

Cowboy churches are local Christian churches within the cowboy culture that are distinctively Western heritage in character. A typical cowboy church may meet in a rural setting. Baptisms are generally done in a stock tank. The sermons are usually short and simple. Some cowboy churches have covered arenas where rodeo events such as bull riding, team roping, ranch sorting, team penning and equestrian events are held on weeknights or even their own country gospel band.

Many cowboy churches have existed throughout the western states for the past forty or fifty years, however just in the past fifteen or so years has there been an explosion of growth within the "movement". Prior to 1980 there were no less than 5 cowboy churches in Texas, now the number exceeds 200, and there are an estimated 750 nationwide. There has been no definitive group that established the movement; rather it seems to have had a spontaneous beginning in diverse areas of the country at nearly the same time. Some of these cowboy churches are an outgrowth of ministries to professional rodeo or team roping events, while the roots of many can be traced back to ministry events associated with ranch rodeos, ranch horse competitions, chuck wagon cooking competitions, cowboy poetry gatherings and other "cowboy culture" events.

The "no barriers" cowboy church model pioneered by Ron Nolen of the Baptist General Convention of Texas has been used by the AFCC (American Fellowship of Cowboy Churches) to plant more than two hundred cowboy churches in sixteen states. This model removes from the worship service the traditions that are believed to have no biblical basis, such as the "altar call" and passing of the collection plate. Tithes and offerings are simply placed in a boot, hat, or wooden bird house at the rear of the meeting room. The model also utilizes a specialized leadership structure that empowers volunteers and teams to execute most of the functions of the church. This model was developed at the Cowboy Church of Ellis County in Waxahachie, Texas, currently the largest cowboy church in North America.

The Southern Baptist Convention have started cowboy churches using their own policy and leadership structure Even though most of these churches are located in Texas and Oklahoma, the number of cowboy churches is expanding rapidly throughout the United States aided by a growing group of formal and informal cowboy church networks.

To find a Cowboy church in your area, go to www.cowboychurch.net and click on your state. You can find listings there.

January 2015

Cowboy Poet, Baxter Black, turning 70 & still going strong

Baxter Black, described by the New York Times as '…probably the nation's most successful living poet,"…thinks it's an exaggeration.

Born January 10, 1945, he can shoe a horse, string a bob wire fence and bang out a Bob Wills classic on his flat top guitar. Cowboy poet, ex-veterinarian and sorry team roper, he has more hair around his lip than on his head. Raised in New Mexico, spent his working' life in the mountain west tormenting cows, now he travels the country tormenting cowboys.

Since 1982, Baxter Black has rhymed his way into the national spotlight and now stands as the best selling cowboy poet in the world. He has written several books, has dozens of audio and video recordings and has achieved notoriety as a syndicated columnist and radio commentator. From the "Tonight Show" and PBS to NPR and the NFR, Baxter's wacko verse has been seen and heard by millions. His works are prominently displayed in both big city libraries and small town feed stores.

Everything about Baxter is cowboy; his cartoonish mustache, his personality and his poetry. He hasn't changed a thing about his subject matter or his delivery. He makes a living shining a spotlight on the flaws and foibles of everyday cowboy life, the day-to-day ups and downs of people who live with livestock and work the land. He demonstrates that it is the truth in his humor that makes it funny. Driven by a left hand sense of humor Black evokes laughter just by being there.

He currently resides in Benson, Arizona, with his wife, Cindy Lou, and has no cell phone, television, or fax machine. One of his philosophies of life claims: "In spite of all the computerized, digitalized, high-tech innovations of today, there will always be a need for folks to be a cowboy, "Ya either are one, or ya aren't!".

This former large animal veterinarian can be followed nationwide through his column, National Public Radio, public appearances, television and also through his books, cd's, videos and web site. . He continues to speak at Agricultural conferences and other social events across the country, write a column, speak on the radio, and has a short segment on RFD-TV.

In a nut shell, there is considerably more to Baxter than just an entertainer. He is the real thing. Because, as he says, "It's hard to be what you aren't." Baxter's philosophy is simple enough. In spite of all the computerized, digitized, high-tech innovations now available to mankind, there will always be a need for someone who can "think up stuff."

January 2015

The Nashville Brat Pack — Kids of the Country Stars!

By Julie Husky (Daughter of Ferlin Husky)

Funny quotes and "Ferlinisms" we remember growing up as kids.

My dad's philosophy on furniture dusting: "You have to wipe the dust off before spraying the polish… otherwise it just makes mud."

Every time we found dad eating in the kitchen, we'd say, "What did you fix us to eat, daddy?" He would reply with his cheeks full of food, "Fingernails and black coffee." (Actually he was a spectacular gourmet cook who was a wizard at regularly creating mouth-watering dishes for his family. Cooking came naturally to him, although, he didn't clean up after himself very well.

He had such a quick-witted, sarcastic sense of humor, that whenever he stood at the door to leave the house, we'd ask him where he was going. He always replied to us with, "I'm going berserk…

wanna go with me!?" Being too young to understand the definition of the word "berserk," we'd always answer with an enthusiastic, "Yes!!! We wanna go too!!! Wait for us!!!!"

His favorite time of year was Christmas. He and mom always filled the house with festive decorations, beautiful holiday music, wonderful home cooking, and warm, thoughtful gifts. He always got so excited when snow was in the forecast, and did his diligence

in maintaining a roaring fire in our living room fireplace to enhance the Christmas mood for us all. We can still vividly remember picturing him dressed in his long johns (long underwear) coming in from the cold outside, carrying loads of firewood in his arms with a big smile on his face, "Kids, it's supposed to snow…we might have a white Christmas this year!" Of course, we had very few white Christmases with him, but cherish them all. Miss him more and more each day.

January 2015

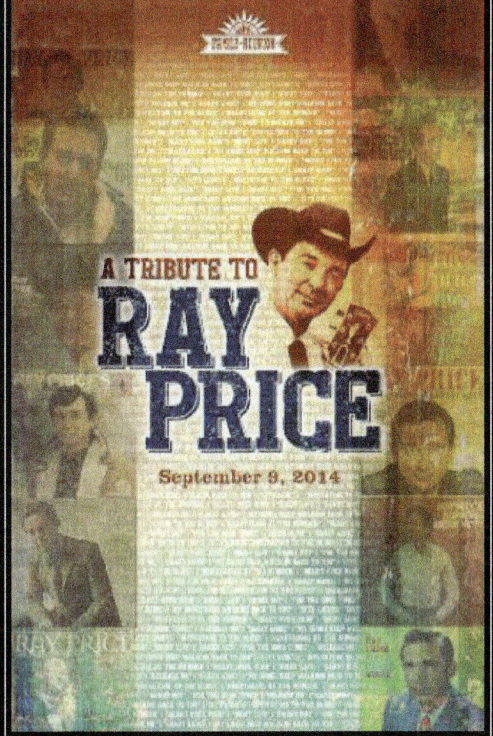

January 2015

 # Stage Clothes of the Stars

By Claudia Johnson

Dottie West: Sunshine and Spandex

She may have been raised on country sunshine, but her style became pure Hollywood.

Dottie West began her music career in 1950s, garnering commercial success in the early 1960s. Album covers and publicity photos from those years show a fresh-faced young woman in demure poses with bouffant red hair, sometimes sporting a long, curled ponytail. Usually attired in calico or gingham dresses, West's clothes had plenty of ruffles and lace. Her more elegant dresses incorporated silk and satin, sometimes with full skirts over stiff crinoline.

On her 1965 "Country and West" album cover with her dark hair lightened to strawberry blond and cut into a conservative puff she is almost unrecognizable. She's wearing a drab green business suit with a paisley neck scarf, looking earnestly at the camera with eyes made wider by false lashes. Two years later on the "With All My Heart and Soul" album cover she poses before a schoolroom blackboard dressed very "teacherly" in a teal suit, subdued makeup and a dark red flip hairdo.

As the '60s turned to '70s, West's look reflects all the fashion trends – maxi dresses, knee boots, velvet suits, bleached blond hair, patchwork and denim. A 1973 Dottie West paper doll book provides Western-inspired pant ensembles, flowing calico frocks with matching large-brimmed hats and vibrant-colored, ruffled evening gowns, perfect for dressing the award-winning singer and songwriter whose current hit, "County Sunshine," was topping pop and country charts and hawking Coca-Cola.

West's legendary paring with Kenny Rogers began with their 1978 hit "Every Time Two Fools Collide." Publicity photos show West in turtle-necks, denim or corduroy suits and the feathered hairstyle made famous by Farrah Fawcett.

Enter Bob Mackie, the Hollywood stylist who designed for performers like Cher, Carol Burnett, Diana Ross, Ann-Margret and Tina Turner. The only country star to wear Mackie's designs, the tall, thin West had the perfect body for the over-the-top costumes he created just for her. Cowgirl boots had high heels and fringe. Denim was replaced with shiny spandex. Capes shimmered with sequins. Plunging necklines teased with marabou. Evening gowns sparkled with rhinestones.

On West's 1980 "Wild West" album she thanked the designer, stating, "To the man whose clothes make women look good, Bob Mackie."

Apparently, her new look instilled confidence. At age 50 she was the subject of a 12-page pictorial and interview in Oui, a popular men's magazine.

"They didn't ask me to appear nude, but they asked me to reveal more than I wanted to," she told reporter Gene Triplett in a 1982 interview about the release of the magazine.

January 2015

In contrast to early album covers with West standing in fields of daisies or swinging on a veranda, her "Full Circle" album released the same year has her propped on a calico covered brass bed wearing a multicolored ruffled peasant dress, sleeves precariously slipping off both arms.

In a television interview conducted at her Nashville apartment in January 1991, West, wearing a more demure outfit with a fox tail scarf, envisions herself her future self.

"When I'm 87, I'll still be walking on the Grand Ole Opry stage and singing 'Here comes more tears to cry'," she told her interviewer, assuring her fans that at 58, she had no intention of retiring.

Less than eight months later she was gone, killed in a car crash as a neighbor rushed her to a slated Opry performance, denying West and her fans the chance to see the evolution of her style as an octogenarian.

Mountain Faith is living the bluegrass

Mountain Faith is an awarded, accomplished bluegrass group based in the mountains of North Carolina. They have been singing and traveling together for 14 years.

Coming up on Larry's Country Diner on January 31 were Sam McMahan, on bass, Luke Dotson on guitar and harmony vocals, Dustin Norris on Mandolin, Summer McMahan on fiddle and harmony vocals, and Brayden McMahan on banjo and harmony vocals.

Mountain Faith has a unique style that offers a variety of different genres of music. Audiences applaud their ability to offer numerous styles from traditional and contemporary bluegrass, classic and modern country, folk, acoustic and contemporary gospel and a little rhythm and blues! This band is fresh, pure and upbeat.

They perform frequently at Dollywood becoming a crowd favorite over the years. They travel the bluegrass festival circuit, running alongside bluegrass' top bands, all over the United States and Canada. Concert venues include civic centers, auditoriums, arenas, fair grounds, parks, churches and other locations. Recently at the SPBGMA awards, they were the only band to have all members, but one, nominated for instrumental awards.

Sam McMahan

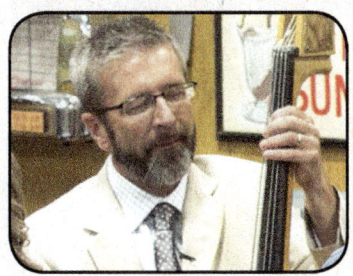

Sam McMahan is the oldest member of the group. He is the father of Summer and Brayden. When Sam is not on the road, he helps his brother run their tire shop and gas station. Sam can also be found in the summer months occasionally hosting his own bluegrass festival on his farm. His festivals are always charitable events raising money for local charities. Sam certainly has a servant's heart.

Sam has traveled with his two children and nephew for 14 years. The kids started playing at 7, 8, and 9 with a passion for the music and people. Sam wanted to nurture that passion by traveling with them. He began reconnecting with the bass, which led him to 2014 bass player of the year nomination with SPBGMA in Nashville, TN.

Sam was thankful to be raised in a Christian home. He is thankful for his Salvation and for the opportunities that God has allowed the band to have. He has passed that heritage and love for Christ on to his family.

Summer McMahan

Summer was born July 1st, 1993. She is currently a junior at Western Carolina University in Cullowhee, NC. She is seeking a degree in Business and Entrepreneurship. She has been playing the fiddle since she was 6. By 8, she was traveling with her dad, brother and cousin most every weekend, all the while, growing her passion for music. "I cannot imagine life without music." Summer says. Summer's role models for music are

January 2015

Alison Krauss, Lee Ann Womack and Sonya Isaacs. Many have told her that she reminds them of Alison. She was honored to meet Alison at IBMA a couple of years ago. She has had the privilege to sing with Sonya at a local bluegrass festival.

Summer has a love for country music. She has recently completed a solo project. She is excited about what the future holds with music.

Summer is thankful for her salvation. She feels blessed to have been a lot of places in the United States all because of music. She has met many fine artists and musicians along the way.

Brayden McMahan

Brayden McMahan was born July 7th, 1994. He and his sister are barely one year apart in age. Brayden and Summer have always done everything together. Being able to be together has brought about some of the finest family vocal harmonies.

Brayden is an accomplished musician. He was nominated for banjo player of the year at recent SPBGMA in Nashville, TN. Although Brayden is the banjo player, he also plays a variety of instruments. He boasts a smooth, melodious sound.

Brayden is currently seeking a degree in Engineering. He is a college transfer student at a local community college.

Brayden says he is thankful to have been raised in church. He is thankful for Christ as Lord and Savior. He considers it a blessing to play in the churches across the United States.

Luke Dotson

Luke Dotson was born January 11th, 1990. He is originally from Boone, N.C. Luke has a degree from Western Carolina University in Parks and Recreation Management.

Luke has been playing the guitar seven years. He has always enjoyed listening to bluegrass music. Among Luke's influences are Tony Rice, Doc Watson, The Hayes Family, and Charles Johnson and the Revivers, which all respectfully reflect his variety of music covering several genres of music.

Luke is the newest member of Mountain Faith, replacing Sam's nephew, John Morgan. He offers excellent instrumentation, strong vocals, either solo or melodic harmonies.

Luke grew up in church and is thankful for his heritage and for his relationship with Christ.

Dustin Norris

Dustin Norris played mandolin with Mountain Faith on Larry's Country Diner. He is from Monroe, NC and has been around bluegrass all his life. He started playing mandolin when he was about 8.

Cory Piatt

Cory Piatt joined the band shortly after the Diner taping taking Dustin's place on mandolin.

Cory is an exquisitely talented young picker who already has a professional resume most musicians would envy. He has been playing almost half his 19 years, and has developed a stunning mastery of his instrument in this short time, as evidenced by his debut solo project, Daydreams, on Patuxent Music.

January 2015

Brown, Vincent & Williams nominated for Grammys!

It's going to be a great year for Country Music. Three great nominations for the 2015 Grammys were announced in December.

T. Graham Brown: Forever Changed Best Roots - Gospel Album

Just following the announcement of the release of his latest album, *Forever Changed*, it was announced that he has received a Grammy Nomination for 2015. Brown is nominated for the Best Roots Gospel Album.

Singer, Songwriter and Entertainer T. Graham Brown teamed up with Mansion/Sony RED for the release of his new Forever Changed album. It is comprised of thirteen tracks that features guest vocal appearances by popular, award-winning artists Vince Gill, Jason Crabb, Leon Russell, Jeff & Sheri Easter, The Oak Ridge Boys, Steve Cropper, The Booth Brothers, Three Bridges, Sony Isaacs and Jimmy Fortune. A line up of talent that collectively boasts 26 Grammys and 37 Dove Awards. Produced by Mark L. Carman, Forever Changed is going to be released January 27th, 2015.

T. Graham Brown will also be the featured guest on Larry's Country Diner on February 14 and he and his wife, Sheila, are guests on the new Country's Family Reunion Sweethearts series set to release soon.

Rhonda Vincent: Only Me - Bluegrass Album of the Year

Rhonda Vincent is nominated for Bluegrass Album of the Year. Her 2014 release Only Me was received with high critical acclaim following its release, and now serves as a final contender for the highest prize in the music industry – garnering Vincent her sixth Grammy nomination. After debuting at #1, where it spent its first two weeks on the chart, the album has proved to have legs. Only Me continues the long line of history-making success that Vincent has enjoyed. Each of her past eight discs hit either No. 1 or No. 2 on the Billboard Bluegrass Album chart.

Rhonda Vincent has been one of the most consistent recording artists in the world of Bluegrass Music, winning the IBMA Female Vocalist of the Year award a remarkable seven consecutive times, and walked away with the top honor of IBMA Entertainer of the Year in 2001. With her band, The Rage – they are the Most Award Winning Band in Bluegrass Music History with over 80 awards. They maintain one of the busiest schedules in the music business today, recently hitting a personal record number of bookings for 2015.

Hank Williams: The Garden Spot Programs, 1950 - Best Historical Album

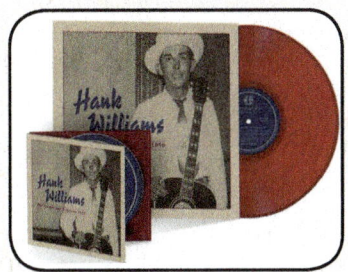

Hank Williams has a release of songs unheard for 64 years that is available on CD, limited-edition red vinyl album and is nominated for a Grammy for Best Historical Album.

Set the time machine for early morning on KSIB, Creston, Iowa. February, 1950. Rescued from obscurity, these shows originally aired over 6 decades ago, and The Garden Spot Programs, 1950 collects material from the four of them now known to exist.

From hits to standards to songs rarely (if ever) performed, this is pure Hank Williams, including playful, between song banter. Fully restored to incredible quality, The Garden Spot Programs, 1950 is more like being in the studio when they were recorded than actually listening to them on the radio!

January 2015

The CD packaging contains rare photos from the collection of set co-producer and Williams biographer, Colin Escott, as well as new liners. Also available on LP, the first pressing will be on limited-edition, translucent red vinyl (with black vinyl to follow), and contains Escott's informative notes and a download card.

"It's incredible to me that we're still finding new recordings by my dad. Great ones, at that! No one even suspected that these recordings existed. We partnered with Omnivore Recordings for this release, and I especially love it that they're taking my dad back to vinyl."

— Jett Williams

The 57th Annual Grammy Awards are set to take place on February 8, 2015 in Los Angeles at the Staples Center. You can learn more about the upcoming awards and nominees at grammy.com.

January 2015

Update on the 'real' Larry's Country Diner in Bellevue

Larry Black says the 'real' Larry's Country Diner is back on track. After negotiations with an existing restaurant fell through, things are back on track to build the Diner on a 1.3-acre parcel just off Interstate 40 at the Bellevue exit (196) across from Shoney's.

Renae Johnson, the vice-president of operations at Gabriel Communications – but better known to the show's faithful as the white-haired, Renae the Waitress – can't wait for groundbreaking.

"Instead of shovels, we're going to be out there with a huge fork and spoon. And if I had my way we'd have the cameras rolling for our fans to see," she says.

"We're excited about the possibility of getting started. I think it will become a destination point," says Larry.

"In our blue-skies approach to things, we even have a vision to have a performance venue out here. I'd take the old country folk who are legends, who are basically sitting around on weekends doing nothing, and give them an opportunity to come out and play for folks. I think that would be a great attraction."

Longtime restaurateur Charlie McCabe, who currently operates the PaSgetti's restaurant in Bellevue and whose family owned the Loveless Café until 2003, will be the Diner's manager.

Nashville, Tennessee

January 2015

FEBRUARY

Huge loss in a tiny package as country music loses Little Jimmy Dickens

James Cecil Dickens was born December 19, 1920, but he was better known as Little Jimmy Dickens. He was not only famous for his singing but for his humorous novelty songs, his small size, 4'11" (150 cm), and his rhinestone-studded outfits (which he is given credit for introducing into country music live performances). He started as a member of the Grand Ole Opry in 1948 and became a member of the Country Music Hall of Fame in 1983. He was the oldest living member of the Grand Ole Opry.

Born in Bolt, West Virginia, Dickens began his musical career in the late 1930s, performing on WJLS radio station in Beckley, West Virginia while attending West Virginia University. He soon quit school to pursue a full-time music career, and traveled the country performing on various local radio stations under the name "Jimmy the Kid."

Dickens was heard performing on WKNX, a radio station in Saginaw, Michigan, in 1948, by Roy Acuff, who introduced him to Art Satherly at Columbia Records and officials from the Grand Ole Opry. Dickens signed with Columbia in September and joined the Opry in August. Around this time he began using the nickname, Little Jimmy Dickens, inspired by his short stature.

Dickens recorded many novelty songs for Columbia, including "Country Boy", "A-Sleeping at the Foot of the Bed", and "I'm Little But I'm Loud".

His song "Take an Old Cold Tater (And Wait)" inspired Hank Williams to nickname him "Tater".

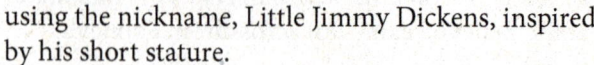

By 1950, Dickens had formed the Country Boys with musicians Jabbo Arrington, Grady Martin, Bob Moore and Thumbs Carllile. It was during this time that he discovered future Country Music Hall of Famer Marty Robbins at a Phoenix, Arizona television station while on tour with the Grand Ole Opry road show. Dickens left the Grand Ole Opry to tour with the Philip Morris Country Music Show in 1957.

Dickens scored his first top-10 country hit since 1954 with "The Violet and the Rose" in 1962..

Then in 1964 Dickens became the first country artist to circle the globe while on tour, and also made numerous TV appearances, including on The Tonight Show Starring Johnny Carson. He released his biggest hit, "May the Bird of Paradise Fly Up Your Nose", reaching No. 1 on the country chart and No. 15 on the pop chart in 1965.

Dickens left Columbia for Decca Records in the late 1960s before moving again to United Artists in 1971. That same year, he married his wife, Mona, and in 1975 he returned to the Grand Ole Opry. In 1983, Dickens was inducted into the Country Music Hall of Fame.

Toward the end of his life, Dickens made appearances in a number of music videos by fellow

Thanks to our loyal reader, Ernestine Hatch for sending us these photos. Notice the autograph in the upper corner.

February 2015

country musician and West Virginia native Brad Paisley. He was also featured on several of Paisley's albums in bonus comedy tracks, along with other Opry mainstays such as George Jones and Bill Anderson.

With the death of Hank Locklin in March 2009, Dickens became the oldest living member of the Grand Ole Opry at the age of 90. He made regular appearances as a host at the Opry, often with the self-deprecating joke that he is also known as "Willie Nelson after taxes."

Dickens played the Opry on December 20 for the last time. He was hospitalized after a stroke on December 25, 2014, days after his last appearance to mark his 94th birthday. He died of cardiac arrest on January 2, 2015. He is survived by his wife, Mona Dickens, whom he married in 1971, and two daughters, Pamela Detert and Lisa King.

Little Jimmy Dickens was on Country's Family Reunion's DVD series, CFR 1, CFR 2, Nashville and Looking Back. Each of these series can be purchased by calling 1-800-820-5405 or by going to www.cfrvideos.com.

What or who is the Martin Family Circus?

They call themselves the Martin Family Circus and if you've ever been to a circus before you know it's filled with bright colors, a lot of characters, and just plain fun! It's 4 kids ranging in age from 6 to 15, representing four generations of musical heritage.

The circus consists of Paul and Jamie Martin, and their four children, March (15), Kell (12), Texas (8), and Tallant (6), the Martin Family Circus may not be a three-ring show in the traditional sense; but what you get from them holds true to the family-fun, happy atmosphere that only a circus can bring. With tight harmonies and a wide variety of acoustic, melody-driven songs, ranging from Toto and The Beach Boys, to Johnny Cash and The Staple Singers, the Martin Family Circus leaves even the hardest music critic satisfied and amazed by the musicality of such young children. Their first CD, titled "In Training," represents their own favorite artists, as well as honors their rich musical roots.

Their background is impressive. Grammy Award Winning artist Paul Martin, AKA "Apostle Paul" from Marty Stuart and the Fabulous Superlatives, and the hit TV show "The Marty Stuart Show" on RFD-TV (also former lead singer/guitarist of country/pop group Exile). Paul met and married Jamie Allen Martin, daughter of Duane Allen of the Oak Ridge Boys & Norah Lee Allen of the Grand Ole Opry's own Carol Lee Singers. They began raising a family that would be exposed to a rich musical heritage from birth. Each of their four children seemed to possess God-given talents, along with the same passion for music as their parents and grandparents. March and his brother Kell flocked to their parents' recording studio early-on, learning to play guitar, bass, drums, and keyboards. Little sister Texas showed talent at the age of 3 for writing songs and singing classic movie melodies, while baby sister Tallant was drawn to the microphone as a toddler.

After several years of singing for fun with the kids (dubbed by Vince Gill as the "Martin Family Circus"), Jamie and Paul decided to set their focus on teaching them how to harmonize and developing their instrumental skills. They spent the summer of 2010 sitting on their patio, making homemade ice cream and working on songs with challenging harmonies. Making sure the children gained a vast appreciation for all genres of music, they learned anything from traditional cowboy music of the Sons Of The Pioneers, to classic rock/pop, to modern day Contemporary Christian artists like Steve Fee.

February 2015

Those practices soon led to family performances around the region.

"It's very humbling and exciting to be standing on the Ryman stage, watching the crowd go crazy for your children. Still, we never lose sight of the fact that we want to keep them grounded and thankful—and to bring some light and a smile to folks along the way," says Paul.

Down Home
with Carol Bass

You have heard the saying, "You can tell the year a woman graduated from high school by the way she wears her hair and makeup!" Just like hair and make-up, a home can show its age too. Here are some dead give-a-ways known as age spots, see if you recognize any. But more importantly, here are some simple practical fixes.

Hope you found this information helpful. Tune in next month for the next instalment in the series; "Is your Room Showing Its Age Spots!"

"AGE SPOT" - FABRICS

Is one of the age spots in your room in the form of the fabrics you are still using? Is it a pattern that has a country feel in blue and mauve? Is it a contemporary splash of color in Miami Vice black and red? Fabric patterns and colors can create that time warp. Fabrics are one of the ways I can tell what year the room was lasted decorated. But buying new sofa and chairs can be expensive. Here are some decorating secrets we use when we create a room-makeover.

Toile Fabric - Not on-trend

Geometric Fabric, - Current Pattern

PRACTICAL SIMPLE FIX

Slipcovers are a great look and very much on-trend. They are relatively inexpensive with many options. Some of my favorite companies are Surefit.net and Domestications.com. I have also found them at Walmart and Big Lots. The cost can be around $80 for a sofa and less for a chair. If the budget allows, have custom slipcovers made. If money is an issue, simply add new pillows in a current fabric. Also consider new window panels in on-trend fabric or solid color. Below are two chairs with slipcovers, one in a fabric that is not on-trend, the other (same chair) in a more current pattern.

**The CFR News
is published monthly by
Gabriel Communications, Inc.
P.O. Box 210796, Nashville, TN
37221
615-673-2846
Larry Black, Publisher
Renae Johnson, General Manager
Paula Underwood Winters, Editor
Subscriptions: $29.95 yearly**

February 2015

Behind the Scenes — **Spotlight**

Thumper Pigg - Gabriel Fulfillment

We have so many talented folks that work behind the scenes of our television shows and tapings that we thought you should meet them. Their talents and experience surely humble us.

Thumper Pigg is the Fulfillment Manager and Mail Marketing Strategist for Gabriel Communications. He is thirty-one years old and has a wife and three-year-old daughter. In addition to working at Gabriel Communications, he is also the Associate Pastor at Stewarts Chapel Baptist Church in middle Tennessee.

"I enjoy all the work in which I am involved as well as restoring my '65 Chevy pickup that has been passed down to me. At some point in the future, I will pass it down to my child, who will be the fourth generation owner," Thumper says proudly. "I am also a 'hobby' musician. I play a variety of instruments and enjoy them all, but the guitar is my favorite."

Like our readers, he is a fan of classic, traditional Country music and is thankful for a company like Gabriel that seeks to celebrate the legacy of Country music. One of the highlights musically was when he was afforded the opportunity to play in jam sessions aboard the 2014 Caribbean cruise. He was able to play with Billy Dean, Rhonda Vincent, Mo Pitney and others, as well as the best musicians Country music has ever seen! "Keith Bilbrey told me that no one could slap the smile off my face. How true that was!"

Thumper says he hopes you are enjoying the series of collections and merchandise we offer. "Our customer service and fulfillment teams take our jobs very seriously and we are working together to serve you better than ever before!"

Thumper is second from right, playing with Mo Pitney, Billy Dean and one of the fans.

Mo Pitney gets Billboard recognition

One of the strongest male vocalists to come along in some time, there's not a lot of vocal acrobatics or technical gimmicks involved with Pitney. Instead, the singer possesses one of the most traditional-sounding vocal styles we have heard in years. Whether covering Keith Whitley on "Miami, My Amy," or turning romantic on "I Didn't Go To Sleep Last Night," Pitney is country all the way. (The latter is one of the most impressive tracks on his debut disc, a co-write with the legendary Bill Anderson.)

February 2015

WORD SEARCH

```
F R I Z Z E L L Q K G H C U C S X F V L
U Y X L C H M W K A Y H O Q E Y A D Z J
W L M C S A I F P R P B N O R A H L E E
H G B R K U H S W E E T H E A R T S C B
Z A Z K A T M F J E O T Y A J U W T L O
S T Q Y G N Q A G U V S W I S A A C S M
D L V G G P D Z M B W O N U X B L R D K
Q I B J S M I E J H B Q H W Z I T V F S
T N I D Q X B W R L O J D T I N X X M T
I P G M T E S C O S H N L U E L V F C G
R P Z D N A U P E V O C K C A E L Z K R
O H O L I W H Q Q E G N N Y W N Y P E A
B T O L E U G M X H D I L R T M E E L H
M W P N A L U K P P V D S E N O T X L A
T O R G D A J O E Y D X B A R S N R Y M
W Y X J F A D P B K N W B W U O C K K Q
H I W D O K H I Z E C B V K X Z R Q B C
I R T G S H E P P A R D S D G J N Y L H
T G F H X Z V P L F G L L I P H T J Y T
E O U U U P K L N D H K S B U O Z T G U
```

SWEETHEARTS	TGRAHAM	GATLIN
HONKYTONK	RHONDA	DUANE
SKAGGS	NORAHLEE	RORY
WHITE	ANDERSON	JOEY
FRIZZELL	VINCENT	TGSHEPPARD
KELLY	ISAACS	

TOUR DATES & TICKETS

Dates	Venue	Location
May 5, 6, 7, 8, 9	Starlite Theatre	Branson, MO
Sept. 22, 23, 24, 25, 26, 27	Starlite Theatre	Branson, MO

For more information: www.starlitetheatre.com or (417) 337-9333

COUNTRY LEGENDS PAST AND PRESENT BY TOM WOOD

ERNEST TUBB

We're still walking the floor for the Texas Troubador, even though the song most closely associated with the long career of Ernest Tubb wasn't a No. 1 hit.

What "Walking The Floor Over You" — which peaked at No. 23 in 1941 — did do, though, was put Ernest in the national spotlight, one which would continue to shine on him for another four decades.

So what was the country music pioneer's first chart-topper? That came three years later with the mournful "Soldier's Last Letter" (1944). In all, Ernest had six No. 1 hits during his career, the next two coming back-to-back in "It's Been So Long Darling" (1945) and "Rainbow at Midnight" (1946).

Fans recognized Ernest Tubb's talent and flocked to him. In a two-year span, he had 24 hit records.

Strange though it may sound, Ernest's most popular No. 1 hit was more closely associated with Elvis Presley. But in late 1948, Ernest was the first record "Blue Christmas" for fans.

His other top hits included "Slipping Around" (1949) and "Goodnight Irene," a 1950 duet with Red Foley. The duo enjoyed a great personal friendship over the years, though they "feuded" on-air.

Ernest returned to his Texas roots for another of his hits. "Waltz Across Texas" became a staple in Lone Star State dance halls when waltz lessons were being given.

Texas may have been home, but Tennessee is where Ernest Tubb made his mark. And his legacy is felt even today.

The first Ernest Tubb Record Shop and opened for business on Broadway, just a stone's throw from the Ryman Auditorium, in 1947 and on May 3, 2014, celebrated its 67th anniversary. The Midnight

February 2015

Jamboree continues to draw crowds to the Texas Troubador Theater near the Grand Ole Opry House, approximately 10 miles from downtown Nashville. Glenn Douglas Tubbs, Ernest's nephew and the writer of his very first hit, performed at the 67th Midnight Jamboree gala.

Here are a few other nuggets from Ernest's golden career.

He was the first performer to play the electric to the Grand Ole Opry stage.

In 1947, Ernest headlined the first Grand Ole Opry show to play Carnegie Hall in New York.

Ernest was the lone inductee to the Country Music Hall of Fame in 1965, and that same year he began hosting The Ernest Tubb Show for a three-year run. Ernest also appeared in Coal Miner's daughter in 1980, along with and Minnie Pearl and Roy Acuff.

He remained active throughout the latter years of his career, making up to 200 appearances. Ernest Tubb died on Sept. 6, 1984.

Country Questions
By Dick Boise, CMH

Send questions to:
Dick Boise, , c/o CFR News,
P.O. Box 201796, Nashville,
TN 37221.

Q. Hi Dick, I was watching an old Wilburn Brothers TV show and they had on Mae Axton and she mentioned her book "Country Singers As I Know Them." Loving old Country music and its artists I have been looking for a copy. Any suggestions?

Thanks, Robert Magee, Christiansburg, VA

A. Thanks for your question and I have never heard of that book. I would like a copy myself. I, too, saw only one available at a very high price. It was published by Hurst: Sweet Publishing 1973 and possibly one of our kind readers may have it available. I'll also keep searching my sources. Maybe we will both be lucky to find copies.

Q. In the late 40s and early 50s I really liked "Texas" Jim Robertson. Do you have any information about him and is there any place I might find records by him other than searching at flea markets?

Thanks. Gerald Derosier, Canon City, CO

A. Gerald, in all my information on country music artists, there has been very little about "Texas" Jim. He was born in Texas in 1909 and died in 1966. He was in the Marines in World War II and entertained in Japan later. I have a friend who may have some copies of his old Victor recordings. I'll send you the form and address to OLD HOMESTEAD RECORDS in Brighton, MI. He sells tapes of old records and is reasonable. I learn from my readers every month, and "thanks."

Q. I'm interested in finding information about a guitarist who used to play for Jim Ed Brown and for Porter Wagoner. I wondered what he is doing now? I think his name was Bruce Osmond, and would like to know more about him.

Bob Bruce Deming, NM

A. Thanks for your inquiry and it caused me to recall the lyrics to a song from around 66 or 67..."Well, there's thirteen hundred and fifty-two guitar pickers in Nashville" and Bruce Osbon is one of them. You are correct. He was with Porter and can be seen on some of the TV show re-runs that were taped on the old Opryland stage. He is now enjoying retirement and he told me thanks for asking.

Q. I want to ask you if you might be able to tell me what Ricky Skaggs' first number one single was? Enjoy CFR News each month here at our house.

B. Norton, Ricky Hill, CT

February 2015

A. Here is the song I believe was Ricky Skaggs. first number one..."Crying My Heart Out Over You." It was big for him around 1981. Many good songs for us to hear since then by that Kentucky born young man. You might enjoy his book, "Kentucky Traveler, My Life In Music." Thanks for the kind words about the News.

By Rebecca Ashworth Parker, Daughter of Ernie "Trembling Lips" Ashworth

I remember traveling with Daddy in the Summer time, how excited we all were to go on a Road trip to unknown places. One of the memories of being on the road was when Kentucky Fried Chicken started franchising, Daddy would get a bucket of chicken & we ate it in the car. You have to remember this was 1964 & there wasn't a lot of Fast Food Restaurants.

Daddy favorite past time was watching TV. After Mama & Daddy moved to Lewisburg. Daddy was one of the first People to have Satellite TV. The Satellite was a big dish delivered on a trailer with a hand crank. Daddy would go down to the dish & we would stand by the window to let him know when he had found a watchable channel.

One of my favorite memories is on my 16th Birthday, Daddy took me with him to the Opry. They called me on stage with Daddy & everyone sang Happy Birthday. Too bad we did not have a movie camera to capture this on tape.

Holding his first grandchild, Patrick above and with the family at right.

Daddy was known for His "Lip Suits." I can see him now, walking around Heaven with his Lip Suit on, looking for a TV.

February 2015

Road Stories

By Claudia Johnson

Jeannie Seely: Saying yes to something special

Life on the road usually holds some surprises and unexpected events, no matter how much you plan, according to Grammy winner and Grand Ole Opry member Jeannie Seeley, who has maintained her reputation as "Miss Country Soul" across six decades.

Seely's career is as diverse as it is durable. She's scored number one hit songs as a solo artist, as a duet partner and as a songwriter.

As a singer, she has recorded more than a dozen albums of her own, and her vocals can be heard on more than 75 additional compilation albums and CDs. For 13 consecutive years Seely placed records on the Billboard country singles chart. She won the 1966 Grammy Award for the "Best Country Vocal Performance by a Female" for the enduring country favorite, "Don't Touch Me."

Songs written by Seely have been recorded by numerous Country Music Hall of Fame members and award-winning artists, earning her accolades and awards for her songwriting.

A member of the Grand Ole Opry since 1967, the beautiful, vivacious blond is credited for wearing the first mini-skirt on the Grand Ole Opry stage. Seely was the first female to regularly host Opry segments and still performs weekly when she is not on the road. She often appears as a headlining artist on the annual Grand Ole Opry Cruise.

As an actress, she's appeared in the movies "Changing Hearts" and "Honeysuckle Rose." She's also starred in major stage productions, "Always... Patsy Cline," "The Best Little Whorehouse in Texas," "Could It Be Love," "Takin' It Home" and "Everybody Loves Opal."

Seely's stage, television and radio appearances are too numerous to mention. Notable, however, is that she served as a radio disc jockey on her own Armed Forces Network Show. She can be spotted in videos with Confederate Railroad and Brad Paisley. She's even published her own successful book of witticisms titled "Pieces of a Puzzled Mind."

No stranger to the road, she has performed throughout the world. She traveled on military tours throughout Europe and Asia. She's also been part of a successful overseas tour with the "Grand Ladies of the Grand Ole Opry." She and her former duet partner, Jack Greene, toured together for more than a decade, performing everywhere from New York's Madison Square Garden to London's Wembley Arena.

However, one call while she was performing at Dollywood stands out.

"Many years ago, I was scheduled to appear at Dollywood in a wonderful production with a very talented and energetic cast of young performers," Seely recalled. "It featured an Opry Star segment, and I was the featured Opry artist for a two week run."

One day she received a call from a friend who asked her to become part of what she thought was a "preposterous" idea for a television show.

"I told him I simply couldn't do it right now, but maybe later if he did some more I would be happy to," she said. "He said 'No, I really need you for this one.'"

February 2015

Seely, quite reasonably, told her friend that she could not work all day, drive home to Nashville at night, tape a television show all day, drive back to Pigeon Forge and work the next morning.

"We were performing three to four shows daily, and while it was really fun, it was also an exhausting schedule, so my plan was to just make sure I got plenty of rest during my off hours so I could keep up," she said.

She tried another excuse, telling him that she was not feeling well, to which he replied, "This will make you feel better."

Not accepting "no" for an answer, her friend proposed that he send a car to Pigeon Forge that would drive her to Nashville and back so she could rest along the way. She gave in.

"How could I say 'no'?" she asked, admitting, "Obviously his idea wasn't so preposterous after all. The show was called "Country Family Reunion," and we're still doing them."

Seely said there is a moral to her story.

"If Larry Black calls you with an idea, go for it!" she said. "Now, he might tell you a different version of this story, but believe mine!"

Larry's Country Diner RFD Show Schedule Feb. 2015

PREVIOUSLY AIRED

COLLIN RAYE
Saturday, February 7
10:00 p.m. Central
Sunday, February 8
6:00 p.m. Central

NEW SHOW

T. GRAHAM BROWN
Saturday, February 14
10:00 p.m. Central
Sunday, February 15
6:00 p.m. Central

NEW SHOW

RONNIE McDOWELL
Saturday, February 21
10:00 p.m. Central
Sunday, February 22
6:00 p.m. Central

NEW SHOW

MARTIN FAMILY CIRCUS
Saturday, February 28
10:00 p.m. Central
Sunday, March 1
6:00 p.m. Central

February 2015

Joey + Rory

Sheila & T. Graham Brown

Sharon White & Ricky Skaggs

Sonya Isaacs & Jimmy Yeary

Linda Davis & Lang Scott

Songs of love color so many moments in each of our lives…. from a first kiss, to a first dance. Country's Family Reunion decided to celebrate Love by getting together some country music couples to share their love stories and some great love songs in an all new series Country's Family Reunion Sweethearts.

You'll fall in love with the songs and stories, and you'll get the background scoop on some of country's most loving couples—

AND, there's something else. Because so many of you have asked for an audio version of the songs from our series, Country's Family Reunion has produced an Audio CD with all of the songs from the taping so you can listen to the music wherever you want to go along with the new DVD series.

You get the Sweethearts DVDs, plus the Backstage, plus the audio CD for only $79.80 plus free shipping if you call 1-800-820-5405 and tell them the promo code "FREE SHIPPING."

This is such a unique series, and we hope you love it as much as we do.

T. Graham Brown & Sheila
TG Sheppard & Kelly Lang
Duane & Norah Lee Allen
Ricky Skaggs & Sharon White
David Frizzell & Jo
Jimmy Fortune & Nina
Linda Davis & Lang Scott
Sonya Isaacs Yeary & Jimmy Yeary
Rhonda Vincent & Herb Sandker
Joey + Rory and Heidi Feek
Larry Gatlin & Janis

Rhonda Vincent

TG Sheppard & Kelly Lang

Duane & Norah Lee Allen

Larry Gatlin

 presents....

Starting February 6 on RFD-TV
Fridays…7 p.m. central
Saturdays…11 p.m central

Own the complete series
$79.80 plus $6.95 s/h
www.cfrvideos.com 1-800-820-5405

February 2015

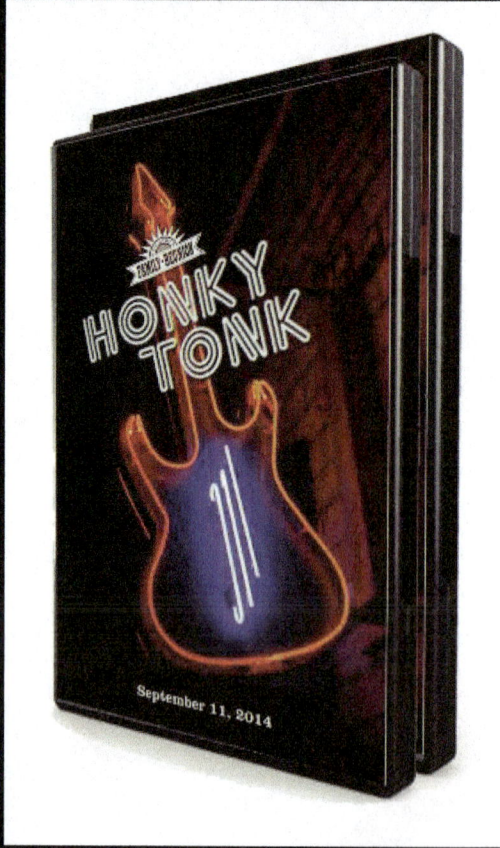

ALL NEW HONKY TONK REUNION

Did you know that MOST of the country artists you know and love today got their starts in places called Honky Tonks? That's right… from Patsy Cline to Ernest Tubb, Honky Tonks are an important stop in the careers of some of the brightest country stars. And the music you'll find in Honky Tonks is like none other on the American landscape. Designed to get your feet tapping and your mind off your troubles, this is music you can't sit down to!

Here at Country's Family Reunion, we enjoy ALL types of Country Music… and Honky Tonk certainly applies. So, we recently hosted a HONKY TONK reunion! The music is so unique, but still uniquely country. We recorded all the people who came out and put it on 5 DVD's for your enjoyment.

Hosted by Bill Anderson, this series features tons of your favorite country music legends such as Moe Bandy, David Frizzell, Tony Booth, John Conlee, Darrell McCall, The Whites, Jim Lauderdale, David Ball, Jim Ed Brown, Ray Pillow, Junior Brown, Eddy Raven, Rhonda Vincent, Dale Watson, Roy Clark, Becky Hobbs, Wade Hayes, and many more!

It's almost 6 hours of content and is just 79.80 plus free shipping if you call 1-800-820-5405 and tell them the promo code "FREE SHIPPING."

February 2015

Musical Sweethearts

♥ October 26, 1969 - Jessi Colter married Waylon Jennings in Mesa, Arizona. They both contributed to country music's first platinum album, Wanted: The Outlaws, and Waylon frequently hailed Jessi as a major force in helping him conquer his cocaine addiction. Waylon passed away on February 13, 2002. In 2006, Jessi released her first traditional studio album in 20 years, and their son Shooter Jennings has followed in mom and dad's footsteps as a recording artist.

♥ March 1, 1968 - Johnny Cash exchanged vows with June Carter at the Methodist Church, in Franklin, Kentucky. Both had previous marriages that produced yet more country stars: Johnny and his first wife, the former Vivian Liberto, welcomed Rosanne Cash; and June's wedding to Country Music Hall of Fame member Carl Smith yielded Carlene Carter. Johnny and June lasted long enough to observe their 35th anniversary. Sadly, June died on May 15, 2003 and Johnny died later that same year on September 12.

♥ February 16, 1969 - George Jones married Tammy Wynette in Ringgold, Georgia, six months after they first announced they had already wed. The duo travelled together in a bus bearing "Mr. & Mrs. Country Music" on the side, but in reality they had a very rocky six years together. Both required at least four marriages to find the one that really took: Tammy married songwriter George Richey in 1978, remaining with him for her last two decades. George and his wife, Nancy, went to the altar in Woodville, Texas, in 1983. And here's a whopper of a tale: Demonstrating just how down-to-earth the couple was, George and Nancy had dinner on their wedding night at a Burger King. George passed away in April of 2013.

♥ May 30, 1966 – Who doesn't love a good mystery? Dolly Parton married Carl Dean in Catoosa County, Georgia, and to this day, he's managed to remain in the shadows publicly, with many of her fans wondering what her husband looks like. In 2006, they returned to the church where they first exchanged their vows to celebrate 40 years together.

♥ December 10, 2005 - Garth Brooks and Trisha Yearwood said "I do" at their home in Owasso, Oklahoma. They had known each other for more than 15 years and sung on each other's records, and Garth's public proposal on one knee remains one of the most enduring country images of 2005. The couple will return to the stage now that their children are out of high school for Garth's 2014 Comeback Tour which could last as long as three years.

♥ December 31, 1947 - Roy Rogers married Dale Evans at the Flying L Ranch in Murray County, Oklahoma. The two were already co-stars, but the union allowed them to travel many happy trails together on a daily basis. Oddly enough, Roy was late for the ceremony—he was detained putting out a fire started by a cigarette butt in another room. And, for the record, even though they spent plenty of time with their horses, Trigger and Buttermilk, she did not consider her flowers a "bridle" bouquet!

♥ April 14, 1948 - Two months after leaving Bill Monroe's band, Earl Scruggs married Louise Certain in Gaffney, South Carolina. She became the manager of Flatt & Scruggs and had a huge role in putting bluegrass in an upscale light. In the ultimate demonstration of family ties, their sons—Gary, Steve and Randy—played with their dad during the '70s in the progressive band The Earl Scruggs Revue. Earl passed away in March of 2012.

♥ March 10, 2000 - Vince Gill married Christian singer Amy Grant in Nashville, with about 75 people attending. Amy took her vows barefoot, and six weeks later, Vince took her to the Grand Ole Opry, where she made her debut, duetting with her husband on "How Great Thou Art."

♥ March 15, 2003 - Brad Paisley married actress Kimberly Williams in Malibu, California. How could she say no to someone who wrote a song as sweet as "Little Moments" about her? The couple now has two sons, Huck and Jasper. Ironically, Brad had seen Kimberly star in Father of the Bride years before when his career was just starting to take shape and she was in one of her first major roles and had harbored a crush on her. He asked her to be in his "I'm Gonna Miss Her" music video and the rest is history.

♥ July 8, 1997 – Grand Ole Opry star Marty Stuart married fellow Opry member Connie Smith on the Pine Ridge Indian Reservation in South Dakota. Marty met her at one of her concerts when he was just 12 and predicted to his mother that he would one day marry Connie. He says committing to her is "probably the most right thing I've ever done in my life."

♥ October 18, 1952 – Having divorced Audrey just three months earlier, Hank Williams married Billie Jean Jones Eshliman in Minden, Louisiana. It was not the most auspicious wedding night: On the way back to Shreveport, their car ran out of gas. The following day, Hank and Billie Jean repeated their vows in front of a packed house in New Orleans. Hank died just 10 weeks later.

♥ January 13, 1948 - Buck Owens married Bonnie Campbell, who sang in his band. The marriage lasted only a few years, though they remained friends until both of them died in 2006. Incidentally, after Bonnie left Buck's band, she went on to sing background for Merle Haggard, whom she also married.

♥ January 7, 2012 – Lady Antebellum's Hillary Scott (daughter of singer Linda Davis) married drummer Chris Tyrell in an intimate ceremony in New York in January 2012. The couple, who met in college and then reconnected when Lady Antebellum and Love and Theft – who Chris was playing drums for at the time – joined Tim McGraw on tour, announced their marriage with a video posted on Lady Antebellum's website. They have one daughter, Eisele Kaye, who shares her birthday with Prince George.

♥ August 4, 1981 - Ricky Skaggs married Sharon White, the lead singer for the family bluegrass group The Whites. Both Ricky and his in-laws joined the Opry within the next three years, and Ricky and Sharon had a sentimental hit together with "Love Can't Ever Get Better Than This."

♥ June 3, 1989 – Marrying your manager doesn't always work out for the best, for Reba McEntire did just that when she wed her manager, Narvel Blackstock, in a Lake Tahoe ceremony on June 3, 1989. Narvel handles the day-to-day workings of Reba's iconic career and together, they have one son, Shelby. Reba's stepson, Brandon Blackstock, is married to pop superstar Kelly Clarkson.

We Love Our Customers!

Because you subscribe to the CFR NEWS we are giving you FREE Shipping!

Simply write **FREE SHIPPING** on your order!

Expires 3/31/15

Send your order along with a check or money order to:
CFR NEWS, P.O. Box 210796, Nashville, TN 37221
and don't forget to write "FREE SHIPPING"!!

February 2015

Keeping the music alive at the Fiddle & Pick: Musical Heritage Center of Middle Tennessee

By Paula Underwood Winters

Despite the music industry's attempts to turn country music into nothing more than pop music with a twang, there are still places that teach traditional country music. Young and old come out to Pegram, a little town just 20 minutes from Nashville, to hear great country music, participate in jam sessions and learn and practice their craft.

The Fiddle & Pick also houses The Musical Heritage Center of Middle Tennessee. They have private lessons, classes, house concerts, dance parties, workshops, writers nights and a lot more.

On New Year's Eve they hosted a rare appearance by Radiola, made up of David, Jan and Emma Harvey, Brian and Nichole Christianson, John Weisburger and Tim May. Tim and his wife, Gretchen Priest-May, own and run the Fiddle & Pick to keep the music alive.

In January the Center hosted the 'Eighth of January' Old Time Music Weekend, filled with workshops, lectures, concerts and jam sessions.

During the two day workshop sessions there were workshops in guitar, fiddle, mandoline, banjo, mountain dulcimer, singing, and even flatfooting and ukulele.

George Gruhn, owner of Gruhn Guitars in Nashville came and gave a lecture on older instruments that everyone enjoyed.

Some of the workshop teachers were The Stuart Brothers, who are world renown for their masterful performances of Appalachian fiddle and banjo duets; Tim May, who played on Charlie Daniel's 2005

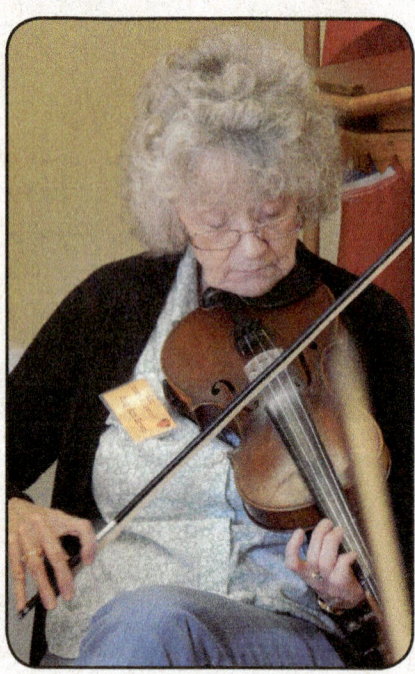

release of 'I'll Fly Away' which was nominated for Country Instrumental Grammy that year and co-author of 'Flatpickers guide to Old-Time Music'; Jay Bland, who is the winner of numerous national and regional dance competition including the prestigious flatfoot competition at Cliftop, VA 3 years in row. He is also 2-time National Champion, as well as GA, KY and TN champion. Kelsey Wells is an award-winning fiddler from Middle Tennessee who placed first in the 2012 Uncle Dave Macon Days traditional fiddle competition. Alan O'Bryant is an iconic music legend and founder of the Nashville Bluegrass band, an international touring act with numerous award winning records. He has a love for playing and teaching old time tunes on both mandolin and banjo.

This April they will be featuring a Celtic concert. So next time you're in the neighborhood, give them a call and see if they've got something happening. And thank them for keeping it real. Country, that is!

The Fiddle & Pick is located at 456 Hwy. 70 in Pegram, TN. You can reach them at 615-646-9131 or 615-812-2192 or you can visit them on the web at www.fiddleandpick.com.

February 2015

Stage Clothes of the Stars

By Claudia Johnson

Bill Anderson: Respectful Glitz

When young singer-songwriter Bill Anderson moved to Nashville half a century ago, the successful country music stars were easy to identify with cowboy boots, western hats and embroidered, rhinestone-studded and fringed clothing.

"I was from Georgia, and I had never dressed like that," Anderson said, "I always admired the way Ferlin Husky dressed. He wasn't gaudy, but he looked like a star when he stepped on stage. He commanded respect from the audience before he even opened his mouth to sing."

Respect for Anderson's audiences has always been a primary consideration when choosing his stage attire.

"They don't pay their money to come see me dressed just like them, and they don't want to see me looking like I just came in from plowing the south forty," he observed.

He has also made a point to adjust his wardrobe to the surroundings.

"I wouldn't wear the same things onstage at Willie's 4th of July picnic that I would wear onstage at Carnegie Hall," he said, characterizing his style "flexible."

Initially, he tried dressing in a showy but decidedly more casual style, but he later became one of Nudie's Rodeo Tailor's, best customers.

"Nudie created a bolero-style short jacket and matching pants design for me back in the '60s – almost a Tex-Mex look – and I had one in every color imaginable," Anderson recalled. "I never felt more like a 'star' than I did when wearing one of those outfits."

Anderson still owns a few of the Nudie Suits but has donated some to various museums for display. A white one is in a glass case at the Ryman Auditorium, a dark blue one is in the Tennessee State Museum and a light blue trimmed in gold is in the new Songwriters Hall of Fame in Nashville.

"For many years it was mostly Nudie, and later his former sidekick, Manuel, who kept me outfitted in clothes designed specifically for the stage," Anderson said. "In recent years, I've gone back to a more casual approach overall."

Currently, his friend, Vickie Salas, who is the head tailor at Nashville's leading men's store, works with Anderson on the more casual aspects of his wardrobe.

"Sometimes during a concert, I will dress casually for the first half of the show then glitter things up a bit for the second half," he said.

It's not always glitz for one of most awarded songwriters in the history of country music who's also a million-selling recording artist many times over, a television game show host, network soap opera star, spokesman for a nationwide restaurant chain and a consummate onstage performer – not to mention current host of "Country's Family Reunion."

"I can be pretty casual and laid back when I'm at the office or just kicking around the neighborhood," he admitted. "I like sweatshirts and hoodies in the cool weather, usually accompanied by jeans and walking shoes. I'll toss a ball cap on my head when I'm too lazy to style my hair. In the summer, it's mostly shorts and loose-fitting shirts. I don't 'dress up' when I don't have to."

Anderson said that he never had a "stylist" but allowed his stage appearance to evolve naturally.

"Occasionally, I'll go back through old photographs and wonder what I was thinking at the time, but I can't rewrite history," he said. "It is what it is and it was what it was."

February 2015

MARCH

Jim Ed Brown in remission, doing well, back at the Opry

Jim Ed Brown looked happy to be back on the stage of the Grand Ole Opry January 30 and 31. He also took time to autograph copies of his new CD for fans including Judy Kirby pictured here.

Jim Ed Brown returned to the stage of the Grand Ole Opry the weekend of January 30-31, after getting the news that he is cancer-free.

He announced that he had been diagnosed with lung cancer in September 2014 in a post to Facebook. His doctors advised him to take four months off to undergo a regimen of chemotherapy and radiation.

In a press release dated Wednesday (Jan. 28), he revealed that the treatment worked. He got the news that he was free of cancer on January 19.

"I am in remission," Brown stated. "There are not enough thanks for the prayers, well wishes, and support I've received during the toughest time of my life. I am so grateful."

Brown rose to fame in the '60s as a member of the Browns, a trio that included his sisters, Maxine and Bonnie. They joined the Opry in 1963 at the invitation of Ernest Tubb. He launched a solo career shortly after, scoring hits including 'Pop a Top,' his signature song. He also teamed with Helen Cornelius for a string of hit duets in the '70s and '80s that included 'I Don't Want to Have to Marry You' and 'Saying Hello, Saying I Love You, Saying Goodbye.'

The gracious star was invited to join the Opry in 1963, when Ernest Tubb asked Jim Ed and his sisters Maxine and Bonnie, to join the Opry as The Browns. As a 50-plus year member, Brown considers the Opry his "second home," and can think of no better place to re-launch his remarkable stage shows.

He went on to enjoy a prolific solo career and also formed an award-winning duet partnership with Helen Cornelius. Jim Ed and Helen won the 1977 Country Music Association award for Vocal Duo of the Year.

Jim Ed turned 80 this past April and recently released his latest album, In Style Again which he signed for fans following his Opry appearance. The record features guest appearances by Vince Gill and Helen Cornelius.

Jim Ed has several things to be excited about these days. Besides being in remission he is touring again. His schedule for March is:

Mar 13, 2015 - Abilene, TX Civic Center Auditorium with

T.G. SHEPPARD
LEROY VAN DYKE
JIMMY FORTUNE
HELEN CORNELIUS

Mar 14, 2015 - Midland, TX Wagner Noel Performing Arts Center with

T.G. SHEPPARD
SUZY BOGGUSS
LEROY VAN DYKE
JIMMY FORTUNE
HELEN CORNELIUS

Mar 15, 2015 - Amarillo, TX Amarillo Civic Center Auditorium with

T.G. SHEPPARD
LEROY VAN DYKE
JIMMY FORTUNE
HELEN CORNELIUS

March 2015

Reviews for the new CD are also a reason for him to be excited.

USA TODAY (Brian Mansfield)

Jim Ed Brown sounds as smooth, as charming as ever on 'In Style Again,' an album that reflects on every facet of a long and varied musical career. Makes me wish he'd gotten into the studio more over the years, because it's crystal clear nobody else sounds quite like he does.

BILLBOARD (Chuck Dauphin)

Some things never change, nor should they. The vocal style of Jim Ed Brown is one of those things. In Style Again showcases that rich and warm voice in such a way that would make Chet Atkins and Jim Reeves proud!

AXS.COM (Allen Foster)

Jim Ed Brown's voice is as warm and comforting as sitting in front of a gently crackling fire. There's a rich history in every single note that rises from his exquisitely seasoned vocal cords. His music is a poignant nostalgia that can bring even the most hardened soul to the brink of tears.

THE NASHVILLE BRIDGE (Brad Hardisty)

IN STYLE AGAIN spotlights Jim Ed Brown at the top of his game with pristine production that rivals latter day works by Loretta Lynn, Porter Wagoner, Charlie Louvin and Ray Price.

MUSIC NEWS LOS ANGELES (Rick Moore)

This recording will no doubt be one of the year's most memorable albums of any genre.

Jim Ed has been on most of the Country's Family Reunion series.

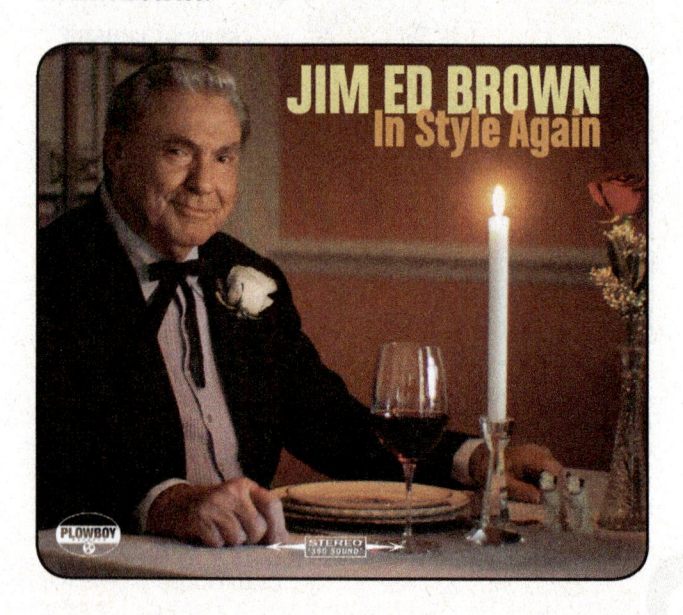

A funny thing happened...

My neighbor was working in his yard when he was startled by a late-model car that came crashing through his hedge, ending up on his front lawn.

He rushed to help the very elderly lady driver out of the car, and sat her down on a lawn chair.

He said gently: "Ma'am, you appear quite elderly to be driving."

"Well, yes, I am." she replied proudly. "I'll be 97 next month, and I'm now old enough that I don't even need a driver's license anymore."

"What!!" exclaimed my neighbor.

"That's right." she said. "The last time I went to my doctor, he examined me, then asked if I had a driver's license.

"When I showed it to him, he took some scissors out of a drawer, cut the license into little pieces, threw the pieces in the waste basket, and said: 'You won't need this anymore.' So I thanked him and left!"

March 2015

Tex Ritter's Co-star White Flash

By Claudia Johnson

It's a confident star who will share billing with another performer. It's a loving one that shares it with his animal. Country singer and Western movie star Tex Ritter was one of those.

When Ritter began his film career in the late 1930s, horses were rented for his use. Soon, however, he acquired a horse of his own, White Flash. The beloved animal appeared in 20 films with Ritter. Old movie posters and press books show a handsome young Ritter and a beautiful white steed, always hailing the movie as starring "Tex Ritter and his horse White Flash."

When the real White Flash was too old to perform in full-length movies, other white horses were used to portray White Flash. Still, White Flash traveled with Ritter, garnering a dedicated fan base of his own. When Ritter stopped making movies, he and White Flash appeared together in live stage shows.

Ritter's wife, Dorothy, recalled in an interview that the popular White Flash received numerous fan letters, all of which were "answered."

"Tex and I would ink up his hoof and 'autograph' pictures for all the fans," said Arizona-born Dorothy, the daughter of a cowboy who had been put on a horse before she could walk.

Being from East Texas, Ritter's musical influences were not purely Western, but he became identified early in his career with the Texas cowboy image.

"That is not how he started out," said Tommie Ritter Smith, Director of The Texas Country Music Hall of Fame/Tex Ritter Museum in Carthage, Texas. "Though he loved cowboy songs, he decided on a law career and in 1922 began attending The University of Texas at Austin."

Smith said that Ritter left college just before graduation in 1928, traveling to New York City where he secured a minor role in a Broadway show.

"After a final stab at finishing law school, he returned to New York in 1931 and landed a featured role in the Broadway play, 'Green Grow the Lilacs,' where he got his nickname Tex," she said.

Born Woodard Maurice Ritter, the cast began to call him "Tex" because of his accent and the name stuck.

"Tex starred on Broadway and worked as a radio star on shows such as The Lone Ranger, Tex Ritter's Campfire and Death Valley Days," Smith said. "Though he had a string of country-western hits, his recording career was significantly less successful than his film, radio and television career. He appeared in 85 movies. For nearly seven years, Tex was ranked among the top ten money-making stars in Hollywood."

In 1953, his recording of "Do Not Forsake Me," the theme from the 1952 Gary Cooper film "High Noon," became a pop hit. The movie won the Academy Award, and Ritter performed the song on the first televised broadcast of the awards ceremony in 1953.

Ritter was founding member of the Country Music Association, was the fifth person and first singing cowboy in the Country Music Hall Of Fame, was inducted into the Western Performers Hall of Fame at the National Cowboy and Western Heritage Museum in Oklahoma City and even has a star on the Hollywood Walk of Fame.

When he joined the Grand Ole Opry in 1965, he and Dorothy moved from California to Nashville, where he died of a heart attack in 1974. He was returned for burial to Panola County, Texas, the county where in 1905 he had been born. In 1993, The Tex Ritter Museum was founded there to honor his memory and house memorabilia.

"The museum soon expanded to include friends of Tex and other Texas-born country music legends," Smith, said explaining its evolution. "The Texas Country Music Hall of Fame/Tex Ritter Museum opened in August 2002 in a $2.5 million state-of-the-art facility. Since then, more than 30,000 country music fans from every state and dozens of foreign countries have stepped back in time to re-live great moments in country music history."

What happened to his co-star and friend, White Flash? After 25 years together, in 1961 the animal had become infirm and blind. Like any merciful and loving animal owner, Ritter had the horse put down. Today, eight decades after the pair began a career together, many of the movies they made can be viewed in digital form.

Behind the Scenes — **Spotlight**

We have so many talented folks that work behind the scenes of our television shows and tapings that we thought you should meet them. Their talents and experience surely humble us.

Phil Johnson - Photographer, Singer, Songwriter

One of the guys behind the scenes at Larry's Country Diner and Country's Family Reunion is Phil Johnson. You might hear Larry Black refer to him as the guy on the ladder taking photos but this is only one of his many talents.

Phil Johnson is a veteran Christian songwriter and producer. He worked for over 30 years with Grammy and Dove award winning artists….Dottie Rambo, Bill and Gloria Gaither, The Oak Ridge Boys, Dallas Holm, Gordon Mote, Alison Krause, The Imperials, Steven Curtis Chapman, The Martins, Mark Lowry, Evie, Christy Lane and many more.

His songwriting talents have landed him recordings by major Country and Christian artists such as "The Day He Wore My Crown," "Give Them All To Jesus", "Mercy Walked In", "More Than You'll Ever Know" and one of Elvis favorites "When It's My Time" that was sang at his funeral.

His music career consisted of 18 years as director of A & R for The Benson Company/Zondervan Music and 10 years as General Manager for Bill Gaither's company, Springhill Music Group. He toured in the late 80's with Holm, Shepherd, Johnson and recorded two albums plus a solo album.

Phil was invited on the Country's Family Reunion "Old Time Gospel " series where he sang "The Day He Wore My Crown". He is currently working on a new project to be released this year.

His creative talents as a photographer for Gabriel are like the icing on the cake.

T.G. Sheppard on tour

It's shaping up to be a busy year for Country legend TG Sheppard as his winter/spring concert tour is getting underway. The singer will headline shows in cities across North America, featuring his groundbreaking music and signature songs. The tour coincides with the 40th anniversary of the phenomenal hit, "Devil in the Bottle."

TG Sheppard says the strong support and broadening of his fan base now makes hitting the road even more meaningful. "I'm constantly amazed to see such a wide age range of people who are showing up for our concerts night after night. Country music fans have never been fickle and will never leave you as long as you're true to them and your music. They are growing larger in numbers all the time." He adds, "I'm looking forward to my upcoming tour dates along with playing closer to home at the incredible Franklin Theatre with my talented wife, Kelly Lang. I haven't done a show locally in years. It will be fun doing a concert this close to Nashville."

The winter/spring engagements for TG Sheppard will include stops in Arizona, North Dakota, Florida, Tennessee and Texas. More shows are being added to this year's tour schedule. So, be sure to check for updates on performances and special appearances.

March 2015

For more information, visit: tgsheppard.com.

2015 Winter/Spring Concert Tour

Sat, Jan 31 – Cruise / Miami, FL (Country's Family Reunion)

Sun, Feb 1 – Fri, Feb 6 – Cruise/at sea (Country's Family Reunion)

Fri, Feb 13 – Crossville, TN (Palace Theater)

Sat, Feb 28 – Fort Yates, ND (Prairie Nights Casino)

Fri, Mar 13 – Abilene, TX (TBA)

Sat, Mar 14 – Midland, TX (Wagner Noel Performing Arts Center)

Sun, Mar 15 – Amarillo, TX (Amarillo Civic Center)

Thu, Mar 26 – West Palm Beach, FL (Private Event)

Fri, Apr 10 – Stafford, TX (Redneck Country Club)

Sat, Apr 11 – Corsicana, TX (Opry & Event Center)

Fri, Apr 17 – Tyler, TX (Shriners Country Fest/ Texas Woodstock)

Sat, Apr 25 – Franklin, TX (Franklin Theatre)

Sat, May 16 – Shipshewana, IN (Shipshewana Event Center)

TOUR DATES & TICKETS

Dates	Venue	Location
May 5, 6, 7, 8, 9	Starlite Theatre	Branson, MO
Sept. 22, 23, 24, 25, 26, 27	Starlite Theatre	Branson, MO

For more information: www.starlitetheatre.com or (417) 337-9333

Nadine's Corner

I know many of you saw me sing on the Diner with Linda Davis. It was one of the highlights of my visits to Larry's Country Diner. So.... I decided to try out of the church choir. After several Sundays I came to the conclusion that more men should join. I mean it !!! And here are my top 10 reasons.

MEN SHOULD JOIN THE CHOIR

The top reasons men should join the church Choir:

10. Rehearsals are every Wednesday night. Which means that for those few hours, you will significantly reduce your risk of contracting tendinitis from nonstop operation of a television remote control or computer mouse.

9. Because you wear a choir robe every Sunday, you are liberated from the task many men find quite challenging: finding clothes that match properly.

8. From your special vantage point every Sunday, in which you look out at the entire congregation from the choir seats, you will develop interesting new hobbies. Among these is a little guessing game called "Who's Praying, Who's Sleeping?"

7. On the other hand, sitting in full view of 200-300 people on a weekly basis makes it much less likely that you yourself will give in to a chronic lack of sleep. Although it has been known to happen.

6. If you think your singing in the shower sounds good now, just wait till you've been singing with us for a few weeks.

5. Singing in a choir is one of the few activities for men that does not require electronics equipment or expensive power tools. This could be good for the family budget.

4. For the fitness buffs, singing in the Choir is not only heart healthy, it's soul healthy. But there are no monthly membership fees, and it's a lot easier on the knees than jogging.

3. If you think you've done everything there is to do, and there are no great challenges left in life, try singing with us guys and staying on pitch.

2. Choir rehearsal lasts half as long as a professional football game but is at least twice as satisfying.

AND then number 1 reason men should join the choir:

1. When people ask you whether you've been behaving yourself, you can say with the utmost sincerity, "Hey I'm a Choir Boy."

Check out Nadine's website www.nadinenadine.com

March 2015

Louvin Brothers honored at 2015 Grammy Awards

They went around the world, but they also stopped in Music City as the Recording Academy selected its 2015 Lifetime Achievement Award winners, from Australia (The Bee Gees) to Liverpool (George Harrison) and France (composer Pierre Boulez).

Legendary country duo The Louvin Brothers were among the Lifetime Achievement Award recipients on Saturday, February 7 during the Grammys' annual Special Merit Awards ceremony.

The selection comes four years after the death of Charlie Louvin. His brother Ira Louvin died in a car accident in 1965 — two years after they'd parted ways. The pair never picked up a Grammy during their run, but a tribute album did win for best country album in 2004.

"This is a long way from the hills of Tennessee," said Ira's daughter, Kathy Louvin, who accepted the award along with her sister Denise and cousin Charlie Louvin Jr.

"The Louvin Brothers possessed a skill to make others want to sound like them. And they had the courage to sing about things that were painful, true and memorable. Greatness is too often scarred by the humanness of us all. Maybe that's because only God is great. I'm sure from their spot inside the pearly gates, they're all smiles tonight."

The occasion couldn't have had a better audience. The historic Wilshire Ebell Theatre was filled with 2015 Grammy nominees and their guests, and they gave standing ovations to songwriters, technological innovators and music educators alike. Other honorees included blues guitar great Buddy Guy, Tejano accordionist Flaco Jiménez; inventor Ray Kurzweil, songwriting duo Barry Mann and Cynthia Weil; producer Richard Perry and jazz saxophonist Wayne Shorter.

COUNTRY LEGENDS PAST AND PRESENT   BY TOM WOOD

ERNEST TUBB

What a classic storyteller!

There are many catchphrases to describe the talent and career of Red Sovine, but "overnight sensation" would not be one of them.

Red burst into national prominence in 1955 when he recorded a duet with Webb Pierce, a cover of the George Jones hit "Why Baby Why." It quickly rose to No. 1 on the charts, and two more songs in the top 15, "Hold Everything (Till I Get Home)" and "If Jesus Come to Your Home," over the next year earned Red a membership in the world's most exclusive country Club. The Grand Ole Opry.

It seemed the baritone's star would only continue to rise. But he met a series of setbacks (during a time when he helped kickstart Charley Pride's recording career), and it would be another decade before Red reached the top of the charts again.

It required something of an image makeover, a left turn, one might suggest, to get back on the road to stardom. And it would not be through singing. Uh, not exactly.

Red's ticket to success came through his oral telling of a story set to music, a genre known as "trucker songs".

March 2015

Their popularity dates back to the 1940s, and provided Red with the perfect avenue to restart his career in a positive direction up the charts.

"GiddyUp Go" rose to No. 1 in 1965, some 10 years following his first chart topper. But the success of the song, cowritten by Red and Tommy Hill, showed he had finally found his vocation.

Similar songs were churned out one after another and "Phantom 309" reached No. 0 in 1967.

Red had several other songs do well, but it wasn't until 1976 that he reached the top of the charts for the final time, striking a chord with listeners across the country and jerking many a tears with "Teddy Bear," the emotional story of a disabled boy connecting over his late trucker father's CB with a truck driver.

Today, "Teddy Bear" still ranks today at No. 3 on a list of the 50 best trucking songs, according to todaystrucking.com. Another internet site, using that chart to compile its playlist of trucker hits, links to "Teddy Bear" — by Elvis Presley! To paraphrase famed comedian Rodney Dangerfield, Red still gets no respect.

But he certainly deserves it—and has received it over the years from legions of fans.

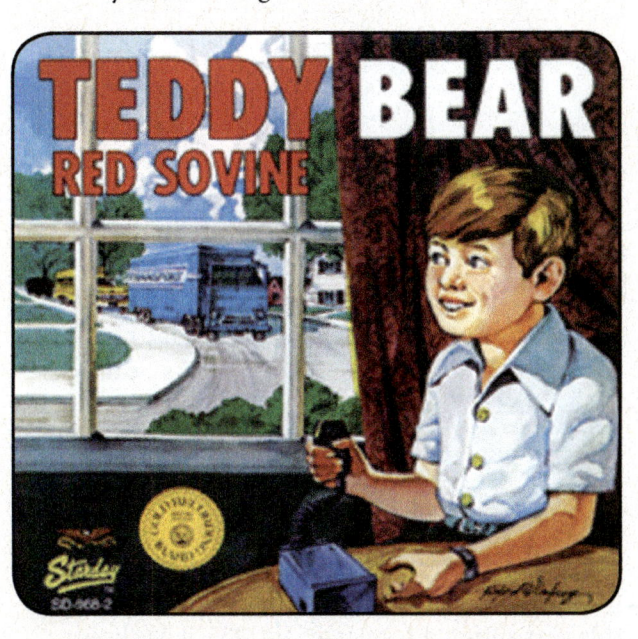

David Ball was last minute add to the Cruise

Fans onboard Larry's Country Diner and Country's Family Reunion Cruise were surprised with the addition of David Ball to the talent line up. "It was a last minute decision," says Black, and ended up being a good one. Mo Pitney who is right in the middle of a six-month radio tour had to leave from San Yuan to fulfill his record label commitments. "I think everyone on the Cruise is hoping he becomes a huge star!! "He kinda feels like one of our kids," said a passenger from Kansas. The send off from the ship was a standing ovation with cheers and well wishes. " We are calling our radio station when we get home and buying his music," said Beth from California.

Just like the country music star he is …David Ball didn't miss a beat. He entertained the crowd with his huge hit song "Riding With Private Malone." And when it came time for the autograph sessions he just drew his own picture in the autograph books that the passengers received. In fact he had so much fun with the passengers that one man even threw him his hat to wear on stage during the finale performance.

The Country's Family and Larry's Country Diner Cruises are all special. You never know what is going to happen during the week. Rhonda Vincent brought her entire band on this cruise and held jam sessions almost every night on the ship. Johnnie Lee signed biscuits and threw them out to the audience. And on this cruise the artist brought their CD's to sell and autograph.

"We are looking forward to the next cruise in 2016." says Darrel and Wilma from Columbus, Ohio.

 ***More information about our 2016 CRUISE coming soon.

March 2015

Brenda Lee's 'In The Mood For Love' featured in Victoria's Secret

Move over Katy Perry! The Super Bowl 49 telecast on had another voice to be heard in the run down of not-to-missed moments highlighting the Patriots-Seahawks face-off.

"I'm In the Mood for Love" – written by veteran tunesmith Jimmy McHugh and co-writer Dorothy Fields, turns 80 this year. Originally released in 1935, it has been recorded by over 100 artists—including celebrated voices spanning the generations of music — Frank Sinatra, Ella Fitzgerald, Sarah Vaughn, Bing Crosby, Rosemary Clooney and Barbra Streisand—to modern turns at the microphone from artists as diverse as the Sex Pistols, Rod Stewart, James Taylor and Amy Winehouse.

In the midst of such stellar competition, now from her rarified perch as a member of the Rock & Roll (and Country) Music Halls of Fame--- Brenda Lee is particularly proud that her vocal rendition got to score a Super Bowl touchdown. She attributes the honor to having had a great coach.

She noted is a recent interview, "As a young artist, I learned from the best—my producer the legendary Owen Bradley. Owen sat me down when we first began working together in the studio and said, 'Brenda, always remember a classic song will live forever.' In the midst of cutting the hits I enjoyed in my teens—songs such as I'm Sorry, All Alone Am I, Break It To Me Gently—Owen would insist we take time in our song searches to listen together and find great, timeless songs such as 'I'm In The Mood For Love' to be included on my album releases. We originally cut the song in 1961 and it was released on one of my best ever selling albums, Emotions, virtually introducing this wonderful piece of music to a whole new generation of listeners."

Brenda Lee proves that great artists and great songs always endure.

Larry's Country Diner RFD Show Schedule March 2015

NEW SHOW
RICKY SKAGGS & SHARON WHITE
Saturday, March 7
10:00 p.m. Central
Sunday, March 8
6:00 p.m. Central

NEW SHOW
JANIE PRICE, JOHN CONLEE, JEANNIE SEELY
Saturday, March 14
10:00 p.m. Central
Sunday, March 15
6:00 p.m. Central

NEW SHOW
BILLY DEAN
Saturday, March 21
10:00 p.m. Central
Sunday, March 22
6:00 p.m. Central

NEW SHOW
CRYSTAL GAYLE
Saturday, March 28
10:00 p.m. Central
Sunday, March 29
6:00 p.m. Central

March 2015

2015 Cruise to the Caribbean

The CFR Band is ready to get started as Larry Black addresses the audience on the Celebrity Reflection.

Rhonda Vincent

Moe Bandy

Bill Anderson

T.G. Sheppard and Kelly Lang

Mark Wills

David Ball

March 2015

Bill Anderson

Gene Watson

Johnny Lee

Teea Goans

Rhonda Vincent and The Rage entertained during their own show.

Mark Wills

Jeannie Seely

Mo Pitney with fan.

Renae smiles for fans.

Rhonda Vincent poses with fans for photos.

Nadine signs her cookbook.

Keith, Nadine, Mo, David and Teea ham it up for fans.

48 CFR NEWS

March 2015

Larry and his wife, LuAnn at the Diner show.

Mo Pitney and David Ball swap stories and songs at the Diner show.

Nadine's comedy show is always a hit!

Michele gets a song.

Mo Pitney introduces his sister, Holly.

Jeannie, Rhonda, Kelly and Teea clowning

Jeannie gets a laugh out of Mo

Johnny Lee had Mark and Rhonda singing backup.

Saying goodbye during the final show.

49 CFR NEWS

March 2015

Country Questions
By Dick Boise, CMH

Send questions to:
Dick Boise, c/o CFR News,
P.O. Box 201796, Nashville,
TN 37221.

Q. I've heard several stories about an old time singer named Vernon Dalhart. Could you give me some information about him? My older uncle says that was not his real name. Thanks.

C. Nichols, Galax, VA

A. Thanks for your inquiry and your uncle was correct about the name. Vernon Dalhart was just one of the many names "Marion Try Slaughter" used to record under back in the early 1920s. It has been said that he released over 5,000 recordings under as many as 135 names. He is noted as having the first million selling copies of the "Wreck of the Old 97." He was from Texas, born April 6, 1883, and passed away September 1948.

Q. I would like to ask of you some information on Carl Smith. Liked his singing and what can you tell me about him? Thanks

J. Burdick, Whitesboro, NY

A. Carl Smith was one of the early country singers and was born in the same town as Roy Acuff, Maynardsville, TN, March 15, 1927. His career with Columbia records gave us many great hits. He married June Carter, they later divorced. In 1957 he married Goldie Hill and they both went into music retirement. He owned a big ranch south of Nashville where he raised and trained quarter horses. He passed away October 11, 2013.

Q. Could you tell me where Hank Williams died? I've heard so many stories and it has been some time ago. Thanks.

Tom Sloan, Ladysmith, WI

A. Thanks for your question, Tom. And you are going back in country music history. I suppose that there are many statements that are being made now days and I happen to have a copy of the Certificate of Death and it states Oak Hill, WV. It was dated January 1, 1953 and though he's been gone some 62 years, his great songs and recordings live on.

Q. I have heard that someone else wrote Buck Owens' hit song "Tiger By The Tail." Is that true? What year was that and thank you for your interesting bits of country history.

Donna Wallace, Springfield, MO

A. Harlan Howard actually wrote the lyrics to "Tiger", and Buck worked out the tune or melody to that 1964 record. The story is told that Buck got the idea from a gasoline poster stating "put a tiger in your tank." He mentioned it to Harlan and soon another hit was in the making for our country music history.

March 2015

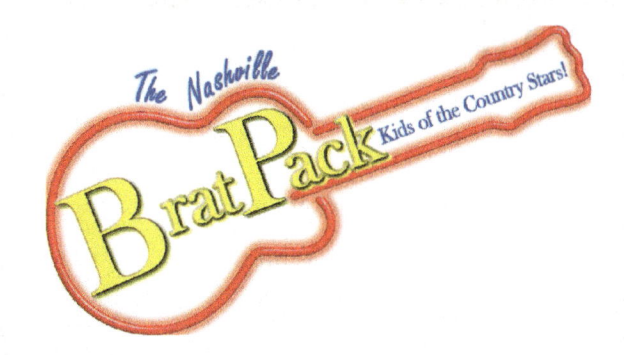

The Nashville Brat Pack — Kids of the Country Stars!

By Nancy Leigh Ann Brown, Daughter of Grant Turner, Voice of the Grand Ole Opry.

Jesse Granderson "Grant" Turner, Texas-born Voice of the Grand Ole Opry, served on that show's announcing staff for forty-seven years.

Back in the days when we, as BRATS, walked in the shadows of our parents, we saw some awesome people visit backstage at the Opry.

Everyone's list will differ, but I got to meet Perry Como, Tom Jones, Steppenwolf rock group, Jerry Lee Lewis, Senator Strom Thurmond, and President Nixon. Agnes Morehead sat on a bench and watched the entire show from start to finish (she was the mom in BEWITCHED).

I always thought it was pretty awesome that these busy people wanted to visit the world famous Opry.

Most of my pictures were destroyed in a house fire, but here are a few that I still have.

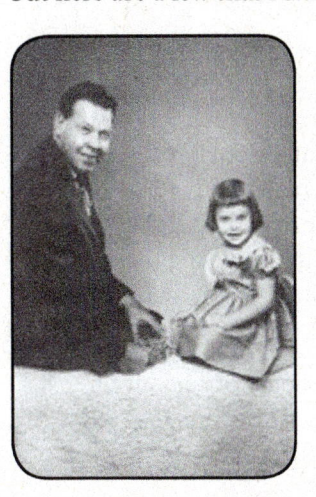

Grant and daughter Nancy as a child and grown up in 1987.

6th Annual Abe's Tractor Cruise Across the Prairie

The 6th annual Abe's Tractor Cruise Across the Prairie will be held Saturday, June 6, 2015. All proceeds from this tractor parade will be donated to the St Judes Children's Hospital. Cost for the ride is $35.00 per entry and application deadline is June 1, 2015.

To participate you must have SMV Sign, Fire Extinguisher, Good Brakes, Tow Chain or Strap.

The parade will depart from Prairieland Heritage Museum, South Jacksonville IL at the corner of Lincoln and Michigan Avenue at 8:45 a.m. and they will make their way North and West of Jacksonville through some very scenic countryside returning to Prairieland in South Jacksonville in approximately 3 hours. Upon returning, lunch will be held at Ponderosa.

This event is sponsored by Prairie land Heritage Museum, Vintage Ag Association, Coke, LG Seeds, Inkorporated Designs, WFMB 104.5 Radio, Larry's Country Diner.& Illinois State Fair Museum.

On Site registration will be available; however your early registration will help us make sure your shirt fits.

For additional information please call us at one of these numbers. 217-494-7105, 217-371-1107, 217-741-3531. Or Email at plhmshow@aol.com.

March 2015

Honky Tonk Reunion filled with great songs

Did you know that some of the biggest country legends ever recorded got their start playing in places called Honky Tonks? That's right. So we here at Country's Family Reunion wanted to pay special attention to that foot-tapping brand of music in a brand new series, Country's Family Reunion Honky Tonks!

All on 5 DVD's for just 79.80 plus shipping and handling, this series features tons of artists who've never been to one of our reunions before—people like Tony Booth, Jim Lauderdale, Eddy Raven and others. And, of course some of your favorite reunion members showed up as well. All sharing their stories and songs from their favorite Honky Tonks.

When you order, you'll receive all 5 DVD's of CFR Honky Tonk with almost 6 hours of content for just 79.80. That includes the special Backstage DVD with more stories and songs not seen on any other part of the taping. All for just 79.80.

All on 5 DVD's with some of the most fun we've ever had at a reunion. So, order CFR Honky Tonk today and you'll be singing and tapping your feet in no time. We had so much fun creating this Honky Tonk series, and we know you'll love it too.

Songs and Artists Featured on Series:

"Bright Lights And Country Music" Bill Anderson

"Hey, Good Lookin' " Moe Bandy

"If You've Got The Money, I've Got The Time" David Frizzell

"The One You Slip Around With" Jan Howard

"The Key's In The Mailbox" Tony Booth

"Waltz Across Texas" John Conlee

"It's The Water" Darell McCall

"Set 'Em Up Joe" Daryle Singletary

"San Antonio Rose" The Whites

"Borrowed Angel" Mo Pitney

"Fraulein" Jim Ed Brown

"Thinkin' Problem" David Ball

"Lord, I Need Somebody Bad Tonight" Jeannie Seely

"(I'm A) Lonesome Fugitive" Jim Lauderdale

"Please Don't Leave Me Anymore" / "The Kind Of Love I Can't Forget" / "Bubbles In My Beer" (swing medley) Ray Pillow

"My Shoes Keep Walking Back To You" Junior Brown

"Burning Memories" Linda Davis

"Tonight The Bottle Let Me Down" Dale Watson

"Walkin' To New Orleans" Eddy Raven

"Buckaroo" CFR Band

"I Do My Crying At Night" Rhonda Vincent

"The Wild Side Of Life" Curtis Potter

"Deep Water" Roy Clark

"Walking The Floor Over You" Tony Booth (featuring Leon Rhodes)

"Jones On The Jukebox" Becky Hobbs

"Let's Get Over Them Together" Moe Bandy and Becky Hobbs

"Let's Chase Each Other Around The Room" Billy Yates

"There Stands The Glass" David Ball

"Dim Lights, Thick Smoke, and Loud, Loud Music" Wade Hayes

March 2015

WORD SEARCH

```
W U R H O N D A R E T T I R W H
Z H K J P I T N E Y R E N A E B
N W O R B D E M I J U M M B U M
N O S R E D N A E E S I U R C F
M O R B G S N L W K M K E E S X
P T T H E R A G E N C Y D N A B
C E S D P E K L U O C R U D H W
E E A S T M A R T E E N B A I S
L A N G U U H S A O E W S N Y T
S M J N S Z D E T M L N H B E T
O G U S G O F X R K Y I E N X H
V S A T O V S P A E N V P A B O
I B N W W A S J C L N U P D A M
N Y C S X G H D T L H O A I L A
E D N E Y H R C O Y O L R N L S
I X T S E E L Y R E J N D E I T
```

FIND THESE WORDS:

	Seely	Teea	StThomas
	Ball	Bandy	SanJuan
JimEdBrown	Pitney	Mark	Ritter
Texas	JohnnyLee	Kelly	Louvin
Woodstock	Rhonda	Nadine	Sovine
Cruise	TheRage	Renae	Brenda
Anderson	Sheppard	StMarteen	Tractor

Country's Family Reunion presents....

HONKY TONK REUNION

Starting February 20 on RFD-TV
Fridays...7 p.m. central
Saturdays...11 p.m central

Own the complete series
$79.80 plus $6.95 s/h
www.cfrvideos.com   1-800-820-5405

March 2015

Stage Clothes of the Stars

By Claudia Johnson

Anna Marie Mitchell: Promise and Bling

Anna Marie Mitchell is walking in the boot steps of some of music's most admired female artists, but she's doing it with a style all her own. The 16-year-old admits that her admiration for her musical heroines, Dolly Parton, Taylor Swift, Tracy Chapman and Bonnie Raitt – all singer-songwriters like herself – not only inspired her pursuit of music as a career but also her stage presence.

"The first time I played in front a crowd, I was 11," Mitchell recalled. "It was at the Grandstand [Minnesota State Fair] with 10,000 people watching. I wore gold and was all glitzed out."

Since then, the Minnesota native has played festivals, arenas, concert halls, acoustic cafes and bars. She's played at both the Bluebird Café and the Commodore Inn in Nashville, pleasing the crowds and garnering positive reinforcement from the Nashville Songwriter's Association International, which chose her song, "West of Boston," to pitch at its annual publishers luncheon and listed her as One to Watch for her song "Broken Glass."

"What I wear depends on where I'm performing," said the ebullient young woman, whose performance and publicity photos depict a spectrum of style.

In one photo, Mitchell wears a short, furry vest, skinny black jeans and a wide-brimmed black hat, conjuring images of Dottie West. In another she's as elegant as Patsy Cline with a strappy, sparkly cocktail dress with its wide satin sash and flouncy skirt. Several videos show her performing in bright but modest, classy dresses reminiscent of Taylor Swift.

More than one image hints at Mitchell's life on her family's horse farm, with her dressed in denim, plaid or calico, not unlike Reba McEntire.

"One of my very favorite things to wear is by the Berry Fit Company," Mitchell said. "It is an amazing vest with a guitar on the back, loaded with Swarovski crystals and appliquéd roses, pearls and beaded fringe."

The vest is so intricately beautiful, it seems Nudie Cohn himself was reincarnated to create it.

"I've never totally given a garment to someone, but when I first saw Anna Marie with the vest on, I knew that I would be giving it to her," said Carolyn Berry, owner and founder of Berry Fit, an Ohio-based company that custom designs, creates and sells one-of-a-kind, handmade couture equestrian and Western wear. "I followed my instinct without thinking of any special result – just doing what I needed to do."

Mitchell said she was particularly honored at the surprise gift, considering Berry Fit's impressive list of clients, including some of the biggest names in the entertainment industry.

"Carolyn is an incredible person and believes in me and my music," Mitchell said. "It is my goal to someday wear the vest on the stage of the Grand Ole Opry!"

It's certain she'll also be donning something else very special wherever she plays.

"I started making guitar straps when Anna did her first 'big' performance," said Anastasia Mitchell, the singer's mother, who is a professionally trained graphic designer. "They were a way for me to help and encourage her from afar."

Mitchell's mother said all the straps carry messages of love written somewhere in the design.

"I usually choose the word 'believe' for Anna, as our wish for her, is to believe in herself – not only as

March 2015

a musician, but as the intelligent and beautiful person that she truly is," her mother said.

Among the recent straps designed for her daughter is one featuring a soaring bluebird.

"This represents the release of her EP 'Little Bird' and our first visit to Nashville in January 2014, when we stood for two hours in the cold waiting to play the Bluebird Cafe open mic," Anastasia explained. "The roses and flames remind me of Anna – beautiful and sensitive, yet strong."

Mitchell acknowledged that her songwriting and musical style continue to evolve, but about her stage style, she's taken a cue from a country music icon.

"A girl's always got to have a little bling," Mitchell observed, sounding a lot like Dolly Parton.

Includes 2 Bonus Audio CDs

DIARY of a TV Waitress
Renae The Waitress

"Every one was finally seated and the theme song played Applause signs began flashing and Bob Barker himself stepped out onto the stage. Okay, mauybe this would be fun. Folks were laughing and yelling and acting pretty silly.
   Names were called, one after another, and audience members ran down to the sstage. Then it happened . My name! Bob Barker was calling my name........."

"Delightful book. I couldn't put it down until I read the whole thing"
Charlotte Webb   PA

" It's so easy to read and I love all of the pictures"
Beth Mobley   Tx

" I bought the waitnress book for my Mom and I couldn't believe how much she enjoyed it. It was easy for her to read and Renae even signed it !!
Jerry Burgess   AZ

" I am a huge Larry's Country Diner fan and "Diary of a TV Waitress" should be on the top sellers list. It is just like the show…fun".

$24.95 plus $6.95 s/h

800-820-5405
www.larryscountrydiner.com

March 2015

APRIL

Don Harron (Charlie Farguharson) of Hee Haw loses battle with cancer

Donald Hugh Harron, affectionately known by Hee Haw fans as Charlie Farguharson, lost his battle with cancer on January 17. Harron, 90, was a Shakespearean actor, a writer and broadcaster. Born September 19, 1924 in Toronto, Ontario, he was one of Canada's most beloved comedic legends.

"I can't remember where I put my pants last night, but I can remember what happened in 1934."

– Don Harron

Harron got an early start as an entertainer and at ten years old, he created his own narrative stories and drawings. He had a head start since his parents were a dye worker and amateur cartoonist. His early performances led him to be cast in the 1936 "Lonesome Trail." He labored during the day as a farmhand in rural Ontario and then worked on his performances at night. He also served in the Royal Canadian Air Force during World War II. Upon returning to Canada, he performed with the CBC radio while studying sociology and philosophy at the University of Toronto. After graduation, he wrote and performed in various plays and then relocated to England where he wrote for BBC radio and performed in London's West End.

He returned to Canada in 1952, starring in the show "Spring Thaw." It was there that Harron debuted his character, Charlie Farguharson. His inspiration went back to his days working on the farm in Ontario.

Harron was busy being a stage actor during the 1950s and 1960s. He performed as Charlie Farguharson all over Canada television, stage and radio.

In 1955, Harron also helped turn the novel "Anne of Green Gables" into a musical for a CBC television production, collaborating with Canadian composer Norman Campbell.

He achieved international fame when he took his character to the U.S. television show Hee Haw hosted by Buck Owens and Roy Clark. His country bumpkin act delivering the news reports often used language and voiced corny jokes. He appeared in the Country's Family Reunion SALUTE TO THE KORNFIELD, filmed in 2011.

In 2000, Harron was recognized for his contribution to the Canadian entertainment industry as a member of the Order of Ontario. In 2007, he was given the Gemini Award for lifetime achievement in radio and television. The Canadian Country Music Hall of Fame also inducted him as a member in 2010 for his work and dedication to the country music industry.

Don Harron entertained generations over the decades and can still be seen through the Country's Family Reunion DVD series and through his performances on Hee Haw.

"A deficit is what you've got wen you haven't got as much as if you jist had nothin."

– Don Harron

April 2015

Southern Raised raised on faith and music

Southern Raised moved to the Ozark Mountains near Branson, Missouri from Northwest Arkansas in 2004. Sisters, Lindsay, Sarah and Emily all began on the classical violin, Emily plays the viola as well and brother Matthew rounded out the group on the cello. They performed in an orchestra and also a quartet together. Growing up in the Ozark Mountains, a love for acoustic music quickly emerged. Having started out in the classical genre allowed them to slide into the acoustic world without missing a beat. The two styles have merged together to create a distinct sound which amazes audiences young and old alike with smooth refreshing harmony.

When asked their faith behind the ministry, Southern Raised says, "He is the reason we sing, the passion that burns, the cause we carry and the One we love! We thank Him for allowing us the honor to share His message with the world!" When Lindsay, Sarah, Emily and Matt were young, their parents prayed that God would give their family a ministry. Years later this prayer has come to fruition through the ministry of Southern Raised. The answer to this prayer is the driving force behind their being COMMITTED TO THE LORD, EACH OTHER AND BRINGING THEIR MUSIC TO THE PEOPLE.

Lindsay, (28) born August 7, 1986, loves all things vintage and loves to work outdoors planting, planting, planting. She has a green house, has planted practically every plant and tree on our farm and there are a lot! She dug by hand her own fish pond built with stone that was gathered from our property. Each fish has a name and she can actually tell them apart! She never tires of zinnias, cone flowers and hydrangeas and believes no home is really quite complete without a fresh flower arrangement! Orange and lime green are her favorite colors and needs her family to temper it for her, however is committed to having an orange Kitchen Aide someday! She loves to cook, makes wonderful homemade cinnamon rolls and homemade bread, loves the feel of dough in her hands. Enjoys writing but has to be encouraged to read. While driving down the road, she loves to roll the window down on a crisp fall day, heater blasting and feel the cool wind blowing on her face. Lindsay loves the fragrance of lilacs in the spring, fresh cut grass in the summer, wood burning fires in the fall and Fraser firs at Christmas. Lindsay considers morning coffee with Mama the perfect start to each day. A perfect day would be her beloved cocker Mabel by her side, hands in the dirt with a flat of flowers waiting for their new home!

Sarah, (26) born November 4, 1988, is the second to oldest. She is more on the quiet, sensitive side. She has spent much of her life riding around in her older sister's back pocket. She loves to sew, cook, read, read, read, especially civil war history, but any good book as well. She has made beautiful quilts and is EXTREMELY meticulous in everything, she appreciates order. She has also made beautiful vintage costumes from the civil war, colonial and renaissance time period. She loves everything vintage and a tall fluffy bed with a good read sitting on her nightstand by her vintage lamp.

April 2015

Her favorite color is purple or is it blue! She has beautiful handwriting and used to write very pretty calligraphy but hasn't done so in years. She makes delicious homemade cookies, enjoys cooking, makes an absolutely wonderful homemade spaghetti sauce and homemade pizza and wonderful homemade noodles! She doesn't do anything half way, once she starts she finishes! She would love one day to have a 1950's vintage truck, preferably baby blue, sit on the tailgate on a warm spring day by the creek and read her favorite book!

Emily Grace, (20) born July 24, 1994, is the baby girl with a bubbly personality, bright dimpled smile and large deer eyes, and a trade mark hat that she usually has on, but not always. Her two older sisters are always trying to teach her to be a lady, but she falls more under the tomboy side. She would be driving a jacked up truck with smoke stacks if allowed. She tends to see more details in life than most, more artistic. She loves to help Matthew check on the cattle, loves to draw, is writing a book, enjoys reading about the civil war and thinks the periodic table is cool. Emily likes the color yellow, mac and cheese, her Golden Retriever Honey and absolutely adores Roy Rogers and Rex Allen and actually owns a gun belt with two Colt 45 Peacemakers (replicas of course). Emily collects cool sneakers, her favorite is a pair of pink sequin high tops. She is very animated and her big eyes seem to take everything in! Expression, expression, expression!!!

Matthew, (17), born December 8, 1997, enjoys all things outdoors. Enjoys shooting his guns, his bow, being the foreman on his cattle ranch and growing herd of Black Angus cattle. Looks for every opportunity to hop on the Kubota with his English Shepherd named General and head out to tame the west. He is more reserved but still loves to cut up and have fun with his family where he feels comfortable. He stands at 6 ft 3 inches with chestnut hair and warm brown eyes and a dimple in his cheek. He is quite proud of his knife collection and he collects coins, however his family thinks he is really just stashing money! Much of life is still an adventure to him, however you would probably only know that if you are in his family, he is quite reserved around people he does not know well. He as well has grown up on Roy Rogers and has a real gun belt with six shooters! Matthew is more sentimental which is a nice way to say he is a packrat! He enjoys reading as well, especially history.

April 2015

Opry loses longtime guitarist James 'Spider' Wilson

James Edward "Spider" Wilson, longtime Grand Ole Opry staff guitarist, died of complications from cancer Thursday, February 26, in Nashville. He was 79.

A native of Nashville, Wilson spent time listening to the music he loved, standing outside an open window of the Ryman Auditorium to hear Hank Williams' Opry performances.

He joined Little Jimmy Dickens' band in the early '50s and also toured with Ray Price before joining the Grand Ole Opry staff band in 1953.

"We would work with anybody who came in and didn't have a band," Wilson explained in an interview for the NAMM oral history program. "Or we would work individually different assignments or just part of (an artist's) band. You always had to be there and ready to go, you know — a very complex job, really."

Fellow Opry guitarist and Country's Family Reunion Band member Jimmy Capps said in the same NAMM interview, "I always called Spider an 'elephant man' because if some artist asked me to work, I'd have to go ask him to hum the intro to it because he'd remember it no matter how far it went back in time."

Wilson was also a popular studio musician, recording with such major acts as Price, Marty Robbins, Bill Anderson, Faron Young and Dolly Parton.

His prominence as a player made him a familiar figure on most of the country music television shows originating in Nashville.

Behind the Scenes SPOTLIGHT

We have so many talented folks that work behind the scenes of our television shows and tapings that we thought you should meet them. Their talents and experience surely humble us.

Dan O'Connell
Post Production

Dan has worked in the Television Entertainment business for over 30 years starting with United Cable TV in a suburb of Chicago, Il back in 1983. He began working in Production and Post Production, producing TV shows and commercials for many of the cable systems national channels.

In 1985 Dan got married and moved from Chicago to Nashville, TN where he lives with his wife, Mitzi, and their three daughters. Here he has worked with many television stations, advertising agencies, production and post production companies.

Dan started working for Gabriel Communications back in 2009 when Larry's Country Diner show began. He and his father can be seen as diner guests on that very first episode. Dan is responsible for Editing and Mastering all CFR & LCD shows and authoring those DVDs for resale. He also helps with productions as a technical advisor.

April 2015

Wade Hayes, honky tonk singer and cancer survivor

Tony Wade Hayes was born April 20, 1969 in Bethel Acres, Oklahoma. His father, Don Hayes, also a professional country musician, inspired him to begin playing music as well. Initially, Hayes had learned to play mandolin, but later switched to guitar after his father bought him one. When he was eleven years old, his family moved to Nashville, Tennessee, where his father signed him to an independent record label. The label soon declared bankruptcy and the family returned to Oklahoma, where Wade later found work as a musician in his father's band.

He attended three different colleges, but dropped out of college in 1991 in pursuit of a career in country music, after seeing bluegrass musician Ricky Skaggs perform on the 1991 Country Music Association awards show. Wade returned to Nashville, where he began recording demo tapes and writing his own material. Eventually, Hayes partnered with a songwriter named Chick Rains, who recommended him to Don Cook, a record producer who has produced albums for several country music artists, including Brooks & Dunn.

Signed to Columbia Records in 1994, he made his debut that year with his gold-certified album Old Enough to Know Better. Its title track, which served as his debut single, reached Number One on the Billboard Hot Country Singles & Tracks (now Hot Country Songs) charts, and three more singles from it all reached Top Ten as well.

Hayes' second album, 1996's On a Good Night, was also certified gold, although its No. 2-peaking title track was the only Top 40 hit from it. When the Wrong One Loves You Right, his third album, produced two more singles, including the No. 5 "The Day That She Left Tulsa (In a Chevy)", although he left the label by 1999. A year later, he signed to the Monument roster, where he released Highways & Heartaches. This album produced no Top 40 country hits, however.

On April 4, 1999, Hayes married former Miss USA runner-up Danni Boatwright, who appeared in the video for Hayes' single "Tore Up from the Floor Up". She also appeared in Hayes' video for the song "Up North Down South, Back East, Out West." Boatwright later was a contestant on the CBS reality television series Survivor. The couple divorced in 2003.

Also in 2003, he founded the duo McHayes with Alan Jackson's fiddle player Mark McClurg. The duo charted one single on the country charts and recorded one unreleased album for the Universal South label, "Lessons in Lonely." He joined the backing band for former Alabama lead singer Randy Owen in the late 2000s, and self-released Place to Turn Around in 2009.

In December 2011, Wade was diagnosed with Stage IV colon cancer. Shortly after learning of his illness, he wrote the song "Is It Already Time," a ballad about his battle with the disease. A year later he was considered being in remission. However, in 2013, Wade once again found himself facing cancer when it returned in his lymph nodes.

Wade was part of the Honky Tonk Reunion filmed in September 2014. That series is on sale now for $79.80 plus shipping and handling, by calling 1-800-820-5405.

April 2015

COUNTRY LEGENDS PAST AND PRESENT   BY TOM WOOD

THE DUKE OF PADUCAH

One of country's original kings of comedy, Benjamin Francis Ford was first known to fans as "Whitey" for his shock of blond hair. Born in DeSoto, Mo. In 1901, the banjo-playing, wise-cracking Ford was dubbed the Duke of Paducah by a band leader during his heydays in the 1940s. The nickname stuck, and so did the pre-Hee-Haw cornpone comedy routine. That multi-layered popularity — he was a crossover hit if ever there was one — that earned Ford a 1986 induction to the Country Music Hall of Fame. Screen credits include Country Fair (1941), Music Caravan (1964), Country Music on Broadway and The Las Vegas Hillbillys (1966).

Whitey Ford did most of his learning at "the University of Hard Knocks," as he joked in his self-deprecating manner to explain that he had only a third-grade education. One irreverent joke was that he met his when he was in the third grade: He was 18, and she was eight!

But the Duke of Paducah was not hindered by that lack of formal education, and the four years he spent in the U.S. Navy from 1918-22 proved life-changing. He learned to play the banjo while in the Navy and first joined a Dixieland Jazz Band following his discharge. It was during this time that he became known as the Duke of Paducah, and he also hosted a number of popular radio shows on stations like WLS in Chicago and KWK in St. Louis.

In 1937, the Duke of Paducah and Red Foley founded the "Renfro Valley Barn Dance" along with John Lair. It proved to be a popular radio show and led to the Duke becoming a regular on Plantation Party from 1942-59 for the NBC Radio Network in Chicago and Cincinnati. The Duke of Paducah joined Grand Ole Opry cast in the early 1940s.

World War II changed everything, but the Duke of Paducah helped lighten the mood on the homefront, when Americans needed a break from the harsh realities of life. The Duke of Paducah owned a zany, offbeat — occasionally off-color — sense of humor that was reflected in his sense of style.

His over the top, trademark look included colorful, really loud clothes, sometimes checked, sometimes over-sized. Hats and two-tone shoes were also large and equally loud. The Duke wore a size twelve shoe and he ended every performance with the line, "I'm going back to the wagon, boys. These shoes are killing me!" It became the Duke's tagline and the title of a book he published in 1947. "These Shoes Are Killing Me" was half-biography, half joke book, and full of photos with fellow country stars. One story he shared told of how the Duke of Paducah became an honorary citizen of Paducah, Ky., and was given a key to the city by the mayor and the town.

The world changed in the 1950s, and the Duke of Paducah changed with them. In the mid-1950s, the Duke of Paducah joined the Rock and Roll Revue and shared billing with a young entertainer named Elvis Presley on several occasions. In 1958, he was named host of a Nashville-based television show on WLAC-TV called Country Junction. It ran for several years and was a precursor to Hee-Haw (on which he made one appearance in 1977). He died on June 20, 1986, in Brentwood, Tenn.

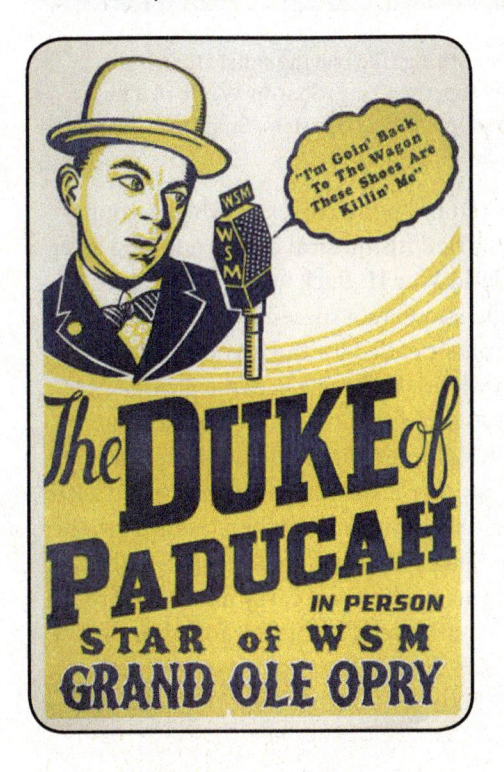

April 2015

The Whites excel in Bluegrass, Country & Gospel

"There's nothing like playing music to bring a family together," says Sharon White of The Whites. The group consists of sisters, Sharon and Cheryl, and father Buck.

The White's story begins in Texas, when a young Buck White started his musical career not long after the end of World War II. Buck worked the dance halls and radio shows in a succession of bands. Honky-tonk music called for the piano and the bluegrass mandolin, and so he became proficient on both. In 1961, White moved to Arkansas, but within a matter of months, he and wife Pat were once again making music. They formed a band with another couple that eventually called themselves the Down Home Folks. Sharon and Cheryl were drawn to music ("Mama said I could carry a tune before I could talk," Sharon recalls.) at first forming the Down Home Kids with the children of other Down Home Folks members in the mid-1960s, then moving up to join their parents in a growing number of bluegrass festival appearances.

The first big break for the Whites came in 1971, when a successful trip to Bill Monroe's Bean Blossom festival convinced the family that the time was right to move to Nashville and pursue a more serious music career. Pat retired from the band in 1973.

The move to Nashville paid off as Buck White and the Down Home Folks began their recording career. The band featured the striking family harmonies and top-notch instrumental work that has characterized their music ever since and they saw a steady ascent in the world of bluegrass, recording five acclaimed albums for various labels and working a busy touring schedule. They also gained a toehold in the country music field thanks to their powerful vocals and broad repertoire. Their talent gained the attention of Emmylou Harris, who brought them in to sing on her Blue Kentucky Girl album of 1979 and then took them on the road with her as an opening act.

The early part of the 1980s brought the band, now called The Whites, to national prominence as their simple, traditionally rooted yet dynamic sound put them on Billboard's country charts with a succession of Top 20 hits. Many of their songs were produced by Sharon's husband, Ricky Skaggs (the two married in 1981). They were inducted as members of the Grand Ole Opry in 1984.

The Whites first all-gospel album, 1988's Doing It by the Book, earned the trio their first award, the fan voted Music City News award for 'Best Gospel Album.'

In 2001, acoustic music blasted onto the mainstream with the smash hit movie and soundtrack, O Brother Where Art Thou? Buck and the girls were hand selected among bluegrass music's finest to participate in the soundtrack and appear in the film. Along with all the industry accolades, The Whites made numerous appearances in promotion of O Brother, including their involvement in the first 18-city 'Down from the Mountain' tour, a stop at David Letterman's "Late Show" with fellow O Brother artist, Dr. Ralph Stanley, and a featured spot on the follow up tours – the 40 plus city 'Down from the Mountain' summer tour in 2002 and the 'Great High Mountain' tour in the summer of 2004.

After years of blending their voices from the living room to the stage, The Whites teamed up with Ricky Skaggs on Salt of the Earth (2007), their first collaborative effort, which earned them a GRAMMY Award for Best Southern, Country, or Bluegrass Gospel Album and a Gospel Music Association (GMA) Dove Award for Bluegrass Recorded Album of the Year. Buck, Sharon, Cheryl, and Ricky share lead vocals with Skaggs' award winning band Kentucky Thunder laying the foundation for their tight family harmony. Traditional hymns, a few familiar favorites, and brand new treasures flow throughout the album providing an intimate look into the heart of one of music's most beloved families..

The Whites have remained some of the most in-demand guest artists to appear on countless recordings including recent works by Kenny Rogers, Charlie Daniels, Connie Smith and Paul Brandt, to name a few. They may not use the name anymore, but Buck, Sharon and Cheryl are still creating music that's as good and as real as everything conjured up by the phrase "down home folks."

Salute to the Kornfield
Enjoy all the memories and stories from the folks you love!

$79.80

We realized no one had ever gathered all the members of the TV show "Hee Haw" into one room and film it, so we decided to do it! What we got out of that taping is incredible, once-in-a-lifetime stuff called Country's Family Reunion: Salute to the Kornfield!

This 5 DVD series features all of the Hee Haw cast we could gather telling stories about one of the most popular TV shows of all time, plus sharing wonderful songs and laughter. And, it wouldn't be a Country's Family Reunion without some of your favorite country stars, many of whom played on Hee Haw when it was on TV.

Some of the guests at this incredible taping include: Roy Clark, Buddy Alan Owens, LuLu Clark, George Lindsey, Gordie Tapp, Buck Trent, Don Harron, Charlie McCoy, Mike Snider, Barbie Benton, Roni Stoneman, Gunilla Hutton, Cathy Baker, Ricky Skaggs, Johnny Lee, LarryGatlin, Gene Watson, The Whites, Moe Bandy... so many people came together for this never-before-done gathering.

And it's all on 5 DVDs for YOU to enjoy. Only 79.80 plus FREE SHIPPING when you use the code 'FREESHIPPING' on your order. Country's Family Reunion: Salute to the Kornfield is a treasure of TV entertainment you've just got to watch. Enjoy!

1-800-820-5405
CFR Videos, P.O. Box 210709, Nashville, TN 37221

Larry's Country Diner RFD Show Schedule April 2015

NEW SHOW
JASON CRABB
Saturday, April 4
10:00 p.m. Central
Sunday, April 5
6:00 p.m. Central

NEW SHOW
DAN MILLER
Saturday, April 11
10:00 p.m. Central
Sunday, April 12
6:00 p.m. Central

NEW SHOW
TEEA GOANS
Saturday, April 18
10:00 p.m. Central
Sunday, April 19
6:00 p.m. Central

NEW SHOW
SOUTHERN RAISED
Saturday, April 25
10:00 p.m. Central
Sunday, April 26
6:00 p.m. Central

April 2015

Randy Travis improving slowly, visits Opry

As of November 2014, Randy Travis is slowly recovering, and can even walk short distances without assistance. He is also relearning how to write and play the guitar, according to his fiancée Mary Davis. Rumor is, he even recently visited the Grand Ole Opry.

Randy was admitted to a Dallas area hospital for viral cardiomyopathy after a viral upper respiratory infection on July 7, 2013. His condition was classified as critical. Three days later, Travis suffered a stroke and had surgery to relieve pressure on his brain. On July 15, 2013, it was reported that Travis was awake and alert after undergoing brain surgery, that his heart was pumping without the assistance of machines, and that he was on the road to recovery. He was released from Baylor Heart Hospital in Plano, Texas on July 31, 2013, and entered a physical therapy facility. Following his stroke, and despite physical therapy, Travis has been unable to sing or speak and has difficulty walking, having

Randy Travis was born Randy Bruce Traywick on May 4, 1959. Since 1985, he has recorded 20 studio albums and charted more than 50 singles on the Billboard Hot Country Songs charts, and 16 of these were number one hits. .

Randy and his brother Ricky were encouraged to pursue their musical talents by their father, who was a fan of Hank Williams, George Jones, and Lefty Frizzell. In 1967, at the age of eight, Randy began playing guitar and sang in church as a boy. Two years later, he and his brother began performing at local clubs and talent contests, calling themselves the Traywick Brothers. Randy often fought with his father and soon dropped out of high school. He spent his getting into trouble with the law.

In 1975, Randy won a talent contest at a nightclub in Charlotte, North Carolina. The club's owner, Elizabeth "Lib" Hatcher, took an interest in the young singer, hired him as a cook, and gave him regular singing jobs at the club. Still in his late teens, Travis had one more encounter with the law. At his hearing, the judge told Travis that if he ever saw the singer back in his court, he should be prepared to go to jail for a long time. Travis was released into the guardianship of Hatcher, who also became his manager. The two began to focus on his career full-time.

He recorded a self-titled album, Randy Traywick, for Paula Records in 1978. The following year, he released two unsuccessful singles, "She's My Woman" and "Dreamin'".

Travis moved in with Hatcher, and in 1982, she and Travis moved to Nashville, Tennessee. It was during this time that an unlikely romance began to form between the two. Travis would later comment, "I think we discovered how much we needed each other." He and Hatcher eventually went public with their relationship and were married in a private ceremony in 1991.

During the early 1980s, Travis was rejected by every major record label in Nashville. His early demo tapes were criticized by record executives as being "too country." To support them, Hatcher took a job as manager of a nightclub, The Nashville Palace, and hired Travis as a cook and singer. In 1982, Travis recorded an independent album Live at the Nashville Palace, and Hatcher used the album to secure a deal with Warner Bros. Records. As part of the contract, label executives insisted they keep their romance a secret, and changed his stage name to Randy Travis. In 1985, Warner Bros. Records released the single "On the Other Hand" which peaked at No. 67 on the country charts. His next single, "1982", became a Top 10 hit single.

Travis and Lib divorced on October 29, 2010 after a 19-year marriage, and their business relationship ended thereafter.

Following Randy's brush with severe medical issues, everyone hopes he is finally on his way to recover.

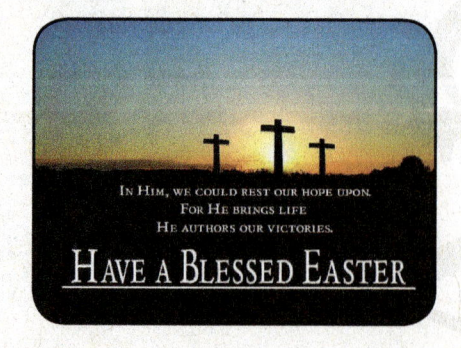

In Him, we could rest our hope upon.
For He brings life
He authors our victories.

HAVE A BLESSED EASTER

April 2015

The Nashville Brat Pack
Kids of the Country Stars!

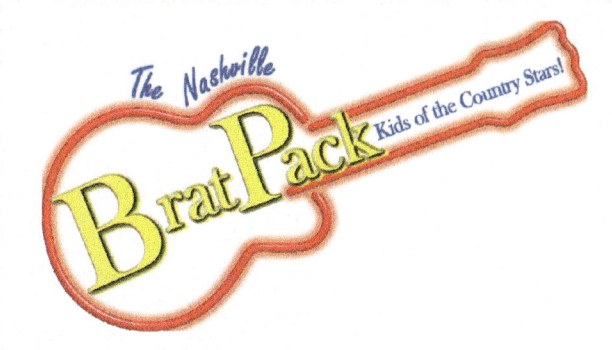

By Karen Wheeler Daughter of Onie Wheeler, Founder of The Ozark Cowboys.

Below left is a 1955 ad for Onie Wheeler who formed The Ozark Cowboys. Onie's Ozark Corral south of Cape Girardeau, The Wilburn Brothers were so new at the time, in fact they misspelled Doyle name.

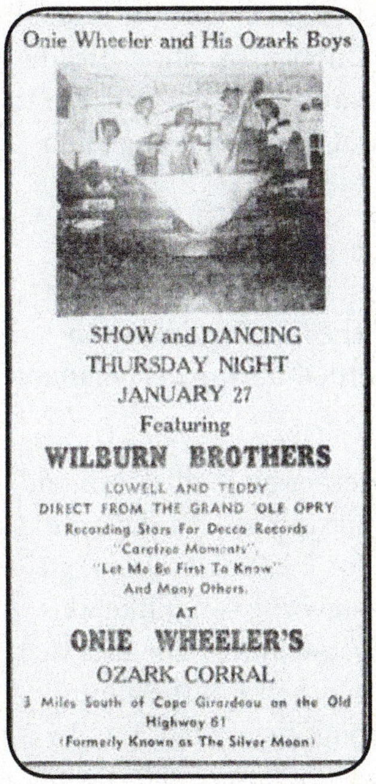

Above is an old photo of me and my mom and dad. Top to Bottom: Karen Wheeler, Carolyn (Nelson) Fosbinder, Jean Wheeler (Mama), A.J. Nelson, and Onie Wheeler (Daddy).

Right: Roy Acuff was a great man. I would make him a skillet of cornbread every week, take it to him, & take him out to eat at "Cracker Barrel" or "Cock Of The Walk" when he lived at the Opryland Hotel.

Below: This was "Johnny Cash & The Country Girls" syndicated show. I'm not sure but I think it was around 1981. Melba Montgomery was in a skit with me & Jeannie C. Riley. We busted through a poster of Johnny Carson! We were singing "Oh Johnny Oh Johnny How You Can Love"

First row at top, left to right: Wendi Holcomb, Jeanne Pruett, Misty Rowe, Ronnie Stoneman, (Behind me) Shelly West, Karen Wheeler, Kitty Wells, Jeannie Seely. First lower row: Kelly Warren, Sue Powell, Connie Smith & Christy Russell.

Below: I was a judge on "You Can Be A Star" TV show hosted by Jim Ed Brown. Along with me is Porter Wagoner and a DJ from Texas, Jerry King.

I have a writer's night at the Maxwell House Hotel in Nashville on April 16 from 8-9:30 p.m.

Far right: Here I am with Ronny Robbins, son of the great Marty Robbins.

65
CFR NEWS
April 2015

Dr. Humphrey Bate and his Possum Hunters

Legacy Recordings released Willie Nelson and Sister Bobbie's December Day, the first installment of the Willie's Stash archival recordings series, on Tuesday, December 2. In celebration, they also released a new three and a half minute video sharing memories of their childhood in Abbott, Texas. The video can be seen on www.wilienelson.com or www.countryweekly.com.

"We grew up working on farms and making our school money picking cotton, baling hay, whatever. It was a great way to grow up," Willie Nelson says. "We learned a little about everything in Abbott. There was no laws up there, so we could pretty well do what we wanted to do, as long as we lived through it, and fortunately we did."

They share the screen with shots of fields and churches, as well as old photos from their upbringing.

"Some of my, really, earliest memories, besides walking through the field, would be us learning music, our grandparents showing us music," Bobbie Nelson shares. "Our grandfather was very much into gospel music — our grandmother, too — and I was trying to learn to play the pump organ. I remember Daddy Nelson showing Willie how to play the guitar, and he taught [him] how to sing so that when he'd go to school, he could sing for the kids."

The two have been playing together since they were kids, starting with performances at church revival meetings. The video is full of laughs and tender moments, which also shows their good chemistry on stage as well.

"There's nothing like playing music with Willie. I get an energy from just sitting with me at the piano, but when I sit with Willie, it's just an all-new energy," Bobbie Nelson says of sharing the stage with her brother. "When we put that all together, you can really feel it."

"We play together, I think, as well as anybody," adds Willie. "When it's just her and I, it's a lot of fun to play. It's nice to know that sister Bobbie is over there because whenever I need someone to take the lead, all I have to do is nod to sister Bobbie, and she's already there. She knows what to do and gives me a chance to relax a little bit and figure out what I'm going to do next."

The album's sound features contributions from other Family Band members, including harmonica player Mickey Raphael and the late Bee Spears on bass on "What'll I Do," recorded during his poignant last session with Willie.

Willie and Bobbie ride together on Willie's bus and spend much of that time jamming on their favorite songs. That is how the idea for December Day came about. 'Why not record our favorite songs like we play them for ourselves?,' Bobbie asked. The idea that 'less is more' is the underlying theme of the album. Everyone has heard these songs before but not like this. The spontaneity born out of familiarity is what this record, December Day, is all about.

The Willie's Stash series will present a variety of releases, personally curated by Willie Nelson, culled from decades of recording and touring, a singular career that's established Willie Nelson as an American musical icon..

April 2015

Musicians on the album include Willie Nelson (Trigger) and Bobbie Nelson (piano, B-3 organ) with Mickey Raphael (harmonica), Kevin Smith (bass), Bee Spears (bass), Billy English (drums, percussion) and David Zettner (acoustic guitar).

December Day: Willie's Stash, Vol. 1 track listing:

1. "Alexander's Ragtime Band"
2. "Permanently Lonely"
3. "What'll I Do"
4. "Summer of Roses"/"December Day"
5. "Nuages"
6. "Mona Lisa"
7. "I Don't Know Where I Am Today"
8. "Amnesia"
9. "Who'll Buy My Memories"
10. "The Anniversary Song"
11. "Laws of Nature"
12. "Walkin'"
13. "Always"
14. "I Let My Mind Wander"
15. "Is the Better Part Over"
16. "My Own Peculiar Way"
17. "Sad Songs and Waltzes"
18. "Ou-es tu, mon amour"/"I Never Cared for You"

Spring Combo Sale
Get both great sets for one low price of only $119.80

Old Time Gospel

Old Time Gospel was filmed in 2011 and was hosted by Bill Anderson, with Rhonda Vincent, Dallas Frazier, Ed Bruce, Con Hunley, Jan Howard, Larry Gatlin & The Gatlin Bros., Gary Morris, Duane, Nora Lee Allen, George Hamilton IV, Linda Davis, Gene Watson, Jean Shepard, Joey & Rory, Phil Johnson, Larry Black, Barbara Fairchild, Dailey and Vincent, The Whites, Jimmy Fortune, Jeannie Seely, T. Graham Brown, Jim Ed Brown, Gordon Mote, and John Conlee. All on 5 DVDs, including the Behind The Scenes' DVD.

Gospel Classics

These performances have been scattered across all of our many collections and is hosted by Bill Anderson and featuring Bashful Brother Oswald, Bill Carlisle, Bill Clifton and Mike Seegar, Billy Walker, Bobby Lord, Boxcar Willie, Carol Lee Cooper, Charlie Louvin, Charlie Walker, Del Reeves, Freddie Hart, George Hamilton IV, Hank Locklin, Jan Howard, Jack Greene, Jean Shepard, Jeannie C. Riley, Jeannie Pruett, Jim and Jesse McReynolds, Jim Ed Brown, Jimmy C. Newman, Jimmy Dean, Jimmy Shumate, Johnny Paycheck, Johnny Russell, Johnny Wright, Justin Tubb, Kitty Wells, Leroy Van Dyke, Martha Carson, Patsy Stoneman, Sheb Wooley, Skeeter Davis, Stonewall Jackson, Stu Phillips, The Browns, The Lewis Family, The Whites, Walter Bailes, Wanda Jackson, and Wilma Lee Cooper. All these on 3 DVDs, plus you get the songbook!

get free shipping by using the code 'FREESHIPPING' with your order

1-800-820-5405
CFR, P.O. Box 210796, Nashville, TN 37221

April 2015

Road Stories

By Claudia Johnson

Hank Snow, a Travelin' Man

Country's ultimate road story may be that of Clarence Eugene "Hank" Snow, whose journey began in Nova Scotia, Canada, in 1914, and ended in Music City in 1999. However, it isn't just the geographic distance he traveled in those 85 years but also the emotional journey that makes the title of perhaps his memorable hit, "I've Been Everywhere," most fitting.

At age 12 he became a cabin boy on fishing schooners to escape physical abuse and neglect resulting from his parents' divorce and the unstable family situation it created. He returned to land permanently at age 16, having survived a storm during which 130 of his fellow fishermen were drowned.

He had learned the basics of guitar as a child but developed a serious interest upon hearing Jimmie Rodgers' recording of "Moonlight and Skies."

"I first heard Jimmie Rodgers when I was in my teens… I became an ardent fan right at that minute," Snow recalled in an interview. "I either had to duplicate his success before I died or bust."

Snow ordered a guitar by mail, practicing constantly as he tried to survive with jobs as stevedore, lumberjack, lobsterman and Fuller Brush salesman. Determined to become a country music star, in 1933 he hitchhiked from his hometown of Brooklyn, Nova Scotia, to Halifax, some 150 miles away, where he worked for CHNS Radio. In 1935 he married Minnie Aalders, but despite his local radio popularity, the couple was not financially secure. Their son, Jimmie Rodgers Snow, was born, at a charity ward of a Salvation Army Hospital.

"My mother told me I slept a lot of nights when I was a baby in a bureau drawer or guitar case," said Jimmie Snow, now 79.

Finally, in 1936 Snow signed a recording contract with Canadian Bluebird, a subsidiary of RCA Victor. In the early 1940s, as "Hank, the Singing Ranger," he toured extensively through eastern Canada, playing at movie theaters during the intermissions between films and teaching guitar lessons.

"Many of Dad's shows were conducted through agreements with priests in the local parishes," said Jimmie Snow. "The church promoted the show and provided a big hall to play in, and Dad spilt the income 50-50 with them."

When Snow became a featured performer in 1942 on CKNB in Campbellton, New Brunswick, the powerful station's broadcast exposed American listeners to Snow, but his label never did U.S. releases of any of his 90 Canadian recordings, many of which were hits.

Snow was determined to become part of the American country music industry. In 1944, he made his first trip to the U.S. performing around Philadelphia, West Virginia and Dallas, where he met Ernest Tubb with whom he later toured. The next year he became a regular on "Wheeling Jamboree" broadcast from WWVA in Wheeling, W. V., but fame and financial stability continued to elude the family.

"Most people don't realize that my dad was an unbelievable trick rider," Jimmie Snow said, recalling

April 2015

the traveling show that had the Snow family sharing a trailer with a horse, Shawnee, for several years. "Dad kept us from starving to death."

The popularity of singing cowboys drew Snow twice to Hollywood, but both times were professional and fiscal disasters.

"Finally he got a call to go to Dallas," Jimmie Snow said. "Bea Terry promoted several artists and had been talking to Dad. She'd convinced some of the bigger radio stations to play several of the Canadian releases, and one of them had become a hit in that area."

Snow found work as a performer in Dallas, though not quite achieving the fame he'd chased so long.

"He played at the Roundup club on the same street where Jack Ruby had his club, the Silver Spur," Jimmie Snow said. "Sometimes Dad would go in to sing a song or have a beer, and when they closed, Jack Ruby would take a bunch of the guys to some of the all-night spots he owed."

Jimmie Snow said his family was shocked when Ruby killed Lee Harvey Oswald because they had remembered his kindness to Hank.

In 1949, RCA Victor finally signed Snow to an American contract after a series of recording sessions at the label's Chicago studios. His first record, "Marriage Vow," hit the American charts that year, sparking a move to Nashville.

Then, with Tubb's influence, early in 1950 Snow played the Grand Ole Opry, receiving a less than enthusiastic reception. Continued disappointments made him consider a return to Canada, not even realizing the Opry was about to drop him.

"Then a miracle happened," Jimmie Snow said. "Dad's song "I'm Movin' On" became a huge hit and spent 44 weeks in the top 100 and 21 weeks at Number 1."

When "The Golden Rocket," another train song, became his second number-one hit in late 1950, the Snow family began to gain some sense of security. After years on the road, the singer bought a home at Madison, Tenn., with a barn and paddock for Shawnee.

"Between 1951 and the end of 1955, Dad had 24 Top Ten hits," Jimmie Snow said. "His single, "I Don't Hurt Anymore," was Number One for 20 weeks in 1954. That is just unheard of today."

Snow was a member of the Grand Ole Opry, was inducted into the Nashville Songwriters International Hall of Fame and the Country Music Hall of Fame, owned a music school and publishing company, founded a charity to help abused children and owned two radio stations.

"Dad recorded 140 albums and had 85 singles on the Billboard country charts between 1950 and 1980," his son said, still in awe of such success when he well recalls the years of struggle the family survived. "In all he sold over 70 million records."

Snow's hit list contained ballads, spoken word recordings, country boogie, Hawaiian music, rumbas, traditional country, gospel and cowboys songs. However, Snow's trademark was – quite appropriately viewed in light of his biography – traveling songs.

Hank Snow and his son Jimmie Snow in a recording session in the 1950s at RCA studios.

April 2015

Country Questions
By Dick Boise, CMH

Send questions to:
Dick Boise, , c/o CFR News,
P.O. Box 201796, Nashville,
TN 37221.

Top: Jerry Jeff Walker
Bottom: Hal Ketchum

Q. We find that most of the country artists are from the states in the south. Is there any from the New York state location? Thanks for any information you have for me.

Larry Wall, Alfred, NY

A. Thanks for your question and there are some from the Empire state. Jerry Jeff Walker (Ron Crosby) was born in Oneonta, NY. Jack Blanchard and Misty Morgan (Tennessee Bird Walk fame) were both from Buffalo. On the other end of the state, Hal Ketchum was born in Greenwich, NY. And this year's hottest Bluegrass due, the Gibson Brothers, were born way up near the Canadian border in a small spot named Churubusco, NY.

Q. I want to know if Ramona Jones remarried? I heard that she is married to a preacher from the Carolinas. Is this true?

Barbara Tuttle, Winston Salem, NC

A. Barbara, Ramona Jones, widow of the late Grandpa Jones, has mentioned on one of the Country's Family Reunion shows that she has remarried and that her new husband is a minister. Gene Gober is a Methodist minister. I do not know where he is from and we wish much happiness to this couple. She is a fine entertainer in her own way.

Q. Could you tell me about the instrument that Bashful Brother Oswald played for Roy Acuff. It looks like a guitar but he played it like a steel guitar.

Pete Young, Stockton, CA

A. That instrument dates back into the mid-1920 and the most popular one is called "Dobro." It is much like an acoustic guitar, however, it has a metal resonator in the top to increase the sound. The name Dobro, comes from the two brothers, originally from Czechoslovakia, whose name was Dopyera. They took the "Do" from their name and the "Bro" from brotehrs, to use as the instrument name. SO, Dobro became famous and nearly every bluegrass group uses one. Thanks for your interesting inquiry.

Q. I overheard someone talking about music and mentioned the name Buddy Killen. I never happen to hear that name and I really know a lot of entertainer's names. Could you give me something about the man?

Florence Thomas, Shamokin, PA

A. The man you asked about wore many, many hats during his time in Nashville. Born in Alabama, November 13, 1932, William (Buddy) Killen came to Nashville soon after high school and played bass for a comedy duo. He also became involved in pitching songs for a new publishing company called Tree Publishing. From this he became to produce record sessions. He also had a very popular restaurant in Nashville called The Stockyard. In my collection of biographies of country "folks," his is my very favorite. It's titled "By The Seat Of My Pants." You should read it! He passed away, November 1, 2006 and is also featured on the Country's Family Reunion Precious Memories series.

CORRECTION: Carl Smith died January 16, 2010.

April 2015

Jason Crabb, his faith gives him voice

Jason Crabb is a small-town, Kentucky boy who has had GRAMMY nods and seventeen Dove Awards. Born and raised in Beaver Dam, KY, Jason was raised with a love of faith and family. He took to the road with his family when he was 14.

As time went on, the family followed different paths and Jason moved into a solo career in 2009, releasing his solo album and watching it move to the top of the charts and earning nomination after nomination.

Jason won Male Artist of the Year at the GMA Dove Awards in 2012. He also took home Artist of the Year. He has won 20 Dove Awards throughout his career, not to mention the GRAMMY Award he took home in 2010.

His own pain, loss and heartache, partially emanating from issues with infertility and miscarriage that he and his wife have lived through, have influenced his life and his music. He is humble and compassionate and his songs reflect those feelings.

"People everywhere are hurting," Jason says. "Their backs are against the wall. They've lost their jobs, their 401Ks. Big corporations are shutting down... We're human and we stumble over everything we're trying to be, to live up to...."

Jason revealed just how human he really is, in his 2011 book, Trusting God to Get You Through, inviting readers to see first-hand the work of God in his life. "I'd love for somebody to think, 'If that boy can make it and there's hope for him, then I can go through these things and there's hope for me as well.'"

Jason is already hard at work on two other books—a children's book and an inspirational book all about dreams.

Long-time friend and mentor Bill Gaither sums it up: "Jason Crabb is the real deal. I love his voice, I love his heart, and I love the unique way he connects people to the hope every human being needs to hear."

GRASSROOTS TO BLUEGRASS & simply BLUEGRASS

Back in 1999, we asked Mac Wiseman to pull together a Who's Who of Bluegrass. He did, and we were able to honor an pay tribute to many of the pioneers of Bluegrass on our Grassroots to Bluegrass series. You'll see and hear Bill Clifton, Brother Oswald, Charlie Louvin, Del McCoury, Doyle Lawson, Eddie Stubbs, J.D. Crowe, James Monroe Jeannette Carter, Jim & Jesse McReynolds, Jimmy Shumate, John Hartford, Kenny Baker, Leroy Troy, Lewis Family, Mac Wiseman, Martha & Eddie Adcock, Melvin Goins, Mike Seeger, Osborne Brothers, "Pappy" Sherrill, Patsy Stoneman, Polly Lewis, Ramona Jones, Ronnie Reno, and Walter Bailes.

Then in 2012 we decided to do it again only this time with Ricky Skaggs hosting Bobby Osborne, Carl Jackson, Dailey & Vincent, Del McCoury, Dierks Bentley, Donna Ulisse, Doyle Lawson, Jerry Douglas, Larry Cordle, Mac Wiseman, Paul Brewster, Ramona Jones, Rhonda Vincent, Ronnie Reno, Sam Bush, Sierra Hull, The Gibson Brothers, The Roys, and The Whites.

Grassroots to Bluegrass (10 DVDS, over 60 songs) plus the Simply Bluegrass Collection (5 DVDs, over 25 songs) AND 2 Audio CD's of Simply Bluegrass If you bought all separately, it would cost over $250 dollars, but with this special offer, you'll get all 17 discs for just $149.75! That's over 100 songs and performances in this 17 Disc collection. It is the ULTIMATE Bluegrass Collection from Country's Family Reunion.

$149.75 plus $16.95 s/h or Free Shipping with code 'FREESHIPPING'

CFR, P.O. Box 210796, Nashville, TN 37221

1-800-820-5405
www.cfrvideos.com

April 2015

Carrie Underwood & husband welcome baby

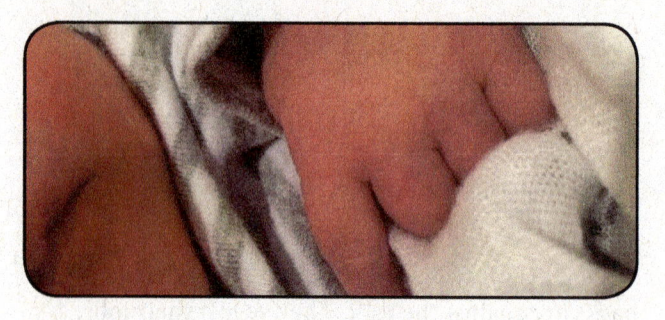

Carrie Underwood and Mike Fisher have announced the birth of their first child, a son named Isaiah Michael Fisher. Underwood shared the above photo of little Isaiah's hand and a short message on social media Tuesday. "Tiny hands and tiny feet…God has blessed us with an amazing gift! Isaiah Michael Fisher – born on February 27. Welcome to the world, sweet angel!"

Moe Bandy – Bulls, Broncos and Country Music

There aren't many musical performers who've been on top of a bucking bull or bronco and on top of the country music charts, but Moe Bandy has.

Before his honky-tonking country sound drew him to the spotlight, Bandy took center stage in another type of venue.

"Dad had an arena called Bandy's Arena where we'd all get together to ride bulls and play some music," the singer said, recalling his youthful amusements. "That was right down my alley."

The family had moved from their hometown of Meridian, Miss., to San Antonio, Texas, area when Bandy was six years old, and by the time Bandy was 16 he and his brother, Mike, were participating in rodeos across the state. Bandy worked as a cowboy on a ranch and competed in bull riding and bareback bronco riding.

"I got tired of bruises and fractured bones," he said, explaining why he finally turned to music as a career.

While growing up, Bandy's mother played the piano and sang, and his father sang and played guitar with a local band called the Mission City Playboys, teaching young Marion, whom he nicknamed "Moe," to play as well.

"Dad wanted me to be a star," said Bandy, whose successful career fulfilled his father's wish by recording 10 Number One smashes, 40 Top Ten hits, 66 charted releases and five gold albums, plus earning an ACM/CMA award for Duet of the Year and being inducted into the Texas Country Music Hall of Fame.

Three of Bandy's recordings, "Bandy the Rodeo Clown," "Rodeo Romeo" and "Someday Soon," were especially appropriate given his longtime connection with rodeo.

After Bandy became a successful country music singer, he played the rodeo circuit receiving the Professional Rodeo Cowboys Association's award for Entertainer of the Year. He was also honored as Entertainer of the Year by the International Rodeo Association, and was named Texas Entertainer of the year by the Rodeo Cowboys Association.

The singer's brother, Mike Bandy, had an impressive rodeo career and was a six-time National Finals Rodeo bull riding qualifier. Both Mike and Moe Bandy were inducted into the Texas Rodeo Cowboy Hall of Fame in 2007.

Bandy continues his relationship with the rodeo through his interest in his Professional Bull Riders bulls, one named MoeBandy.com and one named Bandy's Bad Boy.

"MoeBandy.com made it to the finals four times, but he's getting a little long in the tooth," Bandy said, adding that he goes to watch his bulls in competitions when he can work it into his busy concert schedule.

Now a resident of Branson, Mo., at age 71 he continues to perform regularly in Branson and at a variety of venues throughout the United States.

"I've been playing music for close to 50 years," he said, observing, "I think we're here for a purpose. I've been lucky to have this [music career]."

Bandy said the favorite of all his recordings was "'Til I'm too Old to Die Young," with lyrics that encapsulate his feelings about his life.

"If I could have one wish today and know it would be done, I would say, everyone could stay 'til they're too old to die young."

Moe Bandy on the road still singin'

For over four decades, fans have come to depend upon Moe Bandy for their traditional country fix, and the singer is set to provide that trademark honky-tonk sound in concert throughout 2015. Today, the singer announces a new booking agreement with Battle Artist Agency, joining a list of artists that includes The Bellamy Brothers, Williams & Ree, Eddy Raven, Mickey Gilley, Earl Thomas Conley, and Gene Watson.

"Since we first hit with 'I Just Started Hatin' Cheatin Songs Today,' the fans have been one of the most important aspects of my career," says Bandy. "Getting back out on the road and taking their kind of country to them is what I've always been about, and I'm glad to be working with Battle Artist Agency in that endeavor. Rob Battle is one of the greats at what he does, so we are looking forward to letting him do what he does so well, so we can do what we do."

Bandy followed up that first hit with several more in that traditional vein. Songs like "Barstool Mountain," "Honky Tonk Amnesia," and "Hank Williams, You Wrote My Life" helped to make him one of the most played male artists on the radio in the 1970s. He began a successful recording and touring partnership with Joe Stampley in 1979 with "Just Good Ol' Boys," that led to several awards from the Country Music Association and the Academy of Country Music. Other hits under the Bandy name include "Someday Soon" and the Kevin Welch standard "Till I'm Too Old To Die Young." He is also a frequent guest on such TV Shows as Larry's Country Diner and Country's Family Reunion.

In a career that has seen him work with such heavyweights as The Oak Ridge Boys, Johnny Cash, and Hank Williams, Jr., Rob Battle knows "great" when he says it. He says Moe Bandy easily qualifies. "Moe Bandy is one of the most distinctive talents this industry has ever known," he said. "He has always demonstrated an ability to bring his fans the music that they expect and long for, and this tour will be no exception. I'm just glad to be a part of it."

Moe Bandy Tour Dates:

Apr 10 Smithville Jamboree / Smithville, TX

Apr 11 South Shore Harbour Resort / League City, TX

Apr 18 Orange Blossom Opry / Weirsdale, FL

Apr 19 ACM Awards / Dallas, TX

May 2 Cornyval Fair / Helotes, TX

May 9 Llano Opry / Llano, TX

May 23 Augusta Days / Augusta, AR

Jun 13 Tri-City Speedway / Granite City, IL

July 10 Redneck Country Club / Stafford, TX

July 25 Truman Lake Opry / Tightwad, MO

Aug 14 Lovelady Old Gym / Lovelady, TX

Sep 12 Marmora Jamboree / Marmora Ontario Canada

Sep 19 Texas Theater / Sequin, TX

Oct 25 Andy Williams Moon River Theater / Branson, MO

April 2015

Jimmy Capps honored with Tennessee Senate Resolution

WHEREAS, the members of this legislative body are pleased to recognize citizens of this State who are renowned in their fields of endeavor, especially when those chosen fields are in keeping with Tennessee's pride and heritage in country music; and

WHEREAS, one such renowned musician of the country music genre is guitarist Jimmy Capps, a native North Carolinian who has for many years lived in Hendersonville, Tennessee, and has recorded a fifty six year history of playing music on the hallowed stage of the Grand Ole Opry in Nashville; and

WHEREAS, Jimmy Capps was born on May 25, 1939, in Fayetteville, North Carolina, the son of Tommy and Alice Capps. Raised in Benson, North Carolina, his earliest musical

inspirations were his champion fiddle playing uncle, Lynn Cook, and local guitarist Hayden Ivey, along with country music greats Grady Martin, Chet Atkins, Leon Rhodes, and Spider Wilson; and

WHEREAS, as early as twelve years of age, Jimmy Capps began playing music and performing in person and on local radio stations around both Carolinas. At age nineteen, his professional life moved into orbit when he became the guitarist for The Louvin Brothers, one of country music's all time great duos, and he made his Opry debut in 1958 playing with them; and

WHEREAS, in 1967, Mr. Capps became a member of the Grand Ole Opry Staff Band, and he was honored as a member when that group was nominated by the Country Music Association for instrumental group of the year in 1982; and

WHEREAS, as one of country music's finest guitar players, Jimmy Capps is a true master of smoothness, and he has an amazing ability to move flawlessly from electric to acoustic instruments with a polished and refined touch that he brings to every recording performance of which he is a part; and

WHEREAS, opportunities to work with legendary producers such as Owen Bradley, Billy Sherrill, and Larry Butler are considered by Mr. Capps to be some of the finest moments in his professional career; and

WHEREAS, Mr. Capps has learned from these master producers the art of song production. He has produced albums for artists such as The Wilburn Brothers, Jan Howard, Jim & Jesse, and Roy Drusky; and

WHEREAS, he has received numerous awards from the National Academy of Recording Arts & Sciences. In 1978 and 1979, he was recognized as a member of that organization's Superpickers Band, and he was voted Most Valuable Acoustic Player in 1978; and

WHEREAS, Jimmy Capps has been recognized for his musical excellence in his home state on multiple occasions: an executive proclamation was presented to him in 1998; his hometown of Benson regaled him with "Jimmy Capps Day" in 2009; and in 2014, he was inducted into both the Musicians Hall of Fame and Museum in Nashville and the North Carolina Music Hall of Fame; and

WHEREAS, Mr. Capps is an absolute marvel in country music, his artistic skills are matchless, and the blessings he has received throughout his professional endeavors in music are boundless; and

WHEREAS, he is deeply appreciative of the love and support he has long enjoyed with his wife, country singer Michele Voan Capps, and he is exceedingly proud of his sons, Jeff and

Mark, and his grandchild, Summer Capps; and

WHEREAS, Jimmy and Michele Capps are regular members of one of RFD TV's most popular shows, Larry's Country Diner; and

WHEREAS, Jimmy Capps is an outstanding citizen of Tennessee and is surely among those considered to be the greatest musicians of all time; his contributions to the genre have

April 2015

been defining and monumental; and his love of his profession is tried and true; now, therefore,

BE IT RESOLVED BY THE SENATE OF THE ONE HUNDRED NINTH GENERAL ASSEMBLY OF THE STATE OF TENNESSEE, THE HOUSE OF REPRESENTATIVES

CONCURRING, that we recognize and applaud the illustrious career of Jimmy Capps as a highly acclaimed guitarist and as having played on the stage of the Grand Ole Opry for fifty six years.

Call Renae the Waitress on the phone for DINER CHAT

If you just can't get enough of Larry's Country Diner join Renae the Waitress every week for a NEW one-hour talk show by phone. "The format is going to be pretty simple," says the Diner waitress. I know there are a lot of folks who aren't comfortable with face book so this is a way to get weekly updates not only about our TV shows on RFD but the construction of Larry's Country Diner and other news about their favorite country music artists. I think we do a pretty good job with our monthly CFR NEWS paper but there is nothing like talking to folks."

So how does it work? A few minutes before 3:00 EST every Thursday just dial one of the two telephone numbers on your phone. "It's just like calling a friend, " says Renae. You can listen while driving down the road, doing the dishes, or rocking in your easy chair. In addition the folks that love their computers can go to www.larryscountrydiner.com and click on the DINER CHAT link and listen via the web. International folks will even be able to connect via SKYPE. You can log in early prior to the call.

At 3:00 the theme music will begin and the show will start live. "The hour will go by pretty fast so I will use the first few minutes to outline our call. Everyone will know immediately what we will be talking about and if we have a special guest scheduled. The last 30 will be for questions and answers," says Renae." All you have to do to ask a question is press *2 on your phone. This signals Renae and she un-mutes your line to talk. SIMPLE.

" One of things I hope will be helpful each week is to have our Customer Service on our calls. A lot of folks don't realize that we have our own customer service and fulfillment center. So I am excited to answer any questions about our TV offers, Sponsors, Artists, Shows, Cruise, etc. Some folks may just need our phone number, and that's okay".

And of course the highlight will be special guest callers. More than anything ….I think we are going to have a lot of FUN ! I see it as an extension of our TV shows. Who knows…maybe we can get some of the artists to call in from the road…wouldn't that be cool!!

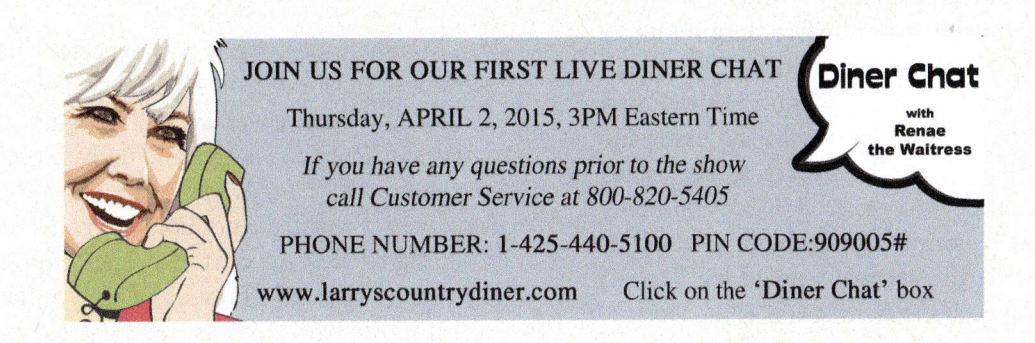

JOIN US FOR OUR FIRST LIVE DINER CHAT

Thursday, APRIL 2, 2015, 3PM Eastern Time

If you have any questions prior to the show call Customer Service at 800-820-5405

PHONE NUMBER: 1-425-440-5100   PIN CODE:909005#

www.larryscountrydiner.com   Click on the 'Diner Chat' box

Diner Chat with Renae the Waitress

April 2015

MAY

Keith Bilbrey inducted in to Radio Hall of Fame

Keith Bilbrey is being inducted into the Tennessee Radio Hall of Fame at a ceremony in Murfreesboro, TN on May 2, 2015.

GKeith moved to Nashville to begin working for WSM in 1974, first as a substitute announcer for WSM-FM and then as a full-time disc jockey on WSM's FM and AM stations. Throughout his career, Keith worked every single time slot at WSM and became an iconic voice in the modern history of the station and fan favorite.

He began announcing on the Grand Ole Opry in 1982, joining a long tradition of legendary Opry announcers, including George D. Hay, Grant Turner, Ralph Emery, and Hairl Hensley. When The Nashville Network (TNN) began televising a thirty minute portion of the show in 1985, the young announcer became the first host of Grand Ole Opry Live. He hosted Opry Live, along with the Opry warm-up show, Backstage Live, until TNN stopped airing the show in 2000.

Keith's affiliation with the Opry earned him additional opportunities in the world of country music television and radio. He was the announcer for Ernest Tubb's Midnight Jamboree, from 1982 until Tubb's death in 1984. He was the announcer for CBS's telecast of the Country Music Association (CMA) Award Show for three years, as well as the CMA's 35th Anniversary Special. Keith continues to announce the non-televised portion of the CMA Award Show. He also served as emcee for a variety of television specials, including the TNN/Music City News Awards, An Evening of Country Greats, Honky-Tonkin' at the Wildhorse, which featured Aaron Tippin and Marty Stuart, and the American Federation of Musicians' 100th Anniversary Show. He also played the role of historian for the A&E biographies of Buck Owens and Ronnie Milsap. In 2006, Bilbrey received the prestigious March of Dimes Air Awards Lifetime Achievement Award.

In addition to his career in country music, Keith spent twenty-four years as an air personality for WSM-TV, NBC's Nashville affiliate. He served the majority of this period as the weatherman on the nation's top-rated local morning show, The Ralph Emery Show, which featured live music and skits in addition to the traditional news, weather, and sports.

Keith Bilbrey and wife Emy Joe at Larry's Country Diner.

In March 2009, Keith was unexpectedly let go from WSM and the Grand Ole Opry. The news drew a great deal of local coverage, including numerous articles in The Tennessean and daily stories on the local news affiliates, as well as anger from many fans, who circulated a petition that collected over 4,000 signatures. According to The Tennessean, the decision to release Bilbrey was simply a matter of cutting costs with advertising revenue slumping. At his last Opry show, many performers dedicated songs to him, and Marty Stuart brought Keith to the front of the stage for a final word and a standing ovation.

May 2015

He co-hosted "Nashville Country Cookin'" with his wife, Emy Joe, on the Rural TV network and he hosted Classic Country Today, a weekly two-hour program on approximately 175 stations nationwide.

Keith is currently the announcer on "Music City Roots", a live weekly radio and TV show live from The Factory in Nashville on Wednesday nights (www.musiccityroots.com), as well as the host of the "Roots Radio Hour" on Hippie Radio 94.5 out of Nashville. He is also currently the announcer and Larry's sidekick on the highly rated "Larry's Country Diner" TV series on RFD-TV (www.larryscountrydiner.com), including live performances in Branson, Missouri.

He is pursuing a variety of business opportunities and writing his memoir.

80s hitmaker, Sylvia, guest on Larry's Country Diner

Sylvia Jane Kirby, more popularly known simply by her first name Sylvia during the 1980s, was born December 9, 1956 in Kokomo, Indiana. Some sources have her birth name as Sylvia Kirby Allen; however, Allen was her first husband's last name. She consequently used only her first name. There was also a point in time that she used Sylvia Rutledge, but currently uses her married name and is promoted as Sylvia Hutton.

Sylvia enjoyed crossover music success with the song "Nobody" in 1982. It charted at No. 15 Pop and No. 1 Country. The song earned her a gold record certification and a Grammy Award nomination for Best Female Country Vocal Performance. Although "Nobody" was Sylvia's only single to reach the Billboard pop charts, her other big country hits include "Drifter" (#1 Country, 1981), "Fallin' in Love", "Tumbleweed" and "Snapshot". In 1982, she was named Female Vocalist of the Year by the Academy of Country Music. She is also credited with making the first "concept" music video clip to air on Country Music Television (CMT), with "The Matador".

She began her career in music at age three when she was asked to sing at a small church near her hometown of Kokomo, Indiana. With a burning desire to become a recording artist like her idols Patsy Cline and Dolly Parton, Sylvia packed her bags and a demo tape and headed for Music City. On December 26, 1976 she arrived in Nashville, where she ultimately landed a job as a secretary for producer/publisher Tom Collins, who produced records for both Barbara Mandrell and Ronnie Milsap.

After auditioning for Dave & Sugar, Sylvia was signed as a solo artist by RCA Records in 1979. Her first RCA single was called "You Don't Miss a Thing". The song reached the Country Top 40, which got her name noticed. In 1980 she released another single, "It Don't Hurt to Dream". That same year, she finally made it to the Top 10 with "Tumbleweed". In 1981 her song "Drifter" hit No. 1 on the country charts, and two other songs, "The Matador" and "Heart on the Mend" landed in the Top 10. "The Matador" was country music's first conceptual music video to air on CMT. Drifter was the title of her 1981 RCA debut album. The album contained several top-ten songs, including "Tumbleweed" and "Heart On The Mend".

Sylvia continued to record for RCA until the end of 1987, charting 13 Top Ten and No. 1 songs, and sold more than four million records.

Over an eight-year period, Sylvia crisscrossed America many times with her popular concert performances (over 200 per year), and she was a frequent guest on network television talk shows and specials — from The Today Show and Good Morning, America to Dick Clark's American Bandstand and the Country Music Awards.

Her decision to stop touring and recording at the end of the 1980s was not fueled by the grueling schedule, as some might guess, but by her desire to bring more of herself to the music, she turned her energies to songwriting.

Sylvia's first independent album, The Real Story, was released from Red Pony Records. The Real Story was described as a "transition this multi-talented singer/songwriter has gone through over the past few years. Sylvia's re-emergence as a recording artist comes after a period of personal growth that has brought her into contact with some of Nashville's finest songwriters and musicians, as well as her own deeper well. With guitarist/co-producer John Mock lending his exquisite hand and ear, she delves into diverse musical terrain. The album has an acoustic, genuine feel, highlighting Sylvia's warm and clear voice. The songs range from intimate ballads to the up-tempo title song, "The Real Story".

In 2002, she followed with Where in the World, which marked the culmination of an 11-year musical collaboration between Sylvia and John Mock. Another shaping force is songwriter Craig Bickhardt, who penned four of the eleven songs, including the title cut. Craig has recorded, co-written and performed with Sylvia since 1984.

In 2002 Sylvia also released A Cradle in Bethlehem, her first Christmas album.

Since 2002, Sylvia has been a life coach where she helps individuals working in the music industry – singers, songwriters, musicians, recording artists, and music industry professionals. She also coaches people who work at non-profit agencies. She is currently married with the name Sylvia Hutton and lives in the Nashville, Tennessee, area.

Tribute to Tammy Wynette in June

A tribute show, Remembering the First Lady of Country Music, Tammy Wynette, will be held on Saturday, June 6 at 11 a.m. at the Nashville Nightlife Theatre.

There will be an afternoon buffet lunch with performances by Georgette Jones and former band members, and more guests to be announced. Special speakers will be family and friends of Tammy.

"Come celebrate Mom with friends and family," said Georgette, "Food, music and memories….lots of pictures. It will be a great way to honor Mom's memory and her music."

Tickets for the show are $50, which includes a commemorative t-shirt, or $40 without the t-shirt and can be purchased via Paypal using codyadamsmusic@yahoo.com as the 'pay-to' email or by sending a money order to Karen Butcher, 1032 Prestige Blvd., Lancaster, OH 43130. Tickets will be mailed in May.

The theatre is located 2820 Music Valley Drive in Nashville.

May 2015

T. Graham Brown learns to play guitar with the help of Chordbuddy

ChordBuddy is the brand new innovative guitar learning system that is perfect for guitar enthusiasts, no matter their skill level. Founded by Travis Perry, the device easily attaches to the neck of any guitar and allows users to play the instrument in the push of a button. With a 93% success rate, the ChordBuddy guitar learning aid allows users to learn primary chords for the key of G: G, C, D and Em, enabling them to play thousands of songs. Featured on the hit ABC show, "Shark Tank," this Made in the U.S.A. product has become a fan favorite and will be featured on QVC's "Clever & Unique Creations by Lori Greiner" this Friday, April 3rd in the 11 am (ET) hour.

"I plan on teaching Lori how to play 'Sweet Home Alabama' in 5 minutes or less," says Travis Perry.

"I hope that music enthusiasts will tune in to see how easy it is to learn to play guitar."

ChordBuddy has quickly created a legion of celebrity fans, including TODAY's Hoda Kotb, John Rich, and the latest to discover the product is 2014 Grammy-nominated singer T. Graham Brown.

T. Graham is doing something he never thought could happen…PLAY GUITAR! When he was three years old he cut his index finger leaving it ¾ inch shorter than normal -- making it impossible to bend that finger around the neck to play the chords. With the ChordBuddy learning aid attached to the neck of his guitar, T. Graham is now able to play!

"ChordBuddy has given me the opportunity to do something I've always wanted to do-play the guitar. Travis has become a great friend; the partnership was a natural and I can't wait to introduce all my fans to this amazing product!," says T. Graham Brown.

Check out ChordBuddy on QVC.com/

If you love Gospel & Country Music, You're going to love this special DVD offering!

Old Time Gospel

Old Time Gospel was filmed in 2011 and was hosted by Bill Anderson, with Rhonda Vincent, Dallas Frazier, Ed Bruce, Con Hunley, Jan Howard, Larry Gatlin & The Gatlin Bros., Gary Morris, Duane, Norah Lee Allen, George Hamilton IV, Linda Davis, Gene Watson, Jean Shepard, Joey & Rory, Phil Johnson, Larry Black, Barbara Fairchild, Dailey and Vincent, The Whites, Jimmy Fortune, T. Graham Brown, Jeannie Seely, Jim Ed Brown, Gordon Mote, and John Conlee. All on 5 DVDs, including the Behind The Scenes' DVD.

$119.80 + $16.95 s/h

1-800-820-5405

Gospel Classics

These performances have been scattered across all of our many collections and is hosted by Bill Anderson and featuring Bashful Brother Oswald, Bill Carlisle, Bill Clifton and Mike Seegar, Billy Walker, Bobby Lord, Boxcar Willie, Carol Lee Cooper, Charlie Louvin, Charlie Walker, Del Reeves, Freddie Hart, George Hamilton IV, Hank Locklin, Jan Howard, Jack Greene, Jean Shepard, Jeannie C. Riley, Jeannie Pruett, Jim and Jesse McReynolds, Jim Ed Brown, Jimmy C Newman, Jimmy Dean, Jimmy Shumate, Johnny Paycheck, Johnny Russell, Johnny Wright, Justin Tubb, Kitty Wells, Leroy Van Dyke, Martha Carson, Patsy Stoneman, Sheb Wooley, Skeeter Davis, Stonewall Jackson, Stu Phillips, The Browns, The Lewis Family, The Whites, Walter Bailes, Wanda Jackson, and Wilma Lee Cooper. All these on 3 DVDs, plus you get the songbook!

CFR, P.O. Box 210796, Nashville, TN 37221

May 2015

Don Williams announces 2015 Spring and Fall Tour

With his easy-going style and laid back nature, Don Williams has become one of Country Music's most-beloved performers both in the United States, as well as abroad. Williams announces the Spring and Fall legs of his 2015 tour, bringing his hits to fans old and new.

"Mercy, the fans have kept us going for years, and I am glad to share the music with them once again," says Williams.

Williams first came to prominence in the 1960s as a member of the folk group The Pozo-Seco Singers. The trio recorded several hit records, with the biggest being "Time." By 1971, Williams had gone solo, and had signed a publishing deal with Jack Clement. The Hall of Fame producer was so taken with Don's style that he offered him a recording contract with his JMI Records in 1972. Early hits included "Atta Way To Go" and "Come Early Morning," as well as "We Should Be Together," which became his first Billboard top ten hit from 1974. He then moved to ABC / Dot (Later MCA), where the hits increased. Tracks such as "Rake and Ramblin' Man," "Tulsa Time," and "Nobody But You" helped to make him one of the most-played artists on Country Radio in the 1970s and 1980s. He took home the Male Vocalist of the Year trophy from the Country Music Association in 1978, and notched his biggest hit in 1981 with "I Believe In You," which also crossed over to the top-30 on the Hot 100.

Subsequent moves to Capitol Nashville and RCA kept Williams on the charts into the 1990s, as he continued to play for huge crowds on the road. His success in the United States is well-documented, but the music of Don Williams has made him an international star – with followings in such places as England and New Zealand. He has placed 52 singles in the top-40 on the Country charts in the United States, with 17 going all the way to the top spot. Williams was a member of the Grand Ole Opry in the 1980s, and appeared in the films W.W. and the Dixie Dancekings and Smokey & The Bandit II with Burt Reynolds.

Williams' most recent album was 2014's Reflections, which earned the singer his highest peak on the Country Album chart in three decades. Known as "The Gentle Giant," Williams was inducted into the Country Music Hall of Fame in 2010.

Don Williams 2015 Tour Dates

May 14th - Eau Claire, Wisconsin - State Theatre
May 15th - Saint Michael, North Dakota - Spirit Lake Casino
May 16th - Fort Yates, North Dakota - Pavilion at Prairie Knights Casino
May 17th - Onamia, Minnesota - Grand Casino Mille Lacs
May 20th - Omaha, Nebraska - Kiewit Convert Hall at The Holland
May 21st - Salina, Kansas - The Stiefel Theatre
May 22nd - Bartlesville, Oklahoma - Bartlesville Community Center
May 23rd - Lula, Mississippi - Isle of Capri Casino
Sept. 9th - Dodge City, Kansas - United Wireless Arena
Sept. 10th - Colorado Springs, Colorado - Pikes Peak Center
Sept. 11th - Deadwood, South Dakota - Deadwood Mountain Grand Hotel
Sept. 14th - Winnipeg, Manitoba - Pantages Playhouse Theatre
Sept. 15th - Regina, Saskatchewan - Conexus Centre of the Arts
Sept. 16th - Saskatoon, Saskatchewan - TCU Place
Sept. 17th - Edmonton, Alberta - Northern Alberta Jubilee Auditorium
Sept. 19th - Calgary, Alberta - Jack Singer Hall Epcor Centre
Sept. 20th - Kelowna, British Columbia - Kelowna Community Theatre
Sept. 24th - Pocatello, Idaho - Stephens Performing Arts Center
Sept. 25th & 26th - Wendover, Nevada - Peppermill Concert Hall
Oct. 14th - Clearwater, Florida - The Capitol Theatre
Oct. 15th - Bremen, Georgia - Mill Town Music Hall
Oct. 16th - Pigeon Forge, Tennessee - Country Tonight Theatre
Oct. 17th - Pigeon Forge, Tennessee - Country Tonight Theatre
Oct. 18th - Newberry, South Carolina - Newberry Opera House
Oct. 20th - Durham, North Carolina - Carolina Theatre of Durham
Oct. 22nd - Huntsville, Alabama - Von Braun Center Concert Hall
Oct. 23rd - Paducah, Kentucky - The Carson Center
Oct. 24th - Branson, Missouri - Oakridge Boys Theatre
Nov. 12th - Kansas City, Missouri - Ameristar Casino and Hotel
Nov. 13th - Norman, Oklahoma - Riverwind Casino
Nov. 14th - Bossier City, Louisiana - Riverdome Horseshoe Hotel
Nov. 15th - San Antonio, Texas - The Tobin Center for the Performing Arts
Nov. 18th - Stafford, Texas - Stafford Centre
Nov. 19th - Midland, Texas - Wagner Noel Performing Arts Center
Nov. 20th - Austin, Texas - Paramount Theatre

May 2015

COUNTRY LEGENDS PAST AND PRESENT   BY TOM WOOD

GEORGE D. HAY

As a print journalist at the Memphis Commercial Appeal, George D. Hay was an outstanding wordsmith.

He always knew how to choose just the right combination of words to paint whatever picture he wanted in the minds of readers, and just when to use them for the greatest impact.

But he never coined a phrase liked the one that led to the birth of the Grand Ole Opry.

The story has been told and retold, but bears repeating again.

A series of bold career moves led George down a path that would result in the launching of a genre.

George was a reporter at the Memphis Commercial Appeal when the newspaper decided in 1923 to start its own radio station. Did George want to transition to this exciting new medium?

He did, taking the night shift, where his popularity at WMC quickly grew. A little over a year later, WLS in Chicago came calling and George took the reins as announcer for a WLS show that came to be called "National Barn Dance."

Another year passed, and George packed his bags once more, heading back down South to take over as announcer for WSM's version of the "Barn Dance." He had begun promoting his down-home, on-air persona as "The Solemn Old Judge" by this time, and it struck a chord with the station's listeners.

As the volume of "old-time music" that Hay played grew, so did his popularity.

The "WSM Barn Dance" show was preceded by the NBC "Music Appreciation Hour," featuring a mix of classical and grand opera performances.

Well, that format gnawed and gnawed at George so much that on one fateful show in December 1927, "The Solemn Old Judge" decided enough was enough. It was time to issue what would turn out to be an everlasting edict.

Fed up with the classics, George introduced "Harmonica Wizard" DeFord Bailey, who played his rousing train song, "The Pan American Blues". Bouyed by the song and perhaps still fuming about the previous show's format, he proclaimed for all the world to hear:

"For the past hour, we have been listening to music taken largely from Grand Opera. From now on, we will present the Grand Ole Opry."

The tag spread like wildfire and helped launch thousands of careers over the decades.

Over the next two decades, George nurtured and grew the Grand Ole Opry brand like it was his own offspring — which in truth it was. He took the Opry to Carnegie Hall in New York, continued to write about the Opry acts and played himself in the 1940 movie Grand Ole Opry.

In 1966, George was inducted into the Country Music Hall of Fame for his pioneering efforts. He died in 1968 at age 72.

There's no disputing this verdict: Without the wit and wisdom of "The Solemn Old Judge," country music would not exist as it is today and there would be no Grand Ole Opry.

May 2015

'The Browns, Grady Martin & Oak Ridge Boys the 2015 Country Music Hall of Fame inductees

CMA created the Country Music Hall of Fame in 1961 to recognize individuals for their outstanding contributions to the format with Country Music's highest honor. Inductees are chosen by CMA's Hall of Fame Panels of Electors, which consist of anonymous voters appointed by the CMA Board of Directors.

Members are inducted during a special Medallion Ceremony later this year at the Country Music Hall of Fame and Museum in the CMA Theater. During the Medallion Ceremony, friends and colleagues pay tribute to each inductee through words and song. Each inductees' bronze plaque is unveiled that will be on display in the Museum's rotunda.

There are three categories inducted every year which include: (1) Modern Area, (2) Veterans Era, and (3) Recording and/or Touring Musician active prior to 1980. A candidate is eligible for induction into the Modern Era 20 years after they first achieve national prominence, and the Veterans Era Category 40 years after they first achieve national prominence.

The 2015 inductees are:

The Browns: Jim Ed Brown, Maxine Brown, Bonnie Brown – Veterans Era

For more than sixty years, Jim Ed Brown has been a dedicated country performer, radio and television host, and recording artist. He has continued the smooth-singing style of country stars such as Red Foley, Eddy Arnold, and Jim Reeves with television, radio and recordings. With the Browns—a trio he formed with sisters Maxine and Bonnie—as a solo artist, and as a duet singer, he placed hits in the country charts from 1954 into the early 1980s.

James Edward Brown began singing with his sisters in school programs and at church functions when the siblings were teenagers in southwestern Arkansas. In 1952, Maxine entered Jim Ed in a talent contest organized by radio station KLRA in Little Rock. Even though he didn't take first place, Jim Ed was asked to join the cast, Maxine quickly followed. Within two years, the duo was singing on the Louisiana Hayride. Using a KWKH studio, Maxine and Jim Ed recorded their original song "Looking Back to See" for Fabor Records, in March 1954. That summer the record became a Top Ten hit on Billboard's country charts. Soon Jim Ed and Maxine moved to KWTO's Ozark Jubilee in Springfield, Missouri.

After Bonnie joined the act in 1955, the trio's rendition of "Here Today and Gone Tomorrow" also made it into Billboard's country Top Ten. RCA Records, one of the music industry's major labels, signed the Browns, and during 1956–57, they scored Top Five hits with "I Take the Chance" and "I Heard the Bluebirds Sing."

As professional and family responsibilities increased, the three singers thought of quitting the music business, but several of their songs became hits and that led to network TV appearances and overseas tours. In 1963, the Browns garnered a Grand Ole Opry membership.

The Browns disbanded in 1967; Maxine and Bonnie eventually returned to their families in Arkansas to raise their young children, while Jim Ed stayed in Nashville to pursue a very successful solo career.

In 1976 he began recording duets with Helen Cornelius, and a year later they became CMA's Vocal Duo of the Year. Their best-known hits are "I Don't Want to Have to Marry You" (1976), "Saying Hello, Saying I Love You, Saying Goodbye" (1976), "Lying in Love with You" (1979), and "Fools" (1979).

Brown was a natural host, not only on his Grand Ole Opry appearances but also on other programs. In 1969, he hosted the syndicated television show The Country Place, which ran until 1970. He hosted six seasons of the syndicated country television show Nashville on the Road between its debut in 1975 and 1981. During the 1980s, he hosted two televised series on TNN: The Nashville Network—the talent show You Can Be a Star and Going Our Way, which featured Brown and his wife, Becky, touring the U.S. in an RV. He has been on many Country's Family Reunion shows where he continues to be a hit.

May 2015

In 2003 Brown began hosting the weekly syndicated radio program Country Music Greats Radio Show, as well as the short-form Country Music Greats Radio Minute. Both are carried by more than 300 radio stations. In addition, these series are available on the Internet. The Country Music Greats Radio Show includes music from the 1940s through the 1990s, and draws upon an interview archive of country stars past and present. Brown also shares his own stories about his life in the country music industry. Maxine Brown published an autobiography, Looking Back to See: A Country Music Memoir, in 2005.

In 2014 Brown announced that he had been diagnosed with cancer. He has since returned to his radio show. In January 2015, after several months of treatment, he returned to the Ryman Auditorium for the Grand Ole Opry, where he was greeted warmly and his new CD, "In Style Again," is getting rave reviews.

Grady Martin – Recording and/or Touring Musician Active Prior to 1980

Legendary guitarist Grady Martin was a member of Nashville's original "A-Team" of studio musicians. He played guitar on hits such as Marty Robbins' "El Paso", Loretta Lynn's "Coal Miner's Daughter" and Sammi Smith's "Help Me Make It Through the Night". During a nearly 50-year career, Martin backed such names as Elvis Presley, Buddy Holly, Johnny Burnette, Don Woody and Arlo Guthrie, Johnny Cash, Patsy Cline and Bing Crosby. He is a member of the Rockabilly Hall of Fame.

Thomas Grady Martin was fifteen when he became the fiddler for Nashville's Big Jeff & the Radio Playboys. In 1946 Martin briefly joined Paul Howard's western swing-oriented Arkansas Cotton Pickers as half of Howard's "twin guitar" ensemble, along with Robert "Jabbo" Arrington. After Howard left the Grand Ole Opry, Opry newcomer Little Jimmy Dickens hired several former Cotton Pickers as his original Country Boys band. Martin backed Dickens in the studio, though he seldom toured with Dickens.

Martin's role as studio guitarist yielded numerous memorable moments. One of his most famous sessions involved an accidental preamplifier malfunction, when Martin played the distorted "fuzz" guitar solo on Robbins's 1960 hit "Don't Worry." Producers often designated Martin as "session leader," which meant that he directed the impromptu arrangements that became a trademark of Nashville recording and often became the de facto producer. Columbia A&R man Don Law used Martin in this capacity for years.

Martin continued to play sessions through the 1970s, working extensively with Conway Twitty and Loretta Lynn, and producing country-rock band Brush Arbor. His signature lead parts helped to make a hit of Jeanne Pruett's 1973 "Satin Sheets." Martin eventually returned to performing, first with Jerry Reed and then with Willie Nelson's band, with whom he worked from 1980 to 1994.

"He understood some things about music that nobody else understood," said Merle Haggard, who recorded with Martin on songs including "That's the Way Love Goes," "What Am I Gonna Do (with the Rest of My Life)," and "No Reason to Quit." "And when he'd put that down on your record, it was like a gift."

Grady died died from a heart attack on December 3, 2001 in Lewisburg, Tennessee.

The Oak Ridge Boys – Modern Era

The Oak Ridge Boys helped pave the way for the many vocal groups that followed them by injecting gospel-based, four-part harmonies and exciting live shows into country music,. From 1977 to 1987, with a lineup of Duane Allen, lead; William Lee Golden, baritone; Richard Sterban, bass; and Joe Bonsall, tenor – they have had twenty-six Top Ten hits (including fifteen #1s), sold millions of records, won numerous industry awards, filled top-tier performance venues, and notched Top Twenty pop hits with "Elvira" and "Bobbie Sue."

Until 1977, the Oaks had been a gospel act for more than thirty years. They began in 1945 as the Oak Ridge Quartet, a gospel ensemble within Wally Fowler's country group, the Georgia Clodhoppers. The original quartet consisted of Fowler, lead; Curly Kinsey, bass; Lon "Deacon" Freeman, baritone; and

May 2015

Johnny New, tenor. They joined the Grand Ole Opry in September 1945.

The Oak Ridge Quartet became the Oak Ridge Boys in 1962. Golden joined the group in 1965, Allen in 1966, Sterban in 1972, and Bonsall in 1973. By then, they had won a dozen gospel music Dove Awards as well as a Grammy. They signed with Columbia Records to broaden their audience, but three albums of "message" music produced two singles that didn't make the country charts. Having removed themselves from the gospel world, the Oaks were struggling to make their mark in commercial country music.

Conventional industry wisdom held that there was room for only one gospel-rooted vocal quartet in country music (the Statler Brothers), but record executive Jim Foglesong was impressed with the Oak Ridge Boys' versatility and range, and he signed them to ABC/Dot (later absorbed by MCA) in 1977. The group's initial ABC/Dot single, "Y'all Come Back Saloon," was a country radio hit that sparked a remarkable run that included chart-toppers such as "I'll Be True to You," "Leaving Louisiana in the Broad Daylight," "American Made," "Fancy Free," I Guess It Never Hurts to Hurt Sometimes," and "Touch a Hand, Make a Friend."

In 1987, William Lee Golden was replaced by Steve Sanders, a former child star in gospel music who was, at the time, the rhythm guitarist in the Oaks' band. In 1996, Golden returned to the group, which remains a touring and recording force.

DJ Convention to Fan Fair to CMA Fest: The history of a legendary event

Originally, what we now know as the CMA Fest, was known as the DJ (Disc Jockey) Convention. It was organized to honor the Grand Ole Opry while consolidating Nashville's role in the country music industry. The event, which was formed to commemorate the Grand Ole Opry's Birthday Celebration, and was suggested in 1951 by Harianne Moore of WSM's advertising department. The intent was for the country music artists to thank the disc jockeys for playing their records and promoting their concerts, while giving the disc jockeys the opportunity to meet the stars and to tape spots with the artists to be played on their local stations.

The first convention took place in November 1952 with about 100 DJs. These DJs were invited from a list that was furnished by Acuff-Rose Publications, which kept a national list of disc jockeys. They were welcomed to WSM radio and treated to a Grand Ole Opry show. The first year was considered enough of a success that it was repeated the following year and extended over two days, with record companies and publishers hosting receptions. BMI gave its first country music awards for radio airplay. In addition, DJs organized the Country Music Disc Jockeys Association, precursor to the CMA. By 1958 attendance had grown to over 2,000 with more and more entertainers taking part. In addition to the formal and informal parties, they now featured panels on industry issues.

That same year the CMDJ disbanded and the CMA was organized. Since then, the CMA has taken over the event. In 1963, October was declared Country Music Month and the event, which had taken place in November, was switched to October to take advantage of the better weather. As attendance continued to grow, the CMA organized their own awards show, along with ASCAP and SESAC, both industry publishing houses.

Since so many country music fans had begun coming to Nashville for the DJ Convention week, the CMA created a festival for just the fans, which was named Fan Fair. Fan Fair still exists today, but has been renamed the CMA Music Festival, while the Country Radio Broadcasters hold their own event.

While the DJ convention no longer exists as it once did, the Opry's Birthday Celebration, which was one of the primary reasons for the convention starting, continues. The birthday celebration grew into such a big event because the majority of Opry members would be in town for the event. That was how important the DJs were to their careers. However, as time goes on, and while the birthday celebration continues, it is not the primary event that it used to be.

The CMA Fest now boasts over 80,000 attendees for the multi-day festival.

May 2015

Hannah Miller to travel Europe as Wyoming Ambassador of Music

Shortly after the Dan Miller Cowboy Music Revue in Cody, Wyoming opens for its 11th season, there will be a familiar and well-loved face absent.

Hannah Miller, who just celebrated her 17th birthday, will be traveling Europe with the Wyoming Ambassadors of Music for three weeks in June. Hannah was nominated for this honor by her Cody High School choir director on the basis of her talent, character and leadership skills, according the the letter she received from Wyoming governor Matt Mead, notifying her of her selection to the elite group.

Hannah has been an integral part of her father Dan's Cowboy Music Revue since it first opened in 2005. As a precocious six-year-old, her first appearances on stage were simply to recite a cowboy poem, take the dollar bill offered to her by her dad, and exit the stage. Soon after, however, she became fascinated by the fiddle that was being played by members of her father's "Empty Saddles Band," and she began taking lessons. Months of lessons, followed by years of personal dedication to the instrument, led to Hannah's integration as a full-fledged member of the Cowboy Music Revue. Regular guests of the show comment regularly on how impressed they are with the talented and genuinely kind person that Hannah has grown to be.

Hannah, her father Dan, bass player and vocalist Wendy Corr, and guitar player Ed Cook, will open for their 11th season on May 23 at the historic Cody Theatre in Cody, Wyoming.

Hannah's European adventure is anticipated to cost around $6,000, so a GoFundMe site has been set up for anyone who would like to contribute. Details can be found on their website:

www.cowboymusicrevue.com

GRASSROOTS TO BLUEGRASS   &   simply BLUEGRASS

Back in 1999, we asked Mac Wiseman to pull together a Who's Who of Bluegrass. He did, and we were able to honor an pay tribute to many of the pioneers of Bluegrass on our Grassroots to Bluegrass series. You'll see and hear Bill Clifton, Brother Oswald, Charlie Louvin, Del McCoury, Doyle Lawson, Eddie Stubbs, J.D. Crowe, James Monroe Jeannette Carter, Jim & Jesse McReynolds, Jimmy Shumate, John Hartford, Kenny Baker, Leroy Troy, Lewis Family, Mac Wiseman, Martha & Eddie Adcock, Melvin Goins, Mike Seeger, Osborne Brothers, "Pappy" Sherrill, Patsy Stoneman, Polly Lewis, Ramona Jones, Ronnie Reno, and Walter Bailes.

Then in 2012 we decided to do it again only this time with Ricky Skaggs hosting Bobby Osborne, Carl Jackson, Dailey & Vincent, Del McCoury, Dierks Bentley, Donna Ulisse, Doyle Lawson, Jerry Douglas, Larry Cordle, Mac Wiseman, Paul Brewster, Ramona Jones, Rhonda Vincent, Ronnie Reno, Sam Bush, Sierra Hull, The Gibson Brothers, The Roys, and The Whites.

Grassroots to Bluegrass (10 DVDS, over 60 songs) plus the Simply Bluegrass Collection (5 DVDs, over 25 songs) AND 2 Audio CD's of Simply Bluegrass If you bought all separately, it would cost over $250 dollars, but with this special offer, you'll get all 17 discs for just $149.75! That's over 100 songs and performances in this 17 Disc collection. It is the ULTIMATE Bluegrass Collection from Country's Family Reunion.

$149.75 plus $16.95 s/h or Free Shipping with code 'FREESHIPPING'

CFR, P.O. Box 210796, Nashville, TN 37221

1-800-820-5405
www.cfrvideos.com

May 2015

Kenny Rogers Embarks of Farwell South Africa Tour

GRAMMY Award-winning country superstar and music icon Kenny Rogers will be returning to South Africa for the final time, performing his Farewell South Africa Tour in Johannesburg on June 15-16 at the Big Top Arena, Carnival City and in Cape Town on June 18 at the Grand Arena, Grand West, Big Concerts has announced. Kenny will be supported by special guest regional country legends "Big Daddy" Lance James, "Queen of Country" Barbara Ray, "Midnight Cowboy" Clive Bruce and "The Killer" Tommy Dell.

Rogers has enjoyed great success during his storied career of five and a half decades. The enduring Country Music Hall of Fame member and pop superstar has endeared music lovers around the globe with his amazing songs, heartfelt performances, distinctive voice, gift for storytelling and universal appeal.

Rogers has played to millions of fans around the world, performing songs from his catalog of smash hits, including "The Gambler," "Islands In The Stream," "She Believes In Me," "Lucille," "Coward Of The County," "Lady," "Through The Years," "Daytime Friends," "Ruby, Don't Take Your Love To Town," "You Decorated My Life," "We've Got Tonight," and many more.

The first country artist to consistently sell out arenas, Rogers has played to millions of fans around the world and has charted a record within each of the last seven decades ('50s, '60s, '70s, '80s, '90s, 2000's, 2010's). He has recorded 24 Number One hits and sold more than 120 million albums worldwide, making him one of the Top Ten Best Selling Male Solo Artists of All Time, according to the RIAA. Rogers has won many awards for his music and charity work, including three GRAMMY Awards, 19 American Music Awards, 11 People's Choice Awards, eight Academy of Country Music Awards and six Country Music Association Awards, including the CMA Lifetime Achievement Award in 2013.

Rogers' music has always crossed boundaries — his 28 Billboard Adult Contemporary Top 10's is sixth-best all-time, and fourth-best among men, trailing only Elton John, Neil Diamond and Elvis Presley.

Remaining a popular entertainer around the world, Rogers, voted the "Favorite Singer of All-Time" in a joint poll by readers of both USA Today and People, still loves touring and recording new music.

Jerry Reed Tribute and CD release party with daughter Seidina Reed

A JERRY REED TRIBUTE and CD Release night for Seidina Reed's Tribute CD will be held Thursday, June 11, 2015 at 7:30 PM CDT (7:00 PM Doors) at The Cannery Ballroom in Nashville, TN. The show is 18 years and over.

Jerry Reed's daughter, Seidina, worked with her father for many years touring and performing with him in concert, singing on his albums, and doing a little bit of acting in his various projects.

Seidina's debut CD, an album of Jerry's songs titled "Today Is Mine", is her personal Tribute to her father. No doubt it's one of the best albums to come out of Nashville this year.

On top of this terrific line up, there'll be some surprise guests, with The Jerry Reed house band (Bart Pike, Ric McClure, Dennis Wage, Pat Bergeson and Mike Wyatt) holding down the groove for what promises to be an outstanding Nashville night.

Tickets are $30.00 per person at ticketweb.com.

May 2015

The Next Generation: Sons & Daughters of Country Legends honors their parents with show to start off CMA Fest week

Jett and Georgette weren't able to make last year's show, but this group photo shows those who did make it. Left to right: Karen Wheeler, Donnie Winters, Chrystie Wooley, Melissa Luman, George Hamilton V, Robyn Young, Hawkshaw Hawkins Jr. and Dean Smith. There were also some surprise guests.

Step back in time to the days when the CMA Fest was called FAN FAIR with a concert of The NEXT GENERATION: SONS & DAUGHTERS OF COUNTRY LEGENDS. This show is comprised of the children of some of Country Music's most famous entertainers. Originally brought together by Larry Black for two of his DVD series' (Generations and Second Generations), these 'Nashville Brats,' as they call themselves, decided they enjoyed hanging out and singing together.

This year's show at 3rd & Lindsley will be held Thursday, June 11. The doors open at 6 and the show starts at 7. The entertainers for this show include: Jett Williams (Hank Williams), Georgette Jones (George Jones & Tammy Wynette), Robyn Young (Faron Young), George Hamilton V (George Hamilton IV), Hawkshaw Hawkins, Jr. (Hawkshaw Hawkins & Jean Shepard), Chrystie Wooley (Sheb Wooley), Melissa Luman (Bob Luman), Dean Smith (Carl Smith & Goldie Hill), Karen Wheeler (Onie Wheeler) and Donnie Winters (Don Winters). There will be other special guests who will show up and sing a song or two as well!

This year's emcee will be the very talented and popular, Keith Bilbrey. Keith, who works for Hippie Radio, currently also hosts the Music City Roots shows at The Factory, and is the announcer on Larry's Country Diner show on RFD-TV.

Several of the members of the group make their living entertaining, but some just do it for fun, and to keep their parents' names and music alive.

Over the past three years, they have played shows to packed houses at Mickey Roo's in Franklin and the famous Nashville Palace. Audiences love hearing them sing the songs their parents made famous. In the past, several parents have even come and helped them entertain the crowd. This is sure to sell out, so be sure to get your tickets early.

Tickets are $20 each and may be purchased at www.3rdandlindsley.com or by calling 615-259-9891.

May 2015

The Nashville Brat Pack — Kids of the Country Stars!

By Hawkshaw Hawkins Jr, Son of Hawkshaw Hawkins and Jean Shepard

Harold "Hawkshaw" Hawkins, Jr. was born one month after his father Hawkshaw Hawkins died in the same plane crash that killed Patsy Cline and Cowboy Copas. He joined his mom and brother Donnie.

You know, Mama was on the road alot, and we had a lady who we now call "other mama" taking care of us. Kay was her name. One day I snuck outside with a pair of sissors and carved myself a new hairdo. Well Kay didn't say anything to me because she knew that Mama was fixin' to come home from the road later that day.

Sure enough here comes Mama. After getting or hugs and kisses, Mama looked at me and said " Harold what did you do to your hair?"

I said with lying eyes "Whats wrong with it?"

She said "You've cut it to pieces."

And I said "No mama, the sun must have melted it."

That was Mother's Day around 1968 or 1969. Happy Mother's Day!

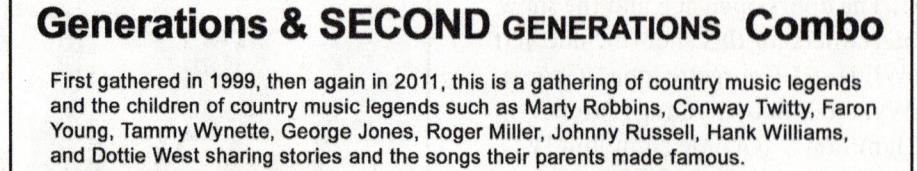

Generations & SECOND GENERATIONS Combo

First gathered in 1999, then again in 2011, this is a gathering of country music legends and the children of country music legends such as Marty Robbins, Conway Twitty, Faron Young, Tammy Wynette, George Jones, Roger Miller, Johnny Russell, Hank Williams, and Dottie West sharing stories and the songs their parents made famous.

ONLY $79.80
plus $6.95 s/h

Robyn Young
Bill Anderson
Karen Wheeler
Michael Twitty
Jean SHepard
Donnie Hawkins
Charlie Rich Jr.
Phil Campbell

George Hamilton V
George Hamilton IV
Hawkshaw Hawkins Jr
Melissa Luman
Chrystie Wooley
Georgette Jones

Jett Williams
Dean Smith
Jan Howard
Will Reid
Langdon Reid
Bill Mack
Dean Miller
Ronny Robbins
Shelly West
Jim Ed Brown

Roy Clark
Bill Anderson
Dean Miller
Michael Twitty
Ronny Robbins
Johnny Russell
Billy Walker
Bobby Lord

Georgette Jones
Jan Howard
Robyn Young
Rex Allen Jr.
Jett WIlliams
Merle Kilgore
Hawkshaw Hawkins Jr.
Del Reeves

1-800-820-5405
www.cfrvideos.com

May 2015

Country Questions
By Dick Boise, CMH

Send questions to:
Dick Boise, , c/o CFR News,
P.O. Box 201796, Nashville,
TN 37221.

Q. Could you give me some information on the song about Mamas and babies growing up like cowboys? Who wrote it and sang it?

Thanks, Leroy, Gilmore, PA

A. Leroy, that song was written by Ed Bruce and his wife Patsy, with Ed having an album recording of it in 1976. Waylon Jennings and Willie Nelson had a number one top of the charts hit with "Mamas, Don't Let Your Babies Grow Up To Be Cowboys" in 1978. Cute reminder for me, I was working in a wholesale building supply and a good friend, Greg Baidel, who was our sales person for Therma Tru, a top residential door, would often come into our locations and repeat, "Mamas, Don't Let Your Babies Grow Up To Be Salesmen."

Q. Dear Dick, Do you have any information on Thom Bresh? He has opened for many acts here n Saginaw, MI, and he was very good. Thank you,

Marvin DeWitt Birch Run, MI

A. Thom Bresh is a very talented man including his entertaining. His father was the late Merle Travis the singer, songwriter and guitarist. Thom is all of that and more. He was a movie stuntman in his youth, working in many movies. His ability with filming videos is one of his other talents. He is most noted for his guitar ability and I believe he is probably one of the top "one man' entertainers in the business.

Q. I have several questions for you and also I enjoy the Reunion DVDs and Larry's Diner. What happened to Jeanne Pruett, have only seen her on one of the shows. Thanks in advance,

Robert L. Hawkins, LaGrange, GA

A. Robert, thanks for your questions and I'll drop you a note with the other answers. Jeanne Pruett announced back in 2006 that she was retiring from the Grand Ole Opry and performing. She was a fine artists to our country music field and is truly missed. She is keeping busy in the music publishing field and song writing that she was noted for.

Q. I would like to know if Roy Clark is married and does he have children? How is his health?

Ruth Otte

A. Ruth, Roy Clark was born April 15, 1933 and so he just turned 82 years young. He has shown some signs of that age in his movements on the Reunion shows, but have never heard of any health issues. Roy married Barbara Rupard on August 31, 1957 so they will have had a 58 year journey together this coming August. That in itself is a remarkable record in this day and age. I have never heard that they have any children. Roy is a remarkable entertainer and I remember back in the mid 1960s. The owner of the Coral Bar in Secaucus, JJ told me as my cousin and I were auditioning our band for a possible full time job playing his his club, "If I could find me another Roy Clark, I would never have to hire a full band again. He has entertained my patrons like no other one man I have seen."

Country's Family Reunion presents....

simply BLUEGRASS
Through May 8 on RFD-TV

SECOND GENERATIONS
Starting May 15 on RFD-TV

Fridays...7 p.m. central
Saturdays...11 p.m central

May 2015

Stage Clothes of the Stars

By Claudia Johnson

June Carter Cash: Modest, Timeless Elegance

For more than six decades June Carter Cash occupied a place in American music culture so large it overshadowed her impeccable fashion sense exhibited both onstage and in her personal life.

June was born June 23, 1929, and at age 10 began playing autoharp and doing comedy bits on the Carter Family's radio broadcasts. A Carter Family promotional photo from that time shows June wearing a plaid wool jumper, a satin blouse with full sleeves and a Peter Pan collar accented with a fluffy satin bow that matches the one in her side-parted hair. She holds her autoharp in her lap, and her legs are crossed daintily at the ankles.

In photos from a few years later when her sisters, Helen and Anita, and their mother, Maybelle Carter, began performing as Mother Maybelle and The Carter Sisters, June is often "cutting up," while the others hold their instruments seriously. They are usually dressed in matching or coordinating costumes. Some are casual floral dresses with tiered shirts and peasant bodices. Others are shirt-waist dresses in bold patterns with full skirts, button-up bodices and self belts that accent the women's shapely figures. The foursome became part of the Grand Ole Opry in 1950, but June soon attracted separate attention.

Some particularly beautiful color images of June taken in the 1950s when she was in her 20s stand out. In one she wears a red-orange and tan paisley shirt, quite fitted to her body, sleeves buttoned to the elbows, exposing thin, pale arms holding lush auburn hair atop her head as she stands in the shadows of a sun-filtered barn. There's a photo most likely made the same day but not so dramatically posed in which she looks directly at the camera, her blue eyes gleaming, wavy hair clasped at the neck and lips tinted a red-orange the exact shade of the paisley shirt. In a separate shoot, June was photographed in various poses at a vintage log structure for Life magazine dressed in a casual striped shirt, wide leather belt and denim jeans rolled to just below the knee.

Another day June is caught in a candid shot as she looks pensively toward the floor. Subtle makeup highlights high cheekbones, and red lipstick contrasts straight, white teeth. Her hair just grazes the line of the boat-neck, white polka dot cap-sleeve, fitted dress

It was in '50s that director Elia Kazan saw her perform at the Grand Ole Opry and encouraged her to study acting, which she did in New York at the renowned Lee Strasberg Neighborhood Playhouse. In 1957, she had the part of Clarise on "Gunsmoke" and was offered a part in a 1961 Woody Allen-written variety show, which she turned down to tour with Johnny Cash for just $500 per week. Cash became her husband seven years later.

Of the hundreds of photos of June Carter Cash, none show her in tasteless, revealing attire – even those that could have appeared that way on other women. There is a formal portrait of her with short hair, rare for her, in which she is draped in an off shoulder satin wrap that manages to be classic as opposed to provocative. An informal, home photo shows her in a fuchsia cocktail dress with a fitted bodice, spaghetti straps and a large skirt held full, no doubt, with crinoline slips. Again, beautiful with no hint of sexuality. A candid stage shot of her wearing similar attire shows her smiling broadly, engaged in a little dance and holding the skirts and slips just slightly above the knees. Another color candid stage

May 2015

shot, which appears to be from the 1950s, caught her dancing, holding her ruffled skirt without exposing even her knees.

After her marriage to Johnny Cash in 1968, when June entered her 40s, she remained a beautiful woman who enjoyed the ever-changing fashion scene. Her wedding dress was a powder blue lace street-length sheath with bell sleeves over a blue satin sheath. She wore a headband of blue and white flowers in her long hair.

When cameras capture photos of her in 1970 with Johnny and their newborn son, John Carter, she was modestly and radiantly attired in a lace and ribbon peignoir ensemble.

Over time June is photographed onstage or on album covers with her husband in a variety of fashions from crocheted dresses to western wear to bell bottomed pants to velvet mini-skirts (though barely qualifying as such by the standards of that era). Sometimes they appeared in matching denim, while other times it was leather for both. A dapper dresser himself, John usually wore his trademark black, while June easily accented his look.

Her dresses, coats, pant suits and evening attire reflect a range of textures and fabrics from velvet to satin to chiffon to fur to lace to hound's-tooth to embroidered silk. She adopted accessories popular for the decade, most noticeable in her choice of hats and boots throughout the years.

One particularly telling photo, not only attesting to her fashion sense but to the undeniable bond between June and her husband, is a candid photo taken during a studio recording session. She wears a maxi dress adorned with Native American patterns, a wide leather belt with silver medallions and leather platform shoes. Her husband's pants are tucked into knee-high lace-up boots, and his arms encircle her from behind.

"She's the greatest woman I have ever known," he said of her in his autobiography. "Nobody else, except my mother, comes close."

When she died May 15, 2003, she was dressed in light blue and placed in a light blue coffin, stylish to the end.

WORD SEARCH

LEGENDS   GOLDEN   JUNE
BILBREY   STURBAN   CARTER
BROWNS   BONSALL   CASH
MARTIN   GENERATIONS MAXINE
OAKRIDGEBOYS REED   BONNIE
HALLOFFAME   SYLVIA   JIMED
GEORGEDHAY   KEITH   ALLEN

Celebrity Waiters event with Renae, Keith & more!

Renae & Barbara Fairchild

The Exchange Club of Murfreesboro held their annual fundraiser for the prevention of child abuse on Thursday, April 2, 2015. The Celebrity Waiters Dinner had a star-studded country music celebrity line up and one TV waitress (me). Celebrities didn't actually wait on the tables but instead had a fun time performing their hits and joining together to sing an array of requests for donations. Keith Bilbrey was the host and had no trouble keeping the entertainment flowing. Among the celebrities was Tanya Tucker, Rex Allen Jr, John Conlee, Lynn Anderson, Lulu Roman, Tommy Cash, Barbara Fairchild, Jan Howard, John Berry, T Graham Brown, and Crook & Chase. Cindy Moore (Minnie Pearl –impersonator) keep everyone laughing as she went from table to table telling everyone to open their wallets and give her some money. One table donated $700 for one of the guests to sing a duet of "I Never Promised You A Rose Garden" with Lynn Anderson. John Conlee handed over a pair of Rose Colored Glasses after his performance. LuLu Roman and T Graham struck up a duet of "You Are So Beautiful" (to me) that had even me gushing. Tanya sang her hit "Delta Dawn" with help from LuLu Roman and Lynn Anderson. Rex Allen Jr. brought the house down with his rendition of "Teddy" during the Teddy Bear song with Barbara Fairchild. Loriann Crook whose name was misspelled "Loraine" joined me as we served coffee at a premium. All of the donations went to a worthy cause but the experience for me was priceless.

Minnie Pearl (Cindy Moore)

John Conlee

Charlie Chase serving coffee

Barbara Fairchild, Renae, Tanya Tucker

Tanya Tucker, T. Graham Brown, Lynn Anderson, Lulu Roman & Keith Bilbrey

May 2015

Midnight Jamboree closes doors due to financial woes

By Claudia Johnson

"Anyone who has been paying attention to what is happening on the internet has to know that the internet has broke the back of the record shop business because people are now downloading music for free instead of buying the records from a record shop," Ernest Tubb's nephew, Glenn Douglas Tubb said. "Consequently, all the big record store chains have gone out of business. Songwriters, artists, publishers and record companies have all suffered devastating losses also. Songwriting is now a hobby for most of us instead of an occupation."

The Ernest Tubb Record Shop was originally the sponsor for the Midnite Jamboree and paid the cost for putting the show on the air every Saturday night, but when people stopped buying records, it became cost prohibitive.

"The bill usually runs between $2,200 and $2,500 each Saturday night, depending on how many musicians are on the stage on any given night," Glenn Douglas said. "Since the record shop was no longer able to support the program, David McCormick, the owner and CEO of the E.T. Record Shops, started paying the bills out of his own pocket, determined to keep the legacy alive that Uncle Ernest started."

Glenn Douglas Tubb said that McCormick has become unable to bear the financial burden alone, forcing the performance, which emanates from Nashville's Texas Troubadour Theatre and does not charge the public to attend the broadcasts, to take a hiatus until June 6.

"The Midnite Jamboree is a piece of Country Music history, and I believe it should be preserved, just like any other National Treasure," he said.

Ernest Tubb Midnite Jamboree was started by Ernest Tubb in 1947, the year he became the first Country music artist to play in Carnegie Hall in New York City.

"That was a pretty eventful year for him," said Glenn Douglas, who is an award winning songwriter.

1947 is also the year Tubb opened the Ernest Tubb Record Shop, providing a venue for country music artists to sell their records.

"Most record shops back then wouldn't sell country music, or, as it was called back then, hillbilly music," Glenn Douglas Tubb explained, adding that his uncle also started the Midnite Jamboree as a means to advertise his records and the records of his fellow artists. "He also decided that the young artists who were trying to get the record companies to listen to them, needed a platform from which they could be heard, not just by the record company producers here in Nashville, New York and Los Angeles but by the public all over America."

The Midnite Jamboree came on immediately following the Grand Ole Opry every Saturday night at midnight when WSM's 50,000 watt-station became a clear channel after most of the smaller stations went off the air.

"This was a powerful tool for letting people know about the new records being offered by Ernest and the other artists," observed Glenn Douglas. "Down through the years, I think most of the Grand Ole Opry members have sung on the Midnite Jamboree at least once. Other artists have sung there too. Even Elvis Presley, the King of rock and roll, sang there when he was starting out."

Glenn Douglas said he remembers Tennessee Ernie stopping in Nashville to sing on the Midnite Jamboree when he was on his way to California in 1947 when the record shop was on Commerce Street."

May 2015

"It didn't stay there very long because it was just too small," Glenn Douglas said. "The people would walk up from the Grand Ole Opry to listen to the Midnite Jamboree, and they would have to stand out on the sidewalk and out in the street to hear the show. The police finally said that something had to be done because the people were interfering with the flow of traffic. So, one night, my dad rented a flat bed truck and me and my brothers moved the entire record shop down to 417 Broadway where it is still doing business today."

Midnite Jamboree is the second oldest radio show in the world, second only to the Grand Ole Opry.

This year, in May, will mark the 68th year it has been broadcasting. The people who have sung on the stage of the Midnite Jamboree would read like a Who's Who of Country music entertainers, some of who have gone on to be superstars and country music legends.

The Midnite Jamboree Association has been organized for the purpose of meeting the weekly costs of keeping this show on the air. Donations may be mailed to The Midnite Jamboree Association, P.O. Box 159326, Nashville, TN 37215. To learn more about the Jamboree, visit www.etrecordshop.com.

Kentucky Headhunters upcoming collaborative bluegrass project

Bluegrass crowd-favorites Lorraine Jordan & Carolina Road along with Grammy award-winning The Kentucky Headhunters have joined forces to record and release "Runnin' Water," a collaboration that can be found on the forthcoming Country Grass, which will be released by Pinecastle Records on June 9.

"We had so much fun making this video, and I think it really shows," says Lorraine Jordan. "This is just a sample of what's to come on this upcoming project."

The video was shot on location in Kentucky, at the legendary Practice House, where The Kentucky Headhunters hit singles have been recorded. In addition to The Kentucky Headhunters, country music hit-makers T.G. Sheppard, Crystal Gayle, John Conlee, Lee Greenwood, Lynn Anderson, Eddy Raven, Jim Ed Brown, Kelly Lang and Jesse Keith Whitley all serve up a little classic country with a bluegrass twist. Stay tuned for more information.

Larry's Country Diner RFD Show Schedule May 2015

NEW SHOW	NEW SHOW	PREVIOUSLY AIRED	PREVIOUSLY AIRED	PREVIOUSLY AIRED
VINCE GILL & PAUL FRANKLIN Saturday, May 2 10:00 p.m. Central Sunday, May 3 6:00 p.m. Central	**SYLVIA** Saturday, May 9 10:00 p.m. Central Sunday, May 10 6:00 p.m. Central	**T. GRAHAM BROWN** Saturday, May 16 10:00 p.m. Central Sunday, May 17 6:00 p.m. Central	**RONNIE McDOWELL** Saturday, May 23 10:00 p.m. Central Sunday, May 24 6:00 p.m. Central	**MARTIN FAMILY CIRCUS** Saturday, May 30 10:00 p.m. Central Sunday, May 31 6:00 p.m. Central

Nathan Stanley Carries on Family Bluegrass Tradition

Rising Bluegrass prodigy Nathan Stanley is gearing up for the re-release of his album, The Legacy Continues, which is available now. The project is appropriately titled, as the Virginia native is the grandson of Bluegrass legend, Dr. Ralph Stanley, who joins Nathan on two epic duets that will leave fans breathless. On the new project, the soulful-grassy singer takes his traditional sound to a whole new level. The album also features a duet with country singer Brad Paisley. The project was released through Nathan Stanley Entertainment.

"I'm very excited about the repackaging of this CD, to which we added two brand new songs," said an excited Nathan Stanley. "I hope it will be a record that bluegrass fans, along with my gospel fans will love."

On the album, Stanley brings emotion that will captivate fans everywhere! Tracks such as "Papaw I Love You," which is a song that Nathan wrote for his Grandfather, is sure to connect with music listeners and take them on a journey. Other tracks like "Calling My Children Home" stretch genre boundaries, giving off a Celtic vibe, while maintaining its traditional bluegrass appeal. By the time you throw in the Brad Paisley duet with "Will You Miss Me When I'm Gone," these graceful harmonies that are sure to be stuck in fans' heads for days!

Nathan Stanley is no stranger to success, which is evident with his previous release, Every Mile. The project (which included a vocal cameo from his grandfather, among other artists such as Vince Gill and T. Graham Brown) was able to gain the attention of Christian audiences, as it took home the award for "Bluegrass Album of the Year" at the 45th Annual GMA Dove Awards.

A longtime member of his grandfather's band, The Clinch Mountain Boys, Stanley has released eight solo records during his career thus far. His 2011 disc My Kind of Country album endeared him to Country and Bluegrass fans alike, and also attracted guest appearances from artists such as Marty Stuart, Patty Loveless, Ricky Skaggs, and Del McCoury. He has appeared on a wide variety of television series, such as The Late Show with David Letterman, TBN's Praise The Lord with Jason Crabb, and Song of the Mountains. In addition, his love of the road is something that is very apparent. Since he was two years old, Stanley has performed more than 200 dates per year.

Diner Chat is like an old fashion PARTY LINE

I remember as a kid we would travel every summer to visit my grandma. She lived in a rural area of Oklahoma and I have such great memories of the train tracks next to her house and the engineer throwing candy as he waved and blew the train whistle. There was an out house instead of indoor plumbing, flooring that was cold when we knelt at night to pray, and a huge tree that had 2 ropes and a board that I would swing and spin for hours.

But the most intriguing thing I remember was the wall telephone! When I picked up the receiver and put it to my ear it was like being a spy from a comic book. No one knew you were there but you could hear people talking. They were talking about everything in their lives and it didn't even matter that I didn't know them, I was spell bound. It was a party line and I found myself checking the phone just to see if anyone was talking.

Party lines were common in that time period where wires had to be run miles to remote farms and houses, which meant shared lines. If you picked up your phone while somebody on your party line was talking, you overheard their conversation (and could join in). The shared line also meant you could not receive a call when the line was being used which would result in a busy signal.

Certain people did get a reputation of being nosey and always trying to listen in on other people's calls to hear the latest gossip. How was this discovered? A coded ring was put in pace. PARTY 1 would be a single ring; PARTY 2 would be two short rings, PARTY 3 would be long short, PARTY 4 would be long –short-long etc. However even though you would be alerted that you had a phone call, you were never alerted when someone was listening. And heavy breathing in those days was not considered a stalker. So you can see how a young girl from California would be entertained by listening in on a party line.

I think **Diner Chat** is the ultimate party line. Every Thursday at 3:00 EST I will be sharing news and answering questions not only about Larry's Country Diner and Country's Family Reunion but also about your favorite country music legend. And just like our TV show…you never know who might call in. We will talk to Jason from customer service along with weekly Diner construction updates and Cruise information. All of the callers will be able to ask questions or just listen.

Here is how you get on our party calls.
By phone you can dial the same number every week
Thursdays, 3 PM Eastern Time
425-440-5100   Pin 909005#

As George Jones use to say, "Make sure you add the "Tick -Tack -Toe" at the end of the pin number) !

To talk to Renae, just hit *2

If you have any questions about what to do prior to the show call Customer Service at 800-820-5405.
To Listen on the Internet: www.larryscountrydiner.com   Click: Diner Chat

May 2015

JUNE

Rory talks about turning 50 & making a movie

Rory Feek turned 50 years old in April of this year. But, he says, "for some reason, in my head and heart, it doesn't feel like it. I still feel like a young man in my late 20s or early 30s at the most."

He says the first birthday he remembers is when his father turned thirty-eight. "We lived in an old farmhouse that we'd rented just outside of Highland, KS and I remember the big "3" and "8" candles on his cake. The funny thing is though…he was already old, at least he was to me. I wonder if he knew he was old then. Or if he felt like I do when he was the age I am now. My father passed away at 51, so I never got to have a conversation with him about growing up or growing old."

He writes in his blog about how life has changed since he wrote his first in January 2014. " I began that year believing that God was going to give us a great story to live and He did. And He's still giving us one today. After a year of writing, filming and sharing scenes from my life, I find myself in awe of where we've been and excited to learn where this journey will lead us next."

Lately Joey has been teaching Indiana to tell everyone how old she is. She asks "how old are you Indy?" and Indiana puts her little hand in the air and raises one finger.

The entire family spent Easter this year in Virginia making a full length movie titled, Josephine. "To undertake something so big is incredibly exciting and completely terrifying at the same time," he says of the project. "Joey and Indy are with me in Virginia and I'm not sure who's more excited about making this movie… Joey, or me. She's here making us all amazing meals and making sure I'm okay and taking care of myself during these long days and short nights – through the stress and the joy that comes with making an epic civil war movie on a small budget. Both of our older daughters, Heidi and Hopie are here working on the film too."

Fifteen years ago, Rory came across some letters that a Civil War soldier from Tennessee named John Robison wrote home to his wife Josephine. Rory tells us, "His grammar and spelling were terrible, but the words he wrote to her were poetic and beautiful. Not long after, I turned those letters into a song called "Josephine" that my wife Joey and I recorded and made a music video for."

In 2013, he received an email from a man in Virginia who had seen the music video and he said he knew of letters that Josephine had also written to John. "When I found and read those letters, I was even more moved by the words she wrote and the love she clearly had for the husband that the war had separated her from."

Over the next year and a half, Rory's best friend Aaron Carnahan and Rory wrote Josephine's story into a full-length screenplay for a movie. Or as Rory says, "Actually we let her tell us the story that she

June 2015

wanted to tell. Page by page, we watched her wait for John until she could wait no more. Then, after burying their only child - in desperation - we saw her cut off her long hair, put on John's old clothes and join the confederate army to find him. We watched a lost and scared girl, dressed like a male soldier, not only learn to become a woman again, but also teach the men around her how to be better men. We followed Josephine and her ragtag unit across three states - over six months, against all odds, with nothing to go on, but the belief in the one thing in the world she had left... love."

Josephine's story tells of the real-world struggles and the reality of war-time and all it entails. "While this is not a Christian film, it's a film made by Christian men who want to tell a real story of redemption and light in a world filled with darkness," Rory says. This is not a movie about the civil war, or the south – and it has no political agendas. It's a love-story that happens to unfold in a war that's hard to understand and even harder to live through.

"We used excerpts from Josephine and John's actual letters in the screenplay," Rory continues. "After Aaron and I had written about half of the screenplay, we learned that in reality hundreds of women like Josephine actually served and fought in the Civil War as union and confederate soldiers."

"If nothing else," states Rory, "We'd love it if you would keep us in your thoughts and prayers over the next few weeks as we walk hand-in-hand down a road we've never been down before."

Renae and her "Diary" featured in Country Weekly Magazine

By Renae the Waitress

Mothers Day was made very special for me with an article by Bob Paxman in Country Weekly Magazine. There is a chapter in my book "Diary of a TV Waitress" titled "Got Pie'?

I was inspired to write the chapter about pies from NADINE, our church lady on Larry's Country Diner. She is addicted to sweets! And eating a piece of Pie at Larry's Country Diner makes her day. But as I explain in my book, when I was growing up it was my Mom's pie that was famous. Everyone had a special pie she would bake for them. I loved Chocolate, my brother loved Pineapple, and my dad loved Coconut Cream and my husband love Lemon. A lot of times we would ask for a pie instead of a Birthday Cake. My mom passed away 2 years ago and we served pie in her memory.

Country Weekly not only took quotes from that chapter but also put my mom's recipe and pie photo in the magazine. I know she was smiling down with pride on this special Mothers Day. Thank you Country Weekly Magazine.

Nadine's Corner

Everyone knows church folk like to cook, and most have their own cookbook. Send me your church cookbook and each month I'll pull a recipe from it and feature it here!

Cookbook, P.O. Box 210796, Nashville, TN 37221.

KING RANCH CHICKEN CASSEROLE

Virgie Mahan

Ingredients
2 cup cooked diced chicken
1 can Ro-Tel
1 can cream of celery soup
1 can cream of chicken soup
1/2 can chick broth or skim milk
1 pkg. corn tortillas, cut into small pieces
1 large onion, chopped
1 cup grated sharp cheddar cheese

Directions

Layer the chicken, tomatoes, soups, chicken broth and tortillas in a greased 2-quart casserole dish.

Add chopped onions, repeat layers and onions. Sprinkle with grated cheese over top and bake at 350 degrees for 1 hour.

MEXICAN CORNBREAD

Mary Ann Woodard

Ingredients
2 eggs
3/4 cup milk
1/2 cup bacon grease
1 cup cornmeal
1/2 tsp. baking soda
1 tsp. baking powder
1 can creamed corn
1 can green chilis
1 cup grated cheese

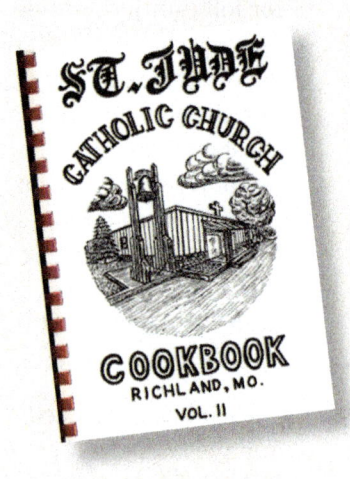

Directions

Mix and put half batter in 9 x 9-inch pan. Then add 1 cup cheese and 1 can chopped chilis. Pour remaining batter over top. Bake at 400 degrees for 40 to 45 minutes.

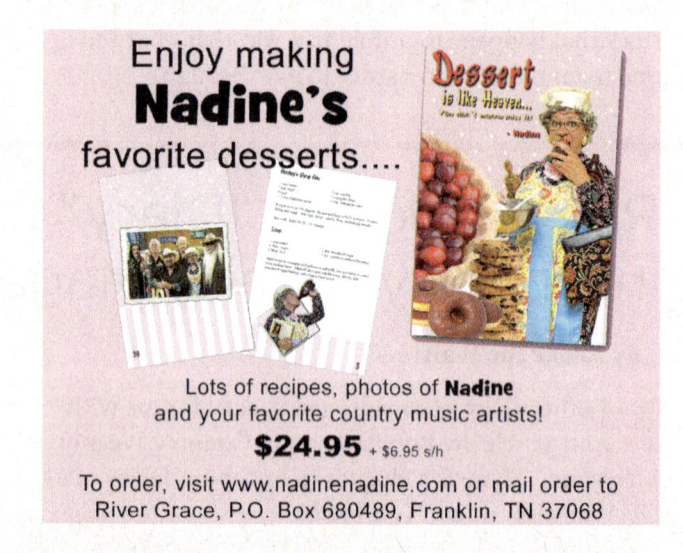

Enjoy making **Nadine's** favorite desserts....

Lots of recipes, photos of **Nadine** and your favorite country music artists!

$24.95 + $6.95 s/h

To order, visit www.nadinenadine.com or mail order to River Grace, P.O. Box 680489, Franklin, TN 37068

Nadine, the church lady

A PERSON IS NEVER SO EMPTY AS WHEN HE IS FULL OF HIMSELF

June 2015

Legendary John Conlee has new single adopted as Tennessee's FOP'S official song for law enforcement

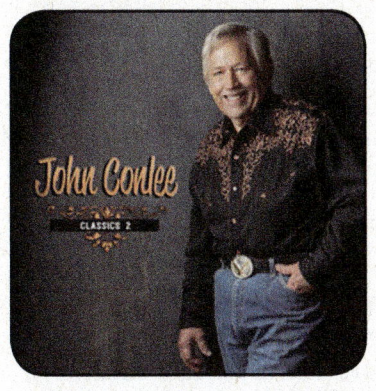

Last week, country music icon John Conlee performed "Walkin' Behind the Star" during an emotional ceremony honoring the members of law enforcement who had given their lives in the line of duty in 2014. The ceremony was held the morning of May 8 at the Legislative Plaza in downtown Nashville. President of the Tennessee's FOP, John Crumby, announced that Conlee's recording was now Tennessee's Fraternal Order of Police official song for law enforcement. "Walkin' Behind the Star" was written by Phil Thomas and the late Ronny Scaife.

Conlee's poignant interpretation of "Walkin' Behind the Star" from his recent 'live' performances and appearances on the Grand Ole Opry have sparked comments from around the country:

Howard R. Sills, sheriff for Putnam County, GA -- "For the last 41 years I have been a police officer and for the last 19 years I have been the Sheriff of my hometown community. Needless to say we in the law enforcement profession haven't been thought of too highly in most of the national media of late. This media coverage has made me more than a little despondent. I was lamenting about all of this when I turned on the Opry show this past Saturday night. It was not too long after the show began before a wonderful breeze of fresh air swept across my veranda and from my old GE radio sitting up on the porch rail. That breeze was the moment I heard you announce to the audience and the world that the Opry wanted to take a moment to honor those who "walk behind the star" and you sang the song with the same title that I'd never heard before. It literally caused me to tear up and it lifted my spirits. I cannot express thanks enough to you, the Opry and WSM-AM for the recognition during your show."

Mike Kelleher, chaplain from San Bernardino County Sherriff department -- "With all the bad press our force is constantly receiving, I would like to thank Mr. Conlee for his uplifting song."

James Bartels, police officer in Patriot, OH -- As a policeman shot in the line of duty, I found John Conlee's comments and his performance on the Grand Ole Opry very moving. I would like to thank him for understanding the terror law enforcement endure every day in the society we live in.

Derik Walker, K102 Country in Spokane/Sandpoint, ID -- Just wanted you to pass along to John Conlee that his song, "Walkin' Behind The Star" was the absolute perfect song to play this week for our fallen officer Greg Moore of the Coeur d'Alene, Idaho police department. I can't tell you how many calls we got regarding the song and how much it meant to folks in the inland Northwest as they deal with this tragedy. Sargent Greg Moore served the people for 16 years, before he was gunned down in Post Falls, Idaho Monday night. Please extend our gratitude to John on behalf of the entire K102 Country family!

David Lyons, police chief in Savannah, GA -- I am a police chief in the state of Georgia, the immediate past president of the Georgia Association of Chiefs of Police and a career police officer. I heard you sing the song, "Walkin' Behind the Star" and wanted to tell you how much I appreciated you. With all that's going on in the world right now along with the attacks on our police officers, it is good to hear some appreciative words. Thank you and God bless you.

Conlee feels the song's message could not be released at a more desperate time in our country. "I wanted to do this song to show support to police officers who are just doing their jobs. With all the turmoil going on I think they are relieved that someone is paying attention the other way and giving them a pat on the back."

"Walkin' Behind the Star" is the first song to be released from John Conlee's latest recording project called Classics 2. Fans can purchase the album on iTunes, www.johnconlee.com or anywhere music is sold.

June 2015

Artists confirmed for 2016 Caribbean Cruise

It's time to start thinking of cruising again. The 2016 Country's Family Reunion and Larry's Country Diner Cruise is now booking! The artists are confirmed and it's going to be a great time.

John Conlee will be the host for this year's cruise and artists are: Joey & Rory, T. Graham Brown, Mo Bandy, Gene Watson, Rhonda Vincent, Mark Wills and Johnny Lee. Brand new to our cruise is Exile! The cast of Larry's Country Diner will be there and you never know who else may decide to come cruise with us.

The cruise is back on the Royal Caribbean's Freedom of the Seas and will sail January 31 through February 7 out of Port Canaveral, FL. We will be visiting four ports of call this time, Labadee, Haiti; Falmouth, Jamaica; Georgetown, Grand Cayman; and Cozumel, Mexico.

This year's shows will be a little different. There will be two Country's Family Reunion Shows and two Larry's Country Diner shows, as well as a Nadine show. And of course, Rhonda will be holding her nightly Jam Sessions.

Seating is assigned in order of booking, so you'll want to book as soon as possible to get the best possible seat in the theatre. But there are NO bad seats, so no matter where you sit you'll be sure to have a great view.

Last year's cruise was featured in the RFD-TV magazine with a two page spread showing this is one of the best times around.

To book or to ask questions, call Customer Service at 800-820-5405.

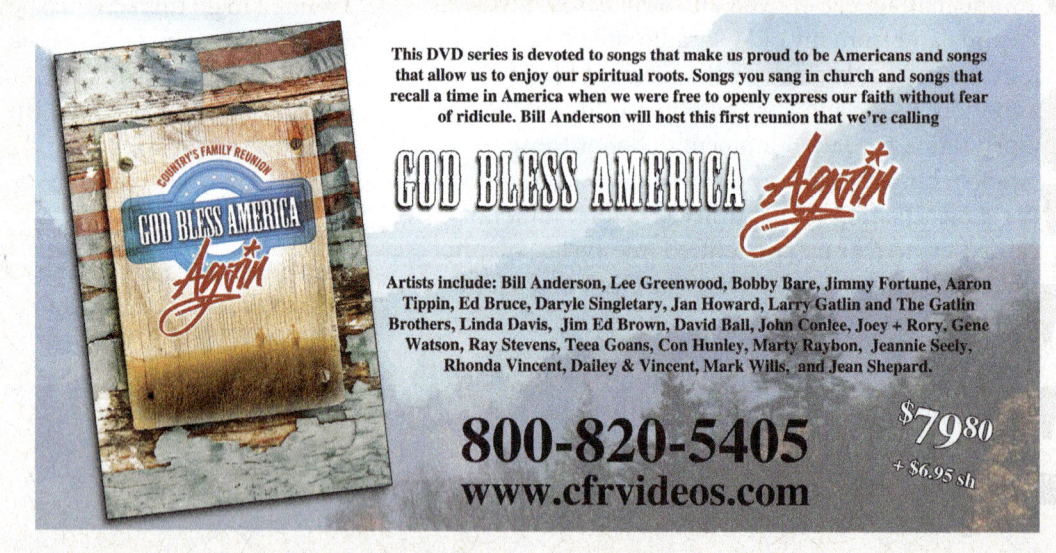

Country's Family Reunion & Larry's Country Diner CRUISE

7 night Western Caribbean Cruise
JAN. 31st - Feb. 7, 2016

JOHN CONLEE • JOEY + RORY • T. GRAHAM BROWN • MOE BANDY • EXILE
RHONDA VINCENT • MARK WILLS • GENE WATSON • JOHNNY LEE • LARRY'S COUNTRY DINER CAST

This DVD series is devoted to songs that make us proud to be Americans and songs that allow us to enjoy our spiritual roots. Songs you sang in church and songs that recall a time in America when we were free to openly express our faith without fear of ridicule. Bill Anderson will host this first reunion that we're calling

GOD BLESS AMERICA Again

Artists include: Bill Anderson, Lee Greenwood, Bobby Bare, Jimmy Fortune, Aaron Tippin, Ed Bruce, Daryle Singletary, Jan Howard, Larry Gatlin and The Gatlin Brothers, Linda Davis, Jim Ed Brown, David Ball, John Conlee, Joey + Rory, Gene Watson, Ray Stevens, Teea Goans, Con Hunley, Marty Raybon, Jeannie Seely, Rhonda Vincent, Dailey & Vincent, Mark Wills, and Jean Shepard.

800-820-5405
www.cfrvideos.com

$79.80
+ $6.95 sh

June 2015

COUNTRY LEGENDS PAST AND PRESENT   BY TOM WOOD
FARON YOUNG

Faron Young refused to be pigeonholed.

Known primarily as a honky-tonk hero of the 1950s-70s, the Singing Sheriff was a genuine multi-media star long before that term came into being.

Good looks and a classic country timbre were Faron's calling card and ensured his spectacular singing career — complete with five No. 1 hits to his credit.

But the Louisiana native was so much more, a major entertainment figure whose legend endures even today.

Faron made his Grand Ole Opry debut in 1951 when "Goin' Steady" started its eventual rise to No. 2 on the charts. But success was not immediate as he was drafted into the U.S. Army. Following his 1954 discharge, the Grand Ole Opry star enjoyed a decade of success that would be hard to match.

Besides a string of charted songs, Faron Young also appeared in movies (the first, Hidden Guns in 1956 led to his nickname), he was an advertising pitchman, made numerous radio, television and personal appearances — and in 1963 even co-founded a highly respected trade journal, the Music City News.

Not only that, but he was a savvy investor on Nashville's Music Row in the 1960s and gave young songwriters breakout opportunities. Guys like Willie Nelson, Kris Kristofferson and Don Gibson owe part of their success to Faron Young and remained lifelong friends.

Indeed, he did it all.

In hindsight, it would be easy to say that Faron Young's relatively short life could be encapsulated in his first No. 1 song, "Live Fast, Love Hard, Die Young" (1955).

His public persona — combined with a sometimes troubled private life full of loves, divorces, numerous health issues and other personal failings including alcoholism — all made for juicy headlines.

And long after his star faded, Faron Young sent shockwaves through the country music world one final time in 1996 when died at age 64 of a self-inflicted wound.

But death did not diminish his continued influence on country music.

Faron had four other No. 1 hits — "Alone With You" (1958), "Country Girl" (1959), "Hello Walls" (1961) and "It's Four in the Morning" (1971) — and spent most of those formative years on the charts.

When CMT first went on the air in 1983, the first video it played was Faron Young's "It's Four in the Morning".

He was inducted into the Country Music Hall of Fame in 2000, four years after his death. Ironically, the trade magazine he founded, Music City News, closed shop that same year.

His works continue to be used in television and movie soundtracks even today.

Pretty heady stuff for a country guy who grew up on a farm in Louisiana.

Randy Travis is married!

Travis' rep has confirmed that the country superstar married Mary Davis on March 21.

The Cooke County clerk's office in Texas told PEOPLE that Travis, 55, and Davis were married by Pastor Tommy Nelson from Denton, Texas.

The legend – who suffered a debilitating stroke nearly two years ago – has been filled with wonderful surprises of late.

Generations & SECOND GENERATIONS Combo

First gathered in 1999, then again in 2011, this is a gathering of country music legends and the children of country music legends such as Marty Robbins, Conway Twitty, Faron Young, Tammy Wynette, George Jones, Roger Miller, Johnny Russell, Hank Williams, and Dottie West sharing stories and the songs their parents made famous.

ONLY $79.80
plus $8.95 s/h

Robyn Young
Bill Anderson
Karen Wheeler
Michael Twitty
Jean Shepard
Donnie Hawkins
Charlie Rich Jr.
Phil Campbell

George Hamilton V
George Hamilton IV
Hawkshaw Hawkins Jr
Melissa Luman
Chrystie Wooley
Georgette Jones

Jett Williams
Dean Smith
Jan Howard
Will Reid
Langdon Reid
Bill Mack
Dean Miller
Ronny Robbins
Shelly West
Jim Ed Brown

Roy Clark
Bill Anderson
Dean Miller
Michael Twitty
Ronny Robbins
Johnny Russell
Billy Walker
Bobby Lord

Georgette Jones
Jan Howard
Robyn Young
Rex Allen Jr.
Jett Williams
Merle Kilgore
Hawkshaw Hawkins Jr.
Del Reeves

1-800-820-5405
www.cfrvideos.com

Singer/songwriter Mitchell Torok wrote songs for Snow & Reeves

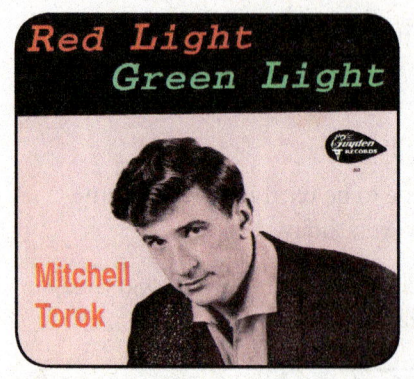

Mitchell Torok was born October 28, 1929, in Houston, Texas. He started playing the guitar when he was about 12 years old. He had his heart set on a music career while still in high school, but finally decided to go to college.

In 1953, while Torok was still at college, his songwriting paid off. Jim Reeves' recorded a song Torok had written, called 'Mexican Joe' on Abbott Records, and it became a smash hit number 1 on all charts. Torok, who at the time did not know anything about Jim Reeves, had hoped that Hank Snow would be given the song. His wish came true the following year when his song 'My Arabian Baby' appeared as the b-side of Snow's hit 'I Don't Hurt Anymore'.

Torok was himself signed to the Abbott label and later that year, he had a number 1 in both the Billboard country and juke-box charts with his song 'Caribbean'. The song, which remained in the country charts for 24 weeks, also became a Top 5 hit in both the Best Sellers and Jockey charts.

He became a member of The Louisiana Hayride on KWKH Shreveport. In 1954, Torok gained a number 9 country hit with the ridiculous-sounding 'Hootchy Kootchy Henry (From Hawaii)', and in 1956/7, he even had success in the UK pop charts with his songs 'When Mexico Gave Up The Rhumba' and 'Red Light, Green Light'. This success led to him touring in the UK in 1957. Torok made further recordings for Mercury, RCA, and Starday, and his last US chart entry was 'Instant Love', for the Reprise label in 1967.

He continued to write songs, mostly working in partnership with his wife (she has used both Gayle Jones and Ramona Redd as pseudonyms), and some of those songs have been recorded by top artists including Skeeter Davis, Kitty Wells, Glen Campbell and even Dean Martin. Hank Snow recorded 'The Mysterious Lady From Martinique' on one of his last RCA albums and 'Redneck' was a Top 20 hit for Vernon Oxford in 1976.

Torok joined Cedarwood Music in the late 70s and worked on a recording project telling the history of Nashville from 1780 to 1980. He is also a talented painter and painted a mural on display in the Elvis Presley Museum in Nashville.

June 2015

George Jones Museum opens with interesting twist

The new George Jones museum opened Thursday, April 23 in downtown at 128 N. 2nd Ave. Those seen walking the red carpet were Naomi Judd, Ricky Skaggs, Lee Greenwood, Moe Bandy, Joe Stampley, T. Graham Brown, John Rich, T.G. Sheppard, Dierks Bentley, and Lorrie Morgan. Jan Howard strolled the museum and shared first-hand stories of the years she knew Jones. The 44,000 sq. ft. facility that has plans for a restaurant and music venue, along with many exhibits on the life and times of George Jones. The opening comes just days before the 2nd anniversary of George Jones' death on April 26th, 2013.

Included in the museum is a gift shop that features numerous George Jones-branded items, including "White Lightning" moonshine that raised some eyebrows since Jones had such struggles with alcohol his entire life. The museum will also feature a moonshine tasting bar, but in an odd twist of fate, they may have to find a new place to make the moonshine to sell there.

The Silver Trail Distillery in Hardin, Kentucky who makes the George Jones White Lightning moonshine exploded Friday, April 24, just one day after the opening of the museum. Two workers were injured in the explosion, and were airlifted to a local hospital with major burns. Spencer Balentine who owns the distillery, was not at the facility at the time of the explosion. The distillery was working on a large order of moonshine for the George Jones museum at the time of the explosion.

Many of George's personal items are on display at the museum including cars and his 'Possum Hollar Pickup" which was brought in by crane through an upstairs window.

The property was purchased by George's widow Nancy in January and everyone was on a rush schedule to get it open by the anniversary date of George's passing. . Construction workers and designers worked around the clock to meet Nancy's timetable.

Also among the museum's first attendees was Jones's sister, Helen Scroggins. Now 93, she is the last remaining of eight Jones siblings. Nashville Mayor Karl Dean, U.S. Rep. Marsha Blackburn, and Tennessee Lt. Gov. Ron Ramsey were among the dozens of celebrities, government officials, and hundreds of music industry professionals who turned out to honor Jones and his legacy.

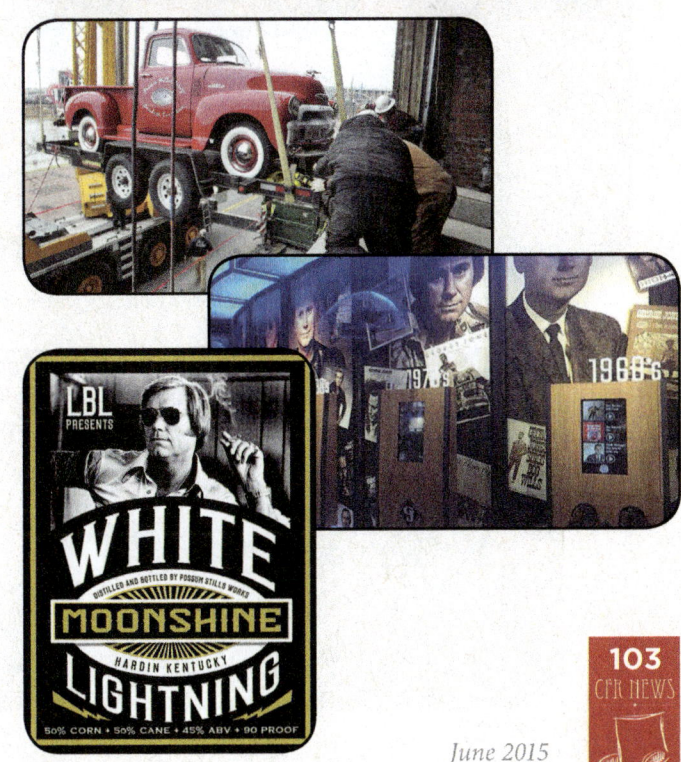

June 2015

Larry's Country Diner show sells out shows at Branson's Starlite Theatre

The Starlite Theater was the place to be in Branson, MO, May 5-9.

The whole cast from Larry's Country Diner TV Show on RFD-TV was they're performing live on stage. Each night a country music legend would join Larry, Keith, the Sheriff, Renae the Waitress and Nadine along with a surprise visit from Billy Dean and Barbara Fairchild,

The sold out shows included Gene Watson, Jimmy Fortune, The Whites and Daily & Vincent. And just like on TV there were tables and chairs on stage for a few lucky audience members to sit and eat pie served by Renae the waitress. It was the best ticket in town with great entertainment and lots of laughs. Make your plans and buy your tickets early for September 22-27 (Daily & Vincent, Jimmy Fortune, Gene Watson, The Whites, Joey and Rory) 417-337-9333

Jimmy Fortune performed on May 6 and again on May 8!

Jimmy and Nadine clowning around!

The Whites performed for the first time on Larry's Country Diner in Branson on May 7 to a sold out crowd.

The cast of Larry's Country Diner all had a blast entertaining everyone. Nadine danced her way through the performances.

June 2015

PFI brought a special mule (Homer?) to the theatre to surprise Nadine.

Dailey & Vincent cracked up when comedian Jarrett Dougherty showed up.

Nadine Dancing

Gene Watson always entertains the audience.

Emy Joe Bilbrey, Renae the Waitress & Nadine

Renae happily signs autographs and chats with fans.

105
CFR NEWS

June 2015

Brown & Gilley are a hit at ACM Awards

Jim Ed Brown's IN STYLE AGAIN has taken the #1 spot on The Roots Music Report's TOP 50 True Country Album Chart, and the Country icon charmed all as he strolled down the Academy of Country Music Awards' Red Carpet this past weekend in Texas.

The Grand Ole Opry star conducted over 30 interviews with high-profile media outlets during a marathon one-and-a-half hour stroll down the Red Carpet. Reps from Access Hollywood, Associated Press, ACM Backstage.com, CBS This Morning, Inside Edition and Fox News got camera-time with the legendary star. Jim Ed was thrilled to chat with radio and print reporters from ABC News Radio, Café Nashville, United Stations Radio Networks, KTHK-FM, Billboard, Cowboys & Indians Magazine, CultureMap Dallas, Dallas Observer, Southwest Airlines Magazine, Fort Worth Star-Telegram and more. During the Awards' weekend, Brown also spoke with drive-time programmers from stations in markets that included: Atlanta, Seattle, Orlando, Kansas City, Los Angeles, Chicago, Pittsburg and more at Westwood One's Radio Row event. Additionally, the singer spent time with personalities from Nashville Nights Live and NASH TV.

This has been a banner year for Brown so far. In January, doctors gave him a clean bill of health after he underwent treatment for lung cancer. Last month, the Country Music Hall of Fame® announced that THE BROWNS will become the newest members of the revered organization in the 2015 "Veterans Era Artist" category, and now, after a 30-year hiatus from recording, his current CD goes to #1. "It's definitely shaping up to be a big year for me and for all of the Brown family," Jim Ed admits. "To be able to share these honors with my sisters and my fans is remarkable. We've all had a long journey to get here, and I am more thankful than I can say."

The legendary Mickey Gilley is celebrating a new milestone as the recipient of the 2015 ACM Triple Crown Award. It's the Academy's recognition of artists who have previously won ACM Awards in all three of the following categories: New Artist (1974); Male/Female Vocalist and/or Vocal Duo/Vocal Group (1976); and Entertainer of the Year (1976).

The Triple Crown Award was presented to Gilley by multi-platinum singer Darius Rucker during ACM Presents: Superstar Duets which was taped for a two-hour television special at Globe Life Park on Friday, April 17 in Arlington, Texas. It was part of the 3-day 50th Academy of Country Music Awards® celebration and is set to air on Friday, May 15 on the CBS Television Network.

"Receiving the ACM Triple Crown Award is truly an honor of a lifetime. I'm thankful for the recognition and grateful to all those who helped me reach this incredible mark of achievement as I celebrate more than 50 years in the entertainment industry," Gilley says.

In addition to being honored with the 2015 ACM Triple Crown Award, Mickey Gilley is marking the 35th anniversary of the Urban Cowboy movie and taking the spotlight across North America with this year's concert tour.

June 2015

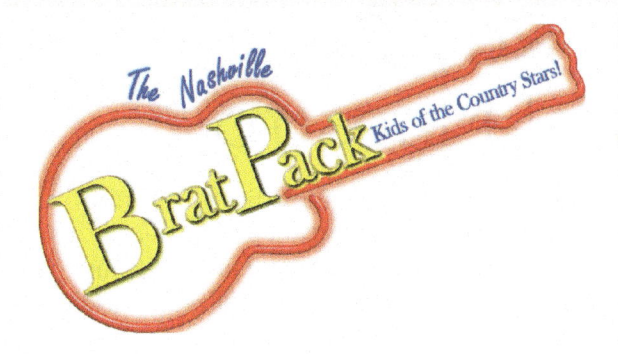

The Nashville Brat Pack — Kids of the Country Stars!

Donnie Winters, Son of Don Winters

(Don was part of the Marty Robbins Trio for over 20 years)

Dennis, Jackie, June, Don, Joyce, & Donnie on a family trip to Florida.

We moved to Nashville from Florida in 1953. He recorded for RCA Victor and Coin Records and Columbia. You can find some of those on YouTube. He has a rockabilly kind of cult hit out today called Pretty Moon and the flip side is Be My Baby, Baby.

Dad had a single out on Decca Records called Too Many Times and on the flip side was Shake Hands with a Loser. It was kinda like a two sided hit. But he was having trouble with management getting him booked onto shows and Marty Robbins approached him backstage at the Opry one night, probably early 60s when dad was employed with Webb Pierce. Marty told him if he wasn't doing so well on his own did he want to come to work with him. And dad looked at him and said, "When do I start?" And he worked with him almost 23 years.

I'd play with my dad at home and he'd teach me stuff. We wrote a little bit together which is where my first cut, Do Me A Favor, came from. Do Me A Favor was my first song that Marty Robbins recorded. Do Me A Favor will be on my new country CD that we're working on.

My first car was a gift from Mel Tillis. It was a 1955 Ford which I commenced to drive the wheels off of. Then my dad bought me a Rambler, which I wasn't real crazy about, but it was transportation. It served as our first band vehicle.

I got to play guitar for Marty on the Opry for a year after his first heart attack.

When we moved out to Franklin, we lived across the road from Marty on his property. There was this old shack that Dennis and I turned into a band room. That's when Jack Pruett, son of Jack and Jeannie Pruett, played bass joined us for the first Winters Brothers Band.

Then we became friends with Charlie Daniels and ended up being on two of the Volunteer Jam albums.

Never a dull moment growing up in the music business.

L to R: Don, Marty, Dennis & Donnie in the studio recording.

COUNTRY'S FAMILY REUNION presents....

SECOND GENERATIONS
June 1 & 8 on RFD-TV

GOD BLESS AMERICA Again
Starting June 15 on RFD-TV

Fridays...7 p.m. central
Saturdays...11 p.m central

June 2015

Hobbies & Interests: Roy Clark, the Multi-Dimensional Maestro

By Claudia Johnson

The name Roy Clark has become synonymous with "Hee Haw," not just for the viewers who watched the country musical comedy, variety show during its three-year run from 1969- 1972, but also for the generations who have watched it in syndication.

For fans of Clark's television and film work there's no doubt the versatile entertainer is a first class banjo picker and just downright funny as a comedic host and actor. Before there was Hee Haw, Clark made guest appearances on shows like "The Odd Couple" and "The Beverly Hillbillies" and was a frequent guest and sometimes host of Johnny Carson's "Tonight Show." Andy Williams and Bob Hope sought him out as a guest for their specials, and he was playing Las Vegas when his competition was Frank Sinatra and Sammy Davis Jr.

In addition to playing multiple instruments, Clark has several well-documented interests outside his long and acclaimed professional life, including fishing, horses, drag racing, sports, philanthropy and flying.

When he was young, he participated in sports, playing both football and baseball, and has admitted in interviews that he remains a "sports nut." He was even a boxer for a time, having been paid for winning 15 out of 16 bouts.

A humorous publicity photo of Clark from the early 1980s, decades after he boxed professionally, shows Clark "squaring off" in the ring at Reno's Golden Nugget against pro mauler Bruce Finch.

"It's a real joy to know Roy," said Angelo Dundee, manager to some of the 20th century's greatest boxers. "Boxing's loss was music's gain. I was real impressed with his knowledge of boxing."

Clark was a licensed pilot who owned several planes since learning to fly in the early 1950s.

"Flying is the only thing that totally relaxes me," Clark told People magazine in the Sept. 26, 1977, issue. "I leave my problems on the ground, and I don't pick 'em up till I get down."

Though he has since had others, at that time he told People he had a 1941 vintage biplane (a Stearman PT-17, originally built as an Army trainer), a seven-passenger turboprop (a Mitsubishi MU-2) and single-engine Piper Tripacer built in 1953.

He donated the Piper, on which he had learned to fly, to Wings of Hope, a Nobel Peace Prize-nominated charity based in St. Louis, Mo., that works throughout the Midwest transforming the lives of kids with profound birth defects, to be raffled for charity.

Clark's philanthropy has been a long-time commitment. He's staged fundraising concerts and other events for hospitals in Virginia, Tennessee and his hometown of Tulsa, Okla. His charitable work has benefited a language disorder clinic in North Carolina, a Los Angeles youth center and an elementary school in Tulsa. He has supported dozens of college programs, like the Roy Clark Music Scholarship, established in 1995 in memory of Clark's parents, Hester and Lillian Clark, funded in part by a benefit concert each December.

Clark used his love of golf to raise more than $800,000 for the Children's Medical Center in Tulsa by hosting a Celebrity Golf Tournament there for several years.

"Roy, I've known a long time now," said the late Bob Hope, one of the many celebrities who traveled to Tulsa to participate in the annual tournament. "It's pretty hard to play golf with him because it's hard to putt over a guitar cord. He's just super… and a beautiful guy, and he's my type…and he's a fair golfer."

For several years, he headlined a golf tournament for St. Jude Children's Research Hospital in Memphis, Tenn., where a floor was named in his honor.

On Dec. 28, 1985, Billboard published an aptly named special section, "Roy Clark: A Multi-Dimensional Maestro," in commemoration of Clark's 25th anniversary in the entertainment industry. It included testimonials from friends and colleagues, along with photos and interviews.

"He's a big-hearted man with a humanitarian's sense of purpose," Billboard concluded. "Often unsung but always appreciated in his constant dedication to needy causes."

In 2015, the Grand Ole Opry member turns 82, celebrates 58 years of marriage to his wife, Barbara, and has been entertaining fans for 55 years.

Fortunately, he still finds time for the hobbies that give him pleasure.

June 2015

Country Questions
By Dick Boise, CMH

Send questions to:
Dick Boise, , c/o CFR News,
P.O. Box 201796, Nashville,
TN 37221.

Q. I would like to ask when and where Gene Autry was born? Talks for your help with this.

Lyle Walton, Lake Fork, ID

A. Orvon Gene Autrey was born September 29, 1907 in Tioga, Texas. He worked a few small radio stations before going on the National Barn Dance show on WLS in Chicago. He later got a part in a Ken Maynard movie doing some singing. After that he became one of America's favorite cowboy movie stars. Gene died October 2, 1998. He left us many, many wonderful memories.

Q. I would like to ask how Mickey Gilley is doing? I heard that he had a mishap and had to take some time off.

Mary Smith, Hamilton, OH

A. Mary, thanks for your question, as many others have mentioned Mickey's condition as well. In 2009 he was helping some friends move a sofa and tripped in the process. He injured his back and was paralyzed for several months. He is now back to appearing at his theatre in Branson and walks out on stage to sing his hits as only he can do.

Q. I overheard someone at a blue-grass show mention the name Tony Trischka. I wondered if you would tell me about this bluegrass person.

Thanks, B. Johnson

A. Tony Trischka is a very talented man who plays several instruments. He is most noted for his five string banjo playing. He has had several instruction books and video tapes of instruction. I know this will be hard for many who enjoy bluegrass to believe, however, Tony was born "way upstate" in Syracuse, NY. He received a degree in fine arts from Syracuse University. Before you

Q. My father used to tell me about his favorite singers and he called them Lula Belle and Scotty. Could you give me some information about them?

Paul Morris, Kingwood, WV

A. They were a very popular singing due on the WLS Barndance in the mid 1930s. Her real name was Myrtie Cooper and she was from Boone, NC. Scotty, who was from Ingalls, NC, met her at the National Barndance show in Chicago. They teamed up together to sing and later married. Some of the favorites were, "Have I Told You Lately That I Love You," and "Remember Me." Your father had good taste in his choice of singers.

June 2015

Legendary fiddler, Johnny Gimble, passes

Legendary fiddle player Johnny Gimble has passed away. The influential Western Swing musician died on Saturday, May 9, just weeks before his 89th birthday.

Born John Paul Gimble in Tyler, Texas on May 30, 1926, Gimble grew up in Bascom, Texas. He began playing in a trio called the Rose City Swingsters with his brothers at age 12 before moving to Louisiana to play with Jimmie Davis.

He joined Bob Wills' legendary Texas Playboys in the late 1940s, where he helped to pioneer the five-string fiddle. He broke away to form his own band, but re-joined Wills in 1953, where he stayed until the 1960s. During that period, he also played on Marty Robbins' No. 1 hit, "I'll Go on Alone."

After leaving the business entirely for a period, Gimble began to record again in 1969, both with Wills and as a session musician for artists like Chet Atkins and Merle Haggard. During his first tenure with Wills, he had played on Marty Robbins' No. 1 "I'll Go on Alone." Gimble also toured with Willie Nelson, released solo albums and, in 1983, earned a hit song with "One Fiddle, Two Fiddle," which also featured Ray Price.

In 1983, Gimble formed a Western Swing group that featured Ray Price and scored a country radio hit with "One Fiddle, Two Fiddle," which was featured in the Clint Eastwood movie Honkytonk Man. He was also nominated for a Grammy award for his performance on the 1993 Mark O'Connor album, Heroes. In his later years, he made guest appearances on Austin City Limits. Gimble was awarded a National Heritage Fellowship in 1994.

Gimble had suffered a stroke in 1999, but continued to play well into his 80s, appearing on A Prarie Home Companion and releasing an album titled Celebrating With Friends in 2010, featuring collaborations with Haggard, Vince Gill, Dale Watson, Ray Benson and more.

John Berry gearing up for 19th Annual Christmas Tour

It might be springtime, but blink a couple of times, and it will be time for chestnuts roasting on open fires, mistletoe, and the alluring scenes of red and green indicating that Christmas 2015 isn't too far away.

Country star John Berry is getting a head start on the season by announcing plans for his annual Christmas tour. A holiday tradition that the Aiken, South Carolina native started in 1997, the show is a mixture of such radio staples as the award-winning "Your Love Amazes Me," "Standing On The Edge Of Goodbye," "Change My Mind" and "I Will If You Will," in addition to such Yuletide-themed standards as "O Holy Night," which Berry first recorded in 1994 – and has become one of the most-played 'Songs of the Season' on Country radio during the holiday period. Other Christmas offerings include "Let It Snow, Let It Snow, Let It Snow," "I'll Be Home For Christmas," and "Little Drummer Boy." The concerts promise to be a night full of music, with over two hours of music planned each night.

Berry recently announced the first leg of the Christmas tour, with more dates to be announced soon. For further concert updates, go to www.JohnBerry.com

John Berry 2015 Christmas Tour Dates
11-20 Marietta, Georgia
12-05 Ashland, Kentucky
12-06 Chillicothe, Ohio
12-13 Kalamazoo, Michigan
12-15 Franklin, Tennessee
12-17 Gainesville, Georgia
12-18 Macon, Georgia
12-19 Bremen, Georgia
12-20 Augusta, Georgia

June 2015

Traditional country artists shine at Van Dyke's Country Gold Tour

Not many artists can say they were on the CMA Board of Directors during the planning and formation of the inaugural Fan Fair which took place at Nashville's Municipal Auditorium in 1972. Even fewer can say they will have the honor of performing their mega-hits at this year's CMA Music Festival – but, Leroy Van Dyke has earned these bragging rights!

"We are proud to bring our Country Gold Tour to this year's CMA Music Fest," says Leroy Van Dyke. "In the formative years, I don't think any of us could have foreseen the magnitude to which Fan Fair (CMA Music Festival) has grown, reaching its present importance and impact on the industry. It is a phenomenon!"

If you are fortunate enough to know him, you know Leroy would never brag. It's just not in his nature. However, it should be noted that he is the only known entertainer who is also an internationally renowned licensed auctioneer. The hit song "Auctioneer" was written solely by Van Dyke while living in a squad tent during his stint in the U.S. Army. Leroy was a Special Agent, U. S. Army Counterintelligence Corps, in Korea. The debut single, in 1956, became an instant multi-million seller. In 1961, Leroy struck pay dirt again releasing his next mega hit "Walk On By." This chart topper stayed at Number One for 19 weeks and remained on the charts for an incredible total of 42 weeks. Billboard Magazine named it "the biggest country music single in recorded history" based on sales, plays, and number of weeks on the charts!

Since its modest inception a quarter of a century ago under the direction of Gladys Van Dyke, Leroy Van Dyke's Country Gold Tour, in various configurations, has been presented in 25 states and four foreign countries.

"COUNTRY GOLD TOUR" performance for the CMA Music Festival is on Sunday, June 14 on the WSM Durango Music Spot Stage at 1:30p (with after-show autograph party!) – here is the lineup:

Leroy Van Dyke & The Auctioneers
Steve and Rudy Gatlin (The Gatlin Brothers)
Jim Ed Brown
Helen Cornelius
Rex Allen, Jr.
Leona Williams
Bobby Bare
Narvel Felts
Janie Fricke
Charlie Rich, Jr.

June 2015

Diner Chat is so EASY...

Even Rio can do it!

Young children are surrounded by technology. They learn how to drag objects on the screen, push buttons, and watch YouTube videos. Not only are smart phones smarter than us, but now toddlers are learning how to play games, take photos and surf the Internet before they are potty trained.

What about social skills...you know, the old fashioned picking up the phone and talking instead typing your conversation. There is so much to be learned through conversation and hearing what is being said.

On Diner Chat we are all about conversation. My once a week - one hour - phone call chat is doing it the old fashioned way. All you do is dial the DINER CHAT number (425) 440-5100, then when you hear the operator tell you to enter your conference number... you just enter our special code 909005# and you are connected to DINER CHAT. It's that simple!

Just like at the Diner, you never know who might call in and ask the same question you have. If you can't remember when to call, just give Customer Service a call at 800-820-5405 and we will send you a DINER CHAT magnet to put on your refrigerator.

Remember to call...

Thursdays, 3 PM Eastern Time

425-440-5100   Pin 909005#

As George Jones use to say, "Make sure you add the "Tick -Tack -Toe" at the end of the pin number) !

To talk to Renae, just hit *2

If you have any questions about what to do prior to the show

call Customer Service at 800-820-5405.

To Listen on the Internet: www.larryscountrydiner.com Click: Diner Chat

Larry's Country Diner RFD Show Schedule June 2015
(These shows have previously aired)

RICKY SKAGGS SHARON WHITE
Saturday, June 6
10:00 p.m. Central
Sunday, June 7
6:00 p.m. Central

JOHN CONLEE, JEANNIE SEELY and JANIE PRICE
Saturday, June 13
10:00 p.m. Central
Sunday, June 14
6:00 p.m. Central

BILLY DEAN
Saturday, June 20
10:00 p.m. Central
Sunday, June 21
6:00 p.m. Central

CRYSTAL GAYLE
Saturday, June 27
10:00 p.m. Central
Sunday, June 28
6:00 p.m. Central

June 2015

JULY

Huge loss as cancer claims life of Jim Ed Brown

Jim Ed Brown, a star of the Grand Ole Opry for more than fifty years and a newly elected member of the Country Music Hall of Fame, died Thursday, June 11. 2015 at Williamson Medical Center in Franklin, TN after battling cancer.

Jim Ed scored major country hits as a solo artist, as a duet singer, and as a member of The Browns with sisters Maxine and Bonnie. The Browns' 1959 crossover smash "The Three Bells" topped Billboard's country chart for ten consecutive weeks, and it spent four weeks atop Billboard's all-genre singles chart.

In September 2014, Jim Ed was diagnosed with lung cancer. While he was undergoing treatments, Plowboy Records released In Style Again, Jim Ed's first solo effort in 40 years. Fellow Opry stars Vince Gill and Sharon and Cheryl White joined him on the critically acclaimed album. In March 2015, Jim Ed and The Browns were elected along with Grady Martin and The Oak Ridge Boys as the newest members of the Country Music Hall of Fame.

"Fame is fleeting, hit records change every week, award show winners and nominees change every year, but being inducted into the Country Music Hall of Fame will be forever," Jim Ed said, in response to receiving country music's highest honor.

While The Browns' official induction into the Country Music Hall of Fame was to take place in October, CMA CEO Sarah Trahern, Hall of Famer Bill Anderson and Country Music Hall of Fame and Museum CEO Kyle Young, made a surprise visit to him in the hospital on June 4th to present him with a medallion commemorating his Hall of Fame membership.

Jim Ed appeared on Larry's Country Diner with Jason Crabb. This show will air again on July 4.

Following the presentation, Bill Anderson wrote the following on his website,

Jim Ed sat up a little straighter in the bed and removed the ball cap that he had been wearing. I said in a halting voice: "Jim Ed, on behalf of the membership of the Country Music Association, it's my pleasure and privilege to welcome Jim Ed Brown and The Browns to your rightful place in the Country Music Hall Of Fame." I slipped the ribbon over his head and watched as he proudly lay the Medallion itself on his chest. There was not a dry eye in the room.

He thanked everybody in his very weak voice and said again what a thrill it was. "I had almost decided this was never going to happen, and I told myself it was all right. I had had a pretty good run. But this means more to me than you'll ever know."

I don't know what made me do it, but suddenly I started singing, "Will The Circle Be Unbroken" there at the head of his bed. Everyone in the room joined in, just as we do on Medallion Night at the Hall of Fame each year. Jim Ed was even mouthing the words. It was sad, but somehow it seemed fitting.

As the people began to say their goodbyes and drift out of the room, Jim Ed told Kirt Webster he wanted to ask me a question. I walked back to his side.

"Do you think I'll be able to sing again when I get to heaven?" he asked weakly. "Because I sure can't sing now."

I was taken back by his question. I thought a minute and said, "Well, Jim Ed, if you can't sing, just send word to me and I'll loan you my 'whisper'!" He smiled.

And then I added, "But you'll have to watch Dickens. He'll try to drown you out."

I think the thought of seeing his old friend again stirred something special inside Jim Ed. He looked up at me and broke into a grin. Then the grin turned into a chuckle. And then the chuckle turned into a belly laugh. He finally got to laughing so hard that tears were running down his cheeks. He said, " 'Tater would do that, wouldn't he?" I nodded, and he reached for my arm. I squeezed his hand, told him I loved him, and I turned away. I wanted to remember him laughing.

Jim Ed died at peace with himself and with his place in country music.

Jim Ed appeared on Larry's Country Diner with Jason Crabb. This show will air again on July 4.

Cowboys and Indians magazine recently had an article featuring Jim Ed.

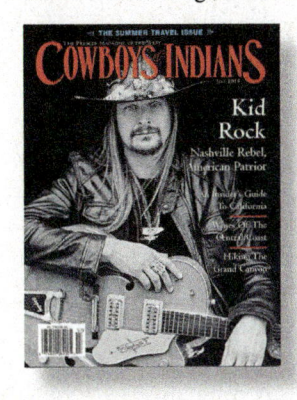

Trisha moves back to Nashville & back to Douglas Corner

Trisha's Southern Kitchen

Trisha Yearwood and husband Garth Brooks moved back to Nashville from Oklahoma last year. The songstress and her husband packed their bags because Brooks' youngest daughter left for college last fall, making them empty nesters for the first time. The reason they moved to the Sooner state in the first place was to be closer to Brooks' three daughters from his first marriage, so there's nothing tying them there now.

Along with Brooks launching back into his singing career with a stint in Ireland last summer that likely will lead to more gigs, Yearwood also is in demand with recording music, writing cookbooks and starring on her own show on the Food Network.

Trisha Yearwood hung out with some her biggest fans at her Fan Party at Douglas Corner Cafe in Nashville on June 13th. She was playing Douglas Corner when she was discovered years ago.

Her show "Trisha's Southern Kitchen" can be seen on the Food Network.

Thu 5:30|4:30c

Fri 1|12c

Fri 5:30|4:30c

Sat 10:30a|9:30c

July 2015

Country Stars Sharing Recipes for Happiness

By Sasha Kay Dunavant

Country songs have a way into our hearts. The stars that perform them are good for the soul. When we see them we light up. We know every word to every song, and we know just the right song to create the ambiance for every special occasion. Just as a song can take us back, cooking can traverse time as well, taking us back to our grandparents' table, remembering how "mama made it" or how holidays "used to be."

Food connects people through generation and congregation. Recipes are like lyrics to a song. They have to be just right and measured with love. Like a taste for good music, legendary country artists enjoy a taste for great cuisine. It turns out that some stars have taken action to showcase their passion for food.

Trisha Yearwood lets the world know of her love for cooking through writing bestselling cookbooks. Georgia Cooking in an Oklahoma Kitchen was published in 2008, and Home Cooking with Trisha Yearwood was published in 2010. Yearwood launched the Emmy Award winning show "Trisha's Southern Kitchen" on the Food Network in 2012 that features recipes from the singer's family and her own collection. Yearwood has stated that husband Garth Brooks craves her tortellini and asks her to include it in many of his meals. She's eager to indulge his and her fans' taste buds but also remains mindful of health concerns. In March 2015, Yearwood published Trisha's Table, My Feel-Good Favorites for a Balanced Life. The star's third cookbook is health promoting and includes nutritious ways to eat comforting, home-style meals.

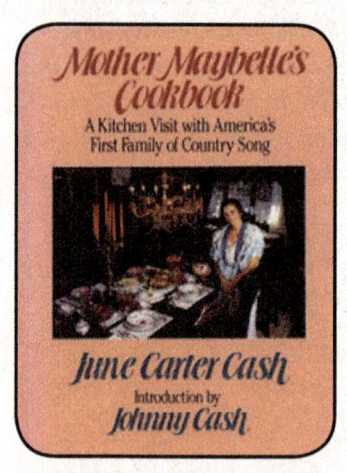

Mother Maybelle Carter was a country music pioneer, but her children remembered her as a wonderful mother and an amazing cook. She named her family's dining table "the family altar," believing that meal times helped families grow closer. Her love for home and hearth was captured by her daughter June Carter Cash in a 1989 cookbook entitled Mother Maybelle's Cookbook, a Kitchen Visit with America's First Family of Country Song. The cookbook's introduction was written by Johnny Cash, a long-time fan of Mother Maybelle's contribution to country music and her Southern cooking. June Carter Cash involved her singing sisters, Alena and Helen Carter. Together they filled the cookbook with delicious recipes and Carter family memories of growing up in the Virginia Appalachian Mountains.

Everyone knows church folk like to cook, and most have their own cookbook. Send me your church cookbook recipe, who submitted it, along with the name of your church and each month I'll pull a recipe from it and feature it here!

Nadine, the church lady

YOU DON'T HAVE TO WALK ON WATER, IT'S HOW YOU WALK ON LAND.

July 2015

Nadine's Corner

Everyone knows church folk like to cook, and most have their own cookbook. Send me your church cookbook and each month I'll pull a recipe from it and feature it here!

Cream Cheese Cut Out Cookies

by Michelle Stevens

1 cup butter
1 - 8 oz pkg cream cheese
3 1/2 cups all-purpose flour
1 1/2 cups sugar
1 egg
1 tsp. baking powder
1 tsp. vanilla
1/2 tsp. almond extract

Beat butter and cream cheese in a large bowl with electric mixer at medium to high speed about 30 seconds or until softened and blended. Add about half of the flour, all the sugar, egg, baking powder, vanilla and almond extract. Beat until thoroughly combined. Scrape sides of bowl occasionally. Stir or beat in remaining flour. Chill about 1 1/2 hours. Cut out cookies. Bake on ungreased cookie sheet at 350 degrees for 7-9 minutes. Frost when cool.

Cookie Glaze

Combine 2 cups sifted powdered sugar, 2 T. milk and 1/2 tsp. vanilla. Stir in additional milk, drops at a time until desired consistency is reached. Tint with desired food coloring. Spread over cooled cookies.

Yield; 36-48 cookies

Through July 4

GOD BLESS AMERICA Again

Beginning July 11

A Tribute To Ray Price

Fridays...7 p.m. central
Saturdays...11 p.m central

July 2015

Joe Bonsall's new book 'On The Road With The Oak Ridge Boys'

For more than 40 years, The Oak Ridge Boys have entertained countless fans across the country, sung for numerous U.S. Presidents, and earned every award in the industry, including their upcoming induction into the prestigious Country Music Hall of Fame. From their roots in southern gospel to their chart-topping career in country music, the Oaks have become one of America's most beloved music groups.

"When the lights dim, the theme music begins to play, and our band members begin to take up their positions, it's just as exciting today as it has always been throughout our long history," says Joe Bonsall, tenor of the group and author of On the Road with The Oak Ridge Boys. "We know that people have gathered to hear us sing our songs, and we never take one person in the audience for granted."

The Oaks got their start back in the 1940s when a group from Knoxville, Tennessee began performing country and gospel music in the town of Oak Ridge, where the atomic bomb was being developed. Over the years, the group gained popularity and soon appeared on the stage of the Grand Ole Opry. From there, members came and went but in 1973, the current group of Bonsall, William Lee Golden, Duane Allen, and Richard Sterban began singing together, and the rest is history.

"Through all these many miles we've traveled and everything we've been through together for more than 40 years, we haven't really changed much as we've gotten older," says Bonsall. "Singing, doing things right, honoring God and families in our lives… these things are still what really matter the most to each of us."

In On the Road with The Oak Ridge Boys, Bonsall takes readers on a backstage tour of life in the country music industry and the multi-faceted career of the Oaks. Through colorful stories and a touch of nostalgia, Bonsall shares about the history behind the group, introduces readers to each of the Oaks, and gives readers a front row seat to what it's like to travel the country in a tour bus equipped with lounges, technology, and multiple television sets. He also shares numerous stories of legendary fans (like 100-year-old Addaline Huff) as well as celebrities the Oaks have sung for and rubbed shoulders with throughout the years, including country stars like Garth Brooks and Kenny Rogers and Presidents from Gerald Ford to George W. Bush.

"When we're asked about our most memorable moments as Oak Ridge Boys, we often recall the honor of singing in the White House and our friendships with many of our nation's presidents," says Bonsall. "And why not? It's simply the truth that these events have provided us with some of our greatest memories."

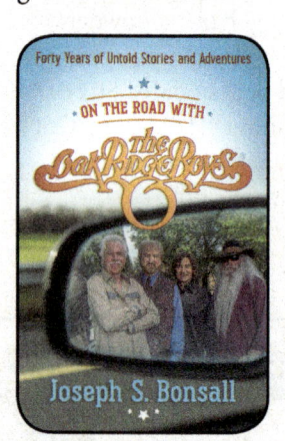

Over the decades, the Oaks have recorded and sung hundreds of songs, with their runaway hit, "Elvira," racing to the top of the charts in 1981. "Elvira" crossed over into the pop market and the song won every applicable music award. The Oaks even found themselves at one time singing it with the prestigious Mormon Tabernacle Choir. Today, contemporary groups are still singing "Elvira," even on the stage at the Grand Ole Opry.

"Our little song has passed down through the generations," says Bonsall. "Perhaps it's a big reason The Oak Ridge Boys are still around. Our music, our shows, and our own American spirit have been passed down from grandparents to parents to young couples and even on to their children. We see them all at our shows—still singing 'Elvira' with the Boys!"

For more information or to order, visit www.oakridgeboys.com.

July 2015

An uplifting update on Glen Campbell's condition

You never know what you'll see on Facebook. Recently, Jimmy Webb posted an update on Glen Campbell that was a nice surprise. It's good to hear that he is doing well. Here's what Jimmy had to say:

I visited my friend Glen Campbell Wednesday in Nashville. Laura and Kim Campbell were there as well.

You may be aware that Glen has bravely been living with Alzheimer's Disease. Along with his strong and courageous wife, they have changed the face of Alzheimer's forever. The world watched as Glen traveled from city to city, to continue doing what he loves to do: perform and share his music. Doctors were amazed at how the music and activity appeared to slow the pace of the disease for a while. With his family, they showed the world that you don't have to hide when you become ill. They raised awareness, and in turn, funds for Alzheimer's research.

Glen is currently residing in a memory support community—it reminded me of one of the nice hotels he would stay at while on tour. Kim has found this place for Glen that is safe, where he is cared for 24 hours a day. The ratio of caregivers to residents astounded me--he is never alone. And there are only 17 other residents; his neighbors are former lawyers, doctors, teachers and others who are living with the same challenges that dementia brings. Glen has been my friend for a long time and I love him like a brother. I am sure that Kim has made the right choices for and with my friend of 50 years.

Glen has his private room and bathroom, all decorated by Kim with custom paint, lots of photos murals and framed memorabilia. The place is bright and clean. He loves color and still wears his blue suede shoes from time to time!

The memory center has elaborate arrangements for activities. There are many different rooms and spaces for him to experience each day, each furnished tastefully and safely.

There is an airy screened-in porch where Glen likes to sit and where we visited with him. He has a full time caregiver, Brody. Brody is in his early twenties with long blond hair--he looks like a surfer! Brody is patient and kind. He plays the guitar with and for Glen. They sing, they walk around the grounds and converse almost constantly. We instantly fell for Brody and thanked him for the care he gives to Glen and the important breaks he gives Kim so she can rest and work.

Glen has always been a happy guy and a jokester. He still is. For longer than I'd like to remember, he has imitated Donald Duck and during the visit, he did his Donald voice for us. He sings in a low register all the way to high clear notes that are reminiscent of the performances we are all familiar with. He seems almost to go from song to song, under his breath at times. He looked at me after singing one song and said, "that was a good song wasn't it?" Music is still at the very center of who he is. It is almost as though he is giving a never-ending performance.

The last thing he said to me when it was time for us to go was, "Was it a good one?" like he used to say to me at the end of a concert. That phrase made me think that he recognized me, that and the fact that he said my name to Kim and Laura when I left the room briefly.

He sees his family all of the time; Kim and two of his younger children live just a few minutes away. And his oldest daughter Debby was visiting just the day before.

He is loved. He is cared for. He is respected. And most of all, he has his dignity. We can all be comforted by that.

Yours very truly, Jimmy L. Webb

SPREAD THE WORD

CALL **DINER CHAT**
THURSDAYS 3:00 P.M. EASTERN
1-425-440-5100 ID CODE: 909005#
Talk to Renae the Waitress Live!

July 2015

Lee Greenwood invites another generation to stand up for America with new book

By Claudia Johnson

It's almost impossible to hear "God Bless the U.S.A." without eyes brimming with tears and a heart bursting with pride.

"What's never stopped surprising – and humbling – me is when the crowd stands up," said Lee Greenwood, who pinned the classic more than three decades ago and has performed it before thousands of audiences.

Greenwood said when he wrote the song at age 41 he felt the same emotions it so clearly continues to evoke in others when they hear it.

"We're proud of our home," he said. "We're proud of our country. We think about how grateful we are to have been born here or become a citizen of this country, and that without being here, we might be someplace that's war-torn or not be able to have your own business or raise your children the way you want to or live your life the way you want to. That emotion rolls out."

"God Bless the U.S.A." has become an anthem for generations of Americans, and Greenwood said he wanted to ensure that future generations experience the unifying strength of the lyrics as well.

"Given the unrest in America today, I felt it was time to give the next generation something to hold and read that tells in a very simple way why it's good to be an American and why we should be proud of it," he said.

Greenwood said the idea of using the lyrics of "God Bless the U.S.A." to create a children's book was inspired by memories of reading to his own children.

"My wife and I would read the same favorite books over and over every night to our kids when they were little," he recalled. "I wanted to write a book that children would be read again and again, and later they'd read it themselves. I wanted it to help them understand the sovereignty of our country."

Greenwood used the lyrics to his beloved song to create Proud to be an American. Released over the 2015 Memorial Day weekend, the inspiring hardback book was the No. 1 bestseller on both Amazon's "Children's Books on the U.S." and "Children's Multicultural Story Books" charts. It features artist Amanda Sekulow's colorful illustrations of scenic farmland and cityscapes throughout the country as well as places like Arlington Cemetery, the Statue of Liberty and other national points of interest.

"The book gives a geography lesson," he observed. "It gives a reason to be a patriot and what it means to be a patriot. There's a lesson on loving your country – the things that represent us, the flag, the eagle – a very good beginning on why it's important to embrace our country that still stands for freedom."

Greenwood pointed out that in the book a gray-haired couple is accompanying a young boy to places and events through which he can experience various aspects of American life, including those involving American military men and women.

"I want parents and grandparents and even teachers to be able to use this book to teach about patriotism," he said. "It is my goal that every school child in the country would have a copy of this at an early age for teachers to use in the classroom."

Included with the book is a free download for a never-before-heard rerecord of the song "God Bless the U.S.A." with the full set of lyrics for all stanzas printed in the back. Greenwood said he wanted to ensure that those who receive Proud to be an American have every opportunity to experience the message of "God Bless the U.S.A."

The Grammy-winning country music star has embarked on a national concert tour this summer, spanning the country from sea to shining sea. For a full list of upcoming tour dates and additional information on his children's book or his new album, "Snapshot: Lee Greenwood," visit www.leegreenwood.com.

July 2015

Asking for prayers as Joey battles cancer again

by Rory Feek

Sunday, Jun 14, 2015

There are few words scarier than the word "cancer". In our culture these days, we usually think that's as bad as it can get. But when you hear a doctor say the words "the cancer's come back"… it's a whole new level of scary.

Last year – this exact time last year actually – Joey went in to surgery for cervical cancer. The doctors felt like they got everything and after a few weeks of healing, she made a full recovery. And now here we are again, faced with a similar situation.

Over the last couple of months, Joey hasn't been feeling well. She had hoped that it was just a stomach virus or an intestinal issue, but after many tests and biopsies, it turns out that it's more than that.

On Thursday, Joey had a port put in for chemotherapy and radiation. She starts the treatments in the coming week.

Here's what the doctors think…

With six weeks of chemo and radiation, the tumor may reduce in size and possibly even go away completely, and if so, she won't have to have any further surgeries. If the chemo and radiation doesn't work like they hope, Joey will be in for an even tougher road ahead.

Here's what Joey and I know…

God has a plan, and His plan is our plan. Each day that we're given is a beautiful gift from Him to us. And while we will pray each day for a miracle, we're gonna live each day as if it's a miracle. And it is.

"Lord, as believers… we trust you completely and pray for your will to be done. Not ours.

But as flesh and bone, husband and wife… we pray for complete and total healing in Joey's body, so we can grow old together, holding hands in rockers on our front porch watching the sun go down.

So that our sweet little baby Indiana can not miss one precious moment with her mama.

Amen. Amen. Amen."

July 2015

Some of our favorite country artists who served in the Armed Forces

To these and all those who are serving and have served...Thank you!

July 2015

Moe & Gene New TV Special...

Could be Steers & Gears, or Cars & Cows, tune it to see!

Look for a NEW Moe Bandy and Gene Watson special produced by Larry Black and Gabriel Communications. It will air as an upcoming Country's Family Reunion special. The show will have footage with Moe and Gene singing together from a concert filmed on May 12th. It will also have footage of both of them sharing their love for cars and bulls. "As of right now….we don't have a title for the show," says Larry Black. However some of the suggestions have been " Cars and Cows", "Steers and Gears", "Moe and Gene", and of course "Gene and Moe".

Here are some behind the scenes photos.

July 2015

The Nashville Brat Pack — Kids of the Country Stars!

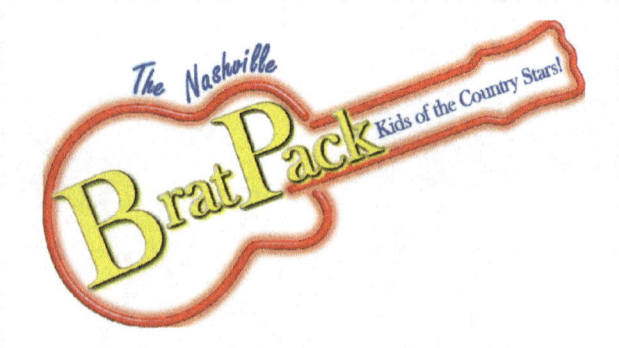

The Brat Pack (or Next Generation: Sons & Daughters of Country Legends) held a concert on Thursday, June 11 at 3rd & Lindsley in Nashville to a sold out crowd. Starting off Fan Fair (CMA Fest) with a bang, the 'kids' did a wonderful job. The artists, left to right were: George Hamilton V, Hawkshaw Hawkins, Jr., Chrystie Wooley, Melissa Luman, Robyn Young, Donnie Winters, Jett Williams, Georgette Jones, Dean Smith, (special guests Mandy Barnett and Chris Golden), and Karen Wheeler. Emcee for the evening was Keith Bilbrey.

Next year's show promises to be bigger and better, so keep reading the CFR News to find out when and where the show will be. Many of the 'kids' are playing shows around the country including a show August 8th in Carthage, Texas inducing Tracy Byrd into the Texas Country Music Hall of Fame. That show will include Hawkshaw Hawkins, Jr., Jett Williams, Georgette Jones, Shelly West, George Hamilton V, Melissa Luman and Robyn Young. Neal McCoy will emcee the event. Keep watching for more news on the Nashville Brat Pack, keeping alive the music of their mothers and fathers.

Photo by James Raymond Pillow

The life of George Jones to become a movie

28 Entertainment and the George Jones estate announced today that they have brought on board writer/producer Alan Wenkus (STRAIGHT OUTTA COMPTON) to fast-track development of their George Jones authorized biopic NO SHOW JONES, which tells the life story of the country music legend. Wenkus is finalizing the script after doing extensive research, conducting dozens of interviews and working closely with George's widow Nancy Jones, who is an executive producer on the film. 28 Entertainment's Brian A. Hoffman along with the original writer, Dennis Baxter, are producing the project.

The film's story is primarily focused on Jones' rise in country music from the 1950's to the 1970's, his legendary struggles with drinking and substance abuse, his turbulent 7-year marriage with singer Tammy Wynette and his marriage to Nancy Jones, who George credited with saving him from his demons.

The producers spent many hours with George in his later years. George Jones died in 2013 at the age of 81.

"We are very excited about moving into the next phase of bringing George's remarkable life to the big screen. We are thrilled that so many talented people have shown a great deal of interest in this project," said 28 Entertainment's Hoffman.

"George Jones literally saved country music when rock and roll almost swallowed it up. He had such an entertaining life. It's got it all. Love, loss, redemption and a lot of whiskey…basically everything George was singing about," added Wenkus.

Wenkus is well known for his extensive research while writing the COMPTON script for director F. Gary Gray.

Known as "No-Show Jones" and "The Possum," George Jones was arguably best-known for ballads like "He Stopped Loving Her Today" and "She Thinks I Still Care" that went beyond heartbreaking by his emotional and moving performances. But George also had a fun side to his personality that would pop up in sunnier songs like "White Lightning" and "The Race Is On."

The amazing success of the George Jones Museum which opened in downtown Nashville on April 23rd of this year has brought new attention to the country music legend that had an unprecedented collection of top 10 hits that spanned 6 decades.

Jones was inducted into the Country Music Hall of Fame in 1992, named a Kennedy Center Honoree in 2008 and in 2012 was presented with a Grammy Lifetime Achievement award. Along with his induction into the Country Music Hall Of Fame he received countless other awards and accolades from ACM, CMA, Country Music Television, and of course, The Grand Ole Opry.

Where is the son of the "King of the Cowboys"?

People have often commented how difficult it must be for Roy "Dusty" Rogers Jr. to stand on stage in his father's shadow. Dusty quickly responds, "As Roy's son, it is NOT my job to stand in my father's shadow; but, it IS my job to lengthen it, and that is what I try to do on stage every day."

As the only natural born son of Roy Rogers and raised by the famous entertainment couple, Roy Rogers and Dale Evans, Dusty has been acting and performing since birth. As a small child, Dusty appeared in his parents' TV series "The Roy Rogers Show" on NBC. He performed with his parents during their summer tours at rodeos and state fairs. As a young man, he appeared in the movies "To Forgive a Thief" for Cathedral Films and "Arizona Bushwhackers" for Paramount Films. He was a disc jockey for WBKC in Chardon, Ohio, and has made numerous radio appearances throughout the United States. Dusty had his own television show on WEWS out of Cleveland, Ohio, "The Roy Rogers Jr. Show." Other TV appearances throughout the years have included the Dennis Hunt Show in Las Vegas, The Tommy Hunter Show in Canada, KMEX Television in Los Angeles, Nashville Network's I-40 Paradise, The John Davidson Show, Entertainment Tonight, The Merv Griffin Show, The Fall Guy, Good Morning America, The TODAY Show, FOX & Friends, and he currently appears weekly on RFD-TV.

Prior to assuming his music career full time, Dusty ran his own construction company. In 1986, he released his biography, "Growing Up With Roy & Dale." In 1989, he became manager for Roy Rogers. Shortly thereafter, Dusty served as President of the Roy Rogers-Dale Evans Museum—a California 501c(3) nonprofit—until its closing in December 2009.

As for entertaining, it was only a matter of time before Dusty followed in the footsteps of his parents and launched his own recording career. He formed his own band, The High Riders, in 1982. He has recorded for Chart Records in Nashville, Teletex Records in Dallas, and Vistone Records in Los Angeles. Dusty's singing has taken him to many concert halls and dinner houses throughout the United States and Canada. In 2003 and 2004, he had the distinct honor of performing at the esteemed Carnegie Hall in New York. From 2003 through 2009, Dusty performed in his very own "Happy Trails Theatre" in Branson, Missouri, located inside the Roy Rogers-Dale Evans Museum. In 2010, Dusty moved his show to the Mickey Gilley Theatre in Branson where he continues to perform his live morning show. This year in 2012, Dusty will be performing in the afternoons at RFD-TV The Theatre, in Branson, MO. During off season in Branson, "Roy Rogers Jr. and The High Riders" take the show on the road to perform at various venues, festivals, and conventions. In the spring of 2008, Dusty's son —Dustin Roy Rogers—joined his father on stage to sing in the tradition of his father and grandfather before him.

Whether appearing by himself or with his band and son, you will experience a wide variety of emotions as you listen to Dusty sing. You will appreciate his transparency as he shares with the audience stories of growing up with his famous parents as only Dusty can do. Dusty continues the legacy of Roy Rogers & Dale Evans by providing quality entertainment for the entire family. An honor of which he is very proud, FAME (Families Advocating Moral Entertainment) named Roy Rogers Jr. their 2009 and 2010 "Western Artist of the Year."

Roy and Dale's memory is kept alive through their son, Roy "Dusty" Rogers Jr., and grandson Dustin Roy Rogers. Their live music show in Branson, Missouri, at the RFD-TV The Theatre, was dedicated to continuing the legacy of Roy Rogers & Dale Evans.

For six seasons, the museum was home to Roy Rogers Jr. and the Highriders until it closed at the end of 2009. The "Roy Rogers Jr. Show" then moved to the Mickey Gilley Theater for two seasons before calling RFD-TV The Theatre home for their last season.

"RFD has been a great home for the show, even Trigger and Bullet call it home," Rogers said. "Patrick Gottsch, (owner of RFD-TV and the theater) has an admiration for the American cowboy, so moving the show was a natural fit."

According to Rogers Jr., getting on the road has become very important.

"We decided to stop waiting for folks to come see us," he said. "Now, we're just going out to see them. It's time to mosey on."

Larry's Country Diner RFD Show Schedule July 2015
These shows have previously aired

JASON CRABB
Saturday, July 4
10:00 p.m. Central
Sunday, July 5
6:00 p.m. Central

DAN MILLER
Saturday, July 11
10:00 p.m. Central
Sunday, July 12
6:00 p.m. Central

TEEA GOANS
Saturday, July 18
10:00 p.m. Central
Sunday, July 19
6:00 p.m. Central

SOUTHERN RAISED
Saturday, July 25
10:00 p.m. Central
Sunday, July 26
6:00 p.m. Central

Country Questions
By Dick Boise, CMH

Send questions to:
Dick Boise, , c/o CFR News,
P.O. Box 201796, Nashville,
TN 37221.

Q. I saw Roy Drusky on one of the Reunion shows and enjoyed his voice. Did he have any number one recordings? And also, where was he born. Thanks.

Beverly Kuhn, NY

A. Thanks for asking, Beverly. He was one of my favorites with his smooth style of singing. I believe he had a number one hit with the song, "Yes, Mr. Peters." It was a duet with the late Jerry Reed's wife, Priscilla Mitchell. I think there was another number one later on, titled, "Long, Long Texas Road." He had many, many hits that landed about the number 3 spot in the charts. He was born in Atlanta, GA on June 22, 1930.

Q. One of our local country stations played an old song by Elton Britt called, "There's A Star Spangled Banner." When was that first recorded? Enjoyed hearing it.

Bill Thomas, VA

A. Elton Britt had a huge amount of radio play on that RCA Victor record in 1942. It was very popular during that period of WWII. He, being a yodeler, was really noted for his song "Chime Bells." Another favorite was "Someday" (You'll Want Me to Want You. Only use older folks recall Elton Britt.

Q. I saw an old TV show that had a pair of brothers that were very funny. Had a name that sounded like Geezer or something. I thought they were very good. Do you have any information about them?

Lonnie Loomis, Toledo, OH

A. I would guess you saw the Geezinslaw Brothers. They were very popular on many TV variety shows in the 70s and 80s. They were from Texas and they were not really brothers. Sam Allred was the spokesman for the duo and he called the "quiet" one, "Son." His real name was Raymond Smith. I saw them many times and enjoyed their funny and clean routing. They began around 1959.

Q. I have listened to T.G. Sheppard for several years and would like to ask what is his name. Someone told me that it is not his real name. Enjoy him very much.

Wanda Davern, Charlotte, NC

A. This fine singer's real name is William Browder, and he was born in Humboldt, TN. His uncle was Opry comedian Rod Brassfield that used to do skits with Minnie Pearl. He has stated that the T.G. can stand for what every you wanted it to. He is married to the fine singer, Kelly Lang and they have just released a CD together. With those two voices, it has to be great!

A Tribute To Ray Price

Rarely in life do we get to honor someone whose singing style ushered in a new way to do it. Ray Price passed away December 16, 2013 and Country's Family Reunion honored Ray's memory by getting together those who knew him best and have a CFR Ray Price Tribute!

$79.80 plus $6.95 s/h

Janie Price, Ray's widow, joined Bill Anderson and a room full of Ray's friends, band members and Country artists to pay tribute to his songs, his style and his life including: Jim Lauderdale, Johnny Bush, David Ball, Wade Hayes, Linda Davis, Ray Pillow, Roy Clark, Jeannie Seely, Gene Watson, T. Graham Brown, Janie Fricke, Darrell McCall, Larry Gatlin, Teea Goans, Moe Bandy, John Conlee, Tracy Lawrence, Curtis Potter, Jan Howard, Johnny Lee, Mo Pitney, Jim Ed Brown, Dean Miller, Buddy Emmons, and Bill Mack.

1-800-820-5405

July 2015

Fan Fair Facts

• The first CMA Music Festival was called Fan Fair in 1972 and brought 5,000 fans to Municipal Auditorium. Roy Acuff, Tom T. Hall, Loretta Lynn, Dolly Parton, Minnie Pearl, Ernest Tubb and others performed.

• The 1974 Fan Fair saw the last performance together of Dolly Parton and Porter Wagoner.

• What is now the Celebrity Softball Tournament began in 1975 as the Fan Fair Softball Tournament.

Joe Bonsal (with the Oakridge Boys), Karen Wheeler & Ranger Doug (Green) playing in the Celebrity Softball game at Fan Fair.

• Fan Fair moved to the Tennessee State Fairgrounds in 1982.

• In 1996, Garth Brooks signed autographs for 23 hours with no breaks!

• Waylon Jennings' final Fan Fair appearance was in 1999.

• In 2001, Fan Fair moves to downtown Nashville.

• Fan Fair became CMA Music Festival in 2004.

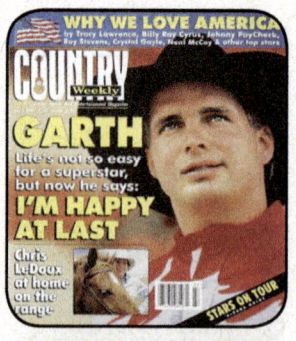

• The now annual Kick-Off Parade and Block Party began in 2005.

• The 2012 festival brought 71,000 fans from all 50 states and 24 countries to Nashville to see 450 artists perform for more than 200 hours of concerts.

Artists who perform at CMA Music Festival do so free of charge. Proceeds from the event benefit Keep the Music Playing, funding school music programs. $7.6 million has been donated to date. Each year more is added to the CMA Festival with attractions such as Fan Fair X.

Update on the REAL Larry's Country Diner

The new Diner is moving along. Slowly, but moving. The plan passed the Planning Commission and is now before the Metro Council for approval. We should get that in July and hopefully be able to break ground in August or September!

After that, we're off and running! They say it will take 8 to 9 months to complete, so it should be ready to open in the spring.

Jared will be happy not to have to mow the property and Larry is so excited to show off the drawings at the recent tapings of the show!

128 CFR NEWS

July 2015

Christmas In July offers for CFR News Subscribers

Special Christmas in July offer! You don't want to miss these four special combo offers only for YOU our subscribers. Just send your order to CFR NEWS or call customer service and order using our special "HOLIDAY" Code for the month of JULY only. Order one combo or all four and receive $20.00 from your order.

CFR NEWS BOOKS includes complete newspaper articles and photos from each year less some advertisements. That is 12 months of monthly newspapers preserved in a beautiful 8 ½ x 11" color book. We are preserving country music for years to come by featuring our country music greats. If you are not a CFR Newspaper subscriber these books are a MUST !!! There are photos and information you will not get anywhere else. Each book retails for $29.95 plus s/h. (Each book has specific months and pages)

THREE BOOK COMBO

CFR NEWS BOOK Year One   (2011-2012 190 pages)

CFR NEWS BOOK Year Two   (2012-2013 208 pages)

CFR NEWS BOOK Year Three (2013-2014 267 pages)

LARRY'S COUNTRY DINER APRONS include the Larry's Country Diner decal right on the front. Just like Larry wears on the show. The Butcher style is longer with an adjusted neck strap. The Waitress style is shorter with Islet lace at the bottom with an adjusted neck strap. Both are hand wash recommended. Press with a warm iron on the reverse side. Butcher Aprons retails for $30.00. Waitress Apron retails for $35.0

LARRY"S COUNTRY DINER TV SHOWS take you back to the beginning with 3 SEASONS of live shows aired on RFD-TV. Starting in 2009. If you love Larry, Keith, Renae the waitress, The Sheriff and our funny Church lady Nadine these TV shows on DVD are a must for your video collection. Each season sells for $59.95

LARRY'S COUNTRY DINER Season 1 Guests include: Bill Anderson, Jim Ed Brown, Jeannie Seely, The Whites, Bobby Bare, Larry Gatlin, T.Graham Brown, Gordon Mote, Charlie McCoy, James Gregory, Ed Bruce, Gene Watson and John Conlee.

LARRY'S COUNTRY DINER Season 2 Guests include: Ray Stevens, Sonny Curtis, Riders In The

Sky, George Hamilton IV, Jimmy Capps & Ronnie Robbins, Time Jumpers, Bill Anderson & Jan Howard, Billy Dean, Mike Snider,

Shelly West, Dan Miller, Moe Bandy, Mandy Barnett, Billy Grammer, Dallas Frazier, Johnny Counterfit.

LARRY'S COUNTRY DINER Season 3 Guests include: Joey & Rory, T.Graham Brown, Buddy Greene & Jeff Taylor, Justin Trevino, Ralph Emery, Jimmy Fortune, Neal

McCoy, Carl Jackson & Larry Cordel,

Con Hunley, Barbara Fairchild, the Grascals, Suzy Bogguss, Aaron Tippin, Dailey & Vincent, Jeannie Seely, Doyle Lawson & Quicksilver

----

Country's Family Reunion Christmas DVD & Marty Robbins Christmas CD will make Christmas in July really feel like Christmas. This 2 DVD CFR Christmas series is the original filmed in 1998 with a Christmas Dinner and many legends who are not with us today. It retails for $49.95. Then we have added Marty Robbins Christmas CD that was released in 1987 which include 10 Christmas songs sung only the way Marty could sing them. Retails for $14.95.

July 2015

COUNTRY LEGENDS PAST AND PRESENT   BY TOM WOOD

JOHNNY RUSSELL

Every July, this grand old country celebrates its independence with festive red, white and blue explosions and patriotic music.

You can always count on grand old country music fans as being among the most fervent defenders of freedom and liberty in the United States of America.

In keeping that red-white-and-blue color scheme, every day can be considered a celebration of the late Grand Ole Opry member (1985) Johnny Russell and his quintessential anthem of a generation.

Yes, Russell's "Rednecks, White Socks and Blue Ribbon Beer" takes a few liberties with this month's patriotic theme, but it still strikes a deep chord with country music fans who continue to burst praise on the 1973 hit that climbed to No. 4 on the Billboard Hot Country Singles chart and was nominated for a Grammy Award.

"Great song about all of us with roots. This is the life that many of us are comfortable with," one person posted in a comment on the YouTube video of "Rednecks, White Socks and Blue Ribbon Beer," which has over 856,000 hits.

Indeed, Johnny Russell was one of the true-blue (make that red, white and true-blue) country legends of the past and present.

He was born in Moorhead, Mississippi, on January 23, 1940, and died in Nashville on July 3, 2001 at age 61 (making for a sad 4th of July holiday that year) of diabetes-related complications that spawned from a lifetime battle with obesity and heart problems.

Just before his death, stars like Garth Brooks, Vince Gill, Roy Clark, Loretta Lynn and others paid tribute to Johnny at a fundraiser to pay for his mounting medical expenses.

Though Johnny achieved success as a singer, he really made his mark on country music as a songwriter. As a tribute to those talents, he was inducted into the Nashville Songwriters Hall of Fame in 2001.

Johnny's lifelong lover of music began at an early age. He grew up listening to the Grand Ole Opry and performers such as Ernest Tubb and Lefty Frizzell. His sharecropper/mechanic father moved the Russell family to Fresno, California, when Johnny was 11 years old, and that's where his career as a singer-songwriter originated.

He started writing songs and performing in talent contests while in high school and soon found his voice. In 1958, the year he graduated from high school, Johnny penned his first recorded hit — "In a Mansion Stands My Love" — for Jim Reeves. It was the flip-side track for the Gentleman's 1960 hit "He'll Have to Go."

Still, it was a good start to a decades-long string of successes for Johnny.

The 1996 book by Ace Collins, The Stories Behind Country Music's All-Time Greatest 100 Songs, recounts the tale of how Johnny "co-wrote" the 1963 chart-topping "Act Naturally" for Buck Owens and the Buckaroos.

In a nutshell, Johnny wrote the song in a two-hour span in 1961 but it was two years before it was recorded. He shopped it around to no avail — until he began writing with Voni Morrison. She thought it would be a natural for Owens, with whom she also had a working relationship, and Johnny agreed to give her a songwriting credit to get it into his hands. The rest, as they say, is history. It was even recorded by the Beatles in 1965.

Other hits soon followed for Johnny, notably "Catfish John" (1972), "The Son of Hickery Holler's Tramp" (1976), and "Butterbeans" (1987) with Little David Wilkins. In 1984, George Strait had a No. 1 hit with "Let's Fall to Pieces Together" written by Johnny, Dickey Lee and Tommy Rocco.

But as great as all those songs were, none stirs the passions of Johnny Russell fans more than "Rednecks, White Socks and Blue Ribbon Beer."

Clearly, it's a song for the ages, one in which we all see a little bit of ourselves.

Author Tom Wood, who writes thrillers and Westerns, is a regular contributor to Country Family Reunion News. Reach him at tomwoodauthor.com

New CD Release from Sammy Kershaw

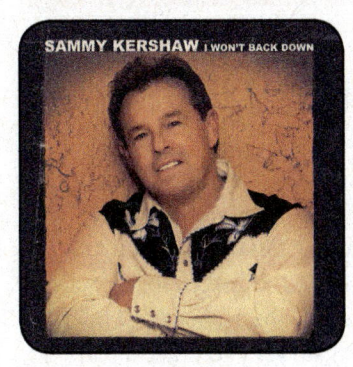

With a legacy that stretches across three decades, encompasses gold and platinum sales, and includes numerous iconic hit singles, Sammy Kershaw is gearing up for the June 9th release of I WON'T BACK DOWN on Cleopatra Records.

Kershaw – a native of Kaplan, Louisiana, first broke onto the Country Music scene in 1991 with the sing-along hit "Cadillac Style." He became one of the most-played male acts of the 1990s with such radio staples as "She Don't Know She's Beautiful," "Love Of My Life," and "I Can't Reach Her Anymore." He has earned Gold and Platinum recognition for such albums as 1991's Don't Go Near The Water, 1993's Haunted Heart, and 1997's Labor Of Love. Kershaw recently achieved his highest peak on the Billboard Country Albums chart in fifteen years with Do You Know Me, his tribute record to longtime friend and hero George Jones.

I WON'T BACK DOWN is a mixture of all things Kershaw, ranging from the romantic yearnings of "Lay Back Down" and "Let's Lay Here Forever" to the heartfelt regret of the haunting "I Had To Give That Up Too." He also ventures into a light-hearted feel on up-tempo cuts like "Fixer Upper" and "Grillin' and Chillin." As is the case with any Kershaw album, you can always count on a cover – and I WON'T BACK DOWN adds two to the mix – "Take A Letter Maria," originally a No. 2 hit for R.B. Greaves on the Billboard Hot 100 in 1969, and the title cut, familiar to Pop listeners as a hit for Tom Petty from 1989.

I WON'T BACK DOWN is the first all-original album from Kershaw in five years, and the singer is excited to bring new music to his fans. "At all of our shows, or wherever go, people keep asking for new music. I'm glad to have a new record coming their way. They've waited a while. Hell, I've waited a while," he said with a grin. "The other aspect of the new album that makes it exciting is getting a chance to work with Tim Yasui and all the staff at Cleopatra Records. Together, we're ready to get it out to the people."

"Sammy Kershaw is one of those voices that you know the moment you hear it. We at Cleopatra are excited to work with an artist of Sammy's caliber," says Cleopatra Records President Tim Yasui.

I WON'T BACK DOWN Track Listing:

1. Take A Letter Maria
2. Lay Back Down
3. Grillin' and Chillin'
4. Fixer Upper
5. Groove
6. I Won't Back Down
7. I Had To Give That Up Too
8. I Can't Wait To Waste A Little Time
9. Send In The Rodeo Clowns
10. Don't Move
11. Why You Wanna Do Me This Way
12. Let's Lay Here Forever

About Sammy Kershaw

Sammy Kershaw is one of the most recognizable voices on Country Radio, with a list of hits that include "Cadillac Style," "Don't Go Near The Water," and "Third Rate Romance." To date, he has amassed 25 Top-40 hits on the Billboard Country Singles chart, as well as three Gold and three Platinum-selling albums. Kershaw has appeared on such television series as Prime Time Country, Hee Haw, and Hannity. In addition to his hit singles, albums, and concert appearances, he is also devoted to his home state of Louisiana, participating in two elections as a candidate for Lieutenant Governor. He has also collaborated with such artists as his hero, George Jones, on the 1993 single "Never Bit A Bullet Like This," as well as fellow performers Joe Diffie and Aaron Tippin for the well-received "Roots & Boots" tour.

Resource Sammy Kershaw online at: www.SammyKershaw.com

July 2015

AUGUST

Larry Black Hospitalized After ATV Accident

Larry Black, host of Larry's Country Diner and creator/producer of Country's Family Reunion, spent a month in the hospital and rehab unit in Billings, Montana following a serious ATV accident on June 18.

He sustained a severe laceration on his left arm requiring surgery, two punctured lungs, torn rotator cuff on his right arm, broken ribs and several breaks to his back which required surgery to place a rod.

Randy Little, owner of PFR/Bootdaddy, and his wife Johnelle, were also in the accident. Randy was hospitalized with a head laceration and concussion. Johnelle was not seriously injured and they are back home in Missouri where Randy continues to recover.

Larry was flown back to Nashville on Tuesday, July 21. He continues to improve and is doing well in his physical therapy

A wife's 'heart-stopping' moment

By Luann Black

The following is my account of the accident with my husband Larry and our friends and Bootdaddy sponsor, Randy and Johnelle Little on June 18th, 2015. Thousands of you have prayed, sent cards, texts, email and Facebook messages with your concerns and well wishes. Because of that, I wanted to personally share with you, our Country Family Reunion and Larry's Country Diner Families, the events of that day.

Many of you know that several years ago we built a place in Montana for our family, 3 sons and wives and our 10 grandchildren. Montana is such a beautiful place, we often tell people, "God lives there!" Every year between our June and August tapings of Larry's Country Diner, we spend our vacation there with friends and family. This year was no different. Randy and Johnelle Little joined us for a few days. The day before they were to fly home, they along with Larry, wanted to drive the "mule" (a 4-seater ATV) and explore the property. I decided to stay at the cabin. About 45 minutes later, Johnelle called asking me to come get them because they had a flat. (That was her smokescreen). So I jumped in the car and headed down the hill. As I topped in the next hill, I saw a medical helicopter, two ambulances, 2 fire engines, sheriff cars and lots of people rushing around. My first thought was someone has had a terrible accident! Then it dawned on me who that someone was. I ran down the hill and the first person I saw was Randy then Johnelle. Johnelle was up and walking around. Randy was on the ground with paramedics tending to him. I kept looking for Larry and when I saw him, he was facedown with the ATV on top of him.

Many of you have in your life that "stop your heart moment", so you know what I am talking about. It is so surreal. I ran to him and he was able to respond to me. It took at least an hour to get him out from under the ATV. In the meantime, Randy was transported via helicopter to Billings Hospital with a severe concussion and broken facial bones. Larry was taken to a small local hospital and when they

August 2015

couldn't get him stable, they knew he had to be sent to Billings also, which was an hour away. Tom Kuntz, our neighbor drove me and Wally Zook, another neighbor drove Johnelle. We got to the ER and I saw him for a moment as they rushed him in. The chaplain walked me out of the room to sit and wait-and wait-and wait. Then she moved me to a private room. I remember thinking that when they do that on TV it usually means the news isn't good. Not long after the trauma doctor came in and said, "You have a very hurt guy in there. When we got him in the ER, he had no pulse or respiration. We had to fight to get him back."

At that point I felt a miracle had happened. He suffered a broken back, broken ribs, two collapsed lungs and severe injury to his left arm. He was on a ventilator for 6 days in ICU. He is slowly getting better after back surgery and surgery on his left arm and they discover a torn rotator cuff on his right arm. They have moved him to rehab where he is working on regaining his strength and stamina.

When you ask Larry what he can remember about the accident, he said he remembers backing up the ATV to see a friend with some horses. The back wheel of the ATV caught a soft edge of a 20 ft. sheer drop off. He and Randy looked at each other and over they went. He remembers hearing the sound of horses galloping and bones cracking. Then no more memory of what happened after that.

Two days ago the trauma doctor came to see him and Larry said, "I know what people are telling me, but can you tell me what condition I was in when I made it to the ER?" The doctor related the same information to me that had been told to me in that room. Then the doctor revealed another piece of the miracle. She said, "In the field-at the accident scene or during medical transport-when someone has suffered blunt chest trauma, with the vital signs Larry had, they would "call it" and abort transport. Injuries too severe. That day the communication system between the ambulance and the ER malfunctioned and they couldn't receive any information on the patient being transported. So the ambulance kept coming. Gives me chills to think about it. I really feel Larry's guardian angel was carrying out God's orders to scramble that communication.

During this time, I have been so grateful to our 3 sons, Ian, Adam and Jared as they have tagged teamed each other to be with me and their dad. My sister, Carol and brother-in-law, Bill, who immediately flew in to be with us. Also, very grateful to Dorathy and Richard Pippin who have become dear Montana friends. They are the kind of friends you can count on. To our neighbors, Wally Zook and Tom Kuntz. Also, Renea, Paula and our office staff for holding down the fort. Very grateful to all the EMTs, ER Staff in both hospitals. Thanks for all you did to save Larry's life! Also, thanks for taking such good care of Randy and Johnelle. And to Brad Edwards, thank you for calling 911!

So, to all of you dear fans and dear friends-Thanks again for your prayers and continued prayers for Larry, Randy, and Johnelle for their complete recovery.

Remember earlier I said that we always say that Montana is so beautiful that "God lives there"?...... I am so grateful he was home that day!

P.S. I thought I would share with you the saying that Larry has framed right next to his desk. It will give you a glimpse into the main that he is.

"Life is not a journey to the grave with the intention of arriving safely in a body pretty and well-preserved body-but rather to skid in broadside-thoroughly used up-totally workout and proclaiming, "Wow, what a ride!"

Country Stars Sharing Recipes for Happiness

By Sasha Kay Dunavant

Country songs have a way into our hearts. The stars that perform them are good for the soul. When we see them we light up. We know every word to every song, and we know just the right song to create the ambiance for every special occasion. Just as a song can take us back, cooking can traverse time as well, taking us back to our grandparents' table, remembering how "mama made it" or how holidays "used to be."

Food connects people through generation and congregation. Recipes are like lyrics to a song. They have to be just right and measured with love. Like a taste for good music, legendary country artists enjoy a taste for great cuisine. It turns out that some stars have taken action to showcase their passion for food.

Tammy Wynette

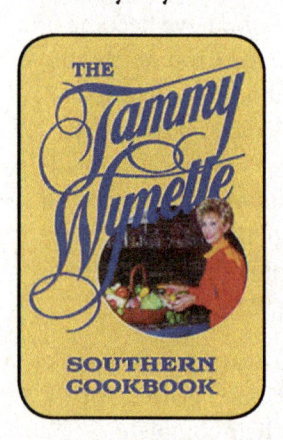

When The First Lady of Country Music published The Tammy Wynette Southern Cookbook in 1990, the late singer highlighted the specific brand of Mississippi-style, Southern cooking she grew up eating on a sharecropping farm in Itawamba County, Miss. Wynette shared her family favorites, usually prepared by herself and her family from memory. Wynette wrote about how she developed a love for cooking as a child, which kept her from being forced to work in the cotton fields. She diligently provided detailed recipes and the history behind each particularly special meal. Two recipes that seem to be a little different from cookie-cutter country cooking are the "Mississippi- Style Stuffed Bell Peppers" and "Cornmeal- Fried Potatoes." In her Southern Cookbook, she also shares her grandmother's recipes and her fondest memories of being with her mother and grandmother in the kitchen with the scent of Fried Apple Pie in the air.

Dolly Parton

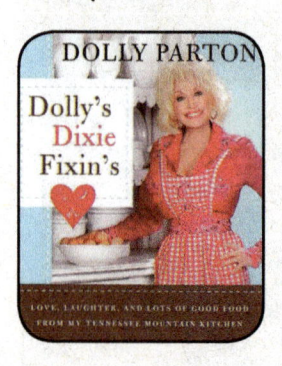

Dolly Parton shared more than 150 of her favorite recipes in the 2006 cookbook, Dolly's Dixie Fixin's, Love Laughter and Lots of Good Food from My Tennessee Mountain Home, which is filled with family dishes, pictures and some of Dolly's most treasured memories of growing up as the fourth of 12 children. The Parton family table may not have included a great variety or quantity of food, but the beloved performer remembers and shares the kinds of recipes her family savored from Fried Taters to Salmon Patties, and Bread and Butter Pickles to Left-handed Biscuits and Gravy. The cookbook also contains some of the crowd-pleasing favorite recipes – like Garlic Cheese Biscuits, Creamy Vegetable Soup – from the menu at Parton's famous dinner and entertainment venue, The Dixie Stampede in Pigeon Forge, Tenn.

The deprivation of education and rampant illiteracy was the unfortunate reality of many Mountaineers. In fact, Parton's own father could not read nor write. With this in mind, she donated all cookbook proceeds to a charitable organization called" Imagination Library," which she established in 1996 to promote the importance of reading and creative thinking in the minds of children. It's clear that the recipe for Parton's charitable project calls for a hard-working mountaineer type nature and an unbelievable amount of heart.

These are only a few of the country stars who, like the rest of us, love food, and have found an entertaining way to share the passion with their fans.

Everyone knows church folk like to cook, and most have their own cookbook. Send me your church cookbook recipe, who submitted it, along with the name of your church and each month I'll pull a recipe from it and feature it here!

August 2015

Nadine's Corner

Everyone knows church folk like to cook, and most have their own cookbook. Send me your church cookbook and each month I'll pull a recipe from it and feature it here!

Gladys Maynard's FUDGE PIE

1 cup sugar
1/4 cup cocoa
1/4 cup flour
2 eggs
1 stick butter
1 tsp vanilla
dash of salt
1 unbaked pie shell

Melt butter, stir in sugar, cocoa, flour and salt. Add slightly beaten eggs and vanilla. Pour in unbaked pie shell and bake at 325 degrees for 30 minutes.

For something a little different, add a dash of cayenne pepper. You'd be surprised at the flavor it adds.

Serve warm with a little ice cream!

Nadine!

The Best of Nadine DVD	$29.95
Nadine's 101 Favorite Church Signs Book	$12.95
Nadine Nadine! Comedy CD	$14.95
Nadine - Out to Sea CD	$14.95
Nadine Coffee Mug	$12.95
Dessert is like Heaven Cookbook	$24.95
Nadine Dessert Glass	$19.95

800-820-5405
P.O. Box 210796, Nashville, TN 37221

add $6.95 s/h

Nadine, the church lady

YOU HAVE TO FACE THE MUSIC BEFORE YOU CAN LEAD THE BAND

August 2015

Outpouring of kindness overwhelming & appreciated

By Johnelle Little

Larry Black, Randy Little, and I were enjoying the great outdoors when "the Accident" occurred. The RTV took a tumble down a steep embankment, knocking unconscious both Larry and Randy. Luckily, horseback riders saw the accident and immediately called 911. Within minutes emergency responders were swarming over the scene. Ambulances, a fire truck, a helicopter, and various other patrolmen, sheriff, fire and police chiefs were on the scene.

Randy was airlifted to Billings, MT and Larry and I were transported to the local hospital. Larry was then transported on to Billings by ambulance. My injuries were minor. Wonderful people made sure that Luann and I arrived in Billings. The outpouring of kindness was and continues to be overwhelming.

The following 48 hours became a balancing act of trying to stabilize both Larry and Randy and assess their injuries. Larry sustained a broken back, 3 broken ribs, a broken arm, and a two punctured lungs. Randy sustained a severe concussion, lacerations of the face, 4 cracks to the cheekbone, and a broken finger.

Randy spent 5 days in the hospital, then returned home to recuperate, where he is steadily improving. Larry has remained in Billings in a rehabilitation program as he recovers from his injuries.

Larry, Randy, and I wish to thank everyone for their overwhelming expressions of love, prayers, cards, texts, emails, and phone calls. Recovery will continue, but the shows will go on.

COUNTRY WEEKLY MAGAZINE sends Larry Get-Well Wishes. There were get-well wishes in a recent issue of Country Weekly Magazine. Thanks goes to them!

Larry's Country Diner RFD Show Schedule August 2015

Previously Aired 
VINCE GILL & PAUL FRANKLIN
Saturday, Aug. 1
10:00 p.m. Central
Sunday, Aug. 2
6:00 p.m. Central

Previously Aired 
SYLVIA
Saturday, Aug. 8
10:00 p.m. Central
Sunday, Aug. 9
6:00 p.m. Central

NEW SHOW 
JAN HOWARD
Saturday, Aug. 15
10:00 p.m. Central
Sunday, Aug. 16
6:00 p.m. Central

NEW SHOW 
RIDERS IN THE SKY
Saturday, Aug. 22
10:00 p.m. Central
Sunday, Aug. 23
6:00 p.m. Central

NEW SHOW 
DAILEY & VINCENT
Saturday, Aug. 29
10:00 p.m. Central
Sunday, Aug. 30
6:00 p.m. Central

August 2015

Dale Watson, an authentic honky tonk artist

Dale Watson is a staunch old-style honky tonk singer who has positioned himself as a tattooed, independent outsider who is only interested in recording authentic country music. He has earned a fervently loyal fan base and has been championed by numerous critics, but due to sticking to his guns about his music, he hasn't become a major star.

Watson was born in Alabama in 1962 but spent his teenage years near Houston, thinking of Texas as his true home state. His father and brother were both musical, and Dale began writing his own songs at age 12, making his first recording two years later. He spent seven years following high school playing local clubs and honky tonks. He moved to Los Angeles in 1988 on the advice of Rosie Flores and soon joined the house band at North Hollywood's now-legendary alt-country venue the Palomino Club. He recorded two singles for Curb in 1990, "One Tear at a Time" and "You Pour It On," and appeared on the third volume of the compilation series *A Town South of Bakersfield* in 1992. He moved to Nashville not long after and spent some time writing songs for the Gary Morris publishing company.

Watson didn't find commercial country much to his liking, and he relocated to the more progressive-minded scene in Austin, Texas, where he formed a backing band called the Lone Stars. He was signed with Hightone Records and released his debut album, Cheatin' Heart Attack, in 1995

In 2000, Watson's fiancée was killed in an automobile accident; devastated, he attempted to drown his sorrows in booze and drugs and nearly died of an overdose shortly after Christmas. He wound up checking himself into a mental institution to recover and re-emerged later in 2001 with the deeply sorrowful tribute Every Song I Write Is for You.

A couple of lower-key releases followed, the holiday album Christmas in Texas (2001) and Live in London, England (2002). In 2004, with his heart still on his sleeve but possessing a thicker skin, Watson released Dreamland.

Watson was inducted into the Austin Music Hall of Fame in 2005, but took a break from music for most of the year, moving to Maryland in order to spend more time with his daughters. He was back playing gigs in Austin by 2006, and a documentary on Watson, Crazy Again. Directed by Zalman King (who at one time hoped to star Watson in a drama about country music that was never produced), the film charted Watson's mental breakdown following the death of his fiancée.

In 2014 he appeared as a guest on the Honky Tonk Reunion series for Country's Family Reunion singing "Tonight The Bottle Let Me Down."

Watson and the Lone Stars continued to deliver their honky tonk sound on another Red House release, Call Me Insane, in 2015.

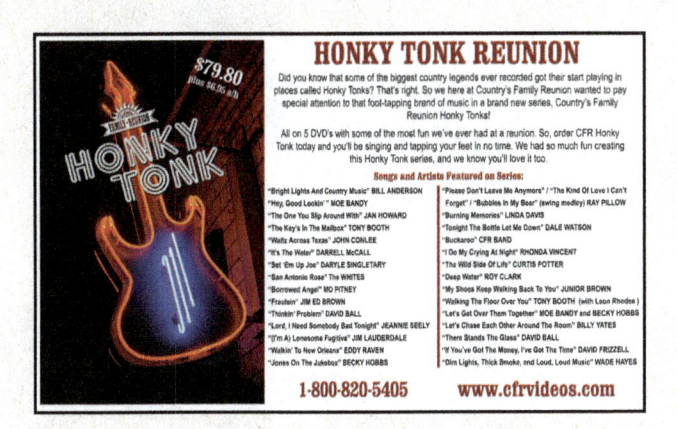

August 2015

COUNTRY'S FAMILY REUNION SCRAPBOOK: DON WINTER

Don and wife, Joyce

DON WINTERS

Don playing the drum with Marty

Don as a Beatle

Don and Marty

Don, Marty, Don's sons Dennis & Donnie

Don and wife, Joyce

Don, Carl Perkins and Donnie

Don & Joyce at Donnie's wedding to Paula

Don Winters was Marty Robbins' road manager, featured singer, best friend for over 20 years.

August 2015

Recollections of Early Days of Elvis, Col. Parker and Life on the Road Captured in New Book

By Claudia Johnson

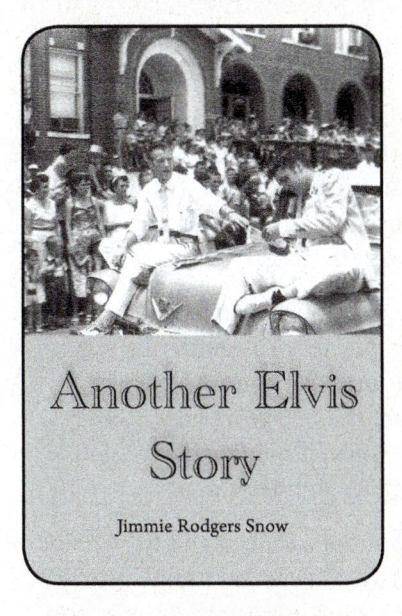

Before Elvis Presley was the King of Rock 'n' Roll, he was an unknown boy from the hills of North Mississippi whose voice and stage presence caught the attention of two men who became music industry legends themselves. One was Col. Tom Parker, who would later be Presley's controversial manager. The other was singer, songwriter and Grand Ole Opry star Hank Snow.

Parker and Snow formed a partnership, Hank Snow Enterprises/Jamboree Attractions, in 1955 that staged traveling shows across the country – something Snow had been doing most of his career already. One of those headliners was Hank Snow's son, Jimmie Rodgers Snow, whose new book, Another Elvis Story, recalls life on the road in Presley's pink Cadillac before both young men's lives took dramatic, divergent turns.

"The first time I saw Elvis Presley perform was Feb. 13, 1955, at the Fair Park Coliseum in Lubbock, Texas," Snow said, who at the time was under contract with RCA as a recording artist. "Elvis had a serious magnetism about him, such as I had never seen in a performer, and I had been raised in the entertainment business."

Though Presley was under other management, he and his accompanying musicians Scotty Moore and Bill Black, soon joined Hank Snow Enterprises/Jamboree Attractions as a special attraction. Presley was 20 and Jimmie Snow was 19, so it was natural the two would become friends, especially since they, as younger performers, traveled together.

"Once we were in Florida in his pink Cadillac," Snow said. "I was in the front seat, and suddenly Elvis swung off the road, ran into a store and came out with a bucket of paint. He then proceeded to paint his name on the doors on each side of his car."

Snow, now 79, has a photo of Presley and himself sitting on the hood of the Cadillac, the passenger door open and the hand-lettered "Elvis" clearly visible. Presley's presence brought another dimension of excitement to an all-star lineup that included some of the most popular acts of the 1950s, such as Faron Young, Bill Haley and his Comets, Mother Maybelle, the Carter Sisters, Slim Whitman, the Duke of Paducah and a comedian named Andy Griffith.

"You haven't lived until you've been chased by a couple of hundred screaming women across the football field, holding your instruments in your hands!" Snow laughed. "Because of the excitement and frenzy of the crowd, if they couldn't get Elvis, they would choose one of the other members of the cast, which meant any of the rest of us. I would jokingly say that I ran a little slower than the rest."

August 2015

Throughout the Another Elvis Story, Snow shares photographs from his and his father's personal albums and collections as well as still shots pulled from the hundreds of hours of home movies shot by his family. He's included advertisements and promotional materials from some of the early Presley tours and a complete copy of the original Parker/Snow business agreement. He also discusses in depth the infamous act of deception by Parker toward Presley's parents and Parker's betrayal of Hank Snow that so fatefully intertwined Presley's life with Parker's.

"It's very interesting how Tom Parker was able to manipulate the contract signings, making him the exclusive manager of Elvis Presley, excluding my father from his 50 percent of Elvis Presley," Snow said. "Can you imagine how much money that 50 percent would've generated for my father through the years of superstar Elvis Presley? I guess we'll never know."

Snow tells the story of his last visit with Presley at Graceland for 10 days in January 1958 and the conversation that changed their paths.

"I told him that when I get home, I'd be leaving my career and going into full time ministry," Snow said. "Elvis looked at me questioningly for a number of seconds, and then finally he said, 'Well, I think that's wonderful Jimmie, and I wish you the very best.' I could tell that he really meant that too. He took me to the airport, and we said goodbye. That was the last time I saw Elvis Presley. I went in one direction and he another."

Snow describes his transition in walking away from recording, television appearances and public performances to preaching the gospel.

"My conflict was why couldn't I stay in show business where I had influence and share Jesus with people?" he explained. "I reasoned that I would surely have more influence than if I gave up my career? I would also be making a lot of money that would give me some kind of stability in my life, and I could use it to help the Christian cause."

Snow did, of course, leave secular music for ministry. For nearly a quarter of a century he was the host of Grand Ole Gospel Time at the Grand Ole Opry, and for more than 30 years he pastored Nashville's Evangel Temple, providing a familiar place of worship for many country stars.

This first-hand account of a crucial and transitional period in the lives of two singers and in the history of American music is anything but Another Elvis Story.

For information on purchasing Another Elvis Story, visit facebook.com/anotherelvisstory.

August 2015

Ronnie McDowell: following his dream

By Claudia Johnson

There's only one explanation for the breadth and diversity of Ronnie McDowell's artistic talent and professional success.

"I'm just very blessed," he said simply.

He's written dozens of songs recorded by artists of multiple genres. He's charted more than 30 Top 40 hits on the Billboard country music charts. Two of his singles, "Older Women" and "You're Gonna Ruin My Bad Reputation," reached Number One on the country charts, while eleven more reached Top Ten. An artist since childhood, McDowell's secondary career as a painter has proven commercially successful, recently attracting the attention of Disney Fine Arts and spawning a five-year contract for the sale of his work worldwide. McDowell readily admits that even he is amazed as he looks back at his life from the vantage point of a 65-year-old.

"Not only did I get to do Ronnie McDowell's thing, I got to be Elvis Presley," McDowell observed. "If someone had told me that when I was a little boy, that I would be Elvis Presley's voice in the movies I wouldn't have believed it."

One of 11 children, he grew up in a small town near Nashville with no particular connection to the world of entertainment and art he now inhabits. Yet, he said he can pinpoint foreshadowing moments from his happy, simple 1950s childhood.

"In 1953-1954 every day my ear would be glued to a great big Philco radio my mother had," he said. "Hank Williams had just passed away, and they were wearing his records out. I was listening to all kinds of music already, but I knew in 1954 when my sister, Linda Sue, brought a record home called 'That's All Right, Mama,' that it was different."

All five McDowell sisters watched when Presley made his first television appearance on The Dorsey Brothers Stage Show in February 1956. McDowell, who was six years old, remembers the gaggle of screaming, jumping, overly-excited sisters, but he also recalls the impact it had on him.

"It was like somebody poured a bucket of water over me," McDowell said. "I knew for absolute certainty, without a doubt, that was what I wanted to do."

It was more than a decade later that McDowell first performed before an audience when he and two friends entered a variety show onboard the U.S.S. Hancock during his Vietnam War Naval service. Just before he stepped onto the makeshift stage to sing "When My Blue Moon Turns to Gold Again," an old man told McDowell that Presley had performed in the same spot in April 1956 during a live broadcast of the Milton Berle Show.

"I feel like Elvis and I have always been crossing paths," he said.

As McDowell matured his "burning passion, drive and initiative" was fueled by admiration for his musical idols like Presley, Williams, George Jones and Conway Twitty and by his growing recognition of their genius. McDowell's own innate talent for songwriting, which he calls his "first love," and for the visual arts – drawing and painting – provided an outlet for his creativity and gave dimension to his career. However, it is largely because of Presley that McDowell has shared his magnificent voice for nearly four decades.

August 2015

When Presley died in 1977, McDowell released an original song he quickly penned in Presley's honor, "The King Is Gone," that has since sold more than 5 million copies. McDowell was the obvious choice to record the 36-tune soundtrack for the television movie, "Elvis," produced by Dick Clark, who became a lifelong friend. He was also the singing voice for a television movie "Elvis and Me," an ABC series titled "Elvis" and a 1997 Showtime special "Elvis Meets Nixon."

Fittingly, one of McDowell's most popular and best-selling prints is from his painting "Reflection of a King," which depicts Presley as a small boy peering into a mirror reflecting an image of Presley performing. McDowell surprised his friend and avowed Elvis fan Dolly Parton with a painting, "Last Night I Dreamed about Elvis," of her and Presley picnicking in a Smoky Mountain meadow. He impressed Disney officials with "Immortal Icons," a painting that shows Presley teaching Micky Mouse to dance on The Ed Sullivan Show.

Along with throngs of other fans, McDowell stood for hours in the Memphis heat to pay his respects when Presley's body lay in state at Graceland, only to be among the thousands sent away when the long waiting line was abruptly closed. He has since become friends with Priscilla Presley and others close to Presley. In an unexpected turn, in 1994 Presley's friend and guitarist, Scotty Moore, acknowledged McDowell's respect for Presley with an irreplaceable gift that is McDowell's most prized possession.

Moore had been present in Las Vegas in 1956 when a jeweler presented Presley with a new custom-made watch. The performer took off the Elgin he was wearing and gave it to Moore.

"Scotty took that watch home and put it in a drawer," McDowell said. "On my birthday when I turned 44 years old, Scotty said 'hey, I got you a gift,' and it was that watch. I have three pictures of Elvis wearing it. It's the same watch Elvis wore on the Dorsey show I watched with my sisters in 1956."

McDowell said he finds it "funny" sometimes how life works out.

"I have a sister who's 80, and she'll ask me 'Do you know how blessed you are to get to do the things you only dreamed of when you were a little boy?'" McDowell said, adding, "It always makes mE stop and realize how true that is."

A new autobiography is in the works and should be ready by Christmas. An article will ge in the CFR NEWS to announce when it becomes available.

Photo by Claudia Johnson

Daryle Singletary releases album *There's Still a Little Country Left*

Daryle Singletary sounds like a man on a mission in his latest album, There's Still a Little Country Left, which drops nationwide in music stores and online July 28th. The album is his first release since 2009's Rockin' in the Country. With his latest album, Daryle remains true to his roots, which he describes as "hardcore country traditionalist."

"When I moved to Nashville in 1990, I left Georgia telling my Daddy, 'I want to make my living in country music,'" Daryle says. For him, country music means the kind of traditional country he grew up listening to. Each selection on There's Still A Little Country Left harkens back to Country at its core. Daryle takes a no-holds-barred approach to the subject as well, underscoring his theme with the album's opening number, "Get Out of My Country."

Hailing from rural Georgia, Daryle grew up listening to Keith Whitley and Randy Travis, his all-time favorite. It was a relationship that would grow over the years, culminating with Daryle's 1995 Giant Records release Daryle Singletary, an album Travis co-produced. That album led to several hit singles, including "Too Much Fun" and "I Let her Lie." Daryle's love for hardcore country is as visible now as it was in 1995, and his passion for songwriting shows. Daryle says his album was written for his fans.

"My fans are not fans of the bro-country movement, which doesn't bother me a bit," he says. "They're people who like it real, and that's what I give them."

Fan's don't have to wait too much longer, either. There's Still a Little Country Left hit music stores July 28.

COUNTRY LEGENDS PAST AND PRESENT   BY TOM WOOD

Bob Luman

To paraphrase his first Top 10 hit, let's think about Luman.

Bob Luman scored his first major hit with "Let's Think About Livin'" and he was so talented that he could have wound up playing for a professional baseball club. Instead, he wound up playing in the world's most exclusive country club, the Grand Ole Opry.

Only the best of the best make that team's lineup.

Bob Luman joined the Opry in 1965 and is a member of both the Rockabilly Hall of Fame, where he cut his teeth in the music business, and the Texas Country Music Hall of Fame (2007).

Born in Blackjack, Texas, on April 15, 1937, Robert Glynn Luman was raised in Nacogdoches, and received his first guitar at age 13 from his father, Joe, who played the fiddle, harmonica and guitar.

But Luman was just as adept with a baseball during those formative years, quickly making a name for himself on the diamond at Kilgore High School in the mid-1950s.

The year 1955 proved to be a pivotal one for the 18-year-old Luman, who was trying to decide on whether to pursue a career in sports or music after high school.

Two things happened that year. Several baseball teams liked his abilities and the Pittsburgh Pirates gave him a tryout and negotiations were under way — and then he saw Elvis.

Bob's life course was set, and altered.

Up to that point, Bob had patterned his musical sound after two of his country heroes, Lefty Frizzell and Webb Pierce. A 1999 article posted at Rockabillyhall.com recounts an interview Luman gave about seeing Elvis for the first time and the impact it had on him.

"This cat came out in red pants and a green coat and a pink shirt and socks, and he had this sneer on his face and he stood behind the mike for five minutes, I'll bet, before he made a move. Then he hit the guitar a lick, and he broke two strings. Hell, I'd been playing ten years, and I hadn't broken a total of two strings. So there he was, these two strings dangling, and he hadn't done anything except break these strings yet, and these high school girls were screaming and fainting and running up to the stage, and then he started to move his hips real slow like he had a thing for his guitar. He made chills run up your back, man, like when your hair starts grabbing at your collar. For the next nine days he played one-nighters around Kilgore, and after school every day me and my girl would get in the car and go wherever he was playing that night. That's the last time I tried to sing like Webb Pierce or Lefty Frizzell."

Rockabilly — considered a blend of the country and rock and roll sounds with a little R&B and Western swing — was perfect for Luman and his rip-it vocal style.

Bob won a 1956 talent contest that landed him a television spot on the Louisiana Hayride. That led to an appearance on the Town Hall Party in Los Angeles and his good looks and strong voice earned him a small, but featured role in the 1957 movie Carnival Rock with David Houston.

He recorded "Let's Think About Livin'" in 1959 and it was released in 1960 — while he was in the U.S. Army, climbing to No. 7 on the Billboard charts. Following his military discharge in 1962, he moved to Nashville, putting the Rockabilly sound mostly in the rearview mirror. He and his new bride Barbara soon moved to a Hendersonville home along Old Hickory Lake, where their neighbors included Johnny and June Carter Cash and Roy Orbison.

The early 1970s were the good times for Bob, scoring Top 10 hits with 1972's "When You Say Love" (No. 6) and "Lonely Women Make Good Lovers" (No. 4), followed by a pair of No. 7's in 1973 with "Neither One of Us" and "Still Loving You" as well as several other Top 100 hits.

Health problems began to crop up, suffering a heart attack in 1975. He recovered—and even had one last Top 15 hit with "The Pay Phone" in 1977—but contracted pneumonia and died on Dec. 27, 1978 at the age of 41. Johnny Cash sang at his funeral and Ralph Emery gave the eulogy.

August 2015

Oak Ridge Boys honored for work against PTSD

When country music supergroup the Oak Ridge Boys were preparing to launch the 25th annual Christmas Night Out tour, they wanted to add a little something extra--a one-night only television special honoring the work of The American Legion and its efforts to aid veterans suffering from post-traumatic stress disorder. The last thing the Oak Ridge Boys had on their minds was receiving a major television award for A Salute to Christmas.

"PTSD can be a debilitating disease for service members returning home, but it can be treated," said Oak Ridge Boys singer Duane Allen. "The American Legion's work with veterans facing PTSD is among some of the most important in the country, and we wanted to help them support that work with the kickoff of our Christmas Night Out tour."

Working with the American Legion also led to a number of PSAs for the legion, which aired on multiple national and cable networks, as well as the one-hour Christmas special which aired in markets across the U.S. A Salute To Christmas received a 2015 Telly Award for outstanding television production.

Established in 1979, the Telly Awards are the premier award honoring outstanding local, regional, and cable TV commercials and programs, video and film productions, and web commercials, videos, and films. Showcasing the best work of the most respected agencies, production companies, television stations, and cable operators, the Telly Award is a highly respected international competition, receiving more than 12,000 annually from around the world.

In addition to the Oak Ridge Boys, A Salute to Christmas featured Larry Gatlin and the Gatlin Brothers, Martin Family Circus, and Mary Sarah. The special was produced by Tracy Trost of Targeting Concepts Marketing, of Tulsa, OK. Trost was surprised by the Telly Award.

"This project is very special because the heart of it is to bring attention to the needs of our veterans. For me personally, being able to work so closely with the Oak Ridge Boys has been a highlight in my career," said Trost. "Winning this award just shows how excellent they and The American Legion are. I am honored to be a part."

Allen agreed with Trost, and added that any recognition the Christmas special garners helps call attention to a good cause.

"If this award can help us tell the story of the men and women suffering with PTSD, and of the help that The American Legion is providing to them, that's a great thing. We're honored to have received this award, but we're more honored that we got to be a part of helping those who've given so much to our country already," Allen said.

The Telly Award for A Salute to Christmas is just one of the accolades received by the Oak Ridge Boys this year. In addition, the Oak Ridge Boys released a critically acclaimed album of new gospel recordings, "Rock of Ages", which broke the Top 10 on Billboard's Christian Albums chart. Earlier this year, the Country Music Hall of Fame announced that the Oak Ridge Boys will be inducted into the hall of fame in October.

The Nashville Brat Pack
Kids of the Country Stars!

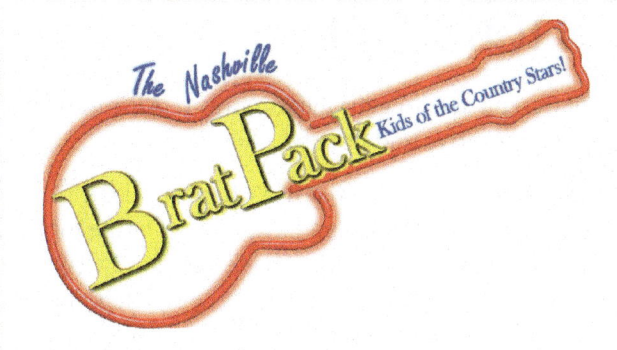

By Lisa Sutton, Daughter of Lynn Anderson and Glenn Sutton

My Dad, Glenn Sutton, wrote many great songs and produced hit records for folks like Jerry Lee Lewis, Bob Luman and Tammy Wynette. He was dubbed "The Merry Prankster" and his antics are legendary. He married my Mother, Lynn Anderson in '68, I came along in '70 and Mom was winning her Grammy by the summer of '71. With songs like "Rose Garden," "Milwaukee" & "I Don't Wanna Play House" between them, they were riding a major wave and were one of the "it" couples in the business.

Being the kid of a star can be difficult and a little lonely. Mostly, Mom was on the road and Dad was on Music Row. Still, they stayed married 10 years, creating some of the biggest selling country records of that decade. None of this really phased me as a kid. I got to show horses, attend concerts and ride on airplanes. It was cool beans when you're 9!

I remember hanging around back stage at Mom's shows, catching glimpses of her doing interviews & getting into wardrobe. I always liked making the trip with her from the dressing room to the stage. On those walks you really felt how famous she was! It was exciting! People staring, concert staff and crew scurrying aside, making room for her to pass. Sequins and hair pieces rustling through dark, gear lined hallways to then emerge into the hot spotlight in front of 1000s of people. I'd sit down behind the curtain, my feet dangling from the edge of the stage, catching smiles from the band or a wink from Mom. Watching all those faces in the audience staring at her. It was impressive! Almost like a dream really.

I couldn't get past the idea that the greatest family gathering I've had lately was my father's funeral. His death was unexpected and I was devastated and that's when my family came around me. I just remember a great gathering of every single person in my family and all this love and mutual respect. It changed my life and it changed my family. I realized all families go through tumultuous times. Maybe if you've got a famous person in your family, the highs seems a little more high and, well, the lows are public record. That might be a little tough on us kids. But I think it also made me a little tougher as a woman.

For all the success my family has achieved, it's because they devoted a massive amount of their time to their fans, their careers and this industry. But I looked back over pictures through the years to prepare for this article and I see both of my parents, even years after divorcing, at every big event in my life. Graduations, Horse Shows, Business Adventures, Broken Hearts! Even though their lives had taken different directions, they came back together, every time, for me. I'm so thankful and proud now of the characters & talent in my family. I'm a lucky girl who gets to benefit from the blood, sweat & tears my family devoted to the music business. But I really hope I'm a better person for all the time they devoted to raising me.

August 2015

Update on Joey's condition

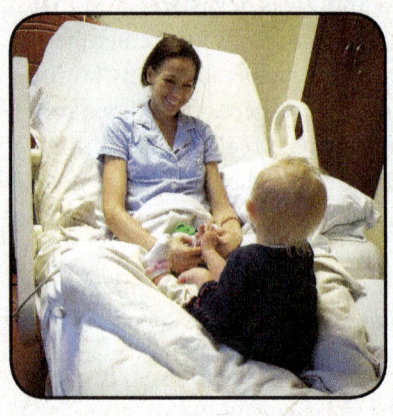

Rory posted this on the night of Joey's surgery, July 10.

"The surgery took almost ten hours, so we didn't get to talk to the doctor or see Joey until after 10 pm last night. When Joey's surgeon finally came out into the waiting room and sat down with us, he was so kind and wonderful and he talked with us for a long time. He told us that everything had gone well in the surgery and that he believes that they were able to get all of the main tumor removed, along with two infected lymph nodes and other places that were affected. They also did intra-operative radiation on some areas where they weren't able to get a clear margin. All-in-all, he was very positive and hopeful. So we are too.

"Joey is going to be in recovery here at CTCA for 7 to 10 days, and then we'll be able to go home for a week or two, then we'll come back here for 5 weeks of chemo and radiation. Once that is completed, Joey will start a more aggressive form of chemotherapy here that will last for 18 weeks. And during that phase, she's going to be given the opportunity to look more like our sweet little Indiana. She's gonna lose all of her pretty dark hair."

On Thursday, July 16, Rory posted a photo of Indy and said, "Grocery shopping with Papa. Mommy might get out of the hospital today and get to stay in the hotel with us." Then they will be home for a few weeks before heading back for chemo treatments.

We continue to pray for a full recovery.

Diner closer to being real

Groundbreaking for the new Larry's Country Diner will be held in August 2015 and construction should start shortly after.

The Metro Nashville Council held the public hearing (below) on July 7 and then the final reading and passing of the bill allowing the diner to move forward was on July 21.

Following the final reading and approval, permits were applied for.

146

August 2015

Kristofferson, Pride, Lauderdale & Halseys get national honor

Charley Pride

Kris Kristofferson

Jim Lauderdale

Sherman Halsey & Jim Halsey

The National Music Council continued its 75th Anniversary Celebrations by bringing its Annual American Eagle Awards presentation to Nashville, Tennessee, for the very first time on July 11, 2015. The highly prestigious Eagle Awards are presented each year in national celebration of an individual's or an organization's long term contribution to America's musical culture and heritage. This year, music legends Kris Kristofferson, Charley Pride and Jim Lauderdale were honored, along with music management icon Jim Halsey and country music producer/director Sherman Halsey. A special award was presented to the Nashville Mayor's Office, Metro Nashville Public Schools, and Country Music Association & Country Music Foundation, for the creation and support of the Music Makes Us arts education initiative.

Dr. David Sanders, director of the National Music Council, notes that the individual recipients are being honored "not just for the incredible gifts they have given generations of music lovers throughout the world with their creative output, but also for their dedication to encouraging young musicians and potential musicians through their great support and commitment to music education."

Past American Eagle Award recipients include Quincy Jones, Herbie Hancock, Clive Davis, Van Cliburn, Benny Goodman, Lionel Hampton, Dizzy Gillespie, Morton Gould, Dave Brubeck, Marian Anderson, Max Roach, Lena Horne, Roy Clark, Elliott Carter, The Oak Ridge Boys, Roberta Peters, Odetta, Leonard Slatkin, Stephen Sondheim, Sesame Street, Hard Rock Cafe and VH1 Save the Music Foundation. This year's event in Nashville marked the 32nd year of formal presentations of the Awards.

The event also featured the New York Emmy award winning animation created by the NMC and the Music Publishers Association of the United States, as part of a primary school lesson plan that encourages kids to think about the ramifications of taking other people's creative works without permission. Sanders frames the animated piece as "part of a world-wide effort by creators to change the narrative in terms of fostering an understanding that the online protection of creative works enhances freedom of speech and the marketplace of ideas, rather than encroaching on them."

The National Music Council is celebrating its 75th year as a forum for the free discussion of this country's national music affairs and challenges. Founded in 1940 to act as a clearinghouse for the joint opinion and decision of its members and to work to strengthen the importance of music in our life and culture, the Council's initial membership of 13 has grown to almost 50 national music organizations, encompassing every important form of professional and commercial musical activity.

Through the cooperative work of its member organizations, the National Music Council promotes and supports music and music education as an integral part of the curricula in the schools of our nation, and in the lives of its citizens. The Council provides for the exchange of information and coordination of efforts among its member organizations and speaks with one voice for the music community whenever an authoritative expression of opinion is desirable.

August 2015

Paul Shaffer guest on Kelly Lang's new album

When Kelly Lang's long-time friend Paul Shaffer visited Nashville for vacation recently, they did what most musicians do. They made music, recording a track for her upcoming album in their first studio session together.

Lang's performance with the former musical director of Late Show With David Letterman is one of several star-studded cuts from her upcoming album, which is set for release later this year. The singer-songwriter was excited to get to record with Shaffer, especially considering the musical magic that they created in their first performance together.

"I've known Paul forever, but we'd never had the chance to perform together," said Lang. "He came down on vacation to see me, check out Nashville, and do a show. After that, we decided, 'Why not record this for the record'?"

Shaffer had originally come to town to visit Lang and to play a July 4th show as Lang's special guest. Lang is a regular performer in the annual Remembering Conway Twitty show at Loretta Lynn's Ranch. This year, she performed "Goodbye Darling," a song she wrote about Twitty. For her second song, she chose "Last Date," a song Twitty fans know for the moving lyrics he wrote to the Floyd Cramer tune.

It was the magic of "Last Date" Shaffer and Lang decided to capture when they made it into the studio. "It's just such a magical song, and Paul brings so much to it, so much feeling and passion," Lang said. "You can hear it all on the record when it comes out. And there's a lot of surprises, too." Lang is playing it close to the vest about the songs she's including on the album. "I've been so blessed in my life to have people like Paul, so many incredibly gifted, talented musicians," she said. "I'm just as blessed to have so many great songs to include on this record."

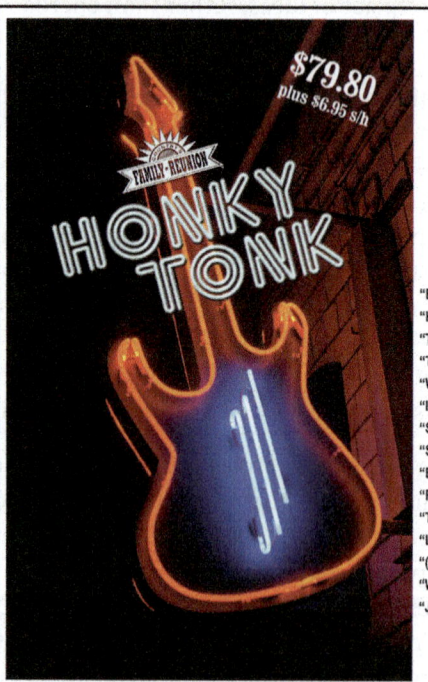

HONKY TONK REUNION

$79.80 plus $6.95 s/h

Did you know that some of the biggest country legends ever recorded got their start playing in places called Honky Tonks? That's right. So we here at Country's Family Reunion wanted to pay special attention to that foot-tapping brand of music in a brand new series, Country's Family Reunion Honky Tonks!

All on 5 DVD's with some of the most fun we've ever had at a reunion. So, order CFR Honky Tonk today and you'll be singing and tapping your feet in no time. We had so much fun creating this Honky Tonk series, and we know you'll love it too.

Songs and Artists Featured on Series:

- "Bright Lights And Country Music" BILL ANDERSON
- "Hey, Good Lookin' " MOE BANDY
- "The One You Slip Around With" JAN HOWARD
- "The Key's In The Mailbox" TONY BOOTH
- "Waltz Across Texas" JOHN CONLEE
- "It's The Water" DARRELL McCALL
- "Set 'Em Up Joe" DARYLE SINGLETARY
- "San Antonio Rose" The WHITES
- "Borrowed Angel" MO PITNEY
- "Fraulein" JIM ED BROWN
- "Thinkin' Problem" DAVID BALL
- "Lord, I Need Somebody Bad Tonight" JEANNIE SEELY
- "(I'm A) Lonesome Fugitive" JIM LAUDERDALE
- "Walkin' To New Orleans" EDDY RAVEN
- "Jones On The Jukebox" BECKY HOBBS
- "Please Don't Leave Me Anymore" / "The Kind Of Love I Can't Forget" / "Bubbles In My Beer" (swing medley) RAY PILLOW
- "Burning Memories" LINDA DAVIS
- "Tonight The Bottle Let Me Down" DALE WATSON
- "Buckaroo" CFR BAND
- "I Do My Crying At Night" RHONDA VINCENT
- "The Wild Side Of Life" CURTIS POTTER
- "Deep Water" ROY CLARK
- "My Shoes Keep Walking Back To You" JUNIOR BROWN
- "Walking The Floor Over You" TONY BOOTH (with Leon Rhodes)
- "Let's Get Over Them Together" MOE BANDY and BECKY HOBBS
- "Let's Chase Each Other Around The Room" BILLY YATES
- "There Stands The Glass" DAVID BALL
- "If You've Got The Money, I've Got The Time" DAVID FRIZZELL
- "Dim Lights, Thick Smoke, and Loud, Loud Music" WADE HAYES

1-800-820-5405   www.cfrvideos.com

August 2015

Road Stories

By Claudia Johnson

Aaron Tippin: Standing for Something for 25 Years and Counting

Aaron Tippin is spending his 25th anniversary in the entertainment industry doing what any "workin' man" would do – entertaining his fans across the country with hit-filled stage performances.

"The fans have been so great to me over the years, and they're still coming out to the shows," he said. "That's why I still sign autographs every night. I just want to get out there and shake their hand and give them a big hug just to say thank you."

Tippin's first hit, the song that endeared him to fans by encapsulating the powerful message about integrity and character into a single line, "You've Got To Stand For Something or You'll Fall for Anything," also caught the attention of Bob Hope. The comedian invited Tippin to join his USO tour in 1990 to entertain the troops who were serving in the Gulf War.

"Performing overseas with Bob Hope is the single most memorable moment in my 25 years," Tippin reflected. "I will never forget it. It started my career and everyone became familiar with my song 'You've Got to Stand for Something.' It also began my desire to give back to our military."

Tippin said the experience began his own tradition of playing for the troops each year.

"Going overseas and performing for the greatest warriors on the planet is the least I can do for the sacrifices they make to keep us free," he said.

During the aftermath of 9/11, Tippin, released "Where the Stars and Stripes and Eagle Fly," a song that he realizes has "become part of the American soundtrack."

"I wanted to talk to Americans about who we are at heart, and the fact that when the going gets tough, that's when we really stand up," he said. "We may have a lot of differences when everything is calm and fine, but when it hits the fan, I think we're the best in the world at sticking together, and rallying around the cause. That song served that purpose very well. I wanted us to be proud as Americans and get back on with living free."

Some of Tippin's biggest hits resonated with a blue-collar, country audience. "There Ain't Nothin' Wrong with the Radio," "My Blue Angel," "Kiss This" and "Workin' Man's PhD" are among those born from his own experience.

"I think several times during my record career, we tried to change and follow trends and stuff," he said. "But, it never seemed to work for me. The most success I had in the business was with songs that I crafted. I'm very proud of that. I think it makes a fan able to identify with me easier because these songs are about me – my life, who I am and how I was raised."

That's not to say Tippin hasn't captivated listeners with heartfelt love songs. Tracks like "Everything I Own," "For You I Will" and the 1995 hit "That's As Close as I'll Get to Loving You" demonstrate his broad vocal abilities not to mention the romantic side of him that has created a loving home with his wife, Thea, for 20 years.

August 2015

"She's got as much stake in this game as I do," he said. "She saw me at my lowest days, stood right there and stayed – even when things weren't great, and I wasn't having hit records. She listened to me whine through it all. I owe her everything."

Tippin has said that his family, which includes his grown daughter, Charla, his granddaughter and teenage sons Ted and Tom, is the center of his universe. The Tippins own a 500-acre farm in Middle Tennessee, complete with a runway (Tippin is a licensed pilot), recording studio and winery. He, Thea and the boys hunt, travel and perform together, and as anyone who follows the Tippins on social media quickly observes, they have great fun together. Tippin has a full performance schedule during his Silver Anniversary year, but a Sept. 4 concert at Stonehaus Winery in Crossville, Tenn., is particularly meaningful. The winery partnered with Tippin to produce a new wine celebrating 25 years in business for both Stonehaus and Tippin.

Aaron Tippin Country Jam, a barrel-selected blackberry wine, was introduced on Valentine's Day 2015.

Tippin has released a 25-song disc that includes a variety of musical genres he's not recorded before – like gospel and big band – along with some of his best-known hits.

"We just wanted to make sure it was everything I wanted it to be," Tippin said, adding in jest, "I don't know if I will make 50 years or not!"

Parton gives 7-year-old actress a thrilling surprise

The singing superstar had a thrilling surprise for the young actress, Alyvia Lind, personally giving her the news that she will play Dolly as a child in the upcoming original movie "Coat of Many Colors." "Coat of Many Colors," named after Parton's song, will be based on Parton's upbringing, with the Parton serving as executive producer.

Parton had called the 1971 track her favorite song she has written. It tells the story of how her mother stitched together a coat for her daughter out of rags given to the family, telling her the biblical story of Joseph and his Coat of Many Colors. But when the girl, all excited, debuts the new coat at school, she is ridiculed by her classmates for wearing rags.

The original coat is now on display in Parton's Chasing Rainbows Museum at Dollywood in Pigeon Forge, TN.

NBC's deal with Parton, includes a series of standalone TV movies based on Parton's songs, stories and life. They will contain music but won't be musicals, with Parton possibly appearing in some. Parton is developing the projects with production partner Sam Haskell of Magnolia Hill Entertainment and Warner Bros. Television.

August 2015

Dolly Parton presents a Kansas teacher with 2015 Chasing Rainbows Award

Dyane Smokorowski was named the 14th recipient of the Chasing Rainbows Award. She enjoyed a weekend trip to Dollywood where Dolly herself presented Dyane with the award. Each year, the National Network of State Teachers of the Year (NNSTOY) honors one outstanding educator with this prestigious award. The honoree is someone who "has overcome great obstacles in his or her life, has captured the rainbow and is helping children." This year's winner serves as the Instructional Technology Coach for Andover Public Schools in Andover, KS.

Smokorowski said, "It is difficult to admit that my personal struggles actually prepared me to be a stronger person today. I wanted to be someone who could inspire others to reach beyond their environments, beyond their extremities, and to do as I have always done—to dream big!"

In 2002, Dolly became the first to receive this award from the NNSTOY. The award celebrated her commitment to fostering a love of reading among children through her Imagination Library. Since then, Dolly has presented the award each year.

Dyane Smokorowski's name will be added, along with past recipients, to the award displayed in the Chasing Rainbows Museum at Dollywood.

For more information on the award and how to nominate an outstanding teacher, visit the NNSTOY website.

CFR News is going International

The CFR News is now available to purchase in a new digital PDF format that can be emailed anywhere in the world! This also makes it great for people on the go or who don't want to wait for mail delivery.

It looks just as it does in print with all the articles, photos and ads, but may be read on your computer or printed out on printer paper and read that way.

If you would prefer to renew your subscription in the new digital format or know someone who wishes to subscribe to the CFR News digial, just call customer service at 800-820-5405 orgo to www.cfrvideos.com and click on the button to subscribe to the digital PDF.

August 2015

SEPTEMBER

Country Legend Lynn Anderson dies unexpectedly

Lynn Anderson, best known for her country hit (I Never Promised You A) "Rose Garden," died Friday, July 31 of cardiac arrest. She was 67.

She had been hospitalized for pneumonia after returning from a vacation in Italy.

Lynn continued to make records until her death … her last, "Bridges" was released in June. Her heyday was in the '70s following the release of "Rose Garden" which would remain her biggest hit to date and earned her a Grammy.

Lynn was born in Grand Forks, North Dakota, on September 26, 1947, and raised in California, Her love of country music is credited to her mother … songwriting great, Liz Anderson. Liz composed such hits as "The Fugitive" and "My Friends Are Gonna Be Strangers" for Merle Haggard. Haggard's band, The Strangers, was named for the latter hit.

Lynn with Glen Sutton and their daughter, Lisa.

Lynn's venture into the music world was when, as a teenager, she entered a singing contest sponsored by the Country Corners program in Sacramento. In her late teens, she became a regular on a top rated network show. When she signed with the Lawrence Welk Show, she became the only country performer featured weekly on national television. By the time she turned 20, Lynn had been with a national recording company for three years, scoring a string of hits: "That's a No No," "Promises, Promises," "I've Been Everywhere," and "Rocky Top."

Lynn moved to Nashville in 1970 and signed with Columbia Records. She and her husband/producer Glenn Sutton, began turning out a steady stream of well-received recordings for the new label. During one of those rare sessions Lynn went to the studio to record Joe South's "Rose Garden." The song was a huge hit and climbed to the top of both the country and pop charts, something that was completely unheard of at the time. "Rose Garden" transformed Lynn Anderson into an international superstar. The album, "Rose Garden," was released after the single in February 1971. It earned Lynn numerous gold albums worldwide and went RIAA Platinum in the United States. She received an astonishing 32 tributes for the recording. "Rose Garden" remained the biggest selling album by a female country artist from 1971 - 1997, when Shania Twain broke Lynn's longstanding record.

In a career that spanned over four decades, Lynn scored 11 No. 1, 18 Top-10, and over 50 Top-40 hits. She earned a total of 17 Gold Albums and won virtually every award available to a female recording artist: CMA Female Vocalist of the Year, Academy of Country Music Female Vocalist of the Year (twice), American Music Award Favorite Female Vocalist, Record World's Artist of the Decade (1970-1980), Billboard's Artist of the Decade (1970-1980) and the prestigious Grammy Award. Her records have sold in the multi-millions worldwide, many of them becoming standards. Her most recent Grammy Award nomination was in 2004 for "The Bluegrass Sessions."

Lynn was equally successful in the equestrian world. She won 16 National Championships, four World Championships and several celebrity championships. She produced a TNN Special, "American Country Cowboy's," which benefited various handicapped groups. Lynn's philanthropic interests are longstanding … one of her recordings was chosen as a theme song for the National

September 2015

Christmas Seal Campaign. She also worked with horseback therapy riding programs for adults and children.

After living in Taos, New Mexico, for 20 years, Lynn decided it was time to move back to Nashville where she had several horses and was still competing at national equestrian events.

Lynn appeared on Country's Family Reunion "Nashville" series as well as "Bill Anderson's 50th Anniversary" series and is on the "Looking Back" DVDs as well.

"It's a funny thing to have lost both parents unexpectedly," Lynn's daughter Lisa said, "Makes me feel like every day should count because it might be the last. (The other day) I noted how the hostas are in bloom and the smell reminds me of gardenias which was one of my Mother's favorite scents. My sister and I had lunch with Mom the week before she died. She'd come home from Venice bearing gifts and mine was this cobalt blue, hand-blown, Venetian glass, perfume bottle. She was so good at giving gifts! I'm realizing this will be the last trinket she will have carried back to me from afar. Makes me sad for sure. Thank goodness for lots and lots of pictures and stories to continue to find new things my Mom accomplished. That's a Music Legacy and Paper Trail that I will gladly follow."

Nadine's Corner

Everyone knows church folk like to cook, and most have their own cookbook. Send me your church cookbook and each month I'll pull a recipe from it and feature it here!

Cookbook, P.O. Box 210796, Nashville, TN 37221.

COFFEE CAKE INTERNATIONAL

CAKE

3/4 cup butter
1 1/2 cup sugar
3 eggs
1/2 tsp almond extract
3 cups flour
1 1/2 tsp baking soda
1 (8 oz) sour cream
1 can (21 oz) cherry pie filling

Preheat over to 350 degrees. Spray 2 - 9" round cake pans. Cream butter and sugar. Beat in eggs until mixture is light and fluffy. Add extract. Combine the flour and soda. Add to cream mixture with sour cream. Divide the batter in 2 pans, spread cherries on top. Sprinkle topping over the cherries. Bake for 25 - 30 minutes until golden brown.

TOPPING

1/2 cup flour
1/4 cup sugar
1/2 tsp cinnamon
Cut in 1/4 cup butter until crumbly

Nadine, the church lady

THE CROSS IS A PLUS SIGN FOR A NEGATIVE WORLD

September 2015

Country Stars Sharing Recipes for Happiness

By Sasha Kay Dunavant

Country songs have a way into our hearts. The stars that perform them are good for the soul. When we see them we light up. We know every word to every song, and we know just the right song to create the ambiance for every special occasion. Just as a song can take us back, cooking can traverse time as well, taking us back to our grandparents' table, remembering how "mama made it" or how holidays "used to be."

Food connects people through generation and congregation. Recipes are like lyrics to a song. They have to be just right and measured with love. Like a taste for good music, legendary country artists enjoy a taste for great cuisine. It turns out that some stars have taken action to showcase their passion for food.

NAOMI JUDD

Naomi Judd's 1997 cookbook, Naomi's Home Companion: A Treasury of Favorite Recipes, Food for Thought and Country Wit and Wisdom, has become a collectible. The hardcover book contains 75 recipes that are easy and delicious, reflecting The Judds' eventful and on-the-go life that includes Naomi Judd's early years as a working single mother and later as half a blockbuster country duo with her daughter, Wynonna. The book also shares personal stories of The Judds' experiences, meals together on the road and life lessons learned. Reviewers say that Judd offers "recipes for life" making the read "so much more than a cookbook."

KITTY WELLS

Deemed the "Queen of Country Music," Kitty Wells numerous recognitions included the prestigious Country Music Pioneer Award in 1976 and The Music City News' Living Legend Award in 1993. Music was in her blood. Along with her sisters and cousin, she formed a girl group, the Deacon Sisters, who were performing on WSIX radio as early as 1936. However, it wasn't just music in this girl's veins. There was also good cooking. Wells shared many of her favorite recipes in her three-volume Kitty Wells Country Kitchen Cookbook series that spanned from 1964-1994. The books include personal photos of her husband, Johnny Wright, and her children, with whom she performed on a 1960s show as well as a family history and stories. In addition to traditional Southern country favorites, Wells features recipes that reflect some of the home-cooking trends of each period. There's 7-up Cake, Tex-Mex, Hawaiian-inspired and Jell-O concoctions. Wells stated in her cookbook that her greatest accomplishment was in being a good wife and mother and that she believed cooking brought together the things in life were valuable to her family.

These are only a few of the country stars who, like the rest of us, love food, and have found an entertaining way to share the passion with their fans.

Everyone knows church folk like to cook, and most have their own cookbook. Send me your church cookbook recipe, who submitted it, along with the name of your church and each month I'll pull a recipe from it and feature it here!

'Larry's Country Diner' wins Gold Cross Award for 'TV Show of the Year 2015' from ICGMA

Renae (The Waitress) accepted the award for Larry's Country Diner.

The International Country Gospel Music Association celebrated their 59th Annual Convention and Awards Show August 6th, 7th, & 8th at the West Plains Civic Center in historic West Plains, Missouri. Again this year the West Plains Civic Center was filled to capacity every night of the event. Artists and fans alike enjoyed outstanding talent as they performed Country Gospel, Bluegrass Gospel, and Southern Gospel Music.

Special guest appearances by fan favorites included country music legend Freddie Hart, Del Way, Chris Golden, formerly with the Oak Ridge Boys, Renae The Waitress from the television show "Larry's Country Diner", and Greg McDougal of Nashville. James Payne and Del Way entertained the crowd with a segment of their "Good Old Boys Like Us" presentation. Christian comedians Barry McGee, Bruce Walker, and Pastor Pudge delighted the fans with their country humor.

The continued growth in the number of new performing artists in the organization added to the enjoyment of the fans, who enthusiastically welcomed this year's talent lineup. Every available booth space in the Exhibit Hall was filled, allowing artists the opportunity to network with other performers, musicians, songwriters, publishers, producers, promoters and broadcasters.

The I.C.G.M.A. honors excellence in 28 categories in their Gold Cross Awards Show. That Awards Show was held on Saturday evening, August 8th. Renae the Waitress was there to accept the Gold Cross Award for "TV Show of The Year". Renae and Phil Johnson were also presenters for the "Album of The Year" and "Comedian of the Year." "We had such a great time attending I.C.G.M.A in Grand Plains, Mo.

COUNTRY'S FAMILY REUNION presents....

September 4 & 11
Sweethearts

September 18
THE ~~GENE & MOE~~
Moe & Gene SHOW

September 25
Tribute Show: Jim Ed Brown

Fridays...7 p.m. central
Saturdays...11 p.m central

September 2015

Gospel & Country Music Icons The Oak Ridge Boys Honored with Two 2015 GMA DOVE Award Nominations

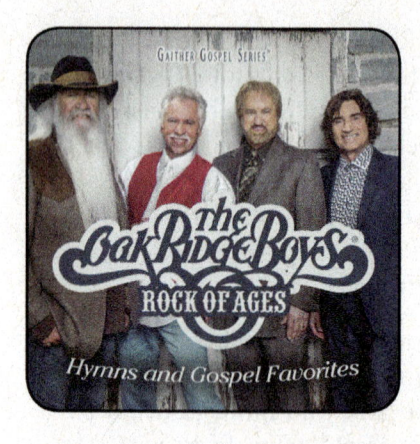

Gospel and Country music legends and American music icons The Oak Ridge Boys received two nominations for the 2015 Gospel Music Association (GMA) DOVE Awards, according to the press conference held Wednesday at Lipscomb University in Nashville, Tennessee.

The award-winning quartet received a nod for Bluegrass/Country Album of the Year for their recent gospel recording, which hit the street on May 26th. Rock of Ages, Hymns and Gospel Favorites (Gaither Music Group), a 15-song project produced by Ben Isaacs (Gaither Vocal Band, The Isaacs) and group member Duane Allen, showcases the group's acclaimed, four-part harmonies and celebrates their musical roots.

The Oaks were also honored with a nomination for Country Song of the Year for their recent country single, "Sweet Jesus," an original song co-written by Kenny Vernon and country music star Merle Haggard, who joined the group for the recording of the song.

"We loved the recitation [within the song] and thought if we could just get Merle to do that recitation we would be thrilled," described Allen. "But then, it worked so well that Merle just kept on singing with us on the last chorus—a once in a lifetime experience for all of The Oak Ridge Boys. It is one of the biggest thrills of my career to get to sing and record with Merle Haggard."

"When I saw that our Rock of Ages album is up for two very special DOVE Awards my heart jumped," stated Joe Bonsall. "This has been a special project. Each of us laid our hearts on the line on this project, and these classic songs are a huge part of our lives and our constant walk with Christ, so to have the Gospel Music Association recognize the work is an honor beyond words! We are so very blessed."

The Rock of Ages, Hymns and Gospel Favorites recording also features guest vocals from the award-winning Isaacs, who joined the Boys for the song "Peace Within."

In April of this year it was announced that the group will be inducted into the Country Music Hall of Fame this October in the Modern Era Artist category.

Rock of Ages, Hymns and Gospel Favorites has been positioned heavily at retail, via catalog placements and through a direct TV campaign on networks including DISH TV, DIRECTV, AT&T U-verse, PBS, GaitherTV, TBN, FamilyNet, CTN, GMTN, Guardian, Liberty, RFD, TCT and TLN. The campaign will also air in Canada on Vision TV, The Miracle Channel, Grace TV and CTS.

Rock of Ages, Hymns and Gospel Favorites is distributed through Capitol Christian Distribution and is available throughout general market stores, including Cracker Barrel Old Country Store®, and the Christian marketplace, in addition to online retailers including iTunes, Amazon and www.gaither.com.

For further information, visit oakridgeboys.com, twitter.com/oakridgeboys or facebook.com/oakridgeboys.

September 2015

An excerpt from an interview with Charlie Louvin

Notes: This excerpt from a 2011 interview with Charlie Louvin is reprinted with permission from the author. To see the entire interview including photos, go to: http://raised country.com/charlie_louvin/

Mr. Louvin often pronounces the name of his late brother, Ira, as "Eye-ree".

EARLY MEMORIES

RC) Can you tell me one of your earliest memories.

Mr. Louvin: Ira was born in April, 1924, and I was born in July of 1927.

Musically, I started singing when I was 8 and Ira was 11.

My daddy loved music, almost any kind of music, especially country or gospel. So, when people would come to see him, he would insist that Ira and I sing these people songs. We were so bashful, it was pathetic.

In the living room there was a bed. In every room except the kitchen there was a bed, because there were 7 kids, plus Mama and Papa.

Mama and Papa slept in the living room. Papa would get up and build a fire. When we finally got up the room would be warm.

We would crawl under Mama's and Papa's bed, which was about 16" off the floor. We'd put our hind ends together and we would sing a song. That's how we learned to phrase together without lookin' at each other, without steppin' on each other's toes, or winkin' at each other. It just come natural.

If the song was gonna get too high for me to sing the lead on, at that instant he'd take the high lead, and I would come under him with low harmony. We learned it that way, and it that kinda mystified other duets who were tryin' to figure out who was doin' the tenor and who was who was doin' the lead.

But, back to papa asking us to sing,

We'd climb out from under their bed after singin', and beat it, … get outta there. We wanted to get out of the house before they could ask us to sing for someone.

I always hated it when people would ask you to do something, then they'd ignore you, like asking you to sing, then having conversation and laughter with each other like you weren't there performing for them.

RC) To get so involved in music at that young age, your home environment must have had a lot of music in it.

Mr. Louvin: Well, my daddy played a 5 string. That was the first instrument that Ira picked up on. That's not too good to sing with. So, Ira switched off to the guitar.

My mama was an extremely good 4 note singer. There was probably 100 songs in this book she had, and she knew every one of 'em, by heart. She would sing the notes, the fah soh lahs, and then she'd sing the words.

Of course, she sang while cookin' dinner, cookin' supper, or washin' the dishes. Whatever she was doin', she was singin' an old song.

That's where the Louvin Brother harmony came from, was the 4 note, Sacred Harp singin's.

That was the style. We grew up in a country setting and at a time where Sacred Harp singin' was the thing. Sure, we had singin' schools where they'd teach it so you could read the music, but we never did that.

FROM PAUL YANDELL TO JIMMY CAPPS

Mr. Louvin: We first had a guitarist named Paul Yandell who was a Chet Atkins worshipper.

September 2015

When we first got the Opry, you know, Chet had cut all our gospel songs, and he's the one who played the guitar for "When I Stopped Dreamin'".

But when he got the executive job with RCA, he didn't have time to cut sessions for just anybody. He had about a dozen artists that he was responsible for – so all his time was eat up with that.

So, we found, with the help of a disk jockey from Mayfield, Kentucky, we found Paul Yandell. Paul worked for us for about 3 years then the draft got him.

He decided he would replace himself. He'd find his own replacement. So, there was two guys in North Carolina who played all Louvin Brothers music, and they had a guitar player named Jimmy Capps.

So, he contacted Jimmy and said if you'll be at a certain place on a certain night, the Louvin Brothers are going to do a show there, and I'll get you an audition, and maybe you'll get the job.

Jimmy Capps was a straight pick man. He now works straight pick, and with his fingers, he can make it sound like he's a thumb style picker.

Anyway, Jim was there. After the show was over, he lugged his amplifier up to the hotel room, and his guitar. He set everything up, tuned his guitar. Everyone was just sitting there.

Paul Yandell's "cuss" word was "by devil." So, he said, "Well, by devil, Jimmy, pick one!"

Jimmy said, "Well, what do you want me to pick."

Paul said, "Well, uh, Malagueña."

That was an instrumental that Chet Atkins had out. Jim kinda looked funny, and he said "You know Paul. I've heard that. I've heard that, but I've never tried to play it."

You could just see the disappointment on Yandell's face. You know, like, I got a guy up here who can't even pick.

And another minute or two passed by with a very uncomfortable silence, and I finally said, "Oh, it's OK, Jim. You don't need to play Malagueña. Ira and I hardly ever sing that song anyway."

It became funny, and Capps turned out to be one of the best pickers, as far as I'm concerned, that ever picked up a guitar. He's still a member of (or the head of) the Opry staff band.

OPRY BAND'S LIMITATIONS

Mr. Louvin: The Opry has disbanded almost everyone except the guest artists.

I've only done one song per show on the Opry since they disbanded. They have me doing about 1 show per month. Last year (2010), I only did 10 songs. I could keep up with that by how much I made off the Opry.

In fact this Saturday night, I'll be working with Jimmy Capps, because I can only use two people on the Opry.

I used to have a full band, only 4 people, that worked the road with me, and I used them for years and years. Then about 6 years ago, the Opry manager, Hal Durham, said that I could only use two people. That was because of a lot of the songs that I do requires harmony. So, I used those two people to put the harmony with the songs.

For the other part of the band, I used the Opry staff band, which are very good musicians.

It's hard to keep a band now. If you can't use them on the Opry, and if you're not working the road, then there's all but two of your men settin' idle.

RC) And you're a regular, not a visiting guest

Mr. Louvin: Regular right – been there a little over 55 years

The good thing about the Opry is that you don't have to pack up and move.

There are no clear channel radio stations left in the US. The Opry is on 65, and I doubt if there are less that 10 or 15 in the US that are exactly on 65.

SHENANIGANS ON THE ROAD

RC) Heh heh. So, tell me. Can you think of the funniest thing that ever happened to you.

Mr. Louvin: Ira and I had a few fisticuffs – I'm only 5 and 1/2 and he was 6 foot. He was just so gawky that before he could even get in the fight, it was over.

September 2015

So, we're comin up the road (we had several of those). I was drivin' and Jimmy Capps was ridin' in the front seat. Ira had been sleepin' in the back seat.

Ira setup in the back seat and said, "Pull it over! Pull it over!"

And we're out in the middle of corn fields, you know. And I said, "We're in the middle of nothin' here. What? Do you want to use the bathroom?"

And he said, "No. No, I don't want to use bathroom. I have just figured out a way to whip your ass."

I just kept drivin'. Jimmy got tickled. Then, I got tickled. Then, a few minutes later, Ira got to laughin', too, and I never did find out what he'd figured out. It was never mentioned again.

But if you ask Jimmy Capps what was the funniest thing to ever happen while he was with the Louvin Brothers, which was a long time, he'd probably mention that incident.

RC) So, knowing that your brother now had a secret weapon, did you ever have another fight? ;o)

Mr. Louvin: <<Laugh>> Nah.

Larry's Country Diner RFD Show Schedule Sept. 2015
NEW SHOWS

WADE HAYES
Saturday, September 5
10:00 p.m. Central
Sunday, September 6
6:00 p.m. Central

JOHN CONLEE
Saturday, September 12
10:00 p.m. Central
Sunday, September 13
6:00 p.m. Central

JOEY & RORY
Saturday, September 19
10:00 p.m. Central
Sunday, September 20
6:00 p.m. Central

CARL JACKSON & ORTHOPHOIC JOY
Saturday, September 26
10:00 p.m. Central
Sunday, September 27
6:00 p.m. Central

September 2015

COUNTRY'S FAMILY REUNION SCRAPBOOK: T. GRAHAM BROWN

T. July 1955, 9 1/2 months

T. and brother Danny

T. Graham Brown and the Reo Diamond Band

With 2 week old son, Acme

T. Graham Brown

T. and wife, Sheila

T. and son, Acme at 2 years

With Granddad, George Washington Brown

With parents, Jackie & Royce Brown

160 CFR NEWS

September 2015

Mickey Gilley's Famous Club Part of American Pop History for 35 Years

By Claudia Johnson

When Mickey Gilley says it's been an incredible ride, he's not necessarily referring to the mechanical bulls at the clubs that bear his name.

"It's been 35 years, and I'm still working the road and working my theater in Branson," he said, adding with a laugh. "Every night when I go to bed, I thank John Travolta for keeping my career alive."

He's referring, of course, to the 1980 movie "Urban Cowboy," which starred Travolta that was filmed in Pasadena, Texas, with much of the action taking place in the 6,000-person capacity Gilley's Club, the world's largest honky-tonk, which was owned by Gilley and former business partner Sherwood Cryer.

"John had just come off 'Saturday Night Fever' when they talked about using Gilley's, so when they said John Travolta would be the star, I thought 'this can be Country Night Fever,'" Gilley recalled. "The movie launched country music into a different stratosphere and gave it a lot of visibility."

Gilley believes "Urban Cowboy" has had a long-term impact on numerous aspects of American pop culture, including a notable influence on fashion.

"The movie opened people up to the idea of western wear – jeans, hats," he observed. "That was back in 1979-80. I look at some of these country acts today and see them dressed just like John's character dressed back then."

Gilley said the "Urban Cowboy" soundtrack has also stood the test of time.

"There are some great songs on there," he said. "They're not all country, but they all work. Boz Scaggs' song 'Love, Look What You've Done to Me' is a great song that's not country, but it was right for the soundtrack."

Gilley's tracks included the bluesy "Stand By Me," which became one of his 17 Number One hits, and a traditional country tune, "Here Comes that Hurt Again."

Since childhood, Gilley played piano and sang with his cousins, rock 'n' roll pioneer Jerry Lee Lewis and televangelist Jimmy Swaggart, working as the years passed to make his living as a performer. He admits he had all but given up when a series of odd twists saved his fledgling music career.

"I struggled for 17 years, and everybody accused me of copying my cousin Jerry Lee," he said. "When I opened Gilley's in 1971, I just threw in the towel on recording. I thought it was never going to happen."

Gilley focused on developing his new business and remembers this as the first time in his life he'd ever made "a half decent living." At Gilley's Club he was the headline act, and some of the greatest stars in the business played there. "Live from Gilley's" was broadcast globally each week on 500 radio stations and Armed Forces Radio between 1977 and 1989. For a while, Gilley even had his own television show on a local channel in Houston.

"One day a lady who owned the juke box at Gilley's was in the club and told me she had heard me sing her favorite song on TV," he said. "She asked me to record it because she wanted it for her 300 juke boxes in the Houston area."

The song was "She Called Me Baby All Night Long," and Gilley was happy to oblige. He needed

September 2015

a B-side, so he chose "Room Full of Roses," an old George Morgan hit. When he purchased advertising for Gilley's Club, he asked the radio station to use his record as background without specifying which side. They chose the B-side, and "Room Full of Roses" became Gilley's first Number 1 hit and launched his recording career in 1974 at age 38.

The original Gilley's Club burned in 1989, but now Gilley has a club in Dallas, three in Oklahoma and two in Nevada.

"I've tried to keep the club out there ¬– it was more popular than Mickey Gilley," said the singer, in his lighthearted, self-effacing way.

Injuries sustained from a serious fall in 2009 has prevented Gilley from being able to play the piano, but he remains confident that he will play again someday. Recently, he's put his theater in Branson, Mo., on the market and bought a tour bus, embarking on an ambitious schedule that includes performances across the country.

"I'm taking the music to the people and having a great time," said the 79-year-old, adding with mischief, "And you know what I've found out? The girls still all get prettier at closing time."

Country music mourns three more loses in one week

Buddy Emmons, Steel player extraordinaire

Buddy Emmons -- one of the most influential musicians ever on the steel guitar -- died Wednesday ,July 29, at the age of 78.

Born Buddy Gene Emmons on Jan. 27, 1937, in Mishawaka, Indiana, his love of the instrument began when his father bought him a six-string lap steel and signed him up for lessons. He quickly took to it, and said Hank Williams' steel player Jerry Byrd and Herb Remington were two of his biggest inspirations. Emmons began playing with local bands around the Indiana area and quit school at the age of 16. Eventually, he moved to Detroit, where he went to work for local musician Casey Clark.

It was during that he caught the ear of Grand Ole Opry star Little Jimmy Dickens. Impressed with his playing, Dickens offered Emmons a job in his band, which meant a move to Nashville. After a year with Dickens, he formed the Sho-Bud Company, which became one of the most successful steel companies in the business. He also became a highly sought-after session player, with Faron Young's recording of "Sweet Dreams" being an early highlight.

In 1957 he became a member of the Texas Troubadours, the touring band for Ernest Tubb. It was on an early Tubb session that Emmons pioneered the use of the "split pedal" sound. By the 1960s, Emmons was continuing to help manufacture steel guitars for Sho-Bud, in addition to his growing session work. He also stayed busy on the road, taking a job in 1962 with Ray Price. As a member of the Cherokee Cowboys, his work on "Night Life" remains one of the definitive licks in the instrument's history. Emmons remained with Price through 1967, by which point he had left Sho-Bud to start his own guitar company. It was during his years with Price that he recorded his greatest work as a solo instrumentalist, 1963's Steel Guitar Jazz. The first jazz record to feature Emmons' trademark instrument, it was critically praised in the pages of Downbeat magazine.

September 2015

He then moved across country to California, where he worked with Roger Miller. His work in the late 1960s and early 1970s can also be heard on many records outside of the country genre, such as that of Gram Parsons, the Carpenters and Ray Charles. He also played the famous steel riff on Judy Collins' recording of "Someday Soon." Emmons returned to Nashville in the mid-1970s and would remain one of the most imitated players of his time. He spent 10 years playing for the Everly Brothers and was inducted into the Steel Guitar Hall of Fame in 1981. In later years, he did some session work with Price, Willie Nelson and Johnny Bush, and also was an occasional player on Garrison Keillor's Prairie Home Companion.

Tandy Rice, Music City's Booking Agent

The distinguished-looking, Music City personality, Tandy Rice, who managed and/or booked such country-music greats as Porter Wagoner, Dolly Parton, Jim Ed Brown, The Kendalls, Tom T. Hall, Helen Cornelius, Jeannie C. Riley, and more, died on Monday, August 3. He was 76 years old. Born Tandy Clinton Rice Jr. in 1938, he was a native of Franklin, TN

Minnie Pearl (Sarah Ophelia Colley Cannon) was a distant cousin and she encouraged him to enter the music business. Tandy Rice began his career as a publicist, representing Waylon Jennings, Chet Atkins, Kitty Wells and Hank Williams Jr., among others. He hit his stride as a salesman for Show Biz, Inc., which distributed syndicated country television shows to stations throughout the nation. He bought the company's booking agency, Top Billing, Inc. after having been there for three years. He developed Top Billing into a Nashville powerhouse. At its peak, the firm booked and/or managed 18 major artists.

Always impeccably groomed and socially polished, Tandy Rice was a master salesman, using his folksy humor, honeyed Southern drawl, evangelistic enthusiasm and skill as a raconteur to charm everyone who met him. He became nearly as well known as the artists he represented. Rice was profiled in Newsweek, The Washington Post, People, Playboy, The New York Times and other national publications. Rice was a judge for the 1983 Miss America Pageant, which crowned Vanessa Williams. He also judged it in 1996, as well as several lesser such competitions.

In 2010, he survived prostate cancer. The following year, he was inducted into the Hall of Fame of the International Entertainment Buyers Association (IEBA). In 2014, Tandy Rice became the inaugural inductee into the National Association of Talent Directors (NATD) Hall of Fame.

He is survived by daughters Cynthia Rice Simonet and Marjorie Rice Mason, six grandchildren and one great-grandchild.

Legendary producer, Billy Sherrill

Legendary country producer and songwriter Billy Sherrill — best known for his work with Tammy Wynette and George Jones, died August 4 in Nashville after a short illness. He was 78.

Sherrill guided dozens of hits for Wynette and Jones, including "He Stopped Loving Her Today." That tune reignited Jones' career in 1980 and is commonly deemed the greatest country song of all time.

Born November 5th, 1936, in Phil Campbell, Alabama, Sherrill was a jazz and blues lover as a child and had a short-lived recording contract as the leader of a blues band. After that didn't pan out, he began a new career as a studio manager for the pioneering rock & roll label Sun Records in 1962, but when the label closed its Nashville operations in 1963, he moved on to Epic Records as a producer. With little experience in country up to that point, he freely mixed elements of pop music into his work.

Sherrill earned his first Number One hit as a producer and co-writer in 1966 with David Houston's "Almost Persuaded." Also in 1966, he signed the then-unknown Tammy Wynette to her first contract and suggested she drop her real name, Virginia Wynette Pugh, in favor of the now-famous stage moniker. Together, the pair topped the country charts with 20 different songs, many of which Sherrill co-wrote. One of those chart-toppers, 1968's controversial "Stand by Your Man," is another frequent entry on the list of the greatest all-time country songs.

September 2015

Sherrill also produced songs and albums for iconic artists including Charlie Rich, Marty Robbins, Johnny Paycheck, Ray Charles, Tanya Tucker and Johnny Cash, among others, but his most famous association was with Jones. Working together for nearly 20 years, he helped the singer revitalize his lagging career, and it was Sherrill who insisted Jones record the Bobby Braddock and Curly Putman-penned "He Stopped Loving Her Today." In the 1996 Jones biography The Life and Times of a Honky Tonk Legend, Sherrill said Jones "hated the melody and wouldn't learn it" because it was "too long, too sad, too depressing."

In 1984, Sherrill was inducted into the Nashville Songwriters Hall of Fame, and he was immortalized in the Musicians Hall of Fame and Museum in 2008. In 2010, he became a member of the Country Music Hall of Fame alongside Don Williams, Ferlin Husky and Jimmy Dean.

A shy man by nature, he said in accepting his induction, "You have to have a lot of help to get here, and I've got it."

Sherrill is survived by his wife Charlene, his daughter Catherine Lale and two grandchildren.

Diner Chat with Renae the Waitress
It's easy...it's fun!!
Listen live by Phone or on the web, every Thursday at 3:00 p.m. EST.
1-425-440-5100
ID code: 909005#
www.larryscountrydiner.com, click 'Diner Chat'

CHAT .... CHAT.... CHAT.... That 's what we do every week on the phone !!

This month of September will be an exciting month for Diner news.

* Groundbreaking for the new "Larry's Country Diner" in Nashville Tennessee is scheduled for September 16th. We are planning a ribbon cutting ceremony and party that will include the whole cast Larry, Renae the waitress, The sheriff, Keith and Nadine. Lots to talk about on Diner Chat.

* You don't want to miss the opportunity to hear about the Legacy Brick Campaign and buy a brick with your name or message on it that will be placed in the legacy walkway at the Diner in Nashville for everyone to see. I have already ordered a brick in memory of our son. There are 3 different size bricks with limited lines to engrave. We have a limited area at the Diner once we start construction so look for ordering details.

* Larry Updates during Diner Chat.....Larry is doing great ! Not much new news except he is now using his walker instead of a wheel chair and has spent some limited time in the office. (I think he missed me serving him coffee?? LOL)

* We have won our very first award !! TV SHOW OF THE YEAR 2015 from the International Country Gospel Music Association! How cool is that and I was there the receive the award. Nadine says she is going next year to the just in case...lol

* Pre-sales will start in October, and I always spill the beans on our weekly show. So look for a pre-sale mailer about our new Christmas show called "HOME FOR CHRISTMAS and " Sweethearts" combo offer.

* We will be doing a monthly give away on our LIVE Diner Chat starting in September. You never know which caller will be picked to receive our free give away. All you have to do is listen in Thursdays 3:00 central time to Diner Chat.

* The cast of Larry's Country Diner will be going to Branson in September for a week of sold out shows at the Starlite Theater. Artists Jimmy Fortune, Gene Watson, Daily and Vincent, The Whites and Joey and Rory will going us for the week long of shows

* More Special Guests are expected on Diner Chat the month of September. Past guests have been Nadine, Ronnie Robbins, Scott England, Keith Bilbrey, Randy Little, LaDonna Gatlin, Jimmy and Michele Capps, Larry and Luann Black and Phil Johnson.

Dont's miss Diner Chat every Thursday at 3:00 Central by phone or listen on the internet.

www.larryscountrydiner.com/dinerchat. REPLAYS are available.

September 2015

The Nashville Brat Pack — Kids of the Country Stars!

By Ronny Robbins, Son of Marty Robbins

This was the closest thing to a family shot, I guess, since I was too young to hold the camera, Mom and Dad had to take turns taking each others picture. The selfie craze had not caught on yet.

The first Christmas I really remember was the one when I got my first guitar (ukulele actually). It was when we lived at the house on Pima Ave. in Phoenix probably Christmas of 1951-52. Judging by the sparseness of the Christmas tree, Dads career was still a little ways off from being successful. I remember playing with the road grader smoothing out our driveway and part of Pima Ave. which was a dirt road back then. Still love moving dirt with a tractor to this day! One thing that really sticks in my mind after all these years, no matter how successful and how much Dad was on the road, he always tried to be home on special days with the family. That didn't always work out for my birthday, since it's in July, the busiest time of the year for concert venues, but Dad was always home for most Thanksgivings and our family was blessed to have 32 Christmas's as a family until the year Dad passed, the only one I missed was when I was in the Army.

The first house we lived in Nashville was on Loney Drive. Here I am with my new dog Mickey, always thought he was a Collie, but now after looking at his ears, I'm thinking he may have come from another country. He was a great dog though, he lived long enough to see me get my driver's license, that's 16 in people years.

Our first Christmas back to Phoenix after moving to Nashville, saying our good-byes for the 3-day trip back home. My uncle Lou (kneeling) made balloon animals, which I thought were the coolest thing, played with mine all the way to Tucson, about drove Dad crazy. L-R Uncle John, Grandma, Momma, Dad and Lou's daughter, cousin Linda.

This photo is a little fuzzy, but a bit of significant history. It's a little know fact that Dad had been working on developing a ventriloquist act, just in case the music thing didn't work out so well. He had this little puppet made up to look just like me...... fortunately the music career took off......and none too soon.

September 2015

Celebrating Marty Robbins' 90th Birthday

Martin David Robinson, better known as Marty Robbins, and his twin sister Mamie were born September 26, 1925 in Glendale, a suburb of Phoenix in Maricopa County, Arizona. His mother was mostly of Paiute Indian heritage. They were reared in a difficult family situation. His father took odd jobs to support the family of 10 children, but his drinking led to divorce in 1937. Among his warmer memories of his childhood, Marty recalled having listened to stories of the American West told by his maternal grandfather, Texas Bob Heckle. He left the troubled home at 17 to serve in the United States Navy as an LCT coxswain during World War II and was stationed in the Solomon Islands in the Pacific Ocean. To pass the time during the war, he learned to play the guitar, started writing songs, and came to love Hawaiian music.

After his discharge from the military in 1947, he began to play at local venues in Phoenix, then moved on to host his own show on KTYL and then his own television show on KPHO-TV in Phoenix. After Little Jimmy Dickens made a guest appearance on Marty's TV show, Dickens got him a record deal with Columbia Records.

On September 27, 1948, Marty married Marizona Baldwin (September 11, 1930 – July 10, 2001) to whom he dedicated his song "My Woman, My Woman, My Wife". They had two children, son Ronny (July 16, 1949) and daughter Janet (January 1959), who also followed a singing career in Los Angeles.

Marty's 1957 recording of "A White Sport Coat and a Pink Carnation" sold over one million copies, and was awarded a gold record. His musical accomplishments include the Grammy Award for his 1959 hit and signature song "El Paso", taken from his album Gunfighter Ballads and Trail Songs. "El Paso" was the first song to hit No. 1 on the pop chart in the 1960s. It was followed up, successfully, by "Don't Worry", which reached No. 3 on the pop chart in 1961, becoming his third, and last, Top 10 pop hit. "El Paso" was followed by one prequel and one sequel: "Feleena" and "El Paso City". Also in 1961, Robbins wrote the words and music and recorded "I Told the Brook," a ballad later recorded by Billy Thorpe.

He won the Grammy Award for the Best Country & Western Recording 1961, for his follow-up album More Gunfighter Ballads and Trail Songs, and was awarded the Grammy Award for Best Country Song in 1970, for "My Woman, My Woman, My Wife". Marty was named Artist of the Decade (1960–1969) by the Academy of Country Music, was elected to the Country Music Hall of Fame in 1982, and was given a Grammy Hall of Fame Award in 1998 for his song "El Paso".

He was inducted into the Nashville Songwriters Hall of Fame in 1975. For his contribution to the recording industry, and has a star on the Hollywood Walk of Fame at 6666 Hollywood Blvd.

Marty has been honored by many bands, including the Grateful Dead who covered "El Paso" and Bob Weir & Kingfish who covered "Big Iron". The Who's 2006 album Endless Wire includes the song "God Speaks of Marty Robbins". The song's composer, Pete Townshend, explained that the song is about God deciding to create the universe just so he can hear some music, "and most of all, one of his best creations, Marty Robbins." The Beasts of Bourbon released a song called "The Day Marty Robbins Died" on their 1984 debut album The Axeman's Jazz. Johnny Cash recorded a version of "Big Iron" as part of his American Recordings series, which is included in the Cash Unearthed box set. Both Frankie Laine and Elvis Presley, among others, recorded versions of Robbins' song "You Gave Me a Mountain", with Laine's recording reaching the pop and adult contemporary charts in 1969.

September 2015

When Marty was recording his 1961 hit "Don't Worry", session guitarist Grady Martin accidentally created the electric guitar "fuzz" effect – his six-string bass was run through a faulty channel in a mixing console. Marty decided to keep it in the final version. The song reached No. 1 on the country chart, and No. 3 on the pop chart.

His song "El Paso" was featured on AMC Breaking Bad's final episode.

In addition to his recordings and performances, Marty was an avid race car driver, competing in 35 career NASCAR races with six top-10 finishes, including the 1973 Firecracker 400. In 1967, Marty played himself in the car racing film Hell on Wheels. He was partial to Dodges, and owned and raced Chargers and then a 1978 Dodge Magnum. His last race was in a Junior Johnson-built 1982 Buick Regal in the Atlanta Journal 500 on November 7, 1982, the month before he died. In 1983, NASCAR honored him by naming the annual race at Nashville the Marty Robbins 420. He was also the driver of the 60th Indianapolis 500 Buick Century pace car in 1976.

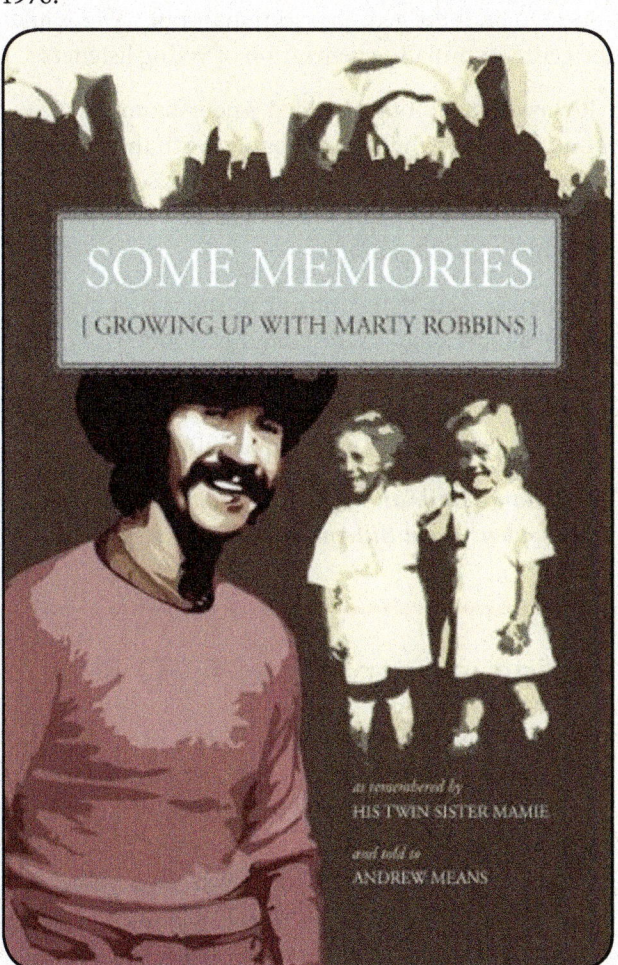

He ran many of the big super-speedway races including Talladega Superspeedway in 1972, when he stunned the competition by turning laps that were 15 mph faster than his qualifying time. Apparently, in his motel room, Marty had knocked the NASCAR-mandated restrictors out of his carburetor. After the race, NASCAR tried to give him the Rookie of the Race award, but he would not accept it, admitting he was illegal because he "just wanted to see what it was like to run up front for once."

In 1972, Marty starred in the movie "Guns of a Stranger" (originally titled "The Drifter") and appeared with Chill Wills and Dovie Beams, released in 1973. The movie is about a drifter forced in the line of duty to kill a young Abilene gunman.

He later portrayed a musician in the 1982 Clint Eastwood film Honkytonk Man.

The last year of Marty's life was climatic. In May 1982 "Some Memories Just Won't Die" made the country Top Ten, and in October Billboard recognized his renewed success by awarding him its Artist Resurgence Award as the performer who had seen the greatest career revival during the past year. On October 11, 1982, he was inducted into the Country Music Hall of Fame. It was only seven weeks before he suffered a heart attack, on December 2. Marty died December 8, 1982, at age fifty-seven just weeks before Honkytonk Man was released.

He was interred in Woodlawn Memorial Park in Nashville. The city of El Paso, Texas, later honored him by naming a park and a recreational center after him.

Marty's twin sister Mamie Ellen Robinson Minotto died on March 14, 2004, when she was partway through writing a book about her brother "Some Memories: Growing up with Marty Robbins" as remembered by Mamie Minotto, as told to Andrew Means. It was published in January 2007.

September 2015

Bill Anderson still plays to sell out crowds

On Saturday, July 18, the marquee sign at the historic Palace Theatre in Crossville, Tennessee read "SOLD OUT," and country music legend Bill Anderson was the headlining name to blame. Bringing top hits like "Po' Folks," "Bright Lights and Country Music," "Mama Sang A Song," "The Tips Of My Fingers," "8X10," "Still," among others, the million-selling recording artist, Grand Ole Opry member, and celebrated songwriter, performer, TV personality and radio host has been touring for over fifty years. Yet still today, he has the ability to capture the attention of millions of country music fans young and old.

Fans can catch Bill Anderson out on the road this fall on the following upcoming stops:

9/4 The Woodlands, Texas | Dosey Doe

9/5 Arlington, Texas | Arlington Music Hall

9/17 Shipshewana, Ind. | Blue Gate Theater

9/18 Shipshewana, Ind | Blue Gate Theater

9/23 Lloydminster, Alberta, Canada | Vic Juba Community Theatre

9/24 Edmonton, Alberta, Canada | Century Casino Edmonton Showroom

10/3 Bossier City, La. | Horseshoe Casino & Hotel / Riverdome

10/10 Ruidoso Downs, NM | Lincoln County Cowboy Symposium

Known as "Whispering Bill," a nickname appointed to him for his soft, gravelly and recognizable voice, Anderson achieved a rare historic distinction in April when his self-penned song "Country," (co-written with Mo Pitney and Bobby Tomberlin and recorded by Pitney) broke through to the Top 40 on the Country Billboard chart. The song makes him the only songwriter known in the history of the genre to have had an entry in the Top 40 on the country charts for seven consecutive decades.

Other career-defining songwriting hits for Anderson include George Strait's "Give It Away," Kenny Chesney's "A Lot Of Things Different," Brad Paisley and Alison Krauss's "Whiskey Lullaby," "Joey" by Sugarland, among others.

At 23 years old, he became the youngest writer to earn BMI's Country Songwriter Of The Year award – a record never broken until 20-year-old Taylor Swift was endowed with the same award in 2010, and to this day, he has still been able to write and record songs that appeal to both the genre's traditional country fans and the genre-dominating generation of young listeners.

Reviewers have long heralded Anderson for his humorous jokes and friendly banter with the audience throughout his live shows, matched by resonant stories of his life milestones and challenges encountered along the way.

Anderson is currently touring in support of his new Gospel album, God Is Great, God Is Good, with over 40 Gospel favorites as well as his original 10-track project, Life, released on November 12, 2013. To purchase, visit iTunes, Amazon or BillAnderson.com.

For show details and information on where to buy tickets, please visit BillAnderson.com.

Country's Family Reunion Tribute Series is coming to RFD-TV!

Country's Family Reunion is producing artist specific shows from over 17 years worth of tapings. For example, did you know that Jim Ed Brown has been on almost every single CFR show since we began? Well, we're going to create a Tribute show just for Jim Ed highlighting his best songs and story moments all in one episode!

We'll do the same for Little Jimmy Dickens, Grandpa Jones and Billy Walker. But it's not just a show for those who are no longer with us. We're creating other Tribute shows around many more of your favorite artists who've joined us multiple times—The Whites, Charley Pride, Vince Gill, Crystal Gayle, Gene Watson, Moe Bandy and others.

All new episodes begin September 25th on RFD-TV.

Bill Anderson gets long lost guitar back

Last year, a man came into the Bell Road Pawn in Phoenix, with the guitar. He never returned for it and didn't respond to the owners, Mike Grauer and Wendy Davis' attempts to contact him. The guitar had water and mold damage, but Grauer, a guitar collector, noticed the "Made for Bill Anderson" label that Billy Grammer pasted inside half a century ago, and he began working with a luthier to restore the instrument.

Grauer found a grainy clip of Anderson playing the guitar on "The Johnny Cash Show" and he emailed photos of the instrument to Anderson's secretary, not expecting to hear back. But as soon as Anderson saw the photo of the custom label inside, he knew it was the guitar he'd been missing for decades and reached out to the Grauers. (He's still not entirely sure how the guitar got out of his possession, but thinks he might have loaned it to a museum and it just never found its way back.)

Grauer told Bill that he and his wife were celebrating their fifth anniversary on the first weekend in August, and that they were both country music fans who wanted to visit the Grand Ole Opry. If Anderson could get them to Nashville, they'd return the restored guitar to him in person.

"You wouldn't believe how quick I bought him an airline ticket," Anderson said onstage at the Opry as he told the story to a packed house.

The couple presented Anderson with his guitar at the Grand Ole Opry in August and then the country singer invited Jamey Johnson onstage to sing "The Guitar Song," which the two men wrote and recorded several years ago about a guitar that was slowly gathering dust in a pawn shop, wishing someone would pick it up and play it again. "This has been a dream come true," said Davis-Grauer backstage after watching the performance.

"It sounds wonderful and I'm so glad to have it back," Anderson said as he and the Grauers sat in his Opry dressing room that night, strumming the guitar he never thought he'd see again. "I just wonder, if it could talk, what stories it would tell me."

Road Stories
By Claudia Johnson

Battle of New Orleans Never Forgotten Thanks to Horton's Catchy Song

The Battle of New Orleans was fought 200 years ago this year, putting an end to the War of 1812. Though countless Americans are descendants of veterans of the bloody three-year war that pitted American citizens against the British and their unlikely Native American allies, most people know very little about the conflict. What awareness they do have may be in part because of the popularity of a song recorded by a country star whose end was as bloody as the battle that brought him fame.

"The Battle of New Orleans" became the song for which Country-Rockabilly artist Johnny Horton is best remembered, though in the 1950s the handsome crooner released a string of other "saga" songs and was a popular performer at live venues. The song was named Billboard's Number One Song for 1959 and won the 1960 Grammy Award for Best Country & Western Recording.

Horton's life offered all the elements of a great movie, but unlike many of his contemporaries, his story has not been told on film. Born in 1925, Horton spent his childhood between Texas and California. He attended colleges in Texas and Washington, playing basketball and studying geology but never graduating. He worked at a variety of jobs from Hollywood studio mailroom clerk to Alaskan gold miner before pursuing music.

In the late 1940s and early 1950s he performed on television and radio on the West Coast, finally landing a guest performance on Louisiana Hayride in Shreveport, La. That's where he got to know Hank Williams and his wife, Billie Jean Jones, who had married Williams in the fall of 1952.

"Hank knew Johnny better than I did," Billie Jean told writer John Prime in a 1987 interview.

September 2015

"Hank was actually a fan of Johnny's and used to listen to every record Johnny would come out with. He would stop the car if we were riding along and Johnny came on the radio."

She told Prime that Williams was convinced Horton would become "one of the biggest stars in the business."

As the new year of 1953 began, somewhere between Knoxville and Oak Hill, W. Va., 29-year-old Hank Williams slipped into eternity in the back of a pale blue 1952 Cadillac, and the iconic singer's young bride became a widow at age 19.

Nine months later, on Sept. 26, 1953, she married Johnny Horton.

Horton continued with his career, and his new wife settled in as a mother to their two daughters and her own from an early first marriage. To relax, Horton hunted and fished, a passion he shared with the man that Billie Jean later told reporters was perhaps the only close friend her husband ever had – Johnny Cash.

Horton's other passion was spiritualism.

Journalist Bill Keith recalled in a 2012 article that during an interview with Billie Jean some years earlier she told him that, unlike Horton, Hank Williams had no interest in mysticism and neither did she.

"[Johnny] had this friend, Bernard, down at the post office who was a real spooky guy," Billie Jean told Keith. "Johnny would invite him out to the house, and they would have séances. I kicked them out of the house, and Johnny built a one-room building in the back yard where they did all that stuff."

Horton experienced premonitions and readily shared them with those close to him. One strong, recurring vision was that he would be killed by a drunk driver. Finally, it happened mid-way across a 320-foot concrete railroad overpass in the center of Milano, La., around 1:30 a.m., Nov. 5, 1960, when Horton's Cadillac was struck head-on by a 19-year-old intoxicated college student. Horton, 35, died en route to the hospital. The driver of the other vehicle, James Evans Davis, suffered only minor injuries and was soon arrested.

"It's ironic that Johnny was killed on a railroad overpass by a drunk driver," Horton's brother, Frank Horton said in a speech many years after the accident. "Johnny had a premonition, a certainty he was going to be killed by a train. He rode on a train for his last appearance on 'The Ed Sullivan Show,' and he never rode another one."

In the fatal accident, Horton's guitar player, Tommy Tomlinson, who was 30, sustained leg injuries that later warranted amputation. Tomlinson died at age 51 of heart failure. Tillman B. Franks, Horton's manager was riding shotgun. He was critically injured but recovered, dying in 2006 at age 86. In his autobiography "I Was There When It Happened" he expressed his disappointment at the outcome of Davis' arrest. Franks said that Davis pleaded "no contest" to "murder without malice" and was given a two year suspended sentence, having served no time in prison. Davis married, raised a family and died at 65 in Bulverde, Texas, where, according to his 2007 obituary, he had taken leadership roles in local community affairs.

In 2013 biographer Robert Hilburn published Johnny Cash: The Life in which he stated that Cash fell in love with Billie Jean Horton after his friend's death and even asked Billie Jean to marry him. She declined, Hilburn reported, because she was scared of drugs. Horton had not used drugs or alcohol, but with Williams, Billie Jean had already experienced their impact. After all, she was a widow for a second time at 27.

The year Horton died he had enjoyed commercial success with "Sink the Bismarck" and "North to Alaska," the theme song for John Wayne's movie by the same name. However, it's the catchy tune about the Battle of New Orleans that the Western Writers of America chose it as one of the Top 100 Western songs of all time and was voted into the Grammy Hall of Fame Award.

It's nice to think that Horton had a good premonition that more than four decades after his death, in 2001, his signature song would be ranked No. 333 of the Recording Industry Association of America's "Songs of the Century."

September 2015

Wade Hayes battles cancer to 'go live life'

Tony Wade Hayes was born April 20, 1969 and raised in Bethel Acres, Oklahoma. His father, Don Hayes, also a professional country musician, inspired him to begin playing music as well. Initially, Wade had learned to play mandolin, but later switched to guitar after his father bought him one. When he was eleven years old, his family moved to Nashville, Tennessee, where his father signed him to an independent record label. The label soon declared bankruptcy. The family returned to Oklahoma, where Wade later found work as a musician in his father's band.

Although he attended three different colleges, Wade dropped out of college in 1991 in pursuit of a career in country music, after seeing bluegrass musician Ricky Skaggs perform on the 1991 Country Music Association awards show. Wade returned to Nashville, where he began recording demo tapes and writing his own material. Eventually, he partnered with a songwriter named Chick Rains, who recommended him to Don Cook, a record producer who has produced albums for several country music artists, including Brooks & Dunn.

With Cook's help, Wade was signed to a record deal with Columbia Records in late 1994. The same year, his debut single, "Old Enough to Know Better", was released, and by early 1995, it peaked at Number One on the Billboard Hot Country Singles & Tracks charts. The single was followed by the release of Wade's debut album, also titled Old Enough to Know Better, which produced three additional Top Ten singles on the country music charts.

On April 4, 1999, Wade married former Miss USA runner-up Danni Boatwright, who appeared in the video for his single "Tore Up from the Floor Up" She also appeared in Hayes' video for the song "Up North Down South, Back East, Out West."

Boatwright later was a contestant on the CBS reality television series Survivor. The couple divorced in 2003.

In 2009, he released the critically acclaimed independent album, A Place to Turn Around, and continued to tour extensively until his world came to a screeching halt when he was diagnosed with stage IV colon cancer in the fall of 2011. It was a surprise to everyone, even the doctors. Because he was so young, doctors initially thought the symptoms were the result of him working out too strenuously and lifting too much weight. After extensive surgery and debilitating chemotherapy, he battled his way back to health only to have the cancer return in the fall of 2012.

"It came back in my lymph nodes, near the original cancer site," he says. "I had to take chemo for several months prior to surgery and then they did surgery again, opened me up nearly in the exact same spot, and got all the lymph nodes out that were affected. I've been cancer free since."

Wade co-wrote "Go Live Your Life" with Bobby Pinson after a conversation with his oncologist. When the doctor told him he was cancer free for the second time, he encouraged the musician to make the most of his new lease on life. "He said, 'Wade, you were stage IV, and now you're cancer free,'" Wade recalls. "He said, 'This is a big deal. I want you to go live your life.'"

In addition to writing and recording, Wade has been back on the road, touring this spring with pals Bryan White and Mark Wills. He also enjoys spending time at his 11-acre farm outside Nashville where one of his favorite hobbies is restoring old pick up trucks. He makes time to share his experience with cancer and encourage others fighting the battle. "I've met so many wonderful people during this journey, especially when I started healing and got out and began speaking. I've met some incredible, brave people that were inspiring to me and told me that my story is inspiring to them. I heard the story of a guy who had cancer similar to mine and he made it back to being cancer free. It gave me so much hope that once I got through the valley I thought, "Man, that's what I want to do for other people.' I want to help them and try to give them inspiration and hope. With God all things are possible. I'm a living example."

September 2015

COUNTRY LEGENDS PAST AND PRESENT BY TOM WOOD

Tammy Wynette

Tammy Wynette didn't just sing Classic Country songs — she lived them.

Known as "The First Lady of Country Music," Tammy's all-too-short life played out like a country song. One with many verses.

"I believe you have to live the songs," Tammy is quoted as saying on her Grand Ole Opry artist bio page.

And live the songs she did.

Over the decades, Tammy's songs tapped into the emotions and resonated with the facets of everyday life that so many of us must deal and cope with — from love and marriage to cheating spouses to D-I-V-O-R-C-E, from home-making to job security, from womanhood to raising a family, from motherhood to childhood, from alcohol to other forms of abusive behavior, from health problems to money problems, from heartache and sadness to livin' and lovin' and happiness, from dreams and schemes to so many other themes.

The Grand Ole Opry member (inducted 1973) and Country Music Hall of Famer (Class of 1998) touched many people with her soulful ballads and the way these songs seemingly bared her heart for all the world to see.

Tammy was one of us. We loved her — and loved her for it.

It's not important now, more than 17 years after her untimely 1998 death, to recount all of the ups and downs of Tammy's well-documented life, but it does give perspective to her music. Or is it the other way around?

Her birth name was Virginia W. Richardson, and life was a struggle from the day she was born (May 5, 1942) on a cotton farm in Bounds, Miss., near the Alabama state line. Hard times filled her childhood as she worked in the cotton fields and she soon was a teen-age bride, living in an abandoned log home (with no indoor plumbing), with her first husband and two children.

In all, there were five marriages, including the tumultuous six years she was wed to George Jones (1969-75), and four children.

Her health issues were many, undergoing more than two dozen major surgical procedures during her lifetime. She died on April 26, 1998, of what a controversial second autopsy performed in 1999 revealed that she had suffered cardiac arrhythmia.

Her music career began in Birmingham, Ala., where she attended American Beauty College to become a hairdresser (she renewed her cosmetology license every year as a fall-back plan in case the music thing didn't work out).

After some moderate success in the mid-1960s, she packed her bags and the children, and moved to Nashville in 1966. That same year, she auditioned for record producer Billy Sherrill, and her first single, "Apartment No. 9" (1967) peaked at No. 44 on the charts.

Her first chart-topper came a year later, the duet "My Elusive Dreams" with David Houston, setting the stage for a phenomenal run for Tammy of six consecutive No. 1 singles hits and a total of eight chart-toppers from 1967-70 (the other two peaking at Nos. 2 and 3).

Two career-defining hits came in 1968 — "D-I-V-O-R-C-E" and "Stand by Your Man" — and both have reached iconic status in terms of controversy and crossover appeal. Who can forget Dan Akroyd and John Belushi's version of "Stand by Your Man" in the Blues Brothers movie?

"Stand by Your Man" was voted the top country song of all time in a 2003 poll of country music writers, producers and stars for a CMT special on the top 100 songs. In 2011, "Stand by Your Man" was named one of that year's 25 recordings to be preserved by the U.S. Library of Congress for the song's cultural significance.

Other No. 1 singles during that fabulous three-year stretch included "Singing My Song" (1969), "The Ways to Love a Man" (1969), "He Loves Me All the Way" (1970) and "Run Woman Run" (1970). Her final No. 1 hit was "You and Me" (1976).

Tammy rhymes with Grammy and she won two of those. A three-time CMA Female Vocalist of the Year, she had 11 albums reach No. 1 on the country charts.

That's a phenomenal success by any measure, and a reason why she continues to rank among the most beloved country music stars we've ever had.

Wynette? Why not?

Author Tom Wood, who writes thrillers and Westerns, is a regular contributor to Country Family Reunion News. Reach him at tomwoodauthor.com

OCTOBER

A 'REAL' Larry's Country Diner breaks ground

Larry's Country Diner hosted a media groundbreaking ceremony on September 16 on a new 6,700 square foot, 135-seat venue that will host the popular TV tapings, a full-service diner restaurant, gift shop and entertainment venue for performances from some of country, bluegrass and gospel music's biggest stars.

Located at 7734 Highway 70 South in Bellevue (Nashville), off exit 196 on I-40 west, the custom-designed facility will be a replica of the diner portrayed in the television show, which airs nationally on RFD-TV. It is slated to open in late spring 2016.

"When we first started this show, we had the vision of creating something that no one else had done - something that was full of family-friendly humor, old-fashioned values, and great music popular in the good ol' days and today. Witnessing its tremendous growth over the past six years that's allowed us to buld a real-life diner where the food is served hot and feels right at home when you walk in is a dream come true," said Larry Black, founder and owner of Gabriel Communications.

In true Larry's Country Diner fashion, the groundbreaking ceremony was complete with a giant fork, and spoons to shovel the dirt and homemade pie.

Councilwoman Sheri Weiner, who according to Larry was involved from day one in helping to clear the hurdles to keep the project on track was there to help shovel the dirt!

A grand opening celebration will be held as soon as the diner is complete!

Some of the Diner's guest artists showed up to shovel, including Marlon and Steve from Exile, Jeannie Seely, Bill Anderson and T. Graham Brown (who lives just down the road). Ronnie McDowell also stopped by to get in on the action.

October 2015

The Americana Music Honors & Awards winners

The Americana Music Honors and Awards Show was held at the Ryman Auditorium September 16. The majority of the program was composed of live performances, beginning with Robert Randolph, the Fairfield Four, and the McCrary Sisters lively rendition of "Rock My Soul." Nearly two dozen artists — who were backed by a top-notch house band led by Buddy Miller — performed over the course of the evening, including all of this year's Lifetime Achievement Award recipients: Ricky Skaggs, Don Henley, Los Lobos, Buffy Sainte-Marie, and Gillian Welch and David Rawlings.

"The Lord has put so many great people in my life," Skaggs said after accepting his award from Ry Cooder. "Getting to play with Bill Monroe, playing with Flatt & Scruggs and with Ralph and Carter Stanley … I'm so blessed."

Sturgill Simpson , a Kentucky native, Nashville-based singer-songwriter, took home the Emerging Artist trophy in 2014. This year he won both Song of the Year for "Turtles All the Way Down" and Artist of the Year.

"Metamodern Sounds in Country Music" was also nominated for Album of the Year; however, those honors went to Americana staple Lucinda Williams for her record "Down Where the Spirit Meets the Bone." This win was a poignant one for Williams: the album title comes from "Compassion," a poem written by her father, Miller Williams, who died on New Year's Day.

Singer-songwriter Shakey Graves, who described standing on the Ryman stage as a "continual, massive, semi-religious experience," was named this year's Emerging Artist.

The Mavericks won Duo/Group of the Year, and John Leventhal, who co-wrote, produced and performed on wife Rosanne Cash's Grammy-winning record "The River and The Thread," received the Instrumentalist of the Year Award.

"Musicians always have been and always will be my heroes," Leventhal said in his acceptance speech.

BB King's beloved guitar Lucille was brought onstage as Keb' Mo paid tribute to the blues legend with a soulful rendition of King's "How Blue Can I Get." King, who died in May would have been 90 years old the day of the awards, was posthumously honored with the Americana Music Association President's Award.

An edited version of the awards show will air on PBS as a special episode of "Austin City Limits" later this year.

2015 winners:

Album of the Year (Award goes to artist and producer)

"Down Where the Spirit Meets the Bone," Lucinda Williams; Produced by Lucinda Williams, Tom Overby and Greg Leisz

Artist of the Year
Sturgill Simpson

Emerging Artist of the Year
Shakey Graves

Duo/Group of the Year
The Mavericks

Song of the Year (Award goes to Artist and Songwriter)
"Turtles All the Way Down" - Sturgill Simpson; Written by Sturgill Simpson

Instrumentalist of the Year
John Leventhal

President's Award: BB King

Lifetime Achievement Award, Trailblazer: Don Henley

Lifetime Achievement Award, Instrumentalist: Ricky Skaggs

Lifetime Achievement Award, Songwriting: Gillian Welch & David Rawlings

Lifetime Achievement Award, Performance: Los Lobos.

Spirit of Americana/Free Speech in Music Award co-presented by the Americana Music Association and the First Amendment Center: Buffy Sainte-Marie

October 2015

Nadine's Corner

Everyone knows church folk like to cook, and most have their own cookbook. Send me your church cookbook recipe, who submitted the recipe, along with the name of your church and each month I'll pull a recipe from it and feature it here!

We also love recipes from our favorite artists. Dottie Rambo had a cookbook out at one time called Seasoned With A Song. Here a few recipes from her cookbook.

JEANNIE C. RILEY'S TEXAS LONE STAR CHILI

4 pounds chili meat
1 large onion, chopped
2 cloves garlic, finely chopped
1 tsp ground oregano
1 tsp cumin
2 Tbsp chili powder
1 1/2 cups whole tomatoes
2-6 dashes hot sauce
salt to taste
2 cups boiling water

Place mean, onions, and garlic ina large skillet or dutch over and cook until browned. Add oregano, cumin, chili powder, tomatoes, hot sauce, salt, and boiling water. Bring to a boil, reduce heat, let simmer for 1 hour. Skim off fat. Serves 10.

JEANNIE C. RILEY'S NACHOS

Tortillas
1 can sliced jalapeno peppers
Grated cheddar cheese

Cut tortillas into quarters and fry in deep fry until brown and crisp on both sides. Drain and put about 1 tsp grated cheese and slice of jalapeno pepper on each quarter. Place in hot oven until well heated and cheese begins to melt. Dish up heartily as a "Texas Side Order" to Jeannie's Lone Star Chili.

JUNE CARTER CASH'S SAUSAGE BALLS

2 cups self-rising flour
1/2 cup shortening
3/4 cup buttermilk
1-2 pounds sausage

Mix flour, shortening, and buttermilk. Roll out in a long roll. Place sausage between waxed paper and roll the same length as dough. Place sausage on top of dough. Roll like a jelly roll. Place in freezer overnight. Slice and bake in 350-400 degree oven until lightly brown.

IF YOU WANT TO HEAR GOD LAUGH, TELL HIM YOUR PLANS!

October 2015

The Oak Ridge Boys' William Lee Golden weds Simone Staley

The Oak Ridge Boys' William Lee Golden is no longer a single man. The Country Music Hall of Fame inductee and country music legend known for his deep baritone voice married Simone Staley in a private ceremony among a small group of close family and friends in Nashville, Saturday, August 29. Celebrities in attendance of course included Golden's confidantes, Duane Allen, Richard Sterban and Joe Bonsall of The Oak Ridge Boys, among others.

The two long-time friends' love story, captured by journalist Matt Bjorke on WilliamLeeGolden.com, is straight out of a fairytale, having re-kindled their friendship after 27 years.

At the age of 18, Staley purchased the Oak Ridge Boys' Together album and was instantly drawn to the picture of Golden on the front of the album cover. She somehow felt as if she would meet him someday, and by the fall of that same year, she was sitting in the front row at her first Oak Ridge Boys concert. Golden threw a scarf her way, and she happened to catch it, as if the two were destined from day one.

In October of 1980, the two finally met at a show at Knott's Berry Farm, and the attraction was instant. They would spend time together over the next couple of years, however, their lives went in two different directions after a show in 1982, and they lost touch.

Fast forward to May of 2009, when they both had recently lost their mothers, they reignited their friendship and bonded over their mutual love of art and painting. Simone painted a portrait of Golden, which she gave to him back in the 80s, that he held on to for all of those years — and even pulled from the destruction after his home was destroyed by a tornado. It was the memory of her that he saw when he looked at it.

"Although it was a portrait of me, I could see her face every time I saw that painting," said Golden.

"I had always wondered if he held onto that painting," said Staley. "It was probably silly to do so, but I just felt very strongly about it after pouring my heart and soul into it."

By summer of 2013, Golden invited Simone to come to Tennessee and go to Alabama and Florida with him to visit family and friends. The time spent traveling together allowed them to get to know one another even better, and it was that trip that solidified what they already knew – that they couldn't be without each other."

The two plan to reside in their home they found together in 2013 in Middle Tennessee with their loving pets — happily ever after.

"It's been the most beautiful experience, together," Golden said.

For more information on The Oak Ridge Boys and to view their upcoming tour dates, please visit www.oakridgeboys.com.

October 2015

Keith Bilbrey's new Reflections series on Heartland Network

The Heartland Network has an all new television series Reflections.. The series premiered on Thursday, August 6 at 8:00 p.m. EDT/PDT and 6:00 p.m. CDT in Nashville and Paducah.

Reflections is a weekly half-hour, one-on-one interview series with Tennessee Radio Hall of Fame DJ Keith Bilbrey. Keith's first season guests include country music legends such as Lee Greenwood, Nancy Jones, Jimmy Fortune, Tanya Tucker, John Conlee, TG Sheppard and many more. Keith's long-time relationships with the iconic artists translate into an intimate and insightful interview with each guest.

A long-time staple in Music City and the country music industry, Keith brings with him decades of experience. During his storied career, Keith has served as a disc jockey for WSM radio, an on-air personality at Nashville's WSMV-TV, a long-time announcer for The Grand Ole Opry and host of TNN's Grand Ole Opry Live.

Reflection's creator and executive producer, Jeff Moseley, said, "For more than 30 years, I've produced country music television series and it's always been my dream to do an in-depth interview series with the greats of country music. With the recent losses of so many legends, I knew we needed to get this project started. Patience paid off as we were able to bring Keith Bilbrey onboard to host. His knowledge of the artists and his enduring friendships with them makes this series a special treat for country music fans!"

Matthew Golden, Luken's Vice President of Programming, said, "When we were first approached with this series, we knew it belonged on Heartland. We are proud to work with CJM Productions and Keith Bilbrey to bring personal interviews with the legends of country music to the viewers who love them."

Airing on September 7, Keith Bilbrey, interviewed singer/songwriter Ronnie McDowell. Country music fans love this new intimate sit-down series as it reveals unknown details about the artist, their music and their videos. For instance, did you know that before Ronnie McDowell had hits on the radio he was a songwriter that had songs cut by Porter Wagoner, George Jones, Tanya Tucker, Roy Acuff, Chet Atkins, Eddie Arnold, Faron Young, Lorrie Morgan among many others? Or, how about the fact that his own mega-hit "Watchin' Girls Go By," recently surpassed one million spins? And, did you know before John Conlee wrote and performed his signature hit, "Rose Colored Glasses," he worked as a DJ for a local Nashville radio station spinning hits of other artists? Or, how about the fact that he was raised on a tobacco farm in Kentucky and that today he still has a passion for his garden and maintains about a ¼ acre plot of home-grown vegetables. These are the kinds of fun facts country music lovers everywhere can discover by tuning into the highly anticipated series "Reflections." These are the kinds of fun facts country music lovers everywhere can discover by tuning into the highly anticipated series "Reflections."

Heartland officially debuted in 2013 with programming comprised of syndicated and first run shows along with digitally restored content pulled from the vaults of Music Row, creating a country music and lifestyle experience that brings delight to lovers of every generation and genre. The program lineup includes The Rick & Bubba Show, Bluegrass Ridge, Country Fix, Country Standard Time, Music City Tonight, Texas Music Scene, Gaither Gospel Hour, classic episodes of Crook & Chase and several popular music video blocks including Country Music Today and Country Music Rewind. For more information about Heartland, visit www.watchheartlandtv.com or www.facebook.com/WatchHeartlandTV.

October 2015

Guest Hosts fill in for Larry during recovery

During the Larry's Country Diner tapings in August, Larry was still in a wheel chair recovering from his ATV accident. Because of that, everyone has the chance to have a two-fer on those shows by having a guest artist PLUS a guest host.

The first show features Ronnie Reno as the artist, with Larry's son, Adam, as guest host explaining how the shows will work. Adam pops in on every show giving updates and reading the Promise. Moe Bandy with Bill Anderson hosting is next followed by Exile with Larry Gatlin hosting, Randy Owen of Alabama with Mark Wills hosting and finally David Ball with T. Graham Brown hosting as the final show in October.

Larry, Luann, Randy and Johnelle are featured in one of the shows talking about the accident and filling everyone in on exactly what happened.

Another great feature for October is that Keith Bilbrey was surprised by being presented with a special proclamation by his State Senator.

As you can tell by the front page ground breaking photos, Larry is up and about and doing great now. He has his walking stick to make sure he keeps his balance, but he is up and out driving himself to work and to physical therapy. He keeps getting better every day and even traveled to Branson the end of September for the Larry's Country Diner live show at Branson!

Larry's Country Diner RFD Show Schedule October 2015
ALL NEW SHOWS

RONNIE RENO
Host: Adam Black
Saturday, Oct. 3
10:00 p.m. Central
Sunday, Oct. 4
6:00 p.m. Central

MOE BANDY
Host: Bill Anderson
Saturday, Oct. 10
10:00 p.m. Central
Sunday, Oct. 11
6:00 p.m. Central

EXILE
Host: Larry Gatlin
Saturday, Oct. 17
10:00 p.m. Central
Sunday, Oct. 18
6:00 p.m. Central

RANDY OWEN
Host: Mark Wills
Saturday, Oct. 24
10:00 p.m. Central
Sunday, Oct. 25
6:00 p.m. Central

DAVID BALL
Host: T. Graham Brown
Saturday, Oct. 31
10:00 p.m. Central
Sunday, Nov. 1
6:00 p.m. Central

October 2015

COUNTRY'S FAMILY REUNION SCRAPBOOK:
SMATHERS FAMILY THE STONEY MOUNTAIN CLOGGERS

"Flying Feet Galore"
THE STONEY MOUNTAIN CLOGGERS
left to right......George Huntley, Darrell Franks, Donnie Henderson, Ben Smathers.....The ladies left to right are Margaret Collins Smathers, Shirley Litrell, Anne Gassaway and unknown.

The Stoney Mountain Cloggers

Ben Smathers, Ray Price, Roy Acuff and Minnie Pearl

Outfitted By BEN SMATHERS & THE STONEY MT. CLOGGERS

Margaret, Sally, Loretta Lynn and Candy

On tour with Charlie Daniels

The Stoney Mountain Cloggers

October 2015

50 Years of EXILE: The Story of a Band in Transition

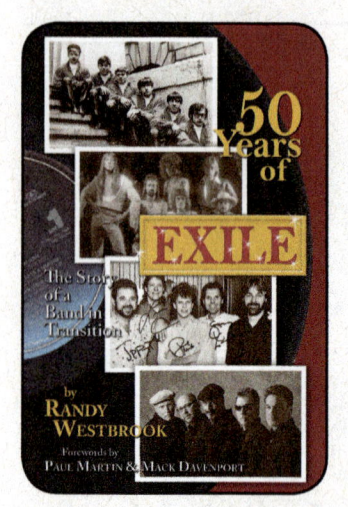

The story of one of the most successful bands in Country Music history has been documented with the recent release of the book 50 Years of Exile: The Story of a Band in Transition. Written by Randy Westbrook, an Eastern Kentucky University musicologist, the book details the group's rise to prominence over the past five decades.

Founded in Richmond, Kentucky by Jimmy Stokley, Ronnie 'Mack' Davenport, Paul Smith, Mike Howard, Billy Luxon, Buzz Cornelison, and J.P. Pennington – while all were still in high school – the band found a following in the Lexington area. But, the Exile story doesn't end there. A stint on the Dick Clark Caravan of Stars in the mid 1960s broadened their audience even more. During that stint, they opened for such Pop acts as the legendary B.J. Thomas.

Continuing to record and tour throughout the late 1960s and early 1970s, Exile's star began to shine bright with the 1978 release of the single "Kiss You All Over." After fifteen years in the business, the band was suddenly an "Overnight Success," with the song hitting number one in the fall of 1978, and selling over 5 million singles. The single's massive commercial success introduced Exile as the new opening act on the Aerosmith tour and then the Heart tour, respectively. The group followed up that hit with another Top 40 on the Hot 100, "You Thrill Me."

In the 1980s, Pennington – along with members Sonny LeMaire and Les Taylor – began to have success a songwriter in Nashville with cuts by Alabama ("Take Me Down"), Kenny Rogers ("Take This Heart"), Janie Fricke ("It Ain't Easy Bein' Easy"). That, combined with the fact that their roots had always been steeped in Country (Pennington's mother, Lily Mae Ledford, was one of the stars of the iconic Renfro Valley Barn Dance), led them to sign with Epic Records in 1983.

Their first single, "High Cost Of Leavin," found success at radio, and set the stage for hit after hit throughout the decade. "Woke Up In Love" became their first chart-topper, and it was followed by songs such as "She's Too Good To Be True," "Hang On To Your Heart," and "She's A Miracle."

50 Years In Exile: The Story of a Band in Transition is an honest look at one of America's most enduring success stories, with anecdotes from many of the band's former and current members, including Paul Martin, who later went on to fame as one of Marty Stuart's Fabulous Superlatives.

Praise for the book has come from a variety of critics and fans, with Randy pinpoints individual performances, instruments as well as the members themselves. Steve Goetzman, longtime drummer of the band, stated "Randy pinpoints individual performances, instruments played and recording techniques used, all in fine detail, yet in a language music fans will enjoy reading. This musicologist's analysis of song after Exile song intertwined with an accurate history of a 50-year-old band might set a new standard for music reviewers. Colorful personalities, career-shaping decisions and solutions for longevity are talked about here."

Keyboardist Marlon Hargis says the book was educational – even for him, "I learned things about the band that I never knew before! An interesting history of Exile from a musician's viewpoint. I recommend it to any Exile fan, or any budding musician wanting a realistic depiction of a band's life!"

Published by Acclaim Press, 50 Years of Exile: The Story of a Band in Transition is available in select bookstores and Amazon. The band continues to tour in 2015, with dates already being added to their itinerary for 2016.

October 2015

Christian singer/songwriter Phil Johnson re-releases CD

By Renae Johnson

Country's Family Reunion and Larry's Country Diner fans are in for a real treat. You have ask for a Phil Johnson CD so here it is. "Just Like You" re-mastered from his 1978 solo record. After Phil appeared on the Country's Family Reunion "Old Time Gospel" series we were flooded with requests for his song "The Day He Wore My Crown". Since I couldn't find enough LP's at yard sales…. I finally convinced him to make a CD! And the CD sounds awesome. It has 10 songs all written by Phil and includes "I've Never Been Out Of His Care". Some of the songs you may recognize that were recorded by many of your favorite Christian artists or heard in a Sunday morning church service. But if not….you will enjoy the smooth voice and uplifting songs by Phil Johnson.

"He Can Hear You", " It'll Be all Right (In The Morning)", "He Didn't Lift Us Up To Let Us Down", "The Day He Wore My Crown", "Somebody Like You", "Don't Take Your Love Away", "I've Never Been Out Of His Care ", "Never Be", "I'm Simply Lost For Words", "Here He Is Again".

(Look for a new Country CD to be released this Christmas "Phil Goes Country" !!)

CD now available

Includes *The Day He Wore My Crown*

To Order call: 1-800-820-5405 or send a check for $14.95 plus $6.95 s/h to Phil Johnson, P.O. Box 210796, Nashville, TN 37221
www.renaethewaitress.com

October 2015

T.G. Sheppard to release 'LEGENDARY FRIENDS & COUNTRY DUETS'

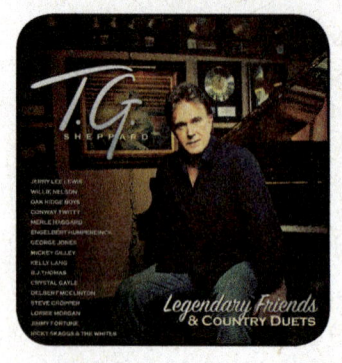

Since leaving home in 1961 to pursue a career in music, TG Sheppard has done it all. He scored a job as a promotions executive for RCA Records, where he became friends with Elvis Presley who believed in his talent so much that he gave him his first tour bus, topped the Billboard Hot Country Songs chart an astonishing 21 times, and left an everlasting mark on Country music. Over the years, the smooth singer/songwriter has made a lot of impressive friends, which inspired the vision for his upcoming album, Legendary Friends & Country Duets, which is set for release on Oct. 30 via Cleopatra Records. On the upcoming project, TG collaborates with some of the most influential artists of all-time and those that he can actually call his personal friends.

"In my 40 years of recording music, this album has to be my most favorite I've ever recorded," says T.G. Sheppard. "I'm very honored that so many of my personal friends came in to sing, with no questions asked, and gave their all."

Listeners will be taken on a journey, with songs that hit the highest of highs and the lowest of lows. Standout tracks on the album include the fun, "It's A Man Thing" which features late country icon George Jones, the relaxing sing-along, "Song Man" with Grammy® winner Merle Haggard, and the inspiring, "In Texas" with country outlaw Willie Nelson. Legendary Friends & Country Duets will bring traditional country music back to the forefront, as the style currently makes a demanding comeback. With the remarkable list of guests on the album, Legendary Friends & Country Duets is a must-have for all music fans to remind them what made country music great.

"As a record company working multiple projects in all genres, it is always special to find an artist and project like what T.G. Sheppard has brought to Cleopatra Records," says Tim Yasui, GM/Cleopatra Records. "T.G. is loved within the Country music community and this project proves that his fanbase is much more than just the country music fans - his fellow artists love him, too! Albums like this come once in a lifetime and Cleopatra Records is very proud to be involved in this iconic recording."

Sheppard has already begun promoting the album, with several upcoming appearances already scheduled. Airing on September 13-14, NBC's "Open House" will take viewers inside the stylish Nashville home of Sheppard and his wife, singer/songwriter Kelly Lang. The show is described as the ultimate insiders' guide to real estate and home design. Next, offering fans a never-before-seen glimpse into the past, present and future of TG's storied career, Sheppard will appear on Heartland-TV's new show "Reflections" on Sept. 14 (check your local listings).

1. Down On My Knees (with OAK RIDGE BOYS)

2. The Killer (with JERRY LEE LEWIS)

3. If You Knew (with RICKY SKAGGS & THE WHITES)

4. It's A Man Thing (with GEORGE JONES)

5. 100% Chance Of Pain (with B.J. THOMAS, JIMMY FORTUNE)

6. Wine To Remember And Whiskey To Forget (with MICKEY GILLEY)

7. The Next One (with LORRIE MORGAN)

8. Dead Girl Walking (with KELLY LANG)

9. Song Man (with MERLE HAGGARD)

10. Why Me Lord (with CONWAY TWITTY)

11. In Texas (with WILLIE NELSON)

12. Have You Ever Loved A Woman (with ENGELBERT HUMPERDINCK)

13. I'm Not Going Anywhere (with CRYSTAL GAYLE)

October 2015

Rhonda Vincent Holiday album features Dolly Parton, Willie Nelson & more!

Rhonda Vincent has been celebrating the season all year; writing new Christmas material, then combining the new originals with the classics. The result is something unique and it's sure to set the perfect tone for this Holiday Season!

This six-time Grammy® nominated artist is set to reveal Christmas Time, on October 30 via Upper Management Music. Among the tunes, you will find the "Twelve Days of Christmas," like you've never heard before! Rhonda calls upon some of her most famous Country music friends to join her in the celebration; including Dolly Parton, Willie Nelson, Charlie Daniels, The Oak Ridge Boys and more (see track listing below).

"It was a dream of mine to create this celebrity version of the 'Twelve Days of Christmas,'" said Vincent. She explains, "As I started sharing my vision with family and friends, my bandmate Mickey Harris, began sharing his ideas, relating the line to specific artists. When I told him I had invited Dolly, he suggested she sing the line 'Eight Maids A Milking.' It was then I set to work to match artists with specific lines, and taking on the task of contacting each artist. Dolly was the first to respond, and the first to record. From there, it became a chaotic coordination of schedules, and a victory celebration with the completion of each artist's contribution. I appreciate every artist that joined me in making this incredible dream come true!"

The upbeat favorite, features vocal contributions from The Oak Ridge Boys, Willie Nelson, Charlie Daniels, Bill Anderson, Dolly Parton, Ronnie Milsap, Gene Watson, Lorrie Morgan, Pam Tillis, Jeannie Seely, Larry Gatlin, and EmiSunshine. Listen closely as each performer sings a line from the famous tune. Another highlight of the album is the "Christmas Medley," which is the closing track of the album. For the first time ever, Vincent sings with only a piano, on a special arrangement of seven classics; including "We Three Kings," "It Came Upon The Midnight Clear," "The First Noel", with ACM award-winner Michael Rojas.

In addition to the large lineup of celebrity guests, Christmas Time also features a who's who of musicians. Along with members of The Rage, joining Vincent on the album is ACM "Fiddle Player of the Year" Stuart Duncan, ACM "Steel Guitar Player of the Year" Mike Johnson, ACM "Piano/Keyboards Player of the Year" Michael Rojas, mandolinist extraordinaire Sierra Hull, and many more, who all come together to bring the Christmas sound to a whole new level. Also assisting Vincent on vocals is the International Bluegrass Music Association's reigning "Emerging Artist of the Year" recipients, Flatt Lonesome.

1. Dreaming of Christmas - Written by Rhonda Vincent

2. God Rest Ye Merry Gentlemen

3. Twelve Days of Christmas (Featuring The Oak Ridge Boys, Willie Nelson, Charlie Daniels, Bill Anderson, Dolly Parton, Ronnie Milsap, Gene Watson, Larry Gatlin, Jeannie Seely, Lorrie Morgan, Pam Tillis, and EmiSunshine)

4. Angels We Have Heard On High

5. Milk & Cookies - Written by Rhonda Vincent

6. Christmas Time - Written by Rhonda Vincent

7. Christmas Time At Home - Written by Rhonda Vincent

8. Away In A Manger

9. Jingle Bells

10. Silent Night

11. O Little Town of Bethlehem

12. Christmas Medley (What Child Is This, We Three Kings, It Came Upon The Midnight Clear, O Come All Ye Faithful, The First Noel, O Holy Night, Hark The Herald Angles Sing)

October 2015

The Nashville Brat Pack — Kids of the Country Stars!

By Chrystie Wooley, Daughter of Sheb Wooley

Packers who grew up with each other in Nashville . I was raised on the West Coast (California). My fathers career in the movie industry mandated him living there . Since Sheb was a real cowboy , he landed many roles in Western classics such as " High Noon", " Giant", "War Wagon" and the hit TV series " Raw Hide". He also had his label home with MGM records for 25 years in Los Angeles .

Along the way Sheb and Johnny Cash became great friends , having strong bonds not only in their music and movie pursuits but how they were raised . My father an Okie and Cash from Arkansas both raised by sharecroppers pick in' cotton. Jonny already made the move from the hustle of LA to Casitas Springs Cali - 2 hours north of Los Angeles - to a beautiful laid back community with a little room to breath . John urged my parents to do the same since LA was neither of their true lifestyle . They needed dirt under their feet ... Shebs dream was to build a house on enough land to raise horses and a little cattle . We ended up neighbors of the Cash family , only 5 miles apart . Our houses were even similar as the same builder designed our home . Ranch style home on a hill . We bought 26 acres in the foothills of the Topa Topa mountains near Ojai and over the hill from Santa Barbara.

Living in the Ojai Valley was where I became childhood friends with the Cash Girls; namely Cindy who was my age . Our parents would attend awards show and I would stay with the girls on many occasions . Cindy and I were very mischievous and caused a little trouble together making the live in maid so mad at us she quit . That didn't go over well with our folks. I also remember Rosanne as a young girl isolating herself to her bedroom for hours writing poetry and songs . That was history in the making .

We had horses and I was taught to ride Western from my father - Nothing Fancy . I learned to barrel race and show in Western Pleasure . This ranch was also the home of Lindsey Wagners parents in the hit series " Six Million Dollar Man " starring Lee Majors . I threw a party the last day of the shoot so my friends could see how a film was made . That lil party turned into 200 crazy teenagers .

Sheb and Johnny went into partnership buying a miniature golf course , tearing it down and building a strip mall . The names it Purple Wagon Mall . Purple after The Purple People Eater and Wagon for the show Raw Hide . John kept one space for his own office and Vivian (his 1st wife) and my mother Beverly opened a beauty shop together . When John moves to Nashville my parents bought him out but the friendship lasted a lifetime ; both passing away only days apart .

In 1975 Sheb put together a show called Second Generation that was held in Yellowstone park . That's where I met some of the Brat Packers for the first time . Robyn Young , Ronny Robbins, Rex Allen Jr, Michael Twitty , Allen Rich , Buddy Allen (Bucks son) . The circle keeps growing as a result of the Family Reunion - Second Generation TV show and I have been so blessed to know other sons and daughters of Country Legends . I laugh a say " we are like a big AA or Alanon meeting." We have an extended family in each other . A soft spot to land were we understand each other and love one another unconditionally .

October 2015

Songwriter Jimmy Payne still enjoys singing around town

Born in Arkansas, raised in Missouri, Jimmy Payne is a Nashville singer-songwriter who has performed both at home and abroad at venues ranging from the Golden Nugget in Las Vegas, to the Wembley Festival in England. His International success is well documented with tours in Japan, the Philippines, South Korea, the Netherlands, Norway and the United Kingdom.

His first major success began when longtime friend Chuck Glaser arranged a live audition between Jimmy and Billy Sherrill. After one song, Billy signed Jimmy to a five year contract with Epic Records.

Jimmy co-wrote the mega hit, "Woman Woman" with his great friend Jim Glaser and recorded the original version himself on Epic Records under the supervision of legendary producer, Billy Sherrill. Gary Puckett and the Union Gap went on to have a multi-million seller with their version of the song and took it to the top of the pop charts in the US in 1967. Since then, it has been recorded around a hundred times and has received nearly five million airplays in the US and became a worldwide pop hit.

With Naomi Martin, Jimmy also wrote the number one hit "My Eyes Can Only See As Far As You" for Charley Pride. Other artists who have recorded Jimmy's songs are Glen Campbell, Tammy Wynette, Tompall and the Glaser Brothers, Dottie West, Jimmy Dean, Levi Stubbs and The Four Tops, Connie Smith, Bill Anderson, Ray Price, Cal Smith, Jeanne Pruett, Jim Glaser, Frank Ifield, Daniel O'Donnell, The Lettermen and many others.

As an artist, Jimmy has had National chart success with " L.A. Angels", "Ramblin' Man", "Where Has All The Love Gone", "Turnin' My Love On" and others. He also entered the British pop charts with his version of "Sweet Fantasy".

Jimmy has recorded for Epic, RCA, VeeJay, Vanguard, Cinnamon, Password and others. He has released six albums, two CD's and numerous singles.

On Jimmy's debut performance at The Grand Ole Opry, the audience rewarded him with three encores. In 2007 he received the honor of being inducted into the Traditional Country Hall of Fame in Anita, Iowa.

Jimmy enjoys writing, recording and playing various writers' nights around Nashville. He has a great sense of humor, and his live performances of his wonderful songs are always infused with his humorous reminiscences. Not to be missed.

October 2015

Diner Chat
with Renae the Waitress

It's easy...it's fun!!
Listen live by Phone or on the web,
every Thursday at 3:00 p.m. EST.

1-425-440-5100
ID code: 909005#

www.larryscountrydiner.com, click 'Diner Chat'

Hey everyone if you are not joining Diner Chat every Thursday you are missing a treat!! And I don't mean Trick or Treat. I have had some wonderful folks calling in and asking questions (Yes...Larry is doing great). Every Thursday at 2:00 Nashville time (check your time zone) me and tens, hundreds, thousands, millions, well….alot of folks chat. It's like the old fashion party line. One number connects us all. Or for those really smart folks you can go to our website at Larryscountrydiner.com/Dinerchat and listen on your computer. AND…all of our calls are recorded to listen to later.

Who are your GUESTS?

We have had some special people join us for Diner Chat: Ronnie Robbins, LaDonna Gatlin, Barbara Fairchild, Nadine, Jimmy Capps, Keith Bilbrey, Moe Bandy, Jan Howard, Scott England, Terry Choate, Phil Johnson and Randy Little to name a few. You never know who might join us !!! And of course my co-host the loveable customer service guru "Jason" is with us every week.

What do you talk about?

All of our shows on RFD are pre-recorded but Diner Chat is LIVE. We will talk about the NEW Larry's Country Diner restaurant under construction, our Cruise, the NEW Christmas series and how to get tickets to our tapings….and anything else happening in Nashville with our Country Music stars. And don't forget customer service…..a perfect time to ask Jason about special offers.

How do I dial the number?

It is so easy to listen to Diner Chat. Just dial 1-425-440-5100. A recording will ask for your conference ID number. You then press 909005# and it will say, "you are being connected". If you are earlier…you will hear music while on hold. At 2:00 Central time the Renae the Waitress theme song will play and we're ready to chat.

How do I talk to Renae or the special guest?

At any time during the call you can just press *2 which gives us a signal that you have a question or comment. Jason then will UNMUTE your line to talk. Simple. Since everyone can't be talking a one time lines are muted unless you press *2.

What if I can't remember to call?

We have cute little magnets that can go on your refrigerator to remind you. Just call Jason at customer service and ask for one to be sent to you. Customer service is 800-820-5405.

Does it cost to call Diner Chat?

NO…if you have unlimited minutes on your phone. However if you have a long distance telephone home package you can call Customer Service and we can give you a LOCAL number in your area that is not long distance. Or of course you can listen free on our website.

How do I know what time Diner Chat is in my area?

Here is a map of where you live and the time zones for Diner Chat.

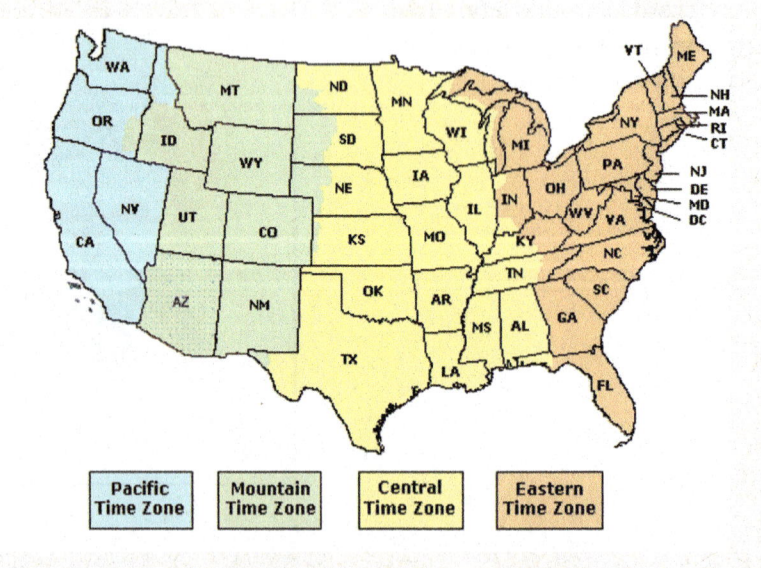

Pacific Time Zone | Mountain Time Zone | Central Time Zone | Eastern Time Zone

October 2015

Buy a Brick and Join the Fun at Larry's Country Diner

The media groundbreaking was held on September 16, and now we're ready to get started building Larry's Country Diner at 7734 Hwy. 70 South in Nashville, TN. The Diner will open in spring of 2016 and we want you to be a part!

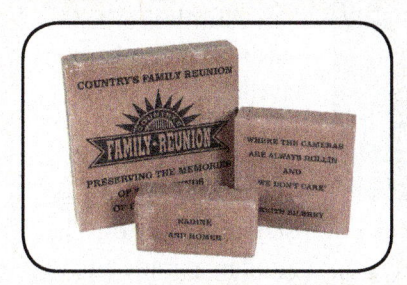

We're inviting you to participate in the "Larry's Country Diner Legacy Walkway" by buying a brick to be placed alongside Larry, Keith, The Sheriff, Nadine, Renae and the legends of country music. Your personal brick will be placed on the "Legacy Walkway" at the Diner for everyone to see!

Buy a brick for a friend, pet, family member, loved one or a corporate brick to promote your business. Be creative or just place your name on it. THEN... come on by, bring some friends and see your brick at the Diner after the Grand Opening (to be announced).

Prices on the brick are:
8 x 4 Red Cement Brick $300

3 engraved lines
8 x 8 Red Cement Brick $500

6 engraved lines
12 x 12 Red Cement Bricks $1000

8 engraved lines and can include a logo

Each line is 20 spaces.

It's time to FALL back!!!

Just a friendly reminder to turn your clocks back Saturday night one hour!!!

Also, now is a great time to change the batteries in your smoke detector when you are "falling back!" Enjoy the rest of this beautiful season!!

Saturday, November 1

October 2015

Rex Allen, Jr. to celebrate Rex Allen Days in Arizona

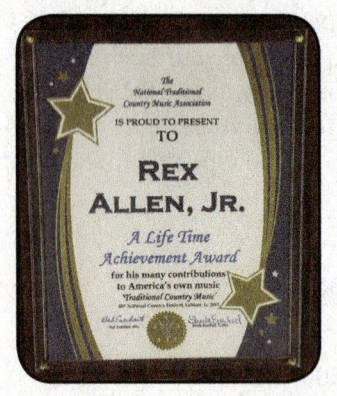

There is good ole fashioned fun to be had in the historic town of Willcox, Arizona at the upcoming Rex Allen Days on October 1 – 4. The Western music weekend is commemorating its 64th anniversary and will celebrate the life and times of the Arizona Cowboy, Rex Allen.

Kicking off the long weekend, Rex Allen Jr., a member of the Western Music Hall of Fame, will do what he does each year and visit the Senior Center on Oct. 1st at 10:30 AM, followed by Willcox Elementary School at 1 PM and then the Northern Cochise Community Nursing Home at 3 PM. This fine gentleman and dedicated artist will also be appearing at his annual "Question & Answer" session to be conducted in Windmill Park on Oct. 3rd at 5 PM where he will then sing his rendition of the National Anthem for the Rex Allen Days Rodeo. Rex Allen Jr. will take part in the annual Parade and will perform two shows on Saturday, Oct. 3 at the Willcox Historic Theater. Show times are 2:00 and 5:00 PM with all seats reserved. To order tickets to Rex's shows, call 520-254-2101.

Rex Allen Jr. says, "Rex Allen Days features many of my dad's favorite events like rodeos, a parade and of course music. We fit in everything we can! So if fans or friends see me out and taking part in the weekend activities, please by all means stop and say hello. This is my favorite weekend of the year and how lucky am I that I get to celebrate and honor my dad with friends that loved him, too!"

Rex Allen Days has been around since 1951. The original event was planned as a benefit for the local hospital. Since then countless other charitable organizations have benefited from the proceeds of the weekend. The proceeds are also used to present scholarships to Willcox High School graduates. The first Rex Allen Days featured a rodeo, parade and an appearance by Rex. That format remains, but has been expanded to four days of fun - "Western Fun ~ Willcox Style". The weekend starts out with the Annual Cowboy Hall of Fame Banquet on Thursday night. Local "cowboys" are inducted into the truly unique group of people who helped contribute to Willcox's history. Friday has a variety of events to choose' including the Rodeo Queen Competition, appearances by Rex Allen Jr., and other entertainers at the elementary school and the NCCH Nursing Home. Afternoon/Evening brings events like gunfights, Antique tractor pulls, Cowboy Poetry entertainers, Rex Jr. Celebrity Panel Q & A, old Rex Allen movie showings and a special Wine & Cheese Benefit for the Rex Allen Museum. Saturday starts with a large parade that goes through Historic Downtown Willcox.

October 2015

Q: Can you give me an update on John Hughey, former steel player for Conway and Vince?

Freda Redifer, Scottsburg, IN

A: John Hughey was born December 27, 1933 in Elaine, Arkansas. In the seventh grade, he befriended a classmate named Harold Jenkins, who would later become a prominent country singer under his stage name Conway Twitty.

Hughey joined Twitty on the road as his pedal steel guitarist, and backed Twitty from 1968 to 1988. He also recorded with various other acts, such as Marty Stuart, Willie Nelson, Elvis Presley, and Dickey Betts. By the 1980s, he began playing for Loretta Lynn, then moved on to play steel for Vince Gill for twelve years. Hughey was inducted into the Steel Guitar Hall of Fame in 1996. In the 2000s, he and several other Nashville musicians formed a Western swing band called The Time Jumpers, who performed every Monday at a club in Nashville.

Hughey died in Nashville on November 18, 2007 from heart complications, one month after having had a stent put in his heart.

For 45 years, Hughey was married to his wife, Jean, who often sat in the audience during The Time Jumpers' performances. Together, they had one daughter.

Q: Could you please tell me about the Stoney Mountain Cloggers who were featured on the Grand Ole Opry?

Linda Gerdes, Centerville, IA

A: For 32 years, Ben Ray Smathers led the popular Stoney Mountain Cloggers dance troupe at the Grand Ole Opry. Organized in the mid-1950s, the group first appeared on the show on September 13, 1958, and was immediately hired for the cast. Largely a family group, the Stoney Mountain Cloggers included at various points Ben's wife, Margaret, and their children Hal, Mickey, Candy, Debbie, and Sally. After the death of Ben on September 13, 1990, the troupe continued until September 11, 1993 when they ended the act.

The other dancers were the Tennessee Travelers. More on them in the next issue.

If you have questions for the Country Music Question &Answers, send them to Paula, CFR News, P.O. Box 210796, Nashville, TN 37221 or email them to paula@gabrielcommunications.

Volunteer Jam 40th Anniversary show had new faces & old friends

Charlie Daniels and Billy Dean

Making waves in the music world in recent years with their blend of Southern Rock and country, Blackberry Smoke was the first surprise of the night. In the 9:00 hour, country mega-star, Eric Church, busted out on the stage in the midst of Daniels' crowd-pleasing performance of "In America," joining Daniels for an electrifying duet. Though both Daniels and Church hail from the state of North Carolina, the two had never shared the stage before – giving the crowd the chance to witness a magnetic inaugural moment.

Ensuring the Jam stayed enthralling to the very end, Lynyrd Skynyrd made their rip-roaring entrance at 11:30 p.m. CT and closed out the final hour of the historically boundless extravaganza with their iconic hits like "Simple Man," "Sweet Home Alabama," "Free Bird," "Gimme Three Steps,"and more.

Jamey Johnson also showed up late in the event, surprising concert-goers, yet again.

The four surprise guests joined billed acts: The Charlie Daniels Band, Ted Nugent, Trace Adkins, Alabama, Terri Clark, Billy Ray Cyrus, Colt Ford, The Grascals, Lee Greenwood, The Kentucky Headhunters, Tracy Lawrence, The Oak Ridge Boys, Ryan Weaver, Wynonna, Craig Morgan, Lee Roy

October 2015

Parnell, Billy Dean, Michael W. Smith, Travis Tritt, Phil Vassar, Montgomery Gentry and Blackberry Smoke, for a jam-packed line-up to remember.

Former Blackhawk pilot, U.S. veteran and rising country star, Ryan Weaver, evoked arguably the most emotional applause of the night with a performance and moving video tribute to his brother and brother-in-law, both lost in combat in the War on Iraq.

A benefit for U.S. Military veterans and their families, the 40th Anniversary Charlie Daniels Volunteer Jam raised hundreds of thousands in proceeds for the 501(c)(3) non-profit organization, The Journey Home Project. It was co-founded by Daniels and his manager David Corlew, seeks to connect donors with veterans' organizations that do the most good in meeting the health care, education and career needs of military servicemen and women and their families. Additional concert proceeds will benefit the Nashville Predators Foundation.

The Volunteer Jam's title sponsor, Henry Repeating Arms, donated a $200,000 check on-stage to The Journey Home Project. Anthony Imperato, President of Henry Repeating Arms, said, "Although we can never repay them [U.S. Military servicemen and women] what they have done for us, Henry's sponsorship of the Volunteer Jam and donation to The Journey Home Project is a small token of our gratitude."

Since 1974, Daniels has commissioned his musical friends and peers to come together on a "volunteer" basis to hang out, "jam" together, and entertain crowds in an unconventional, laid-back fashion unknown to any other concert event -- all while dedicating concert proceeds to worthy causes.

The 40th Anniversary Charlie Daniels Volunteer Jam was co-hosted by conservative talk show host, Sean Hannity, and SiriusXM "The Highway" host, Storme Warren.

COUNTRY LEGENDS PAST AND PRESENT BY TOM WOOD

Little Jimmy Dickens

The only thing diminutive about Little Jimmy Dickens was his size. Everything he accomplished in his 94 years was larger than life.

What a well-lived life it was.

"He was exactly the size we needed him to be. I, for one, don't want to live in a world of 'Big' Jim Dickens," Brad Paisley said at Dickens' funeral service, held at the Grand Ole Opry House following his death on Jan. 2, 2015.

How big was Little Jimmy Dickens?

Big enough that while growing up in Bolt, West Virginia, the 4-foot-11 teenager played on his high school basketball team. Big enough that he was elected class president as a senior.

"Did y'all know I played basketball in high school? Yes, I did," Little Jimmy said a few years back during one of the Country's Family Reunion tapings, surrounded by Bill Anderson, Grandpa Jones, Stonewall Jackson, Boxcar Willie and other country music stars from yesteryear.

"You had to play 16 quarters a year to earn a letter. I got three of those boogers on my sweater."

Following high school—and knowing that sports was not in his future (unless it was as a horse racing jockey, an opportunity he nixed), he poured all his energy into his other passion: making country music.

He came from a musical family and had developed an enormous personality and stage presence (Jimmy went to West Virginia on a drama scholarship), so it wasn't that difficult a transition. Not yet Little Jimmy, Dickens made his first touring and radio appearances as Jimmy the Kid. In 1941, the host of an Indianapolis radio show that hired him suggested the Little Jimmy moniker.

A brand was born.

October 2015

How big was Little Jimmy Dickens?

Big enough that he became a member of the Grand Ole Opry even before he put out a record.

His big break came in 1945 when Little Jimmy first met Grand Ole Opry star Roy Acuff, then opened a show for him a few years later in Saginaw, Michigan. Impressing Roy Acuff is no easy feat, but Roy liked enough of what he heard and saw to suggest Little Jimmy move to Nashville.

Once in Music City, Roy introduced him to Art Satherly at Columbia Records and backed Little Jimmy for membership in the world's most exclusive country club, the Grand Ole Opry. Little Jimmy was initiated in August 1948. He remained an active member up until his final days and was also inducted into the Country Music Hall of Fame in 1983.

Little Jimmy took to the Grand Ole Opry spotlight and made it glitter even more not only with his persona and flair for wild rhinestone costumes. The original Rhinestone Cowboy.

Novelty songs became Little Jimmy's schtick and two provided career highlights.

His only No. 1 hit was 1965's "May the Bird of Paradise Fly Up Your Nose" but he had seven more crack the Top 10 singles chart. His very first hit was "Take an Old Cold 'Tater (and Wait)," which peaked at No. 7 in 1949, and it provided him with another nickname that stuck throughout his career — Tater.

Credit Hank Williams Sr. for that one.

"We were walking down the street one day and he says, 'Tater, let's go in this store here and buy something.' I've been Tater ever since," Little Jimmy recounted on the CFR video.

Little Jimmy and Hank were great friends, close enough that Hank one day offered to write a hit song for Dickens. About 30 minutes after putting pen to paper, Hank had finished "Hey Good Lookin' " and Little Jimmy was excited about recording the sure-fire hit.

"About a week later," he recalled on the CFR video, "we were in the old studios at WSM for the Friday Night Frolic and he said, 'Tater, I cut your song today.' I said, 'Much obliged, Herm. Appreciate that. What a friend, oh my!' "

Little Jimmy took it in stride, much the same way he took life. With a smile and an infectious laugh.

That's how big Little Jimmy Dickens was.

Author Tom Wood, who writes thrillers and Westerns, is a regular contributor to Country Family Reunion News. Reach him at tomwoodauthor.com

October 2, Tribute - Little Jimmy Dickens
October 9, Tribute - Grandpa Jones
October 16, Tribute - Billy Walker
October 23, Tribute - Blake Shelton and Vince Gill
October 30, Tribute - Charley Pride and Crystal Gayle

Fridays...7 p.m. central
Saturdays...11 p.m central

October 2015

NOVEMBER

WE'RE MOVING BACK TO THURSDAY.

Cards and letters really do work! RFD-TV has made the decision to move Larry's Country Diner back to its original day and time of Thursdays at 7 p.m. central time and Saturdays at 10 p.m. central time starting on November 5.

Everyone is very excited about this move back including Nadine! The show will now be in its primetime spot on Thursdays making it more view friendly and for those who attend church on Sundays.

Larry's Country Diner is set in the backdrop of a real-life diner with tables draped in blue and white-checkered tablecloths and a neon "open" sign. Southern sayings fill the wood-planked walls, while Renae The Waitress serves up hot plates of food to the live studio audience. Other characters Larry Black, Keith Bilbrey, Sheriff Jimmy Capps and the witty, sassy church lady Nadine interjects her own brand of humor while watching musical guests perform.

Since its initial airing on August 3, 2009, Larry's Country Diner has produced over 100 episodes and has become one of the most popular shows on RFD-TV. The show welcomes 1.6 million viewers per month and is one of the most-watched shows on RFD-TV, earning top primetime ratings for viewership ages 50 and up (Nielsen).

Tapings of Larry's Country Diner will be changing this coming year as well. With the construction of a REAL Larry's Country Diner the tapings will move from the studio and into the actual Diner. It won't happen until next spring. Another change in the taping schedule will be that instead of taping two days (seven shows), four times a year, the show will switch to one day (four shows), six times a year. For 2016 we will tape in February, April, June, August, October, and December.

Things are still a little up in the air as to how the audience will be scheduled and how many audience members the new diner will hold, so call customer service to find out more information at

800-820-5405.

And remember to watch Larry's Country Diner at its NEW (old) times on Thursdays (7 p.m. central) and Saturdays (10 p.m. central).

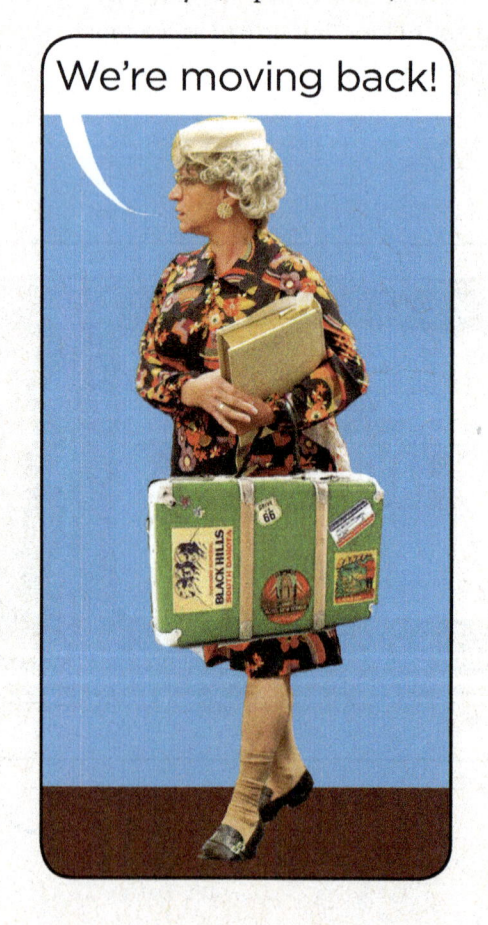

We're moving back!

November 2015

T. Graham Brown's new Christmas DVD

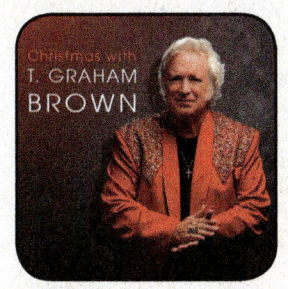

Christmas music this year will have a soulful Country sound, with the upcoming album from T. Graham Brown. The Country chart-topper will release his very first holiday album, Christmas with T. Graham Brown, on October 3. The perfect stocking-stuffer will be released by Mansion Entertainment and distributed by Sony RED Distribution. The project was produced by T. Graham Brown and Tony Griffith.

"I love Christmas! Christmas music makes everyone happy," said an excited Brown. "We hope this album makes you happy and that you'll play it all season long, every year. Merry Christmas!"

Brown chose 11 songs, a combination of classic and new tracks, which he hopes will bring the Christmas spirit to friends and fans everywhere. Standout tracks include the feel good standards, "Have Yourself a Merry Little Christmas" and "I'll Be Home for Christmas," which blends perfectly with Brown's unique style. You'll find a few up-tempo choices to energize the holiday rush and make you feel like dancin' and singin' along. There's a rockin' "Run Run Rudolph," and a fun fantasy tune, "Santa Claus is Comin' in a UFO," penned by T., his wife, Sheila and their son, Acme. There's a little "Merry" music for every Christmas music fan on Christmas with T. Graham Brown.

The future holiday classic is the follow-up to Brown's 2015 Grammy nominated project, Forever Changed. The Country/Gospel/R&B collection was produced by Brown and Mark Carman. It features collaborations with some of T. Graham's closest friends, including Vince Gill, The Oak Ridge Boys, Jimmy Fortune, Sonya Isaacs and many others. The album marked a triumphant return to the studio for Brown, after a 9 year hiatus. It was met with great critical acclaim from the music industry, critics and fans, securing features in Country Weekly, Billboard, CMT and many more.

Christmas with T. Graham Brown track-listing:
Have Yourself a Merry Little Christmas
Here Comes Santa Claus
I'll Be Home For Christmas
Rockin' Around the Christmas Tree
Silver Bells
Run Run Rudolph
Jingle Bell Rock
White Christmas
Santa Claus is Coming in a UFO
Away in a Manger
Mary Had a Little Lamb

Kenny Rogers retiring

Kenny Rogers recently announced that he will retire after he gives his fans one final tour.

The 77-year-old country legend told people he plans to retire during an appearance on The Today Show Friday morning (Sept. 25). "It's happily sad or sadly happy," he says. "I'm going to do a big worldwide tour, and it's going to be my last. I'm going to say goodbye at that point; I've done this long enough."

He was on the show to promote his new Christmas album, Once Again It's Christmas, and he told the audience that he wants to devote more time to his life outside of music. "I wrote in my book that there's a fine line between being driven and being selfish, and I think I crossed that line when I was younger," he explains. "And I really want to be there with my kids and my wife. They're really very important to me, and I don't see enough of them." Rogers and his wife have 11-year-old twin sons, Jordan and Justin.

Rogers also uploaded a video to his facebook page telling his fans about the retirement and his reasons.

Rogers said that he's known retirement was on the horizon for a while, adding that life on the road has gotten harder for him. "I'm sure I will miss it. I swore that I would do this until I embarrassed myself," he says with a laugh. "I don't walk around well, so I've found some new humor. My mobility is really driving me crazy."

November 2015

THE HOLIDAYS

I am sure glad Halloween is over. The grandkids came over for Halloween so Homer dressed the dog up as a cat. Now he won't come when Home calls him. You know I don't believe there are real Ghosts and Goblins around our house, but there are always more trick –or-treaters than neighborhood kids.

Our granddaughter asked Home and me if we were moving to Florida before the holidays. I said " no honey why would you think that?" She said, " well Mimi, you're over 60 and I thought it was the law."

Enjoy some Thanksgiving comedy "Nadine Style"

Q: What kind of music did the Pilgrims like?

A: Plymouth Rock

Q: Why was the Thanksgiving soup so expensive?

A: It had 24 carrots.

Q: What happened when the turkey got into a fight?

A: He got the stuffing knocked out of him!

Q: What do you get when you cross a turkey with a banjo?

A: A turkey that can pluck itself!

Q: If the Pilgrims were alive today, what would they be most famous for?

A: Their AGE!

Q: Why did the police arrest the turkey?

A: They suspected it of fowl play

Q: Why did the turkey cross the road?

A: It was the chicken's day off!

Q: Who is not hungry at Thanksgiving?

A: The turkey because he's already stuffed!

I hope everyone has a blessed Thanksgiving and remember….folks travel thousands of miles to be with people they only see once a year. And then discover once a year is way too often.

Thanksgiving Mini-Pumpkin Pies

- 1 pk. refrigerated pie dough crust
- 1 can (15oz) canned pumpkin
- 1 can (14oz) can sweetened condensed milk
- 2 eggs
- 1 tbsp pumpkin pie spice

Preheat oven to 425 °. You will need a 4" round cookie cutter. (I used a large cookie cutter) & a muffin pan. One box of 2 pie crust is enough for 12 mini pies.

Spray your muffin tin with cooking spray. Cut your circles out of your dough. Press them in your tin.

Mix pumpkin, sweet condensed milk, eggs, spice in a large bowl until smooth. Pour into pastry lined muffin cups. Top with pastry leaf if desired. I sprinkled some cinnamon on top.

Bake 15 minutes at 425. Reduce oven temp. to 350°. Bake 20-25 minutes longer or until a knife comes out clean. Remove to wire rack allow to cool completely. Keep refrigerated.

November 2015

Tim Atwood and Jeannie Seely entertain at R.O.P.E as Seely celebrates 48 years at Opry

Tim Atwood plays piano as Jeannie Seely sings at the R.O.P.E. Banquet and Awards. Photo courtesy of Lynn Woodruff Gray

Jeannie Seely's entertainment career began when she was 11 years old singing on a WMGW morning radio show. She has had success as an actress, author, songwriter, and singer, but mostly she is known as being an amazing entertainer.

While Jeannie considers it a privilege and an honor to perform any night at the Grand Ole Opry, this night was even more special and she wanted to perform a song that is very special to her. "Don't Touch Me" was her first number one song, and even won her a Grammy award in March 1967 for Best Female Country Vocal Performance. More important than that, however, "Don't Touch Me" brought Jeannie to the attention of the country music industry and was a catalyst toward her achieving her lifelong dream of becoming a member of the Grand Ole Opry. In September 1967 that dream became a reality. And this night, on the 48 year anniversary, Jeannie can hardly believe that dream has continued all this time.

Jeannie was first to wear a mini-skirt on the Grand Ole Opry stage. She's been credited with changing the image of female country performers. When not out touring she can be found hosting and performing at the Opry on any given weekend that she is in town.

In October, Jeannie celebrated 48 years as an Opry member. Not only was the evening celebrated by the artists and audience, but also in October, Jeannie entertained at the R.O.P.E. Golden Banquet Awards. R.O.P.E.,)or the Reunion Of Professional Entertainers), began one evening in May of 1983 when forty-three folks in the music industry got together to discuss the idea of having an organization.

Tim Atwood performed and played piano for Jeannie as they performed at the R.O.P.E. Show.

Tim Atwood played for music's elite on the The Grand Ole Opry for many years. During that time, Tim backed legends and legends-in-the-making, including Garth Brooks, Taylor Swift, Carrie Underwood, Darius Rucker, Vince Gill, Merle Haggard, Willie Nelson, Jim Ed Brown, Jeannie Seely, and Little Jimmy Dickens.

Beyond the stage, Tim continues to be a sought-after musician in Nashville, playing on recordings for some of those very artists with whom he shared the spotlight's fringe - artists who include Dolly Parton, Ray Price, George Jones, and Charley Pride.

Winners of the Awards were: Entertainer - Moe Bandy; Musician - Smiley Roberts; Media - Dave Barton; D. J. - Eddie Stubbs; Business - Dallas Frazier and Songwriter - Tommy Cash. Keith Bilbrey was the evenings emcee.

Larry's Country Diner RFD Show Schedule Nov. 2015

THESE ARE NEW SHOWS | **These shows have previously aired**

MO & HOLLY PITNEY
Host: Jeannie Seely
Thursday, Nov. 5
7:00 p.m. Central
Saturday, Nov. 7
10:00 p.m. Central

ASLEEP AT THE WHEEL
Host: Rhonda Vincent
Thursday, Nov. 12
7:00 p.m. Central
Saturday, Nov. 14
10:00 p.m. Central

RONNIE RENO
Host: Adam Black
Thursday, Nov. 19
7:00 p.m. Central
Saturday, Nov. 21
10:00 p.m. Central

MOE BANDY
Host: Bill Anderson
Thursday, Nov. 26
7:00 p.m. Central
Saturday, Nov. 28
10:00 p.m. Central

November 2015

John Conlee honored law enforcement officers on FOX-News

John Conlee, one of the most recognizable voices in country music, honored law enforcement officers around the country with his October 14th performance of "Walking Behind The Star" on the #1 rated cable morning show Fox News' FOX & Friends.

"I wanted to do this song to show support to police officers who are just doing their jobs," says Conlee. "With all the turmoil going on I think they are relieved that someone is paying attention the other way and giving them a pat on the back."

Conlee's poignant interpretation of "Walkin' Behind the Star" has sparked comments from around the country:

Howard R. Sills, sheriff for Putnam County, GA -- *"For the last 41 years I have been a police officer and for the last 19 years I have been the Sheriff of my hometown community. Needless to say we in the law enforcement profession haven't been thought of too highly in most of the national media of late. This media coverage has made me more than a little despondent. I was lamenting about all of this when I turned on the Opry show this past Saturday night. It was not too long after the show began before a wonderful breeze of fresh air swept across my veranda and from my old GE radio sitting up on the porch rail. That breeze was the moment I heard you announce to the audience and the world that the Opry wanted to take a moment to honor those who "walk behind the star" and you sang the song with the same title that I'd never heard before. It literally caused me to tear up and it lifted my spirits. I cannot express thanks enough to you, the Opry and WSM-AM for the recognition during your show."*

Mike Kelleher, chaplain from San Bernardino County Sheriff department -- *"With all the bad press our force is constantly receiving, I would like to thank Mr. Conlee for his uplifting song."*

James Bartels, police officer in Patriot, OH -- *"As a policeman shot in the line of duty, I found John Conlee's comments and his performance on the Grand Ole Opry very moving. I would like to thank him for understanding the terror law enforcement endure every day in the society we live in."*

Derik Walker, K102 Country in Spokane/Sandpoint, ID -- *"Just wanted you to pass along to John Conlee that his song, "Walkin' Behind The Star" was the absolute perfect song to play this week for our fallen officer Greg Moore of the Coeur d'Alene, Idaho police department. I can't tell you how many calls we got regarding the song and how much it meant to folks in the inland Northwest as they deal with this tragedy. Sargent Greg Moore served the people for 16 years, before he was gunned down in Post Falls, Idaho Monday night. Please extend our gratitude to John on behalf of the entire K102 Country family!"*

David Lyons, police chief in Savannah, GA -- *"I am a police chief in the state of Georgia, the immediate past president of the Georgia Association of Chiefs of Police and a career police officer. I heard you sing the song, "Walkin' Behind the Star" and wanted to tell you how much I appreciated you. With all that's going on in the world right now along with the attacks on our police officers, it is good to hear some appreciative words. Thank you and God bless you."*

Conlee's newest release, "Bread and Water" has deep meaning to the veteran Opry legend. "The song was written by Vince Gill and Leslie Satcher and hit me right in the heart the first time I heard it. It is a story of redemption and a reminder that with God, all things are possible."

John continues the long-standing relationship between faith and the country music industry. "Out of concerns for today's America it has affected the way I'm applying my musical energies. I believe in prayer and I feel like now more than ever is the time to be singing about it and hopefully inspiring others to do the same."

Road Stories

By Claudia Johnson

Stars Not Immune to Hazards of the Road

There's nothing more exciting for fans than knowing their favorite stars will be in concert nearby. Many performers schedule dozens, if not several hundred tour stops, including interviews, media opportunities, promotional appearances, book signings, private performances and concerts, as they travel the country or the globe.

Whether by automobile, plane or tour bus, extensive travel means increased exposure to danger. Reports of bus fires and wrecks, plane crashes and automobile accidents are not uncommon, and performers are not immune to the hazards of life on the road.

Not all tour stories have happy endings. Two plane crashes in the early 1960s jolted country music fans. Worldwide sensation Jim Reeves, 40, died in the plane he was piloting when it crashed near Nashville as he returned from a business trip on July 31, 1964. Less than a year earlier, on March 5, 1963, three of country music's brightest stars, Patsy Cline, 30, Cowboy Copas, 49, and Hawkshaw Hawkins, 39, perished when the plane in which they were returning from a charity concert in Kansas City, Kan., crashed near Camden, Tenn.

Grand Ole Opry member Billy Walker had performed at the same charity event but was called to Nashville for an emergency. Hawkins gave Walker his commercial plane ticket and opted to return via private plane with Copas and Cline. Walker died tragically more than four decades later at age 77 on May 21, 2006, when the van he was driving back to Nashville after a performance in Foley, Ala., veered off Interstate 65 in Fort Deposit and overturned. His wife, Bettie, bassist Charles Lilly Jr. and guitarist Daniel Patton were also killed.

On March 17, 1991, seven members of Reba McEntire's band, along with her road manager and two pilots, were killed when the private plane in which they were traveling from San Diego, Calif., to Fort Wayne, Ind., crashed in a mountain area near the Mexican border. All of the deceased musicians were younger than 30 years old and lived in Nashville. McEntire and two remaining members of her band, as well as several members of her road crew, were on another flight.

Country superstar Dottie West, 58, died Sept. 4, 1991, from injuries sustained as the result of an automobile accident in Nashville, Tenn., several days earlier. According to police reports, West's car broke down as she was headed to perform at the Grand Ole Opry, and an 81-year-old neighbor gave West a ride. The driver missed a curve at high speed near the Opry building, crossed an entrance ramp and crashed off the road.

At age 32, country singer, guitarist and fiddler Don Rich, a member of Buck Owens' Buckaroos, died on July 17, 1974, when he struck a center divider after losing control of his motorcycle on Highway 99 north of Bakersfield, Calif., while traveling to Morro Bay for a family vacation after finishing work at Owens' Bakersfield Studio.

"He was like a brother, a son and a best friend," Owens said in a late-1990s interview. "Something I never said before, maybe I couldn't, but I think my music life ended when he died. Oh yeah, I carried on and I existed, but the real joy and love, the real lightning and thunder is gone forever."

Today's stars often find life on the road offers unexpected hazards, and many of them are quick to reassure their fans about their safety using social media or the internet.

Joe Diffie's tour bus caught fire in August 2012 in route to a tour date in Independence, Mo. Charring of a few wires was quickly repaired and performance was not affected.

"Had to stop and evacuate everyone," Diffie posted on Facebook. "Scary for a minute! All ok now!"

November 2015

Singer Willie Nelson announced on his website that he would postpone part of his 2013 tour after three members of his band were seriously injured when their tour bus plowed into a bridge pillar in East Texas during wet roads and high winds. Nelson was not one of the seven people aboard.

In February 2015, Wynonna Judd Tweeted that the generator on her tour bus had caught on fire. She quickly followed up with a Tweet counting her blessings, which included the fact that the crew was not on board and that the entourage made it safely to a show at the American Music Theater in Lancaster, Pa.

"We are so glad you are all okay," she Tweeted to her crew. "Stay safe on the road. Wynonna!"

Country singer Sammy Kershaw's tour bus was struck by another vehicle on Nov. 2, 2012, following a performance in Nocona, Texas. The impact caused major damage to the bus, and the car was totaled. The driver of the car was hospitalized with injuries. Kershaw and the nine members of his band and crew were shaken and sore but not seriously hurt.

"Eleven people were involved in the accident, and no one was killed," Kershaw said in a statement. "It could have gone the other way. Buses and cars can be replaced, but people can't. I'm so thankful that the other driver, my band and crew are all still here. We had a guardian angel."

Fortunately for Lady Antebellum frontwoman (and daughter of country star Linda Davis) Hillary Scott and her husband, their tour manager and bus driver were unharmed when the Lady Antebellum tour bus caught fire on a Dallas-area highway April 16, 2015, forcing a hurried but safe evacuation as the singer was traveling to the Academy of Country Music Awards ceremonies.

"EVERYTHING in the back lounge was destroyed from the flames, except my Bible," Scott Tweeted later. "The outside cover was burned and messed up but NOT ONE PAGE was missing. Yall, God's Word will always stand…My faith is forever deepened because of today. I hope this story deepens yours."

CORRECTION

Thank you to Dee Boedeker who brought to our attention that Johnny Horton's accident was actually in Milano, TX and not Milano, LA as we had stated. She said the student, James E. Davis was attending Texas A & M University in College Station, TX at the time.

November 6
Tribute - Bill Anderson
November 13
Tribute - T. Graham Brown & BJ Thomas
November 20
Tribute - The Whites & Riders in the Sky
November 27
Tribute - Gene Watson & Moe Bandy

Fridays…7 p.m. central
Saturdays…11 p.m central

November 2015

COUNTRY'S FAMILY REUNION SCRAPBOOK: IRA LOUVIN

Daddy 1957

Ira Louvin, Jim Reeves, Charlie Louvin

Ira & Paul Yandell

Gail, Dad, Grandmother
Ira's oldest daughter, Gail

Ira & daughter, Kathy

Ira & Charlie

Mom & Aunt Betty

A groggy Christmas morn. The nights were long

Kathy Louvin

November 2015

Special Memories Made During Larry's Country Diner at the Starlite in Branson

Moe Bandy crashed Gene Watson's show at the Diner and cracked everyone up on stage and in the audience.

A very touching day as The Whites performed (above). Barbara Fairchild gave Larry a hospital gown and a stuffed bear during one of the shows and told him to stay off ATVs.

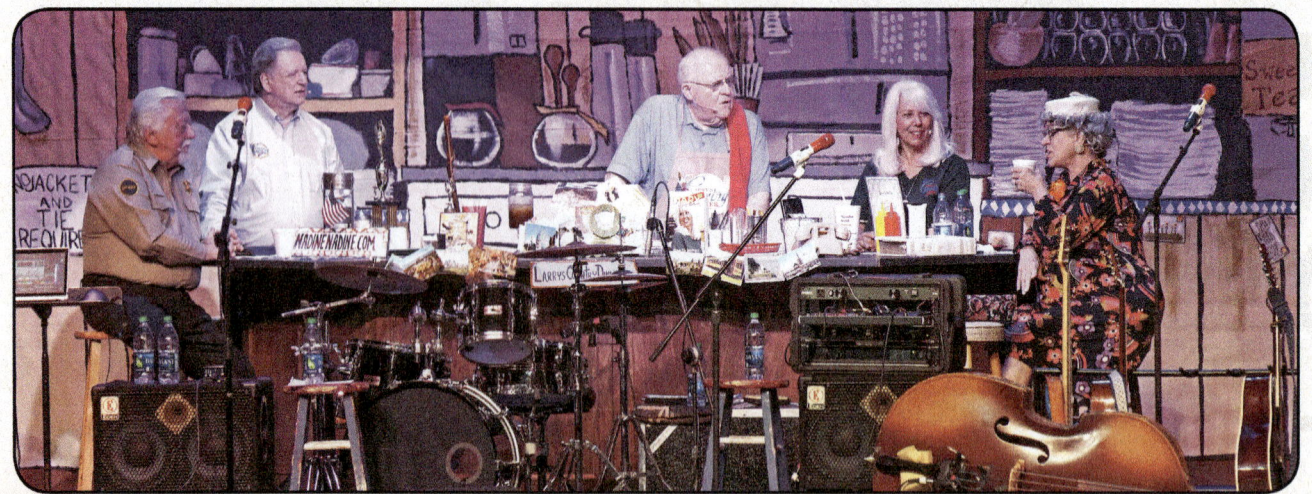

November 2015

Nadine surprises Gene Watson on stage.

Dailey and Vincent are always a hit at the Diner shows in Branson.

Jimmy Capps and Jimmy Fortune pick a few tunes.

Jimmy Fortune croons out a tune.

Just in time for Christmas!

Ahh.... Love songs—Songs of love can color so many moments in each of our lives.... From a first kiss, to a first dance. Well, we here at Country's Family Reunion decided to celebrate Love this time of year by getting together some country music couples to share their love stories and some great love songs in an all new series Country's Family Reunion Sweethearts. All on 4 discs plus an audio CD.

We also gathered a ton of country music legends to share their favorite Christmas stories and songs with each other and YOU. All on 3 DVD's plus an Audio CD with all the songs from the show.

Home for Christmas Series

Artists Include:
The Isaacs
Duane Allen
Rhonda Vincent
Ricky Skaggs
Teea Goans
The Whites
T-Graham Brown
Linda Davis, Rylee Scott and Lang Scott
Joey and Rory plus Heidi Feek
Mandy Barnett
William Lee Golden
Jimmy Fortune

Songs Include:
It's Christmastime Again
Getting Ready for a Baby
Christmas Time At Home
New Star Shining
Jingle Bells
They Saw A King
Hangin' Around the Mistletoe
Mary Had a Little Lamb
Tennessee Christmas
Still Believing In Christmas
Remember Me
Winter Wonderland
Thank God For Kids
Away In A Manger
O Holy Night

Sweethearts Series
Songs and Artists featured:
"Forever Changed" T. Graham Brown (Sheila)
"Islands In The Stream" TG Sheppard & Kelly Lang
"When There's Love At Home" Duane & Norah Lee
"Hearts Like Ours" Ricky Skaggs & Sharon White
"Valentine's Day" David Frizzell (Jo)
"But You Know I Love You" Bill Anderson
"If" Jimmy Fortune (Nina)
"Love Never Gives Up" Linda Davis & Lang Scott
"Only Jesus Could Love You More" Sonya Isaacs Yeary & Jimmy Yeary
"I'll Sing For You" Joey + Rory and Heidi Feek
"When She Holds Me" Larry Gatlin (Janis)
"I Give All My Love To You" Rhonda Vincent (Herb Sandker)
"Thanks Again" Ricky Skaggs

$79.80 each plus $6.95 s/h
OR
both for $119.80 plus $16.95 s/h

800-820-5405
www.cfrvideos.com
P.O. Box 210709, Nashville, TN 37221

November 2015

Reviews on new Hank Williams say biopic not particularly good

By Paula Underwood Winters

The new Hank Williams biopic, which is set for national release on November 27, was shown at the Toronto International Film Festival on September 11. The reviews are less than stellar, some actually calling it 'shockingly bad.'

Many of the reviews have to do with the screenplay itself, however, several of them poo pooed the singing as well. It goes back to if you don't sound like the original, then lipsync. While Reese Witherspoon and Joquin Phoenix did fine jobs with June Carter and Johnny Cash, they were still only mediocre. Sissy Spacek as Loretta Lynn is really the only actress whoever 'nailed it' singing the songs of such an iconic singer.

Steve Pond writing for The Wrap observed, *"The actor turns out to be a fine, convincing country singer, but that's not enough. Williams' voice was high, keening, utterly distinctive and such an integral part of his persona that if you don't get it right, you're missing something huge … The music in 'I Saw the Light,' which should be the heart of the film, is like a very good cover version of a classic song. It's enjoyable and it's sometimes enough, but it's not the real thing."*

But as Hank Williams III—a staunch critic of the film since it was first announced—said when Saving Country Music interviewed him in September of 2014, "But I will say, with or without this movie, Hank Williams' music is still going to do that … No matter, his music is going to be timeless, and movies come and go. At the end of the day, his music and what he did is going to outlast the movie, and be passed on for generations. That is why he is as special as he is."

When the movie makes its offical release, fans of Hank Williams can make their own decisions as to whether this film is worthy. Some fans will be fine with someone else singing Hank's songs, while others may be critical.

Q: Can you tell me if the Hager twins are still living and are they married, and children?

Evelyn Viebrock, MO

A: This is one of those questions we get periodically as new people subscribe to the paper. Both Jim and Jon Hager are deceased. The identical twin brothers died just months apart. Jim Hager died of an apparent heart attack on May 1, 2008 in Nashville, Tennessee. He was 66. Jon Hager, died in his sleep on January 9, 2009, also in Nashville. He was 67, As far as we can tell, neither was married and they had no children.

Renae is finishing a book, Precious Memories Memorials, which will have information on many of the artists who have passed away, where they are buried, etc.

If you have questions for the Country Music Question & Answers, send them to Paula, CFR News, P.O. Box 210796, Nashville, TN 37221 or email them to paula@gabrielcommunications.

November 2015

The Nashville Brat Pack — Kids of the Country Stars!

By Kathy Twitty, Daughter of Conway Twitty

On November 8, 1958 my daddy was in for two big surprises. One was his first single went to number one, not just in our country but it 23 different countries. The song "It's Only Make Believe" would become one of the biggest records of the year, even nominated for a Grammy. Daddy hit the big time! Another surprise was me! I was born on that very day. The headlines of the newspaper in my parent's hometown read "The Itty Bitty Twitty Is Here!" Alongside a beautiful picture of my beautiful mother they told the story of daddy's double surprise that day. I asked years later which one was the best surprise of the day, Daddy always knew how to make my heart melt and said, "There was no question about it Kathy, it was you. I knew I would always have another other records out there, but there would only be one you."

As soon as I could talk I wanted to sing! And singing I did any time I could get on the stage. I knew no fear, as a matter fact, I felt more at home on the stage than out in the real world. And daddy would have to do a "Kathy check" every time the bus left town to make sure I wasn't hiding in there somewhere so I could go and sing with daddy because that's where I wanted to be. And I did just that for 10 years of my childhood traveling and singing with daddy all over the country. He said "If you want to do this for a living, Kathy, it's a business and you have to treat it like a business so I'm going to teach you" and he did. He taught me every aspect of it and he was the best teacher. The funniest part was when I needed someone to play the guitar for me and I had Conway Twitty for my band. Not every girl had that

I was raised in Oklahoma until I was almost 17 and quite honestly being the daughter of a celebrity like daddy made it kind of lonesome not to have anyone else with anything in common with me. I wanted to sing from the moment I came out of the womb and traveled and sang on tour with dad for most of my life. I opened his show from age 13 to 17 so I lived a double life just a girl at school and then all dressed up and singing I front of 20 thousand people kinda left a lonely hole in my life.

Pictured are Michael, Jimmy, Kathy & Joni.

Tanya Tucker and I became friends at the West Coast Awards when we were 12. We hit it off right away and we had two seats between Farrah Faucet and 6 Million Dollar Man husband, Lee Majors. On the other side was James Brolin and like two 12 year olds, we kept getting up and down and they were all so put out with us. But we didn't care. Tanya loved to come visit and stay at our home in Oklahoma because we were as normal a family as we could be and she got to be just a kid. We went to JC Penny's at the Mall and played in the make up and got thrown out! We wanted to get an apartment together when we turned 18 but couldn't figure out how we would get two greyhound buses in the parking lot. We had it all planned out. I saw her recently and her little girl was there. She wanted me to tell her all about her mom when she was her age and I did. Then Tanya and I disappeared from the crowd and sat on the floor in her bedroom and laughed and cried and played in the make-up. It was a wonderful visit. The years fell away and we were 12 again laughing and crying and sharing the stories of our lives …. She is the real deal. She is the same Tanya I meet years before. What a pistol! What a Jewel!

November 2015

We moved to Tennessee and still kinda lonely then at age 30 I thought of a group of country music superstars would be unique ... Wilson Philips did it so why not one in country music. First thought of Patsy Lynn we put our heads together and Cindy Cash wanted to join us and Georgette Jones. Wow big names and we all sang and even though we wanted to be a group- we also wanted to be a group of individuals. Before we knew it Tony Conway wanted to book us and he was the best & RCA wanted to sign us by just seeing this photo! It was a powerful idea and we headed to Canada for 3 weeks to work out our show and sold out everywhere we went. And at the end of those 3 weeks we did a show in the US opening for The Judds! We came out one at a time doing a few songs each the music never stopped and at when the last of us hit the last note Johnny Cash Ring of Fire started and we were all on stage together doing two of our famous parents songs with the others singing harmonies. The crowd went wild it was an unbelievable experience when we came off the stage a member of the press came up and said that was the most powerful show I have ever seen! It was surreal. Sadly it never happened. But those weeks were big fun. We shared cloths make-up takes for hours (the national enquirer would have paid big bucks to hear our conversation especially after we shared a bottle of wine) I treasure each of these wonderful artist. Knew and loved their parents and even though it was not meant to be..... It was worth the ride!

Daddy produced Joni and my albums. He was a gifted producer even producing his own music after parting with Owen Bradley. I was always asked if it made me nervous. "Lord no! Daddy made me feel safe and loved."

His gentle strength was the most powerful energy one can have. The thick glass between the control room and the studio was tinted and I could barely see him through it…but I knew he was there listening to every note….wanting the best for me. Knowing he was there gave me confidence…allowing me to lay my fears aside and stand strongly within my soul and let my talents flow….unobstructed.

After daddy's physical death, I imagine him there in heaven behind the tinted glass…watching me…listening and loving me. Knowing he's there brings me peace and confidence and makes my heart sing.

Charitable Legends – Thankful Stars Help Others Have Food

By: Sasha Kay Dunavant

The most successful performers often express they realize how fortunate they are and how their God-given talents combined with knowing the right folks have gotten them where they are today.

Country music stars have a lot on their plates. They travel by bus for months at a time. They are required to be flawless, sometimes having had very little sleep at all. Of course, it does help to have a personal hair and makeup team and as many amenities as it takes for a comfortable stay in their home-away-from home tour bus. One thing that these stars definitely do not have to worry about is having food. More often than not, they can have their preference of cuisine.

One would presume that hard working yet indulged individuals like these would be caught up in a whirlwind of themselves. It's certainly unexpected that stars would notice the empty plates and stomachs of their fans and specific needs of people around them.

November 2015

When Willie Nelson, John Mellancamp and Neil Young organized the first Farm Aid concert on Sept. 22, 1985, in Champaign, Ill., 80,000 attended. Included among the performers were artists from a variety of musical genres, like B.B. King, Billy Joel and Bob Dylan. Thirty years later, Nelson, Young and Mellencamp still headline the annual star-studded concert performed before hundreds of thousands. The Farm Aid organization continues to raise money through music and as well as donations to www.farmaid.org. The charity has contributed $34,279,821 since 1985 to multiple vital programs ranging from environmental education and necessities of farmers to tornado funds that provide psychological and financial support for farmers who lose crops and homes to natural disaster.

Annually for the past three years, country stars have worked with local dairy farms to stock South Dakota's food banks with dairy products. Milk, a natural source of protein and nine other essential nutrients, is the most requested yet least donated item available for distribution through America's Food Bank Network. Last year the generous trio of Sammy Kershaw, Aaron Tippin and Joe Diffie, who have 42 number one singles among them, presented the "Roots and Boots Tour" at the annual "Be Our Guest" concert to benefit Feeding South Dakota. These caring countrymen have raised more than $29,000.

When it comes to food, superstar Reba McEntire knows exactly how to bring in the canned goods. For example, in January of 2000 she encouraged concert-bound fans not only to bring their love for her music, but she also respectfully requested that her fans support her partnership with U.S.A. Harvest. After just six weeks into her tour, 23,747 pounds of non-perishable items such as canned food, pasta and dried beans had been collected by volunteers at each venue and delivered to local food banks and hospices immediately following the concert.

Last year McEntire was the leading artist for the fourth annual Outnumber Hunger Campaign conducted by Feeding America, the world's largest domestic-hunger relief charity. For the effort, McEntire partnered with Big Machine Label Group, a collaboration of recording labels, General Mills and Feeding America.

"I was raised to treat others with compassion," McEntire said regarding her ongoing charitable work with food. "Knowing that one in six Americans struggle with hunger means my fans and people I see every day need help. The Outnumber Hunger campaign is such a simple way to help your neighbors, so how could you not?"

McEntire and other artists, including Florida-Georgia Line, The Band Perry and Rascal Flatts, were featured on more than 60 million General Mills packages, such as Cheerios, Pillsbury, Yoplait and Nature Valley, etc. Purchasing these products and entering the codes from those packages online secured five meals for the local food bank. Since 2011, with the dedication of country music, Outnumber Hunger has secured 35 million meals. The effort runs through Jan. 31, 2016. Learn more about how to help the artists raise funds at www.feedingamerica.org.

It's inspiring to see country stars serve up gratitude and food through heart and song across the nation.

November 2015

Diner Chat
with Renae the Waitress

It's easy...it's fun!!
Listen live by Phone or on the web,
every Thursday at 3:00 p.m. EST.

1-425-440-5100
ID code: 909005#

www.larryscountrydiner.com, click 'Diner Chat'

GOT COFFEE? I am so excited to share our Larry's Country Diner building progress every Thursday on Diner Chat.

After a week of shows in Branson, Missouri I was so excited to get back to Nashville to see if there was any construction progress at the Diner. We had a few rainy days so I worried there wouldn't be any actual changes. However, as I headed to the office and turned the corner…..there it was….a construction trailer and port-a-potty!! Whoooo hooooo… PROGRESS !! And a few days later machinery arrived to start clearing trees.

One of the areas at the Diner that is so dear to my heart is our "Legacy Walkway". What a wonderful opportunity for YOU to share your legacy with an engraved brick located close to your favorite country artists at Larry's Country Diner. I have talked to so many folks who watch Country's Family Reunion and Larry's Country Diner and say they feel like we are family. We feel the same way and what a special way to be apart of our family right here at the "real" Diner.

I have already ordered a memorial brick with our son's name on it that will be placed on the walkway. And not far will be a special brick with my parent's names on it in their honor.

As the orders have been coming in it is very interesting to see what folks are engraving on their bricks. The 8 X 4 $300 Brick has room for 3 lines and it's amazing how much you can write. The $500 8 X 8 Brick gives you 6 lines and of course the $1000 12 x 12 Brick is huge. You can engrave a custom logo on that size brick and 8 lines. With Christmas coming soon what a great gift that will last for years to come. Call Jason at customer service if you need help ordering your brick. (800) 820-5405.

My Larry update is all-good news……He and Luann have decided to take a road trip for their 50th Anniversary (not on an ATV). Luann is calling it "50 Shades of Gray Hair Tour". I think everyone can agree they deserve some time away from hospitals and doctors. Although Larry wishes he was stronger…. he is doing great!!! He was there for all of the shows in Branson, signing autographs, taking photos and visiting with all of the fans. So again…. thanks for all of the prayers….God is answering prayer.

I hope you are enjoying all of the new Tribute shows on CFR and new shows on Larry's Country Diner with guest hosts. AND don't forget to go back to THURSDAY NIGHTS for Larry's Country Diner starting November 5th. Join me LIVE every Thursday at 3:00 Eastern by phone for Diner Chat and then catch us on RFD –TV for our show at 8:00 Eastern time.

See ya at the Diner!! Renae the Waitress

November 2015

Oak Ridge Boys

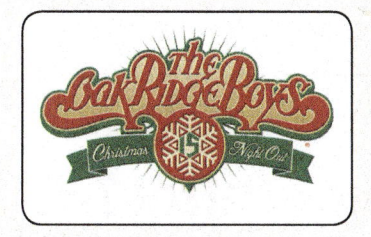

Grammy Award-winning music legends, The Oak Ridge Boys, will once again celebrate the Christmas season with timeless hits and holiday classics on their 26th Annual Christmas Night Out Tour, coming to a city near you. The almost two-hour holiday show transports concertgoers into Winter Wonderland with fan-favorite hits and Christmas tunes new and old, beautiful sets, falling snow—and even a special visit from Santa Claus himself.

"There is nothing quite like an Oak Ridge Boys Christmas Show. This tour has become an Oak Ridge Boys tradition and is a tremendous experience for the entire family. With a revamped stage and a fresh approach, this year's show will be a dynamic mix of music representing every aspect of Christmas from presents and snow, to romance and Santa Claus, on to the real meaning of the season celebrating the birth of Jesus," said The Oak Ridge Boys' Joe Bonsall.

Each year The Oak Ridge Boys' Christmas tour plays to packed houses across America. The 2015 Christmas Night Out Tour will take the group to more than two-dozen cities in nineteen states, from the East to West Coast, mid-November through December 23.

The group—Richard Sterban, Duane Allen, William Lee Golden and Joe Bonsall—have earned prestigious membership in the Country Music Hall of Fame (2015 Inductees) and Grand Ole Opry, among other designations. Known worldwide as one of recording history's most extraordinary musical successes, they have charted single after single and album after album, celebrating over 41 million records sold, two double-platinum albums, and more than 30 Top 10 hits, including No. 1 chart-toppers "Elvira," "Bobbie Sue," "Thank God For Kids," "American Made," among dozens more.

A mixture of traditional and contemporary songs—including religious, romantic, and fun holiday tunes—makes up the set list, which includes songs from the Oaks' six bestselling Christmas CDs.

Bonsall added, "Folks can expect to hear old favorites like 'White Christmas' and 'Jingle Bells' mixed with some very poignant newer songs like 'Getting Ready for A Baby' and 'Mary Did You Know.' A highlight of the evening is the much-loved 'rocking chair' segment where each BOY rocks by the fireplace and shares personal thoughts about Christmas. So we hope you'll come out and see us… and Merry Christmas!"

UPCOMING TOUR DATES – 2015 CHRISTMAS NIGHT OUT TOUR

11.17 | Branson, Mo. | The Oak Ridge Boys Theatre
11.18 | Branson, Mo. | The Oak Ridge Boys Theatre
11.19 | Branson, Mo. | The Oak Ridge Boys Theatre
11.21 | Canton, Ohio | Canton Palace Theatre
11.22 | Newport News, Va. | Ferguson Center For The Arts
11.24 | Portsmouth, Ohio | Vern Riffe Center For The Arts
11.27 | Cedar Rapids, Iowa | Paramount Theater
11.28 | Sioux Falls, S.D. | Washington Pavilion
11.29 | Des Moines, Iowa | Hoyt Sherman Place
11.30 | Topeka, Kan. | Topeka Performing Arts Center
12.01 | Cheyenne, Wyo. | Cheyenne Civic Center
12.02 | Colorado Springs, Co. | Pikes Peak Center
12.03 | Richfield, Utah | Sevier Valley Center
12.04 | Boise, Idaho | Morrison Center at Boise State University
12.05 | Kennewick, Wash. | Toyota Center
12.06 | Lewiston, Idaho | Clearwater River Casino Event
12.07 | Spokane, Wash. | INB Performing Arts Center
12.08 | Eugene, Ore. | Hult Center
12.10 | Shelton, Wash. | Little Creek Casino Resort
12.11 | Lincoln City, Ore. | Chinook Winds Casino
12.12 | Lincoln City, Ore. | Chinook Winds Casino
12.13 | Redding, Calif. | Redding Convention Center
12.15 | Deadwood, S.D. | Deadwood Mountain Grand Hotel
12.16 | Saint Joseph, Mo. | Civic Arena
12.17 | Paducah, Ky. | Carson Center
12.18 | Manistee, Mich. | Little River Casino Resort
12.19 | Wisconsin Dells, Wis. | Crystal Grand Music Theatre
12.20 | Merrillville, Ind. | Star Plaza Theatre
12.21 | Evansville, Ind. | Old National Events Plaza
12.22 | Atlanta, Ga. | Philips Arena
12.23 | Nashville, Tenn. | Country Music Hall of Fame and Museum

November 2015

Mo Pitney engaged to fellow performer Emily Bankester

Mo Pitney, who has been seen on Larry's Country Diner and the CFR Cruises, is engaged to marry a fellow musician, Emily Bankester of the bluegrass family band the Bankesters.

Mo posted an engagement photo on Instagram recently, showing off the ring and their happy smiles, along with a sweet message. He wrote, "I couldn't be happier. The Lord is just dumping love on me. I watched Him form the woman I asked for on my knees. I love this beautiful Jesus loving woman and I'm so excited for a lifetime of serving The Lord together. I'm overflowing with thankfulness for the future Emily Pitney."

He then added Proverb 18:22 ("He who finds a wife finds a good thing and obtains favor from the Lord") and the message, "Love you Em."

Emily plays the fiddle and claw hammer banjo in the Bankesters, and also sings lead and harmony vocals. In 2012, she won the International Bluegrass Music Association's Momentum Award for Vocalist of the Year. She also works as a dog groomer.

Looking for a great stocking stuffer?

Phil Johnson
JUST LIKE YOU

CD now available
Includes *The Day He Wore My Crown*

To Order call: 1-800-820-5405 or send a check for $14.95 plus $6.95 s/h to CFR, P.O. Box 210796, Nashville, TN 37221
www.renaethewaitress.com

November 2015

Rock n Roll Grafitti singer Billy Joe Royal dies

The recent unexpected passing of Billy Joe Royal, on Tuesday October 6, 2015 at his home in Morehead City, North Carolina has shocked fans and friends alike. The 73-year-old singer died in his sleep. He was an American Icon in music leaving behind a legacy that will live on forever.

Billy Joe Royal had a deep history from which to draw.. Born and raised in Valdosta, Georgia, he made his public debut at age five in a first-grade performance for the PTA and got his first paycheck—a five-dollar bill—for playing a New Year's Eve show in Atlanta that also featured Gladys Knight.

He soon became a regular on a local radio show, The Georgia Jubilee, which also featured Ray Stevens, Freddy Weller, Jerry Reed and Joe South. Royal moved on to work in the house band at the Bamboo Ranch in Savannah, a Gilley's-like venue with room for 2,500 people. The club brought in such national acts as Fats Domino, George Jones, The Isley Brothers and Faron Young. In that environment, Royal formed a longtime friendship with Roy Orbison and earned praise from his idol, Sam Cooke.

Elvis and Royal became friends when both played Las Vegas during the '70s. Going By Daydreams, released on B.J. Thomas' new Raindrops Records label, further cements the Elvis connection, since the project is produced by Chips Moman, who oversaw the recordings from The King's comeback period: "In The Ghetto," "Suspicious Minds," "Kentucky Rain" and "Don't Cry Daddy."

In recent years, Royal has been touring with Ronnie McDowell, who had a tour planned with him for November. Royal was one of the featured artists on the CFR Rock N Roll Grafitti series.

November 2015

COUNTRY LEGENDS PAST AND PRESENT   BY TOM WOOD

Hawkshaw Hawkins

It should have been the best of times, but life — as we all know — can sometimes be cruel.

The date was March 5, 1963, and Grand Ole Opry member Hawkshaw Hawkins had a promising new single out — "Lonesome 7-7203" — that had made its first appearance on the Billboard country chart just three days earlier.

That Justin Tubb-penned hit recorded by Hawkshaw in 1962 would go on to spend four weeks at No. 1, but the Hawk never had a chance to enjoy the record's success.

For it was on that infamous 1963 date that death claimed the lives of Harold Franklin "Hawkshaw" Hawkins, Patsy Cline and Cowboy Copas in a private plane crash near Camden, Tenn. The trio was flying back to Nashville from Kansas City, where they had performed at a benefit with Billy Walker.

Following the benefit, Walker got an urgent call to return ASAP to Nashville. Hawkshaw, who had flown commercially, offered to swap tickets and joined Patsy and Cowboy on the small plane being flown by Randy Hughes, who was Patsy's manager and Cowboy's son-in-law. The plane refueled in Dyersburg, then flew into a storm and crashed in a forest near Camden.

The deaths of these three stars shocked not only country music fans, but the industry as a whole and music fans everywhere. Indeed, it was one of those days "the music died," as singer-songwriter Don McLean famously penned about the 1959 death of Buddy Holly — also in an airplane accident.

Hawkshaw, who was 41-years old when he died, left behind a widow, fellow Grand Ole Opry star Jean Shepard, and two sons, Don Robin (named for friends Don Gibson and Marty Robbins), and Hawk Jr., who was born a month after his father's death.

But the story and legacy of "Lonesome 7-7203" didn't end with Hawkshaw's death.

Immediately after the stunning plane crash, the song disappeared from the charts for two weeks, but then returned on March 23 for a 25-week run, including four at the top spot.

"Lonesome 7-7203" was the only No. 1 hit for Hawkshaw, but he also enjoyed chart success with seven other songs in the top 15.

The Huntington, W. Va., first scored singles chart success in 1948 with "Pan American" (No. 9) and "Dog House Boogie" (No. 6). A year later, "I Wasted a Nickel" climbed to No. 15. In 1951, Hawkshaw scored three top 10 hits with "I Love You a Thousand Ways" (No. 8), "I'm Just Waiting For You" (No. 8) and "Slow Poke" (No. 7).

His next hit didn't come for another eight years, when "Soldier's Joy" made it to No. 15 in 1959.

That was his last chart success until "Lonesome 7-7203 came along, a song which Shepard had actually recorded a year earlier but had not been released.

Jean explained in a 1997 episode of Country's Family Reunion how Hawkshaw came to record the heartbreak ballad.

"It laid in the can for a year or so and Hawkshaw told me, 'If they're not going to release that Justin Tubb song, I'm gonna record it," Jean told Country's Family Reunion.

And record it he did. Too bad he wasn't here to enjoy its success.

Author Tom Wood, who writes thrillers and Westerns, is a regular contributor to Country Family Reunion News. Reach him at tomwoodauthor.com

November 2015

DECEMBER

Jean Shepard celebrates 60 years at the Opry & announces her retirement plans

Jean Shepard celebrated her 60th year as a member of the Grand Ole Opry on November 21st making her the longest-tenured member of the current Opry cast and the only female artist to reach that six-decade milestone.

"She's somebody who was there and can tell you firsthand about Opry founder George D. Hay, Rod Brasfield," says Opry announcer and WSM DJ Eddie Stubbs

Jean is proud of her longtime association with the Opry. "Sixty years ago, I loved what the Grand Ole Opry stood for," she said told a Tennessean reporter. "I still love what it stands for, but not quite so much. Isn't it terrible being so truthful?" She doesn't pull any punches. That's one of the things that endears her to so many fans.

As a young girl growing up with nine siblings in Oklahoma during the Great Depression with her nine siblings, Ollie Imogene Shepard fell in love with country music. Every Saturday night, her family would listen to the Grand Ole Opry on a battery-powered radio. When she was still in grade school, her family moved to Visalia, California, about 80 miles north of Bakersfield, a town with a country music scene that would spawn Buck Owens, Merle Haggard and Wynn Stewart, among others.

In high school, Jean formed a band called The Melody Ranch Girls; she sang and played a bass that her parents hocked all their furniture to afford. During one performance, Shepard caught the ear of country star Hank Thompson, who alerted Ken Nelson of Capitol Records about the young singer he'd found in California.

She signed a Capitol deal, and while her first single, "Crying Steel Guitar Waltz" (released in 1953), failed to chart, her second single, a collaboration with Ferlin Husky called "A Dear John Letter," topped the country charts, crossed over to the pop charts and sold a million records. When she began working with Ferlin, she was younger than 21, so her parents had to make him her legal guardian so that the two singers could tour together across state lines.

"It was a wonderful relationship between Ferlin, Ken and myself," she says. "Everybody should have a relationship like that because so much crap goes on with the ins and outs of the music business."

Jean sang "Dear John Letter" with Ferlin for her Grand Ole Opry debut. Taking the Ryman stage for the first time, she said, was "a thrill that nobody can explain to you if you haven't had such an experience. … I don't have any idea what I was feeling, but I knew I better go out there and do my best. And I did."

On November 21st for her 60th anniversary she was back on the Ryman stage where it all began.

On her 22nd birthday — Nov. 21, 1955 — she got the surprise of a lifetime when Opry manager Jim Denny stood on the mezzanine of the Andrew Jackson Hotel and made an announcement that she was to be a member of the prestigious Grand Ole Opry.

"He said, 'We want to wish a happy birthday to our newest Grand Ole Opry member, Jean Shepard. Happy birthday, Jean," she remembers, smiling at the memory. "What a thrill! I'd have liked to wet my britches."

December 2015

Jean met fellow country artist Hawkshaw Hawkins while working on the Ozark Jubilee. The two fell in love and were married in 1960. The two soon welcomed son, Don Robin (named after their two good friends Don Gibson and Marty Robbins). However, Hawkins was killed in the 1963 plane crash that also claimed the lives of country singers Patsy Cline and Cowboy Copas. Jean was eight months' pregnant with the couple's second son, Harold Hawkshaw Hawkins, Jr, at the time.

Jean was devastated by the loss, but the Opry community, including artists Skeeter Davis, Jan Howard and Teddy Willburn, rallied around her, and executives such as WSM President Jack DeWitt told Jean that her job would be waiting for her when she was ready to return.

She came back to the Ryman a few months after the crash and stood on the side of the stage. A few Saturdays later, the she gained the courage to begin performing again, and she worked to support her two small boys.

Fighting for traditional country music is something Jean does and is part of who she is. "It's a good fight for a good cause and I mean that with all my heart," she says. "Today's country is not country, and I'm very adamant about that. I'll tell anybody who'll listen, and some of those who don't want to listen, I'll tell them anyway. ... Country music today isn't genuine."

Because of ongoing health issues, Jean hasn't performed on the Opry in nearly a year. Jean was a guest on Diner Chat with Renae the Waitress the first part of November and she told the listeners the she is planning on retiring. She said she believed it was time.

These days, the other loves of her life include Benny Birchfield, her devoted husband since 1968 and father of her third son, Corey, and the many grandchildren and great-grandchildren who are often at her home, as well as the relationships she's made in music over her truly remarkable career.

In 2014, Jean Shepard published her memoir, "Down Through the Years." It is available on her website, jeanshepardcountry.com.

Nadine The Church Lady

Strawberry Santas

1 lb large strawberries
1 pkg (8 ounce) cream cheese, softened
3-4 Tbsp powdered sugar (or sugar substitute - to taste)
1 tsp pure vanilla extract

1. Rinse strawberries and cut around the top of the strawberry. Remove the top, (enough for a hat). Clean out the whole strawberry with a paring knife, if necessary (some of them are hollow already. Prep all of the strawberries and set aside.

2. In a mixing bowl, beat cream cheese, powdered sugar, and vanilla until creamy. Add cream cheese mixture to a piping bag or Ziploc with the corner snipped off. Fill the strawberries with cream cheese mixture.

3. Once strawberries are filled, top with the 'hats.' Decorate according to photo.

4. If not serving immediately, refrigerate until serving.

December 2015

Album becomes Fortune's first Top 10 Billboard Country Album

After joining the legendary Statler Brothers in 1982, winning countless awards, and being inducted into both the Country Music Hall of Fame and Gospel Music Hall of Fame, Jimmy Fortune is no stranger to success, as he continues to reach new heights. His latest album Hits & Hymns, is off to a roaring start, as it debuts on Billboard's Country Albums chart at No. 10, becoming his first top ten record on the chart as a solo artist. The feel-good album also debuts at #1 on the Southern Gospel Album chart and No. 6 on the Billboard Contemporary Christian Album chart.

Hits & Hymns is available at Cracker Barrel Old Country Store® locations, iTunes, Amazon, and music retailers nationwide.

Accompanying the album is the Bill Gaither hosted DVD special, Jimmy Fortune: Hits & Hymns, which also debuts with strong numbers. The collection debuts at No. 1 on the Billboard Music Video chart, along with No. 1 on the Christian Music Video chart, marking Fortune's first #1 solo project. Fortune traveled to Indiana to tape the hit DVD, with a featured appearance by Bill Gaither. In addition to performing every song on the album, the "Elizabeth" singer opens up about some of his biggest trials and triumphs. Fans got to preview the collection ahead of time, as it made its debut last month on TBN, Heartland, The Miracle Channel, DISH TV, and more.

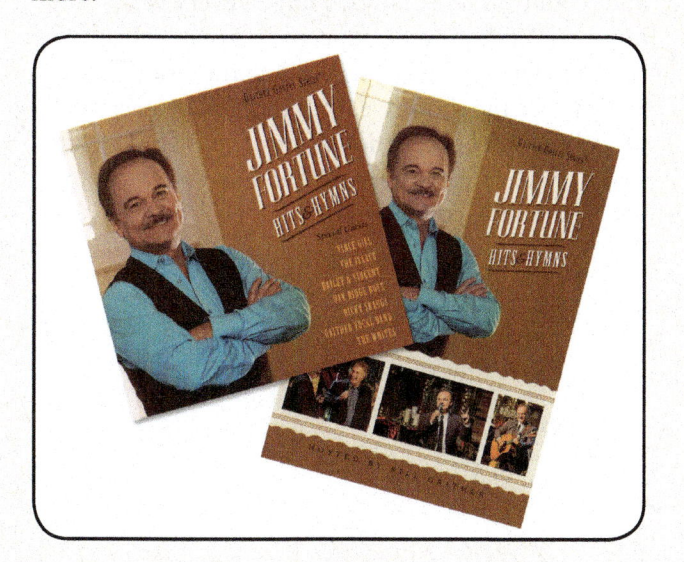

The CD project, which features collaborations with Vince Gill, The Oak Ridge Boys, The Isaacs, Ricky Skaggs, Dailey & Vincent and more, has generated a great amount of buzz. Billboard says that "Jimmy Fortune earned his reputation as one of the purest tenor singers in the format," while the Cleveland Plain Dealer says, "It's a great album, and I suspect it will add even more Dove Awards for gospel music to what has to be a very large trophy case."

Hits & Hymns Track Listing:

1. Elizabeth (with Ben Isaacs & Sonya Isaacs)

2. Life's Railway To Heaven (with The Oak Ridge Boys)

3. Danny Boy (with Ben Isaacs, Gene McDonald, Reggie Smith)

4. More Than A Name On A Wall (with Becky Isaacs, Sonya Isaacs, Ben Isaacs)

5. Far Side Banks Of Jordan (with Ben Isaacs & Charlotte Ritchie)

6. Precious Memories (with Ben Isaacs & Charlotte Ritchie)

7. Just A Closer Walk With Thee (with The Gaither Vocal Band)

8. Rock Of Ages (with Mike Rogers & Sydni Perry)

9. I Believe (with The Whites)

10. How Great Thou Art (with Mike Rogers & Sydni Perry)

11. In The Sweet By and By (with Dailey & Vincent)

12. Too Much On My Heart (with Ricky Skaggs & Sharon White Skaggs)

13. Amazing Grace (with Vince Gill & Sonya Isaacs)

14. If I Was God (with Mike Rogers & Sydni Perry)

15. Victory In Jesus (with Ben Isaacs, Gene McDonald, Reggie Smith)

December 2015

CFR & LCD friends make a visit to Marcy Jo's Mealhouse

On Thursday, November 12, a bunch of the Country's Family Reunion/Larry's Country Diner crowd drove down to Marcy Jo's Mealhouse to eat and sign a giant card for Joey. Included in the day were Larry & Luann Black, Renae & Phil Johnson, Mona & Dave Brown, Jeannie Seely and husband Gene Ward, Michele & Jimmy Capps, Emy Joe & Keith Bilbrey, Jamie Amos & husband Patrick Kennedy. Renae also broadcast her Diner Chat show from there. Rory's sister Marcy welcomed them with open arms and great food!

Grand Ole Opry moves to the Ryman for the winter

This is the time of year that the Grand Ole Opry goes back to its roots and holds all the shows at the Ryman Auditorium. From November through January the shows move from the Opry House out near the Opryland Hotel to the old Ryman in downtown Nashville.

These include the Tuesday 7 p.m. show, Friday 7 p.m. show and Saturday 7 p.m. and 9:30 p.m. shows.

The Opry celebrates 90 years of great country music this year! What began as a simple radio broadcast in 1925 is today a live entertainment phenomenon. Dedicated to honoring country music's rich history and dynamic present, the Grand Ole Opry showcases a mix of country legends and the contemporary chart-toppers who have followed in their footsteps. The Opry, an American icon and Nashville, Tennessee's number-one attraction, is world-famous for creating one-of-a-kind entertainment experiences for audiences of all ages.

It began on the night of Nov. 28, 1925, when an announcer on Nashville radio station WSM introduced fiddle player Uncle Jimmy Thompson as the first performer on a new show called "The WSM Barn Dance." Now, nearly 90 years later, the show Hay started is still going strong. Along the way, it has launched countless country music careers and led the way for Nashville to become Music City.

It's been called the "home of American music" and "country's most famous stage." Every year, hundreds of thousands of people make pilgrimages across town or around the world to the Grand Ole Opry to see the show live. Millions more tune in to Opry broadcasts via a mobile app, SiriusXM Satellite Radio, Nashville's 650 AM WSM, and on opry.com and wsmonline.com.

December 2015

Gene Autry turns Ugly Ducking Reindeer into Christmas Classic

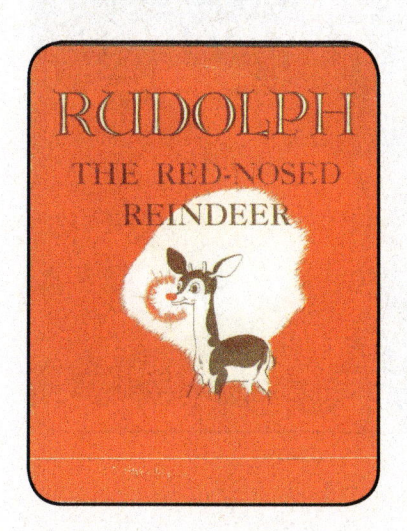

By Sasha Dunavant

You know Dasher and Dancer and Prancer and Vixen or Comet and Cupid or Donner or Blitzen? But, do you recall the most famous reindeer of all? That's right. It's Rudolph the Red Nose Reindeer. He may be climbing in years, but at 76 he remains the best-known reindeer in the world, and it's all because of one of country's most popular singers, Gene Autry.

The song that tells poor Rudolph's story was originally a poem by Robert L. May written in 1939 as a work project for Montgomery-Ward when the department store and mail order company decided that creating its own holiday booklet to give to children would be more cost effective than handing out coloring books bought elsewhere. When the store ceased using the booklet, May, who held rights to the poem, fashioned it into an illustrated children's book.

He also allowed his bother-in-law Johnny Marks, who wrote many of the Christmas songs still popular today, to convert the poem into a song called "Rudolph the Red Nose Reindeer." The composition was sent to and turned down by artists like Perry Como, Dinah Shore and Bing Crosby, who didn't appreciate the song's story line. Love for the song didn't grow over night, but there was a Singing Cowboy that would change all that.

Autry and his sidekick horse, Champion, were known for unforgettable Western movies in the 1930s and '40s that garnered them legions of devoted fans. When Autry was approached to sing "Rudolph the Red Nose Reindeer," like many other artists, he didn't care for the tune. However, his wife, Ina, fell in love with the "ugly duckling" appeal of Rudolph's shiny nose that made Santa choose him while other reindeer had shunned him. Ina encouraged her husband to record the song, and on Sept. 1, 1949, Columbia Records released Gene Autry sings Rudolph the Red Nose Reindeer. The album also included "Here Comes Santa Claus" written by Autry, who was inspired while riding his horse in the Santa Claus Lane Parade (The Hollywood Christmas Parade) in Los Angeles, Calif., when he heard children shouting, "Here comes Santa Claus."

The Gene Autry sings Rudolph the Red Nose Reindeer album sold 1.75 million copies in the Christmas season of 1949 alone. The first time fans ever heard Autry sing the song was on Oct. 8, 1949, on his CBS radio program, Melody Ranch. Autry had previously taken a break in 1942 from his film and music career to enlist in the U.S. Army, where he served as a pilot until 1945. Rudolph the Red Nose Reindeer reintroduced Autry to the music charts as it steadily stood No. 1 the entire first week of 1950. Rapidly gaining admiration, the album would go on to sale 12.5 million copies.

Rudolph the Red Nose Reindeer made another important debut on Dec. 6, 1964, during an NBC Christmas special called the General Electric Fantasy Hour. The program was produced in stop motion animation, which gives the illusion of object movement by moving the object a little during a series of photographed frames. The technique allowed viewers to be entertained by the song's story of Rudolph the Red Nose Reindeer through illustrations and the interacting of characters.

Two of the other very popular Christmas classics performed in the special by Burl Ives, "Holly, Jolly Christmas" and "Silver and Gold," were written by Johnny Marks, the same man who had turned the Rudolph poem into a song decades earlier. The special ran only once a year on NBC until 1972. Since that time, only CBS continues to provide a very limited broadcast schedule of the Rudolph the Red Nose Reindeer Christmas special.

December 2015

Had a beloved country star like Gene Autry not taken a chance on this quirky Christmas tune, generations of children may have missed the joy of one of the holiday season's most beloved characters.

Second only to Bing Crosby's "White Christmas," "Rudolph the Red Nose Reindeer" remains one of the top-selling Christmas singles of all time with estimated sales, including cover versions, at 200 million copies. For decades renowned artists of all genres have recorded the song for their own Christmas albums. A few country favorites such as Dolly Pardon, Merle Haggard and Alan Jackson have added their personal touches to the holiday mantra as well.

However, The Singing Cowboy certainly made the most famous version of all. Autry is legendary, and part of his legend is "Rudolph the Red Nose Reindeer."

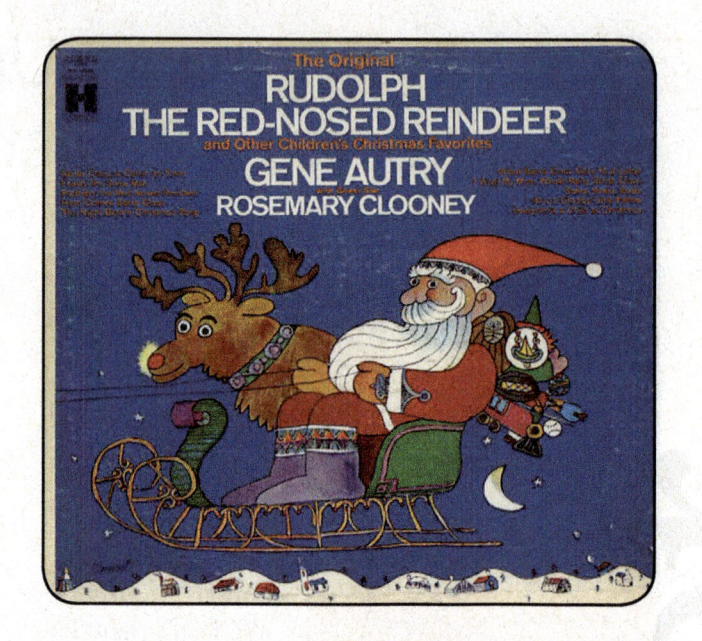

Charlie Dick, husband of Patsy Cline, dies at 81

Charlie Dick, the widower of country legend Patsy Cline, died Sunday, November 8, at his home in Nashville. He was 81.

Dick spent his life working to preserve the legacy of Cline — who died in a plane crash on March 5th, 1963, at age 30 — as one of the most influential singers in country music. In 1980, the Loretta Lynn biopic Coal Miner's Daughter renewed interest in Cline and her catalog. Five years later, Jessica Lange portrayed the singer in Sweet Dreams, with actor Ed Harris playing Charlie Dick. The real Charlie critized the film for some of its glaring discrepancies. He would continue to be an active participant and advisor in Cline documentaries and other projects throughout his life. While Cline was alive, Dick worked at a printing shop in Nashville and also served as his wife's road manager.

Charles Allen Dick was born near Whitehall, Virginia, then moved to Winchester, Virginia, and after high school worked for a local newspaper. Dick met his future spouse at one of her singing engagements in nearby Berryville, VA in 1956. While they were dating, he accompanied Cline to New York in 1956 for her second audition for Arthur Godfrey's Talent Scouts. Dick was drafted and left to join the Army in March 1957. The couple married on September 15th of that year. They relocated to Fayetteville, North Carolina, as Dick was stationed at Fort Bragg, then moved back to Winchester in 1959.

Cline had already hit with "Walkin' After Midnight" in 1957, but was still a few years away from her first major success, which came once the couple relocated to Nashville. Beginning in 1961, she scored three classic singles in a row: "I Fall to Pieces," "Crazy" and "She's Got You."

He was laid to rest in Joelton, TN on Thursday, November 12 with many friends in attendance.

December 2015

COUNTRY'S FAMILY REUNION SCRAPBOOK: CONWAY TWITTY (HAROLD JENKINS)

Conway, Mickey and daughter Kathy

Conway's wife, Mickey

Kathy, Jimmy, Joni, Conway & Mickey

Michael, Jimmy and Conway

L-R: Michael, Kathy, Conway, Joni & Jimmy

December 2015

Christmas Music is the Soundtrack of Our Holiday Memories

By Sasha Kay Dunavant

It's that time of year again, the time of year that the decorations go up and the family comes out. It is the time of year that we look forward to all year long, no matter our age. It's the time of year that gives us hope for the year to come. Music is our favorite part of Christmas, and it began touching our lives decades ago. While some Country Music Hall of Famers record single Christmas songs for the holiday season, some wish to make your season bright with chart-topping albums that are so unforgettable, we absolutely cannot have Christmas without them.

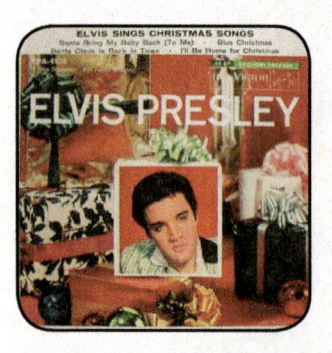

Let's take a look back at some of country's most memorable Christmas albums. Elvis' Christmas Album, the best-selling Christmas album of all time, first hit the racks in October 1957 and has been released four subsequent times. It topped the Billboard Charts for a solid four weeks. The latest stats show that 13 million copies have been shipped in the United States alone. Fans retain tremendous love for the "King," to this day, and even recording artists of all genres say the album is one of their personal holiday "must haves." We couldn't agree more.

Five years after Elvis Christmas Album had its debut, country music legendary artist Johnny Cash introduced The Christmas Spirit, which had taken Cash three years to complete. Cash performed vocals and wrote four songs himself, while eight others were already holiday favorites. June Carter Cash co-wrote the tune entitled, "Christmas as I Knew It" along with Grand Ole Opry Star, Jan Howard. The album included what has become a Christmas classic, "The Little Drummer Boy," which topped both pop and country charts. Cash also recorded "Silent Night," previously recorded by Presley, his former label mate at Sun Record. The Christmas Spirit album made it to No. 7 on Billboard Holiday Album Chart for 1963. The success of The Christmas Spirit album inspired Cash to release three more holiday collections, with one released each decade from the '60s through the '90s. In a career spanning 1954-2003, Cash, his wife and other members of their musical family touched generations. It is inevitable that Cash's The Christmas Spirit dwells in our hearts at Christmas time.

Two beloved Country music stars, Kenny Rogers and Dolly Pardon, joined voices to create 1984's Once Upon a Christmas, accompanied by a popular television special called, "A Christmas To Remember." In 1989 Once Upon a Christmas was named a Double Platinum album by the Recording Industry Association of America. Pardon recorded a second Christmas album comprised mainly of traditional Christmas songs entitled Home for Christmas in 1990. It, too, was accompanied by a television special and gained a Gold accreditation.

Rogers went on to record six Christmas albums. The most recent release is 2015's Once Again It's Christmas. The album entertains its audience through its alliance with up and coming music sensations, such as Home Free and Winfield's Locket. Platinum songwriter and pianist Jim Brickman is featured along with treasured country music artists Allison Kraus and Jennifer Nettles.

"I can't tell you how much fun it was recording a Christmas record again," Rogers said, expressing his love for the yuletide. "I'm excited for people to hear it. I feel like this is a special group of songs — both old and new — and I was particularly lucky to be joined

December 2015

by many talented guest artists and musicians who each have something unique to say."

Country Music powerhouse Leann Rimes released her third holiday record, Today is Christmas, on Oct. 15, 2015. Rimes co-wrote two original songs for the album, including the title track "Today is Christmas" and "I Still Believe in Santa Claus."

"I wait for Christmas all year long – it's my absolute favorite holiday," Rimes said. "I can't wait to share some of my new original Christmas songs as well as my favorite classics. I am looking forward to making more holiday memories with my fans this year."

Rimes, who had her first hit at the tender age of 13, begins her "Today is Christmas" tour on Dec. 4.

These artists make our holiday seasons memorable. They take us back and move us forward. Whether it is on a television special, at a live performance or listening on the radio, their execution of holiday song is mesmerizing, and once we experience it, we cannot get enough.

May your holiday be bright and your heart be light. This is the time of Country Christmas Music. Enjoy.

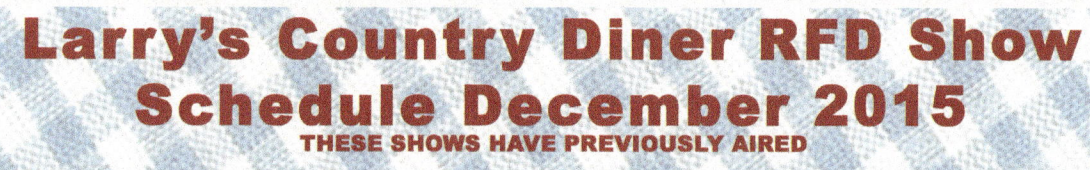

Larry's Country Diner RFD Show Schedule December 2015
THESE SHOWS HAVE PREVIOUSLY AIRED

EXILE
Host: Larry Gatlin
Thurs., Dec. 3
7 p.m. Central
Sat., Dec. 5
10 p.m. Central

RANDY OWEN
Host: Mark Wills
Thurs., Dec. 10
7 p.m. Central
Sat., Dec. 12
10 p.m. Central

DAVID BALL
Host: T. Graham Brown
Thurs., Dec. 17
7 p.m. Central
Sat., Dec. 19
10 p.m. Central

MO & HOLLY PITNEY
Host: Jeannie Seely
Thurs., Dec. 24
7 p.m. Central
Sat., Dec. 26
10 p.m. Central

ASLEEP AT THE WHEEL
Host: Rhonda Vincent
Thurs., Dec. 31
7 p.m. Central
Sat., Jan. 2
10 p.m. Central

December 2015

Just who were the Hoosier Hotshots?

The Hoosier Hot Shots started on a farm near Arcadia, Indiana, about 20 miles north of Indianapolis with the birth of Kenneth Trietsch on September 13, 1903. He was to be one of a family of four girls and five boys, children of parents with musical inclinations that included a banjo-playing father.

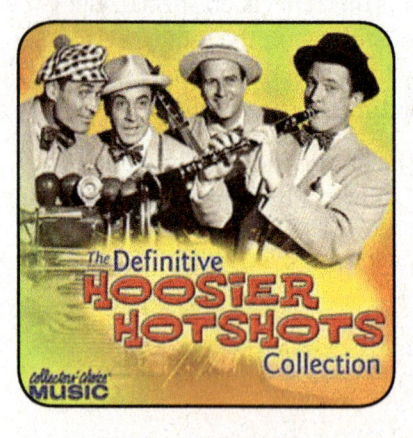

On April 11, 1905, about 18 months after Kenneth's birth, another son was born, who was given the name Paul. It was these two brothers, Ken and Paul, who, because of their love of music and entertaining, eventually formed the nucleus of the Hoosier Hot Shots.

Except for a brief period when the family lived in Georgia and Alabama, the Trietsch brothers spent their formative years in rural Indiana, not far from where they had been born. By the time he was five years old Ken was playing tuba which, since it was almost as large as he was, had to be placed in a chair before he could play it. In high school he won prizes for his corn crops and played in a 65-piece concert band. While still a young man he went off to New York where he played in the Paul Whiteman and Vincent Lopez orchestras.

Besides helping with the laundry, one of Paul's other duties on the farm was bringing home the cows for their evening milking. Every cow had her bell, and to his inventive mind it seemed only natural that he should attach a cowbell or two to the washboard for musical variety. Over the years he wore out more than a dozen washboards before having one specially made of an enduring alloy which he allegedly insured for $10000. Paul's Wabash Washboard became the centerpiece of the Hoosier Hot Shots.

While working for the Buzzington, Ken and Paul made the acquaintance of another member of the band, Charles Otto Ward, Otto began his musical career as a solo clarinetist with the theater orchestra before joining the Buzzington aggregation with which he worked for eight years.

By the end of the 20's, movies and radio were taking their toll on vaudeville, but it was the crash of '29 that ended that source of income for the Trietsch brothers and Otto Ward. They then set their sights on a career in radio and, pooling their talents, landed a job at WOWO in Ft. Wayne, Indiana. It was there that they unintentionally became known as the Hoosier Hot Shots. One day, when they barely made it to the studio in time for their program, a clock-conscious announcer, flustered by the prospect of their being late or not showing up at all, greeted them with the admonition, "Hey, you Hoosier hot shots, get in here!"

In 1933, the Hoosier Hot Shots took their act to Chicago where they had a successful audition at WLS, the Prairie Farmer Station. Here Paul (now known as Hezzie) and Otto (answering to the name Gabe), and Ken were given free rein to develop zany routines that made them one of the station's most popular acts. "What we had to sell was a product called stupid," Gabe once told a newspaper columnist. "That's what it was-stupid-but it was what was needed at the time. Others have referred to the Hoosier Hot Shot's music as "fractured Dixieland" and a "cornball blend of bad jokes, ragtime sounds, [and] a little jazz. Each rendition bore the unmistakable mark of the Hot Shots' distinctive touch, including Ken's opening question-directed at his brother Paul-"Are you ready, Hezzie?"

In august of 1934, the Hoosier Hot Shots added a fourth man to their act. He was Frank Delaney Kettering.

When Frank Kettering left the Hot Shots, he was

December 2015

replaced by Gil Taylor who hailed from Alabama. In 1946 Taylor joined the others as the Hoosier Hot Shots bid farewell to Chicago and departed for the West Coast where they continued to make movies, records and stage appearances.

By the end of the 1950's the Hoosier Hot Shot's career had begun to wind down, but they did not disband until the death of Paul "Hezzie" Trietsch on April 20, 1980. Frank Kettering had died in 1973, and Ken Trietsch passed away on September 17, 1987. The last Survivor of the original Hoosier Hot Shots was Otto "Gabe" Ward, who continued to perform solo after the others had died or retired. Billing himself as the Hoosier Hot Shot he sought bookings as a clarinetist, master of ceremonies and comedian. In the years immediately preceding his death he regularly entertained at a senior citizens center near his home. Otto Ward died on January 14, 1992.

The most famous of the hoosier Hot Shots inspired acts was Spike Jones and His City Slickers.

Thank you to Jean Roberts of Odessa, TX for asking this question!

The Hoosier Hot Shots and June Vincent gather around Kirby Grant and young Tommy Ivo in "Song of Idaho" ('48 Columbia).

Q: Jean Shepard has a record she made back in the 60s named The Melody Ranch Girl. I was wondering if it was possible to get a copy of that record.

L. Carr, Michigan

A: I have not been able to find anything on a single by that name, however the CD boxed set is available through Amazon.com. Used starts at $39.95, or new for $116.00. The five-disc box set The Melody Ranch Girl collects all 151 tracks that Jean Shepard recorded for Capitol Records between 1952 and 1964. It can also be ordered through Barnes and Noble for a higher price. I cannot find a listing of a song called The Melody Ranch Girl anywhere only the boxed set of that name.

Q: What were Goldie Hill's brother's names? I was wondering if Eddie Hill was her brother.

A Fan

A: Eddie Hill was not related to Goldie. Here is a photo of the family sent to us from Dean Smith (Goldie's son with Carl Smith).

Front Row: John Thomas Hill, Sr. (41), Effie Mae Davis Hill (37), Kenneth "Kenny" Charles Hill (15)

Back Row: John Thomas (Tommy) Hill, Jr. (14), Daniel Jefferson Hill (17), Argolda "Goldie" Voncile Hill (9).

If you have questions for the Country Music Question & Answers, send them to Paula, CFR News, P.O. Box 210796, Nashville, TN 37221 or email them to paula@gabrielcommunications.com.

December 2015

Two new upcoming books remember those who have passed

Outlaw country music icon Waylon Jennings' son, Terry, provides an intimate and revealing look at the life and times of his father, on and off the stage in Waylon: Tales of My Outlaw Dad.

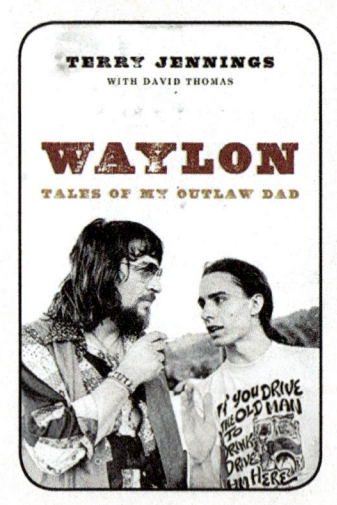

Born when Waylon was only nineteen years old, Terry grew up more like Waylon's brother. On the road together, they toured with legends such as Johnny Cash, Willie Nelson, and Kris Kristofferson, leading a reckless lifestyle centered around music, hard drugs, and women. Critical acclaim, bestselling albums, and sold-out tours were at times overshadowed by the darker aspects of fame, from drug use to womanizing to debt and depression.

Debunking myths and sharing stories never before told, WAYLON is a loving and strikingly honest portrait of a father by his son, one that will resonate for generations of fans.

Terry Jennings is the CEO and founder of Korban Music Group LLC, a full service management, consulting, and publishing company. Well known for his varied experience at all levels of the music industry, Terry was introduced to the business at an early age through his work as production manager for his father, Waylon Jennings. He has also worked for booking agencies, publishing companies, and as a talent scout for major label companies, including RCA Records. He lives near Waco, Texas.

The hardcover book will be 256 pages. It is published by Hachette Books and is expected to be released to bookstores April 19, 2016.

Precious Memories Memorial ….a long awaited book that guides you through the lives, deaths, funerals and cemetery locations of some of Country Music icons.

Renae Johnson's new book honors the memories and legacy of over 80 country music legends from Roy Acuff to Lynn Anderson. She answers so many questions she has been asked over the 18 years she has worked for Larry Black, creator of 'Country's Family Reunion." How did these legends die? When did they die? Who attended their funerals and what songs were sang? Where are they buried?

There are over 13 Nashville cemeteries with maps and photos for those fans that want to visit these special resting places. It includes 14 out-of-town cemeteries in her "Road Trip" section. The photos she includes of each "resting place" might surprise you. Or it might bring back your own memories of how their music touched your life.
But either way you will be glad you own this book.

"Entering through the gates of the final resting place of so many country music legends brought tears to my eyes. I felt an overwhelming sense of reverence, as I studied their names and comments engraved upon their headstones, which represented entire lives and careers. "

Available January 2016 (Hardcover, 244 pages $24.95)

December 2015

The Nashville Brat Pack — Kids of the Country Stars!

Christmas Memories
Melissa Luman (Bob Luman)

My happiest Christmas memory is the last Christmas that my Dad was still with us...Christmas 1977. I had gotten a horse that summer and my Christmas was full of horsey stuff. Then my Dad and I went to the barn where I kept my horse (he bought all my horsey stuff at Loretta Lynn's store in Hendersonville). The good days...

Seidina Reed (Jerry Reed)

My favorite Christmas memory is when I was 10 years old. In those days the whole family came together under one roof. That year we had deep snow! The adults were doing the usual "You'd better go to go sleep! Santa Claus is coming!" routine.

All of a sudden we heard bells and big thumps on the roof. It was so exciting ... and scary! My family was so great at playing up the fun ... "What's that? Do you hear that? That's gotta be Santa Claus!! Look outside and see if you can see him! That's Santa Claus!" Us kids started running around looking out the windows. Finally, there he was, walking through the snow in the front yard! He didn't see us, lol! We all started running and hollering, "IT'S SANTA CLAUS!!!" He walked all the way across the front yard around to the back.

The mothers and aunts told us that he knew we weren't asleep yet, that we'd better get in bed so that he could come back. I wish I could find the words to convey the thrill it was, and how beautiful it was to see. It was the most beautiful, magical moment. The reindeer landing on our roof and Santa Claus walking slowly through the deep snow in our front yard with his bag over his shoulder, snow falling from the sky. It was daddy. He had thrown rocks on the roof and played Santa Claus for us.

Whenever daddy wasn't present, we always assumed he was writing or picking so we never suspected a thing. What a precious, golden memory.

Robyn Young (Faron Young)

Brat Pack Xmas. I do not really have a special memory of Christmas with my Dad. Sometimes he was there. Sometimes he was not. Same thing went for Birthdays & other holidays also. The sad fact is, when you grow up as the child of a celebrity. Many times they are not around. Especially back in the days of our parents. They were out on the road singing and, keeping their careers going. Promoting new records and, maintaining their image as a star for their fans. I cannot count the times that someone has asked me " So what was it like having a Big Star for a parent " ? My answer was always the same " Well, it meant that My Dad was not around near as much as your Dad was. " But, don't feel too sorry for me. I got to grow up in a really big, nice house !

Ronny Robbins (Marty Robbins)

This was my first guitar (ukelele actually) and the first Christmas I remember. This is the house on Pima Ave. in Phoenix probably Christmas of 1951-52. Judging by the sparseness of the Christmas tree, Dads career was still a little ways off from being successful. I remember playing with the road grader smoothing out our driveway and part of Pima Ave. which was a dirt road back then. Still love moving dirt with a tractor to this day......lol. One thing that really sticks in my mind after all these years, no matter how successful and how much Dad was on the road, he always tried to be home on special days with the family. That didn't always work out for my birthday, since its in July, the busiest time of the year for concert venues, but Dad was always home for most Thanksgivings and our family was blessed to have 32 Christmas's as a family until the year Dad passed, the only one I missed was when I was in the Army.

December 2015

Joey gets Hospice care in Indiana

Following the prayer vigil on Thursday, November 5, God gave an answer. It was not the answer anyone wanted, but it was an answer.

"At 4 am on Friday morning we rushed Joey to the hospital in Muncie. Her pain had become too much to bare," Rory wrote in his blog. "A few hours later the doctors told us that the pain was from the cancer tumors continuing to grow and become inflamed and we need to concentrate now on helping her be comfortable."

At print time on November 16, Hospice had been arranged and a hospital bed was delivered. Rory and Joey's family have a play area on the carpet nearby – close enough for Joey to watch Indy play, and for Indy to turn and make sure her mama can see her. Friends were brought up by bus on Thursday to say their final goodbye.

"Joey is at peace with where she is and where she's going. So am I," Rory wrote.

Happening at the Country Music Hall of Fame

The newest inductees into the Country Music Hall of Fame, Jim Ed Brown and The Browns, studio session great Grady Martin, and The Oak Ridge Boys made it official at a star-studded emotional Medallion Ceremony on October 25, 2015. Considered country music's most prestigious event, the ceremony is the official induction of new Hall of Fame members.

"They have made music that endures through decades," said Jody Williams, BMI executive and trustee on the Country Music Hall of Fame and Museum's Board of Officers and Trustees. "Tonight, we honor them—respectfully, formally, and enthusiastically—as country music masters."

In September, Bonnie Brown disclosed that she has been diagnosed with lung cancer. This diagnosis came just three short months after another member of the group — her older brother, Jim Ed Brown — passed away from a different form of lung cancer.

Originally Brown thought that her heart was the source of her health concerns, but on September 2 the 78-year-old was diagnosed with Stage 4 adenocarcinoma in her lung. Brown is fighting the illness with chemotherapy treatments in Little Rock, Ark.

Fans who want to wish Bonnie Brown well can send her letters to P.O. Box 233, Dardanelle, Ark., 72834-0233.

Maxine (left) and Bonnie (right) with Jim Ed's wife Becky, at the Hall of Fame Induction.
Photo by John Shearer / Getty Images

December 2015

Deck The Halls Concert at The Hall of Fame

December 2 - Skaggs Family Christmas with Ricky Skaggs and The Whites

December 16 - An Evening with Lonestar

December 9 - Brenda Lee presents Rockin' Around the Christmas Tree

December 23 - The Oak Ridge Boys A Christmas Night Out.

For tickets contact the Hall of Fame at 615-416-2001 or visit their website at www.CountryMusicHall ofFame.org/DeckTheHall2015.

December 4 & 5
Home for Christmas 1

December 11 & 12
Home for Christmas 2

December 18 & 19
CFR Christmas 1998

December 25 & 26
CFR 1 1997

Fridays...7 p.m. central
Saturdays...11 p.m central

December 2015

Diner Chat
with Renae the Waitress

It's easy...it's fun!!
Listen live by Phone or on the web,
every Thursday at 3:00 p.m. EST.

1-425-440-5100
ID code: 909005#

www.larryscountrydiner.com, click 'Diner Chat'

Hey Guys......look at the progress at Larry's Country Diner !!!!! We had to fill in the foundation with several tons of rock but I don't think it caused any big delays. The days have been mild with a little rain. So we are going FULL SPEED AHEAD.

We have new Diner tapings on December 2nd with Larry back on the show!! Whoooo hooooo. Those shows will air in a few weeks so you can look forward to seeing him back.

My family will be celebrating Christmas this year in Montana, but there will be no ATV rides down the mountain. Our daughter Chi is expecting our second grandbaby in April so we will be sitting in front of the fireplace watching Rio play.

Larry and Luann are staying in Nashville for the Holidays as they welcome their new puppy "Little Lulu". I am sure she will be a big hit with the grandkids.

If you are not joining us every week on Diner Chat then you are missing great fun. We have been randomly selecting one LIVE listener (not listening to the playback) to give a free gift to. I gave away a "HOME FOR CHRISTMAS" signed poster one week. It had signatures of all of the artists on our new Christmas series "HOME FOR CHRISTMAS". A real collectors' item. So tune in every Thursday at 3:00 EST by phone at 425-440-5100 ID 909005#. If you need a local number just call customer service for a toll free number in your area.

So how many folks are glad we are back on Thursday nights???? You ask us to switch back so RFD finally gave us that opportunity. We hope you support the change.

Our Country's Family Reunion and Larry's Country Diner Cruise is almost sold out. If you have been waiting to book your cabin we may be sailing without you. Unfortunately Joey and Rory will not be able to make our Cruise. Joey's has stopped treatment and is spending quality time with her family. TG Sheppard and Kelly Lang have stepped up and will join us again. Everyone loved them last year on our Cruise and we are so happy to have them back with us.

Make sure you stay tuned to Diner Chat every Thursday. The wonderful JEAN SHEPARD was one of my special guests last month. If you miss any of our "Chats" you can replay them on our website and listen any time. See ya at the Diner!!

December 2015

A Country Christmas at Opryland features The Gatlin Brothers

Gaylord Opryland Resort's 32nd annual A Country Christmas® will make memories of a lifetime for the thousands of people who travel from around the world to experience the most captivating holiday resort entertainment, decor and food in America.

There's no better place to be this holiday season than Nashville's iconic Gaylord Opryland Resort with 2 million twinkling lights, acres of larger-than-life decorations, live shows and exciting attractions. New this year with the NEW Christmas dinner show featuring Grammy award-winning trio Larry Gatlin and the Gatlin Brothers!

Known for major hits like "All The Gold In California," "Houston (Means I'm One Day Closer To You)," "Broken Lady" and "I Just Wish You Were Someone I Love," brothers Larry, Rudy and Steve —celebrating their 60th anniversary in 2015—will perform holiday classics and many of their career hits.

"For the Gatlins, Christmas is not just about gifts under the tree," says Larry. "It's about the greatest gift of all, the birth of the Christ Child. To be able to spend this Christmas at home with our families, for the first time in 40 years, singing the wondrous songs about HIS birth, at the fabulous Opryland Hotel, is a double blessing. Just like a bunch of kids... We can't wait!! MERRY CHRISTMAS a little bit early!"

Gaylord Opryland's A Country Christmas kicked off on November 20 with Larry Gatlin & the Gatlin Brothers performing 30 live dinner shows leading up to Christmas. Held in the iconic 2,882-room hotel's Tennessee Ballroom, each show will include a four-course meal prepared by Gaylord Opryland's award-winning chefs.

Larry Black thanks fans for all the get well cards

Larry received thousands of get well cards and wishes following his June ATV accident. In November he posed for a photo with the stacks of cards to print an official Thank You to all of his fans.

Filming for new Larry's Country Diner episodes will feature Larry back at the helm as he hosts the shows. He continues to get better every day and is feeling wonderful. He has been back at his office working since the end of August.

He and his wife of 50 years, celebrated their anniversary by taking a three week road trip up the east coast to visit friends and enjoy the fall colors. With the holidays underway, he wanted to be sure his fans new that he is doing just great and enjoying life and looks forward to the cruise the end of January.

December 2015

Home for Christmas offers new & classic songs

The newest offering from Country's Family Reunion is the DVD series Home for Christmas also features the CD version of the songs from the show. We gathered a ton of country music legends to share their favorite Christmas stories and songs with each other and YOU.

Joey and Rory, along with daughter Heidi, performed Remember Me.

The DVDs and CDs feature The Isaacs It's Christmastime Again, Duane Allen of the Oak Ridge Boys Getting Ready for a Baby, Rhonda Vincent Christmas Time At Home, Ricky Skaggs New Star Shining, Country's Family Reunion Band Jingle Bells, Teea Goans They Saw A King, The Whites Hangin' Around The Mistletoe, T. Graham Brown Mary Had A Little Lamb, Linda Davis, Rylee Scott and Lang Scott Tennessee Christmas, Joey and Rory with Heidi Remember Me, Mandy Barnette Winter Wonderland, William Lee Golden of the Oak Ridge Boys along with Duane Allen and Jimmy Fortune Thank God for Kids, The Isaacs Away In A Manger, and Jimmy Fortune O Holy Night.

This series is the perfect way to get in the Christmas spirit whether watching it on your television or listening to it in your car or home. It's a great blend of newer Christmas songs along with traditional hymns.

Duane Allen, Jimmy Fortune and William Lee Golden singing Thank God for Kids.

This series can be purchased for $79.80 plus $6.95 shipping and handling OR you can purchase the special of Home for Christmas AND Sweethearts for $119.80 plus $16.95 shipping and handling. (You can also use the coupon on this page to get $20.00 off) Just call Customer Service at 800-820-5405 or send a check to Country's Family Reunion, P.O. Box 210709, Nashville, TN 37221. If you order through Customer Service, be sure to tell them to use the Holiday Code 2 to get your discount!

The Isaacs performed It's Christmastime Again and Away in a Manger.

228 CFR NEWS

December 2015

Country singer Tommy Overstreet dies at 78

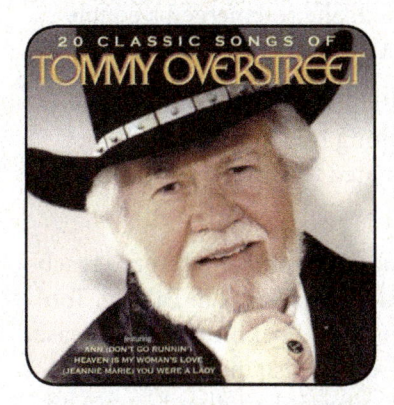

Country singer, Tommy Overstreet was born in Oklahoma City and grew up in both Houston and Abilene, Texas. He decided on a singing career when he was very young, influenced largely by his cousin, "Uncle" Gene Austin. Austin was a singing star of the 1920s and 1930s.

Overstreet's musical career started when he was 17, singing on country and western star Slim Willet's television show in Abilene. In the late 1950s, Overstreet started a group called "The Shadows."

In 1967, Overstreet was hired to manage Dot Records in Nashville, Tennessee. In 1970, he decided to pursue a recording career, quickly establishing himself as a country hit maker that very year with a top five hit, "Gwen (Congratulations)," which peaked at No. 5 on the Billboard country music chart.

Overstreet made frequent guest appearances on the TV variety show Hee Haw. His highest charting Billboard hit was 1972's "Ann (Don't Go Runnin')," which went to No. 2.

His other top-20 hits were "I Don't Know You Anymore" (#5 in 1971), "Heaven is My Woman's Love" (#3 in 1972), "Send Me No Roses" (#7 in 1973); "I'll Never Break These Chains" (#7 in 1973), "(Jeannie Marie) You Were a Lady" (#7 in 1974), "If I Miss You Again Tonight" (#8 in 1974), "I'm a Believer" (#9 in 1975), "That's When My Woman Begins" (#6 in 1975), "If Love was a Bottle of Wine" (#11 in 1976), "Don't Go City Girl on Me" (#5 in 1977), "Yes, Ma'am" (#12 in 1978, and "Fadin' In, Fadin' Out" (#11 in 1978).

Tommy Overstreet died at his home in Oregon on Nov. 2, 2015, just two days ahead of the CMA Awards. He was 78 years old. Tommy had reportedly been suffering from a variety of illnesses over the last few years, and he succumbed this week. "Tommy Overstreet has passed away at his home," fellow country musician Rex Allen Jr. wrote on Facebook. "Tommy was a great guy and headlined the first tour I ever worked. So sad."

New Gene Watson CD to be released in 2016

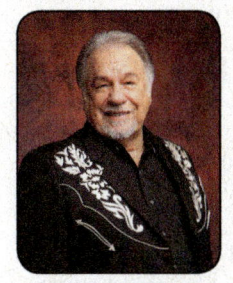

Gene Watson had quite a bit of fun this fall traveling to Pennsylvania, Maine and all around the Southeast, Texas and more. On his new record, he's done most of his part and now Dirk Johnson, his producer, is adding the background vocals. He is hoping you'll love all the songs he chose as much as he does.

"I can tell you one song I chose to re-record is the great Larry Gatlin penned tune, "Bitter They Are, Harder They Fall," says Gene. "Thanks to Larry asking me to duet with him on that song on a CFR show and many times on the Opry, it has become a new favorite so we wanted to be sure fans could get it - as the older version is getting harder to find."

The new CD should be out to the stores sometime early 2016. Gene wants to let all his fans know that he appreciates you and thank you for being a fan of his music. His band members appreciate all of you as well and are glad so many of you have been out to see them this year.

HERE is the TRIVIA QUESTION just for you: Name the CITY and STATE where you will find "GENE WATSON BOULEVARD". EMAIL your answer to GENEWATSONMUSIC@HOTMAIL.com for your chance to win an autographed Tee Shirt!

Now please go to www.GeneWatsonMusic.com to read the very latest Gene Watson newsletter.

December 2015

COUNTRY LEGENDS PAST AND PRESENT   BY TOM WOOD

Skeeter Davis

Look up the word "Skeeter," and you'll find several definitions in the dictionary — everything from slang for mosquito to an iceboat at least 16 feet in length that has a single sail to what you call a person who shoots skeet.

But for country music fans, there's only one meaning. And it is associated with happiness and heartache, joy and sadness, and hundreds of other emotional highs and lows.

That would be Skeeter Davis, whose up-and-down life story reflected her music.

Her unique sound drew fans from around the world and crossed all musical boundaries, especially with her signature song, "The End of the World." The 1962 smash hit reached No. 1 on the adult contemporary charts, was No. 2 on both the U.S. country and Billboard Hot 100, and climbed to No. 18 on the UK charts.

Born Mary Francis Penick on the next-to-last day of 1931, she became known as Skeeter at a very early age when her grandfather marveled at the way she buzzed around family gatherings in Dry Ridge, Kentucky.

The moniker stuck, and she added the surname Davis as a teenager when she performed with high school friend Betty Jack Davis as the Davis Sisters from 1947-51. They scored a sure-fire hit with "I Forgot More Than You'll Ever Know," in late May 1953, and might have produced many more, but tragedy soon struck. Betty Jack died a day after an Aug. 1 auto accident that severely injured Skeeter.

"I Forgot More Than You'll Ever Know" continued to rise on the country charts and spiked at No. 1 from mid-October through mid-November. Skeeter briefly performed with Betty Jack's sister before "retiring" to get married. She re-emerged a couple years later as a solo act.

In all, Skeeter had 10 hits make the country charts as a solo act, first reaching No. 5 in 1959 with "Set Him Free." She was invited to join the Grand Ole Opry that same year.

The year 1960 produced her only other hit to reach as high as No. 2. "I Can't Help You) I'm Falling, Too" was an answer song to Hank Locklin's smash "Please Help Me, I'm Falling," and it also made the pop charts (she previously answered another Locklin hit with 1957's "Lost to a Geisha Girl").

As Skeeter's star continued to rise, so did the upheavals in her life—as if the 1953 auto accident that took her best friend's life wasn't enough.

For every career high point—like touring with Elvis Presley and appearances on American Bandstand and The Midnight Special—there was an abundance of life's low moments, like being kicked off the Grand Ole Opry for 15 months after criticizing Metro Nashville police in 1974, like going through three marriages, and finally waging a three-year battle against breast cancer before dying on September 19, 2004 at age 72.

It might have been the end of her life, the end of an era.

But Skeeter's music lives on as one of the all-time greats.

Author Tom Wood, who writes thrillers and Westerns, is a regular contributor to Country Family Reunion News. Reach him at tomwoodauthor.com

December 2015

PRECIOUS MEMORIES MEMORIAL

Order NOW

Order *Precious Memories Memorial* by Renae Johnson.... a long awaited book that guides you through the lives, deaths and funerals of some of country music greatest entertainers. There are over 80 country music greats in this 288 page book that include:

Marty Robbins, Roy Acuff, Waylon Jennings, Tammy Wynette, Johnny Russell, George Jones, Jimmy Dean, Little Jimmy Dickens, Joey Feek, Kitty Wells, Eddie Rabbitt, Ferlin Husky, Johnny Cash, Ray Price, Roger Miller, Wilburn Brothers, Stringbean, Jim Reeves, Jerry Reed, Justin Tubb and many more.

You will see pictures of their gravesites and find out how they died, when they died and even maps to visit their final resting places.

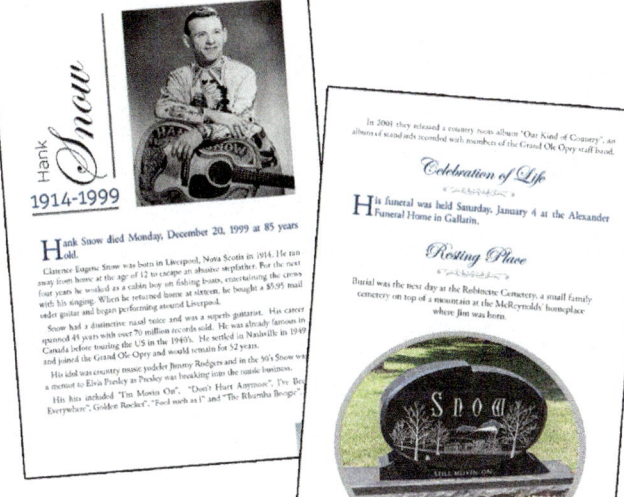

To order:

Send $24.95 plus $6.95 ($31.90) by check or credit card to: PO Box 210796 Nashville, TN 37221. (TN residents, add $2.33 tax)

www.cfrvideos.com
www.Renaethewaitress.com

1-800-820-5405

CPSIA information can be obtained
at www.ICGtesting.com
Printed in the USA
LVOW02s2034210616
493564LV00001B/1/P

9 780989 398916